Final Cut Pro HD

HANDS-ON TRAINING

Includes Exercise Files & Demo Movies

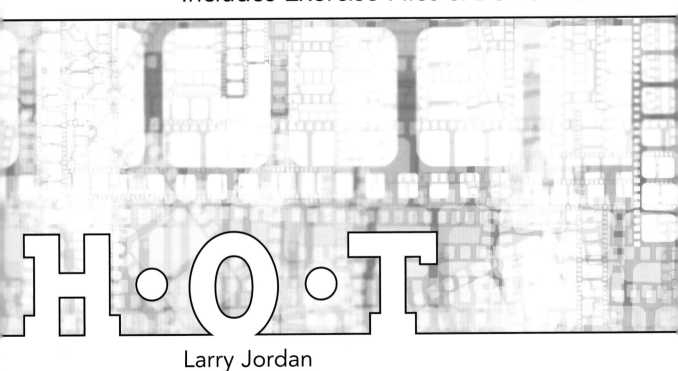

H•O•T

Larry Jordan

Final Cut Pro HD | H·O·T
Hands-On Training

By Larry Jordan

lynda.com/books | Peachpit Press
1249 Eighth Street • Berkeley, CA • 94710
800.283.9444 • 510.524.2178 •
510.524.2221(fax)
http://www.lynda.com/books
http://www.peachpit.com

lynda.com/books is published
in association with Peachpit Press,
a division of Pearson Education
Copyright ©2005 by lynda.com

ISBN: 0-321-29399-1

0 9 8 7 6 5 4 3 2 1

Printed and bound in the
United States of America

H•O•T | Credits

Original Design: Ali Karp, Alink Newmedia (alink@earthlink.net)

Editor: Karyn Johnson

Copyeditor: Darren Meiss

Production Coordinator: Myrna Vladic

Compositors: Rick Gordon, Deborah Roberti

Beta testers: Adam Fischer, Cristy Bond

Proofreader: Liz Welch

Cover Illustration: Bruce Heavin (bruce@stink.com)

Indexer: FireCrystal Communications

H•O•T | Colophon

The original design for *Final Cut Pro HD H•O•T* was sketched on paper. The layout was heavily influenced by online communication—merging a traditional book format with a modern Web aesthetic.

The text in *Final Cut Pro HD H•O•T* was set in Akzidenz Grotesk from Adobe and Triplex from Emigre. The cover illustration was painted in Adobe Photoshop and Adobe Illustrator.

This book was created using QuarkXPress, Microsoft Office, and Final Cut Pro HD on an Apple Macintosh using Mac OS X. It was printed on 60 lb. Influence Matte at Courier.

Acknowledgments

Writing a first book is an act of faith, even more, I suspect, for the publisher than the author. I owe a huge debt of gratitude to Lynda Weinman, of Lynda.com, for giving me this opportunity. And a second huge hug to Lisa Brenneis, for recommending me to Lynda.

This book grew out of my production and teaching experience where I discovered my students and co-workers had a good understanding of their piece of the process, but were weak on how all the different pieces fit together. The goal of this book is to provide both the detail and a greater context of where post-production fits in the grand scheme of storytelling. And this, I think, is what makes my book different from the other Final Cut books that are available. This is more than a "tools" book. It's a book on using Final Cut in post-production. Anyone can teach you how to use a hammer; this book goes further and helps you understand how to use that hammer to build a house.

I also want to thank Garo Green, Vice-President of Operations, for Lynda.com, for his unfailing support, encouragement, and prompt checks, the beta testers for this book, especially Christy Bond, for making sure my exercises were accurate, Sean MacLean for his help with Microsoft Word, Blaine Albios for the video graphics, Darren Meiss for his copyediting (and interesting discussions on the proper capitalization of "playhead"), and Nathan Dugi-Turner for some killer original music compositions.

Finally, I want to thank Mike Hatchett, Waide Hoyt, and Tim Manning at Standard Films (www.standardfilms.com) for providing absolutely stunning snowboarding footage, as well as the still image of Fred Kalbermatten (photographed by Sullivan). Also, Joel Suttles and Ainie Hastings at CNN ImageSource (www.cnnimagesource.com) for the hurricane footage.

Dedication

To Jane, Paul, and Julia,
for allowing me to skip doing dishes
so I could write this book.

Final Cut Pro HD | H•O•T _____ **Table of Contents**

Introduction _____ **x**

I **Get Organized** _____ **2**

What Is Editing?   3

A Few Key Terms   3

The Editing Workflow of Final Cut Pro HD   4

Organize Your Life   7

Exercise 1_Create A Folder System That Works   10

Make Archiving Easy   11

Organizing Final Cut Pro   12

Exercise 2_Setting Preferences–Getting Final Cut Ready   13

Exercise 3_Setting Scratch Disks   16

Summary   19

2 **Understanding the Final Cut Pro Interface** _____ **20**

The Final Cut Pro Interface   21

Editing Flow in Final Cut Pro   26

Exercise 1_Explore the Browser   27

Exercise 2_Explore the Viewer   34

What Is Timecode?   40

Exercise 3_Explore the Timeline   42

Exercise 4_Explore the Canvas   48

Exercise 5_Customize Final Cut Pro   51

Summary   61

3 **Gather Your Media** _____ **62**

The Capture Process   63

About Video Formats   63

Exercise 1_Getting Ready to Capture   66

Exercise 2_Exploring the Log and Capture Screen   74

Exercise 3_Logging and Capturing Media   83

Exercise 4_Using Capture Now   92

Exercise 5_Demo–Reconnecting Media   97

Exercise 6_Importing Media   101

Tools for the Power User   107

Summary   111

4 **Build Your Story** _____ **112**

The Story Is the Heart of Your Video 113

Exercise 1_Creating and Saving a New Project 114

Exercise 2_Viewing and Marking Clips 118

Exercise 3_Building the Timeline 127

Exercise 4_Three-Point Editing 136

Exercise 5_Browser Power Tips 141

Summary 144

5 **Organize Your Story** _____ **146**

Exercise 1_Navigating the Timeline and Selecting Clips 147

Exercise 2_Deleting Clips 150

Exercise 3_Moving Clips 158

Exercise 4_Power Editing Techniques 164

Exercise 5_Storyboard Editing 170

Exercise 6_More on Markers 174

Exercise 7_Creating Subclips 180

Summary 185

6 **Trim Your Story** _____ **186**

What Is Trimming? 187

Exercise 1_General Trimming Tools 189

Exercise 2_One-Sided Trimming 196

Exercise 3_Two-Sided Trimming 202

Exercise 4_An Alternate Way to Edit 208

Exercise 5_Trimming with Timecode 212

Exercise 6_Trim Edit Window 216

Summary 220

7 **Audio—The Secret to a Great Picture** _____ **222**

The Workflow of Editing Audio 223

The Math of Audio 223

Exercise 1_Building the Audio Story 227

Exercise 2_Adding B-Roll for Illustration 234

Exercise 3_Trimming Audio While Staying in Sync 241

Exercise 4_Setting Audio Levels 247

Exercise 5_Adding Music or Effects 255

Exercise 6_Using the Voice Over Tool for Narration 260

Exercise 7_Mixing Your Project 265

A Quick Tour of the Audio Mixer 270

Summary 272

8   **Transitions—Making Change Beautiful** _____ **274**

"Everything Is a Transition"   275

Exercise 1_Creating an Audio Transition   276

Exercise 2_Creating a Video Transition   283

Understanding Rendering   289

Exercise 3_One More Way to Create a Transition   292

Exercise 4_Changing the Default Transition   294

Exercise 5_Create a Favorite Transition   297

Exercise 6_Bonus Transition: A Gradient Wipe   300

Summary   302

9   **Text, Titles, and Graphics** _____ **304**

Exercise 1_Creating a Main Title   305

Exercise 2_Creating Lower-Third and Upper-Corner Titles   314

Exercise 3_Creating a Credit Roll   321

Exercise 4_Understanding Video Scopes   325

Exercise 5_Importing LiveType Projects   332

Exercise 6_Working with Adobe Photoshop Graphics   335

Summary   338

10   **Motion Effects** _____ **340**

What Is a Motion Effect?   341

Exercise 1_Creating a Picture-in-Picture Effect   343

Exercise 2_Working with Wireframe Mode in the Canvas   353

Exercise 3_Moving Images with Keyframes   359

Cool Way to Fade to Black   370

Exercise 4_Moving Text with Keyframes   372

Exercise 5_Creating a Still Frame from a Clip   377

Exercise 6_Running a Clip at Variable Speeds   379

Exercise 7_Moving a Still Image   382

Summary   385

11   **Filters and Keying** _____ **386**

Exercise 1_Using Audio Filters   388

Exercise 2_Using Video Filters   393

Exercise 3_Fancy Filter Tricks, Part 1   399

Exercise 4_Fancy Filter Tricks, Part II   404

Exercise 5_Nesting Sequences   406
Why Color Space Drives Me Nuts   410
Exercise 6_Simple Color Correction   413
Exercise 7_Creating a Luma Key   423
Exercise 8_Creating a Chroma Key   425
Exercise 9_Creating a Traveling Matte   432
Summary   437

12   Output Your Project _____ **438**
Definitions   439
Techniques for Outputting Long Projects   440
Exercise 1_Print to Video   441
Pre-Program Material   444
Striping Tapes   447
Exercise 2_Edit to Tape   449
"But, Wait A Minute…!"   452
So, You Wanna Be an Export Expert?   453
Exercise 3_Exporting a QuickTime Movie   455
Exercise 4_Special Cases: Exporting Audio   457
Exercise 5_Special Cases: Exporting Video   460
Summary   463

13   Archiving Your Project _____ **464**
Archiving Your Project   465
Exercise 1_Changing Reel Names   466
Exercise 2_Protecting Your Project Using Save As   468
Exercise 3_Deleting Render Files   469
Exercise 4_Backing Up Project Files and Trashing Media   472
Exercise 5_Restoring an Old Project   475
Exercise 6_Exploring the Media Manager   480
Summary   485

A   Additional Resources _____ **486**

   Index _____ **498**

Welcome! I'm really glad you decided to buy this book, because I think you'll find it an exciting, interesting, and engaging way to learn Final Cut Pro HD.

At least, I hope so. That's been my goal.

Introduction

| Welcome! | What Is Final Cut Pro HD? | Who Is This Book For? |
| How to Use This Book | System Requirements |
| What's on the H•O•T DVD? |

No Lesson Files

FCP HD HOT DVD

What Is Final Cut Pro HD?

Final Cut is a delightfully powerful tool to help you create, organize, craft, and output the ideas you have in your mind, and in your camera, so that you can share them with the rest of the world.

And "tool" is the most important word in that paragraph. Because even with an incredibly powerful tool like Final Cut, your creative vision is still in charge. Final Cut simply helps you give that vision life.

Which brings me to my first important point: There is nothing you can do in Final Cut that will damage your computer, or the media files you have stored on your hard disk. So feel free to experiment. Choose a menu, or click a button and watch what happens. It may not always look good. It may not be what you want or expect. But, you won't hurt anything. You can always undo your changes. Remember, many a famous filmmaker owes a part of their reputation to blind luck at the right moment.

Voltaire once wrote: "The perfect is the enemy of the good." In editing, this means spending so much time to create the perfect effect that you run out of time to finish the show on deadline.

There is no such thing as the "perfect" way to edit. Final Cut doesn't care if you like the keyboard or the mouse—it allows you to edit either way. Final Cut doesn't care if you are a slow or fast editor—your program plays back at the same speed regardless of how fast you edit.

Final Cut does not giggle. Final Cut does not smirk. Final Cut does not call its friends after you've finished working for the day, exclaiming, "did you see that bizarre edit he did today?" Final Cut does not evaluate your worth as an editor and give you a report card at the end of your project.

So, don't get hung up in the search to edit "perfectly." This book is filled with tips and techniques that will make you a more efficient and proficient editor. Make you faster. Make you more comfortable. Make you more effective. But neither this book, nor Final Cut, can help you be more creative—or improve the quality of your story. That comes from within you.

And telling your story is why you are editing in the first place.

Who Is This Book For?

This book is for anyone who wants to improve their understanding and skills using Final Cut Pro HD. I've written it for the beginning and intermediate editor, especially someone who is self-taught, to round out your understanding of the program and give you a solid foundation you can build on for the future.

This book assumes you are using some form of Digital Video (MiniDV, DVCAM, or DVCPRO-25), although higher-end users can also learn from the techniques in this book.

This book also assumes you are not a computer geek, nor particularly interested in becoming one. This is OK. Final Cut does not require you *understand* a computer in order to *use* a computer.

A recent survey showed that Final Cut was being used to cut documentaries, corporate presentations, broadcast programs, weddings, training, commercials… in short, Final Cut is being used everywhere in all kinds of video production.

This book is focused on the process of editing. Its goal is to help you tell your story—whether you are creating a 30-second commercial or a 2-hour documentary—and to make that process fun along the way.

How to Use This Book

At the core of this book are dozens of hands-on tutorials, provided so you can learn Final Cut by using Final Cut. I believe that the best way to learn is to do—though my students would probably tell you that I also have strong opinions on which ways are better than others. And throughout this book, I'll share those opinions with you as if you were in one of my Final Cut classes.

As you will learn in the next chapter, there is a flow in editing from initial planning to final output and archiving. This book walks you through every step of this process and shows you what you need to know.

All the examples in this book use NTSC video, running at 30 frames per second. If you are a PAL or film editor working with different image sizes or frame rates, you can still benefit from this book, because the techniques are the same, regardless of the media you are editing. This consistent interface is one of the great strengths of Final Cut.

(Also, on a technical note for readers outside North America, you can edit the NTSC video included in this book on your computer with no problems. The only issue is that you can't display NTSC video to an external PAL monitor.)

Final Cut has over 600 keyboard commands. (No, don't panic, you don't need to know all of them to use Final Cut. In fact, you can edit quite happily using only the mouse. The keyboard just makes you faster.)

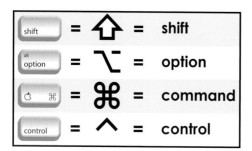

But, the last time I checked, my keyboard did not have 600 keys on it. In fact, it has 104. I just counted them. So, in order to access all 600 keyboard shortcuts, you need to use "modifier keys." These are keys you press and hold while typing other keys. There are, specifically, four:

• Shift

• Control

• Option

• Command

(And here's a note about this Command key. Some people, and I won't name names, call it an "Apple" key. I'm sorry, I don't "Apple" my computer. I "Command" my computer. That's because I'm in charge— at least, most of the time. Now, this may say more about me than it does about my computer, but for the rest of this book, I'll refer to this key as the Command key. You'll see these keyboard commands abbreviated like this: **Cmd+S**.)

Andrew Balis once suggested a good way to think of the Option key is that it is the "opposite" key. If you are using a tool to perform some action, holding down the Option key will often, but not always, perform the opposite action. You'll learn more about this throughout the book.

At the end of each chapter, I list helpful keyboard shortcuts that were either mentioned during that chapter or are relevant to the material covered in that chapter. I've found these lists to be handy in the books I read, and I wanted to provide the same service to you.

Finally, Final Cut has a hidden treasure trove of shortcuts that you can find only with the mouse. They are called **contextual menus**, and you access them by either holding down the **Control** key and clicking, or, if you have a two-button mouse, clicking with the right mouse button.

In this book, I will always refer to these using the term **Ctrl+click**. All Macintosh computers ship with a single-button mouse. This means that if you learn how to use the Ctrl+click to access a contextual menu, you can use Final Cut with any mouse; which is why I teach it this way. If you have a two-button mouse, you can either Ctrl+click or right-mouse-click. It's the same result, just a different procedure.

System Requirements for Final Cut Pro HD

Apple's Web site states the minimum computer requirements for Final Cut Pro HD:

• Macintosh computer with 350 MHz or faster PowerPC G4 or G5 processor and AGP graphics card

• Mac OS X v10.3.2 or later

• QuickTime 6.5 or later

• 384 MB of RAM

• For Soundtrack, 500 MHz or faster single processor or 450 MHz or faster dual processors

• 512 MB of RAM recommended

• For RT Extreme, single 500 MHz or faster PowerPC G4 (550 MHz for PowerBook G4) or any dual PowerPC G4 and 512 MB of RAM

• For DVCPROHD, 1 GHz or faster single or dual processors and 1 GB of RAM

• 1 GB of available disk space for application installation

• 5 GB of disk space for Soundtrack content

• 9 GB of disk space for LiveType content

• DVD drive for installation

However, your editing system is more than just your computer. And, in fact, there are a number of other pieces you will need in order to successfully launch yourself on the road to editing glory...or, um, well, at least to get started.

Minimal System Configuration

Everything on Apple's list, plus the following:

• More RAM. Try to give Final Cut between 1 GB and 2.5 GB of RAM. It will work faster.

• A second hard drive to store media (more on this in a moment).

• A DV camera to use in transferring your media into the computer.

• Final Cut Pro HD.

• A copy of this book.

NOTE | Why a Second Hard Drive?

Although it is technically possible to edit using only one hard drive, it is not a wise idea to do so. This is because your hard drive has many, many, many calls on its attentions: the operating system, Final Cut, any background applications, all background processes, then, finally, and dead last in priority is playing your media.

Yet, unless your media plays smoothly, without any fits and starts, the rest of your editing system is useless.

By adding a second drive you not only provide a whole lot more storage space for your media, you significantly improve the performance of your system by allowing your boot hard disk (that is, the one that contains the operating system and applications) to concentrate on serving the needs of the operating system and Final Cut, while the second disk concentrates on playing all media.

For editing DV (by which, I mean MiniDV, DVCAM, or DCPRO-25), an internal drive will be faster than an external FireWire drive. If you are editing larger file formats, such as DigiBetacam, an external RAID (Redundant Array of Inexpensive Disks) will be faster. It is beyond the scope of this book to detail all the different hardware options you have for storage; however:

- RAIDs are the fastest, largest, and most expensive storage devices. The fastest RAIDs are Fibre Channel– or SCSI-based. There are some new, less expensive FireWire RAIDs, but it is too early to tell how effective they are for video editing.

- Internal hard disks are faster and generally cheaper than FireWire drives, but are not portable. Be sure to get one that spins at least at 7200 RPM.

- FireWire drives are portable and will generally meet the needs of editing DV, provided you get a FireWire drive that has *at least* a 7200 RPM spin, 8 MB cache, and an Oxford 911 chip for FireWire 400 or an Oxford 922 chip for FireWire 800.

- Brand names are not always good guides as to drive performance, so be sure your hard drive meets or exceeds these specs.

In Chapter 14, *"Additional Resources,"* you'll find Web sites and other resources you can use in selecting and maintaining your system.

Suggested Accessories

The following accessories will make your editing environment more efficient and productive. However, not everyone needs all these, so consider this a wish list for future purchases. (In my project studio, I use all of these.)

- **DV deck:** Very useful because it reduces wear and tear on your camera, plus you can wire the deck into your computer and monitors, which means you can stop plugging and unplugging cables whenever you want to switch between shooting and editing.

- **NTSC (for North America) or PAL (for everywhere else) monitor:** Allows you to watch your productions on a TV screen, rather than the computer, which has several advantages:

    - The color display is accurate. Computers don't display video colors accurately.

    - Interlace artifacts disappear. These are the horizontal "forked" lines that appear on your computer monitor when you watch video with fast action.

    - You can, generally, see a larger image on the video monitor than on your computer monitor. However, bigger is not better for video monitors. The best sizes to buy are between 9-inch and 14-inch monitors.

- **Audio speakers:** The tiny speaker on your computer is inadequate for anything, much less working with audio. Again, you can choose among a wide variety of speakers; my recommendation is to spend a couple hundred dollars and buy studio monitor speakers. mAudio, Tannoy, Event, Mackie, and JBL are all good brands. (I use mAudio in my studio.) Also, avoid subwoofers for mixing. Subwoofers are good for listening, but not for mixing your audio.

- **Audio mixer:** This is really useful for monitoring audio from your computer as well as plugging in a mike to record narration or voiceovers. There are lots of mixers to choose from; my favorite, above all others, is Mackie.

- **Final Cut keyboard:** This is a standard computer keyboard with the normal keycaps replaced by brightly colored ones that show which keys to press to select a particular tool, task, or effect. (Final Cut ships with little stickers that you can put on your keyboard as reminders of what the keys do. While useful, I find them annoying. The FCP keyboard is available at a variety of retail and mail-order outlets.)

- **UPS (uninterruptible power supply):** This protects your computer from surges, lightning strikes, and power failures.

- **RAID:** This high-capacity, high-performance storage system is exceedingly useful when you have hours and hours and hours of documentary footage to edit, or you need the ultimate in performance. Not needed for DV, but necessary for all other formats.

- **Software, plug-ins, and other stuff:** Your editing system is, in the end, as individual as you are. Depending on what you are doing, you can add

  - Sound effects libraries

  - Music libraries

  - Graphics software

  - Video effects software

  - Audio production software

  - Effects and transition plug-ins for Final Cut

  - Two-button mice

  - Shuttle controllers

  - And dozens of other accessories

The purpose of all this customization is to give you the creative tools you need for your productions. However, don't feel you need to buy everything at once. Start editing and see what you need—where you are spending your time and what needs speeding up. I can assure you that you will *always* think of something else you "absolutely have to buy."

Sigh…

NOTE | Thoughts on Final Cut and Multiple Users

One of the strengths of Final Cut is that it takes advantage of the multiple-user capabilities built into OS X.

For instance, if you have multiple people who will be using this computer, assign each one of them a separate login and user account (using **System Preferences > My Account**). Final Cut stores each user's preferences separately, so that when Brooke finishes editing and Julian logs in and starts, all of Brooke's customization and preferences are safely stored and replaced by Julian's so that to each user, Final Cut appears exactly as they left it.

Another example is that if you are using Final Cut at home, create a separate user account for your editing. That way, all your editing files and preferences are safely stored when someone else is using your computer.

What's on the H•O•T DVD?

Bound into the back of this book you will find a DVD containing the following:

- Project lessons and media files for this book

- QuickTime movies that illustrate key concepts that are hard to convey in print, but easy to follow in video

The text file **ReadMe.rtf** on the DVD gives you a list of the movies available.

Installing the Project and Media Files onto Your Local Hard Disk

1. Insert the **FCP HD HOT** DVD into your computer. You must copy the files from the DVD to your local hard disk. The DVD player is too slow to run the files directly from the DVD itself.

FCP Projects

2. Create a new folder on your boot disk called **FCP Projects**.

*The boot disk—the one that contains the operating system—is generally displayed in the top-right corner of your computer screen and is often named **Macintosh HD**.*

FCP HOT files

3. Copy the entire **FCP HOT files** folder from the DVD into the **FCP Projects** folder. All the lessons and media for this book are contained inside the **FCP HOT files** folder.

The nice thing about using the FCP Projects folder is that as you create new projects in the future, not just for this book, but during your real-life editing, you store them in the FCP Projects folder. You'll learn more about how to use this organizational structure in Chapter 1.

(After my long rant about the need for two hard drives to edit, why am I telling you to copy all these book files to one drive? Because I've specifically designed these files for this DVD. For these tutorials, you can get away with using a single drive. In real life, you'll need two.)

4. The **Movies** folder you can copy or leave on the DVD, whichever you prefer.

NOTE | How to Open Lesson Files

The lesson and media files that you just installed to your local hard drive are used throughout this book. There are two ways to open lesson files:

Method 1

1. Open Final Cut Pro.

2. Choose **File > Open** (or press **Cmd+O**).

3. Open the boot disk (often called **Macintosh HD**, but not always).

4. Open the **FCP Projects** folder.

5. Open the **FCP HOT files** folder.

6. Open the **Lessons** folder.

7. Select the project file you want to open, for example: **Chapter 02 Lesson**.

8. Click **Open**.

Method 2

1. From the **Finder**, open the boot disk (often called **Macintosh HD**, but not always).

2. Locate and open the **FCP Projects** folder.

3. Open the **FCP HOT files** folder.

4. Open the **Lessons** folder.

5. Double-click the project file you want to open, for example: **Chapter 02 Lesson**.

You can select whichever of these two methods is most convenient for you.

After you've opened a lesson file, you can easily find it again inside Final Cut by choosing **File > Open Recent** and selecting the file you want to reopen.

☑ Bring all windows to the front on activation
☑ Open last project on application launch

Also, the next time you start Final Cut, it will automatically open the last project you were working on, unless you have unchecked **Open last project on application launch**, which is part of **Final Cut Pro > User Preferences** on the **General** tab.

If you want to go back to the original project as it was before you started making changes (or go back to the last time you saved the project), choose **File > Revert**. Click **OK** to agree to losing all changes.

Summary

I find editing to be exciting, frustrating, challenging, and intensely involving. I love telling stories. And Final Cut makes it possible. This book will show you how.

I

Get Organized

What Is Editing?	A Few Key Terms
Final Cut Pro Editing Workflow	Organize Your Life
Organize Your Computer	Organize Final Cut Pro

No Lesson Files

FCP HD HOT DVD

In this chapter, you'll learn a system of organizing your computer and editing projects so that you can concentrate on being creative without worrying where all the pieces are stored.

You'll also learn an editing workflow within Final Cut that will help you concentrate on accomplishing tasks in the right order, without wasting a lot of time. In editing, there is so much to do and so little time. Unless you stay focused and concentrate on working through the steps of your project in the right order, you can easily lose time working on the wrong things.

For instance, spending time creating the perfect transition between two shots before you've even figured out whether either of those shots will be in the final version of your project is simply a waste of time and creative effort.

What Is Editing?

A few months ago, I saw the following anonymous sign taped on the wall of an edit bay at KTLA-TV, Los Angeles:

"What is Editing?

"Editing is the process that transforms a miscellaneous collection of badly focused, poorly exposed, and horribly framed shots containing reversed screen direction, unmatched action, disappearing props, flair, and hair in the aperture; (but not containing any close-ups, cut-ins, or cut-aways) into a smooth, coherent, and effective visual statement of the original script…for which the director gets the credit."

Final Cut Pro won't make you a great editor. But using Final Cut can help you do great editing.

Regardless of whether your story is a feature film, corporate training, or home movies of Jennifer's first birthday, the essence of all video and film production is storytellling.

Compelling media, meaning programs that you want to watch, all have a solid story—with a beginning, middle, and an end—at their core. Now, this story doesn't have to be fictional. Maybe it's a biography of someone you respect, or training for a new piece of equipment, or a news report, or a documentary.

What makes a story compelling is that it stays focused on its mission. It doesn't wander about, highlight irrelevant material, or meander through meaningless backwaters. A good storyteller knows what's essential for telling his or her story, tells it, then stops.

Editing is essential to storytelling. Editing is the process of getting rid of everything that isn't relevant to the telling of your story, arranging the pieces for the greatest impact, then tweaking the timing until it flows smoothly. Only after you have it organized can you "fancy your story up."

In short, editing is a process that requires both logic and creativity to be successful.

A Few Key Terms

A complete glossary of digital video terms would fill an entire book, but here are some key terms you need to know to start working with Final Cut Pro HD. You'll work with all these terms throughout the rest of the book.

Final Cut Pro HD, Final Cut Pro, Final Cut, and FCP: These are all different ways of describing the same great editing package—Final Cut Pro HD. (And, as you'll discover, I use all of them interchangeably.)

Project (or project file): A Final Cut Pro project file stores pointers, or references, to all the different elements that make up your production. Video, audio, graphics, sound effects, text—everything that is in your final edit is stored in the project file. All editing is done in the project file. Generally, when you are done with a project, you archive this file for permanent storage.

Media: I use this to mean the timecode-based video and audio files stored on your hard disk and referenced by your Final Cut Pro project. Although others might also include graphics files, sound effects.

and other elements, when I use the term "media," I'm generally referring to material initially stored on a videotape. Generally, when you are done with a project, you trash all timecode-based media to save disk storage space.

DV: This is a generic term that includes three different media formats: MiniDV, DVCAM, and DVCPRO-25. Although each format writes data to the tape differently, they all have the same basic image compression and quality. For this reason, I describe all three formats using the generic term, "DV."

Clips: These are the individual shots or elements stored inside your Final Cut project file that get edited into your finished project. A clip is anything that is stored in the Browser or located on the Timeline. (You'll learn more about these terms in Chapter 2, "*Understanding the Final Cut Pro Interface*.") Clips are the basic building blocks you use to create your program.

Pointers: Final Cut Pro uses references inside a project file to "point" to the actual media files stored on your hard disk. Using pointers, rather than the actual media, in your Final Cut project helps keep the project file size small. Also, when you make changes to an edit in Final Cut, these changes affect only the pointers, not the actual media files stored on your hard disk, which enables you to easily undo your changes, without damaging quality. You don't actually see these pointers; rather, the clips you see inside Final Cut use pointers to reference the actual media files stored on your hard disk.

Timeline: The Timeline is that part of a Final Cut Pro project that allows you to assemble all the different elements of your program from beginning to end. If clips are building blocks, the Timeline is the table that allows you to lay them all out and get them organized in the order you want to best tell your story.

The Editing Workflow of Final Cut Pro HD

Final Cut doesn't force you to work in any particular order. However, what I've learned during years of editing and working with Final Cut is that I can be more productive, which means I have more time for creativity, if I break each project down into individual steps and focus on completing each step before moving on to the next.

Editing Workflow

1. Plan
2. Gather
3. Build and Organize
4. Trim
5. Add Audio
6. Add Transitions
7. Add Text, Graphics, and Effects
8. Output
9. Archive

There are nine basic steps to editing any project:

- Planning and organization

- Gathering media

- Building your story

- Trimming your clips

- Adding additional audio

- Adding transitions

- Adding titles, graphics, and effects

- Outputting the project

- Archiving the project

The outline of this book follows these same steps, though I've added a few extra chapters to give you a better opportunity to learn the software.

Planning and Organization

By spending a little time getting your project organized at the very beginning, you can save huge amounts of anguish at the end. Hundreds of different elements go into even a medium-sized project. Planning upfront about how files are named, where they are stored, what format they should be in, and what you want to keep (or trash) after the project is over can make the difference between getting a job done by deadline or frantically floundering at the finish.

Planning is covered in this chapter.

Gathering Media

Bringing audio and video elements into a Final Cut project is the subject of Chapter 3, "*Gather Your Media*." Although you can bring elements into your project lots of ways, there are basically two broad categories: "capturing" elements that need to be converted from videotape into a format the computer can read, and "importing" elements that are already digitized and simply need to be brought into a project file. Chapter 3 covers both.

Building Your Story

Once you've assembled the components that make up your story, you need to start putting them together. Chapter 4, "*Build Your Story*," teaches you how to create a new project, view your clips, set Ins and Outs, and edit them together. Then, in Chapter 5, "*Organize Your Story*," you'll learn techniques to easily move clips around in the Timeline.

Chapter 4 teaches you how to view clips and edit them to the Timeline; Chapter 5 teaches you how to get them organized. From a purely editing point of view, Chapter 4 is probably the most important chapter in the book, and you'll probably use its tips the most. (At least, they're the ones I use the most.)

Trimming Your Clips

After you have all your clips organized in the Timeline, it's time to start trimming the fat. Chapter 6, "*Trim Your Story*," teaches you all the different trimming tools built into Final Cut. Also, you'll spend time learning why a particular tool is the best, along with the effect it has on the rest of your Timeline.

One of the key features of Final Cut is that there are multiple ways to do the same thing. My goal is to teach you many different approaches so you can pick the one that works best for you.

Adding Audio

Chapter 7, "*Audio—The Secret to a Great Picture*," brings sound into your project. Great sound makes even mediocre pictures seem interesting. Final Cut gives you some serious audio tools, and Chapter 7 shows you how to put them to work.

Adding Transitions

Purists would argue that a cut is also a transition, but I haven't seen many people get excited about how sexy a cut is. However, I have seen them wax eloquent over whether a page peel is "so 1990," or the intrinsic difference between a 0 dB audio crossfade and a +3 dB audio crossfade. Chapter 8, "*Transitions—Making Change Beautiful*," will teach you everything you need to know to hold your own in these discussions, plus a few tricks that will shut up that know-it-all in the second row.

Adding Titles, Graphics, and Effects

True, this could easily fill an entire book. But, here you'll do it in only three chapters. Chapter 9, "*Text, Titles, and Graphics*," covers a variety of different ways to put text on the screen. Chapter 10, "*Motion Effects*," discusses how you can get your pictures to move. And Chapter 11, "*Filters and Keying*," presents a variety of ways you can give your images a unique look.

Outputting Your Project

Whether you want to show your work on the Web or on prime-time network television, you'll need to get your project out of Final Cut. Chapter 12, "*Output Your Project*," teaches you the best way to get video out of FCP for the Web, CD, DVD, and videotape.

Archiving Your Project

Finally, when everything is over, all the dust has settled, and the client's check has cleared the bank, it's time to back up essential information and trash the rest. Chapter 13, "*Archiving Your Project*," shows you how to tell the difference. Plus, it gives you a wealth of tips on the best settings and fastest ways to get your projects output.

Chapter 13 also includes a section on media management. This is the process of tracking, moving, copying, adding, deleting, or changing just about every file that Final Cut Pro uses. Not every project needs to use this. So, I saved it for the end. You'll either really need to know this, or you'll never use it. After you read this, you can decide for yourself.

Appendix

There's one more section, an Appendix, that provides troubleshooting help and additional resources to keep you current on this frequently changing application.

Organize Your Life

Well, OK, maybe not your *whole* life, but certainly that part of your life that involves editing. Planning your project is critical, so I want to spend the rest of this chapter making sure you start off on the right foot.

There are three stages to getting organized:

- System-wide naming conventions

- Organizing your computer

- Organizing Final Cut Pro

Naming Conventions

I realize that nothing empties a room faster than some intensely earnest person saying, "We need to have a meeting to discuss naming conventions." Most people would rather watch paint dry. But naming conventions are important—especially when it's 11 o'clock at night and you can't find that one graphics file that has the closing animation to the project you've been working on for the last six weeks, because you forgot how it was named or where you stored it.

Perhaps spending a little time thinking about file names isn't such a bad idea after all.

Here's why developing a system to consistently name files is important. A typical Final Cut project contains hundreds of files:

- Video files

- Audio files

- Music files

- Sound effects files

- Graphics files

- Project files

- And narration, backups, alternate versions, and, well, you get the picture

If you already have a naming system in place, great! You can skip to the next section. If not, I can save you the meeting—here's the naming system I use. You can use my system until you think up a better one. Believe me, using *something* is *much* better than using nothing!

Let's create a fictitious client named "Just-a-Moment Productions." In my system with every new client, I create a two-letter code that represents that client, in this case, "JM."

Next, when Shannon at Just-a-Moment calls me with a new job, I assign a job number and create a new, four-digit job code: "JM04," which means the fourth job from client JM.

Now, whenever I create a new file for this project (except media files, which I'll talk about next), the file name *always* starts with "JM04." That way, if a file gets lost, or wanders away, I can easily figure out where it belongs.

On small- to medium-sized projects, starting with a job code followed by a brief description is enough to keep track of most files. For instance, in the illustration above, "JM04_open.psd" tells you that this is the file for the opening graphic. On larger projects, involving thousands of files, I use a more highly formatted name, such as "JM04_anim_a2_intro_v2.mov," which stands for "Just-a-Moment Productions, Job 4, Animation for the Introduction to Act 2, version 2." Remember, file names can't be longer than 31 characters, and you'll find that FCP displays shorter file names more easily than longer ones.

I carry this one step further and label camera master videotapes as "JM04_01," "JM04_02," "JM04_03," and so on, meaning the first, second, or third tape shot for the fourth job for Just-a-Moment Productions. I am a *huge* believer in uniquely labeling all your videotapes as soon as they are shot, and I'll talk about this more in Chapter 3, "*Gather Your Media*." (I also keep a database of all my videotapes so that I can find a shot or location when I need it later, long after the project is over.)

The nice thing about this file-naming system is that files automatically sort by project, file type (animation, image, sound effect, music), act (or location in the project), location within the act, and version. This automatic sorting makes finding a file and understanding where it goes fast and easy. Clean. Simple. Easy. Neat.

Organize Your Computer

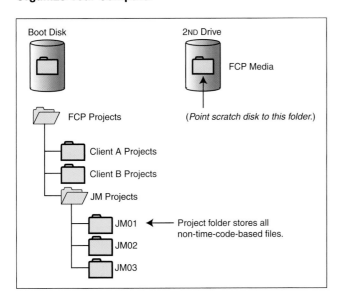

As you read in the Introduction, editing video is at least a two hard-drive proposition—initially because using two hard drives improves performance, but more importantly, because it simplifies organization.

In the next two exercises, you are going to set up your system so that, when you are finished running the tutorials in this book, your system will be ready to edit in the real world.

I. ————————**Create A Folder System That Works**

1. In the boot drive (the drive at the top-right corner of your Mac), create a folder called **FCP Projects**, if you haven't already done so in the last chapter when you installed the exercise files from the **FCP HD HOT** DVD to your computer. You can use this folder for the rest of the exercises in this book, as well as storing later, real-life projects.

*Inside that folder, in addition to storing the files from this book, create a folder for every client, and inside each client folder, create a folder for every project from that client. Although your folders will be different from mine, inside that project folder put **every** file you create that relates to that specific project: Final Cut project files, memos, budgets and spreadsheets, audio files, LiveType and Sound Track projects, graphics files, and so on, everything **except** timecode-based media. ("Timecode-based media" is a fancy term that means all the stuff you capture from videotape.) You'll store this media on the second hard drive.*

2. On the second drive, create a folder named **FCP Media**, which will store media for every project. When the time comes to capture media, tell Final Cut to store all timecode-based media in this one single folder on the second drive. If you have more media than will fit on a single hard disk, create a media folder on every hard disk you plan to use to store media. Later, in Exercise 3, you'll learn how to tell Final Cut where to store this media.

Make Archiving Easy

Media files are huge. An hour of DV footage takes 12 GB of hard disk space to store. And, even though hard disks are getting bigger, they are not designed for long-term archiving. Even a 100 GB drive holds only about eight hours of footage, and that's without including the space needed for render files. You just can't afford to keep your media permanently on your drives. This means you need to trash all your captured media when a project is over, and not use your hard disks for long-term storage.

(Here's another reason: think of any piece of computer equipment you purchased seven years ago that you can still connect to your current computer. Computer technology changes at a dizzying pace—exactly what you DON'T need for media you want to archive for years.)

Nope. The best place for long-term storage of your media is on videotape.

The benefit to this organizational system is that when a project is complete, all your essential project files are stored neatly in the Project folder, and all expendable media is stored in a separate folder. To make a permanent backup of your project files, simply drag the Project folder from your boot disk to a CD (or DVD) for storage. Every file you need to re-create this project in the future is then stored inside this Project folder, and you can now safely trash your media.

Here's the reason I differentiate between timecode-based media and all other files: timecode-based media is most often stored on videotapes. And because this tape has timecode, which uniquely identifies each frame of video, it is a simple matter to capture or recapture this media from tape back into your computer whenever you need it. And this is done using the Batch Capture function of Final Cut, which you'll also learn about in Chapter 3, "Gather Your Media."

That's why your project file is so important—it keeps track of all the media you use, so you can easily recapture it in the future.

NOTE | Storing Videotape

Nothing lasts forever, including CDs, DVDs, and videotapes.

You should always store your videotapes on edge and wound all the way to the end (or beginning). Also, store your tape on end, not flat. Following these simple storage guidelines minimizes the effect of magnetic print-through on the tape, gravity, and the earth's magnetic field. Oh, and try to keep your tapes from getting too hot, too cold, or too exposed to harsh sunlight. In other words, treat them like the valuable records they are.

The lifespan of a videotape stored in a normal environment (not too hot, too cold, too wet, or too dusty) is 20 to 25 years. VHS tapes don't last quite as long, premium tapes somewhat longer. To be safe, assume 20 years. After that, the magnetic oxide that stores all your precious images starts to flake and fall off.

Although there is increasing debate about the life expectancy of CDs and DVDs due to what's called *CD rot*, generally, if you store your discs on edge, away from heat, direct sunlight, and humidity, and don't bang them around too much, they should last at least as long as videotapes and probably longer.

If keeping your media safe for long periods of time is important, be sure to write the date you put the tape, or disc, into service so you'll know when to make dubs to whatever storage media is current at the time.

Organizing Final Cut Pro

There are hundreds of different preferences within Final Cut Pro. Rather than spend dozens of pages creating a laundry list of all possible variations, this book divides preferences into three main sections, spread across three chapters:

- Getting Final Cut Pro set up and organized (Chapter 1)

- Understanding the Final Cut Pro interface (Chapter 2)

- Getting Final Cut Pro ready to capture video (Chapter 3)

And even with these three large categories, there are still a variety of preferences targeted at the professional user that won't be covered in this book; that is, after all, why Apple printed a 1,628-page manual!

2. ———————Setting Preferences—Getting Final Cut Ready

When you first install Final Cut Pro, the installer puts it into your Application folder. In this exercise, you'll move the FCP icon into the Dock to make it easier to access, then start Final Cut, and configure some initial preferences to get it ready to run.

1. In the **Finder**, open the **Applications** folder (press **Shift+Cmd+A**) and locate Final Cut Pro.

2. Click once on the **Final Cut Pro HD** icon and drag it into the **Dock**. Put it anywhere you like, except into the Trash, which would erase the program!

3. To move the **Final Cut Pro HD** icon elsewhere in the **Dock**, simply grab it with the mouse and move it to its new home. Notice how the other icons scuttle out of the way?

4. While you're there, move the **Dock** so it doesn't get in the way. Click the **Blue Apple** and choose **Dock**. Choose **Turn Magnification Off** and **Turn Hiding On**. Then position the **Dock** to the right, or left, side of the screen. You can change this again at any time.

*I prefer putting the Dock on the left side of the screen and hiding it, to get the Dock out of my way. By the way, a neat keyboard shortcut is **Option+Cmd+D**, which hides, or reveals, the Dock.*

5. Start Final Cut by clicking it once in the **Dock**. (You can also start it by double-clicking its icon in the **Applications** folder, but the **Dock** is faster.)

6. If Final Cut is loading for the first time, this dialog appears. (If you are using a video format other than DV, the contents of the two pop-up menus may look different.) For now, accept the top suggested menu item (DV – NTSC) and change the bottom menu to point to your second hard drive. Then click **OK**.

7. This dialog may appear next if you don't have a DV, or other video, device connected and turned on. Because you are simply setting up Final Cut for the first time, turning on your camera or deck is not necessary, so click **Continue** and let Final Cut finish loading. (If you decide to turn your deck on at this point, click **Check Again**, so that Final Cut will look for and connect to your deck.)

8. Chapter 2, "*Understanding the Final Cut Pro Interface*," discusses in much more detail the Final Cut interface that now appears. For this moment, however, concern yourself just with setting some initial preference files. Choose **Final Cut Pro HD > Easy Setup**.

The Easy Setup dialog is your one-stop shop to setting virtually every audio and video preference within Final Cut. If you are capturing and editing DV footage, make sure your menu choices match those shown in the previous screenshot. (If you are outside the U.S., select, DV – PAL from the top pop-up menu.)

If you are capturing and editing other video formats, and you are setting up the system yourself, the following table will put you on the right track. If someone else set up the system for you, leave the settings alone until you better understand how Final Cut works.

Video Format Settings	
Video Format	**Menu Choice (Codec)**
MiniDV, DVCAM, DVCPRO-25 (NTSC – U.S.)	DV NTSC
DVCPRO-25 (PAL - rest of world)	DVCPRO - PAL
MiniDV, DVCAM(PAL – rest of world)	DV-PAL
DVCPRO-50 (U.S.)	DV-50 – NTSC
DVCPRO-50 (PAL)	DV50 - PAL
DVCPRO-HD (1080 interlaced)	DVCPRO HD – 1080i60
DVCPRO-HD (720 progressive 24 frames/sec)	DVCPRO HD – 720p24
DVCPRO-HD (720 progressive 30 frames/sec)	DVCPRO HD – 720p30
DVCPRO-HD (720 progressive 60 fields/sec)	DVCPRO HD – 720p60
Betacam SX (NTSC)	8-Bit Uncompressed NTSC
Betacam SX (PAL)	8-Bit Uncompressed PAL
Betacam SP (NTSC)	8-bit Uncompressed NTSC
Betacam SP (PAL)	8-Bit Uncompressed PAL
DigiBetacam (NTSC)	10-bit Uncompressed NTSC
DigiBetacam (PAL)	10-bit Uncompressed PAL
HD 1080i/1080p, 720i/720p	(Setting depends upon capture card)

3. ——————Setting Scratch Disks

A scratch disk is where Final Cut Pro stores all the media you capture, along with all audio and video render files. Because scratch disks are so important, Final Cut won't even start until you tell it where at least one scratch disk is located. As you learned earlier, I strongly recommend that you store all your timecode-based media (that is, the material you first captured on videotape) to a second hard drive. This exercise shows you how to set up your scratch disks—both for these exercises and real life.

1. Choose **Final Cut Pro HD > System Settings (Shift+Q)**.

This screen allows you to set scratch disks. (Note the Scratch Disks tab at the top of the screen.)

NOTE | Scratch Disks

A scratch disk is a place that Final Cut uses to store the video and audio files that you capture, along with the various render files that it automatically creates as part of the editing process. As you learned earlier, scratch disks are so critical that Final Cut won't even start until you specify where they are. And, just to reinforce this point, it is equally critical that your scratch disk **not** be your boot disk. Put your media files on a separate disk from the operating system.

Final Cut Pro allows you to have up to 16 scratch disks. However, you generally won't use anywhere close to that number because hard disks are getting bigger, allowing storage of far more media than even a year ago. And, the more FireWire drives you add, the slower they go. The general limit for efficient FireWire use is 5 to 7 drives, due to the nature of how FireWire communicates between devices. If you need more hard drive space than that, move up to a RAID.

A RAID (**R**edundant **A**rray of **I**nexpensive **D**isks) is a very high-performance, high-capacity storage system for video editing. It's also the most expensive. For DV footage, unless you have hours and hours and hours of material, a RAID is not necessary. For other video formats, however, RAIDs are often essential.

2. To set your scratch disk, click the top **Set** button, and navigate to the media folder you created earlier on your second hard drive. In this example, I have the scratch disk pointing to the **FCP Media** folder on my second hard drive. Select the **folder** you want to use as a scratch disk (**not** the files in it), then click "Open."

3. If you have multiple hard disks, create a scratch disk on each one of them by moving down to the next line in the **Scratch Disk** window that doesn't have a hard disk assigned to it. Click the **Set** button, navigate to the **FCP Media** folder you created on each disk, select it, and click **Open**.

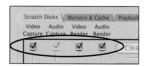

4. Be sure each line has all four columns checked. (It's normal for the **Audio Capture** check box to be grayed out.) If you are using DV video, it is perfectly OK for all four file types to be stored on one disk. There is virtually no reason to ever check the **Capture Audio and Video to Separate Files** check box unless you are in an **HD** environment, and, even then, check with your capture card manufacturer. Capturing audio and video to separate files causes far more problems than it is worth.

5. You can leave the **Waveform Cache**, **Thumbnail Cache**, and **Autosave Vault** set to their default locations. These files are rarely large and can easily be stored on any hard disk.

6. However, you **do** want to change the default setting of **Minimum Allowable Free Space on Scratch Disks** from its default setting of 2048 MB. Hard disks hold only a certain amount of data. Once they are full, they can't hold any more, obviously. What isn't obvious is that a hard disk gets full sooner than you expect.

Essentially, you never want to fill a hard disk any fuller than about 95 percent of its capacity. The reason is that when a hard disk is reading or writing information, it creates invisible, temporary files. If there isn't sufficient room to create these temporary files, the hard disk just plain refuses to work.

So, to prevent the calamity of your hard disk locking up, set **Minimum Allowable Free Space on Scratch Disks** to be 5 percent of the size of the largest hard disk that **isn't** your boot disk. A fast way to determine the size of your hard disk is to select it in the **Finder**, then choose **File > Get Info**. The **Get Info** window will show you the total capacity of your hard disk, how much space is available, and how much is used.

For instance, let's say you have three hard disks:

• Boot disk (internal): 160 GB

• Internal hard disk #2: 80 GB

• External hard disk #1: 120 GB

You would then set **Minimum Allowable Free Space on Scratch Disks** to 6000 MB (6 GB), which is 5 percent of the size of the largest hard disk that isn't the boot disk.

In this exercise, my second hard drive is 120 GB in size, so I set the minimum free space to 6000 MB or 6 GB. (Technical purists will gleefully point out that a gigabyte is actually 1,024 megabytes. And, although they are correct, for the purposes of this dialog, using 1000 megabytes to equal a gigabyte works just fine.)

7. You can leave the **Limit Capture/Export File Segment Size To** box unchecked. This box is useful if you need to make movie file sizes compatible with OS 9 and some versions of Windows. If you work exclusively with OS X, you won't need to use this. If you send movies to OS 9 or Windows, turn this on.

8. For now, leave the **Limit Capture Now To** box checked and at the default setting of 30 minutes. I'll explain more about this in Chapter 3, *"Gather Your Media."*

9. That ends this initial exercise for setting preferences in Final Cut. To save your preferences, click **OK** in the bottom-right corner of the **System Settings** dialog. If you are done working with Final Cut, choose **Final Cut Pro HD > Quit** or press **Cmd+Q**.

Helpful Keyboard Shortcuts	
Shortcut	**Action**
Option+Cmd+A	Open Applications folder (Finder only)
Option+Cmd+U	Open Utility folder (Finder only in OS 10.3.*x*)
Option+Cmd+D	Hide, or reveal, the Dock (all applications)
Ctrl+Q	Open Easy Setup preference window
Shift+Q	Open System Settings preference window
Tab	Move forward between settings in a dialog
Shift+Tab	Move backward between settings in a dialog
Escape	Exit a dialog without saving any changes
Enter (on keypad)	Close a dialog and save all changes
Cmd+Q	Quit Final Cut Pro

Summary

This chapter focused on getting you, your computer, your projects, and Final Cut Pro organized—all starting with a simple and consistent file-naming convention. Next, you'll fire up Final Cut Pro HD and get your hands dirty exploring the user interface.

2

Understanding the Final Cut Pro Interface

| Introduction | Learn the Interface | Navigation |
| Exploring the Browser | Timecode Practice |
| Customizing FCP | Power Tools

Chapter 02 Lesson

FCP HD HOT DVD

In this chapter, you'll come face-to-face with the Final Cut Pro interface.

The good news is that you really only need to read this chapter once. The bad news is that until you read it, you won't be able to take advantage of all the power and flexibility in Final Cut.

So, grab an extra large cup of coffee and snuggle up next to your computer—by the time you're done with this chapter, you'll know everything there is to know about the FCP interface: how to navigate in it, how to customize it, and what keyboard shortcuts you should use to run it.

The Final Cut Pro Interface

There are four main windows in Final Cut Pro. This initial discussion presents their purpose and use. Then, there will be a series of exercises so you can explore the interface further.

During this initial presentation, I use the files that you'll be editing in Chapter 4, "*Build Your Story.*"

Four main windows and two small palettes make up the principal interface of Final Cut Pro:

- Browser
- Viewer
- Canvas
- Timeline

The principal interface also includes two floating palettes:

- Tool Palette
- Audio Meters

 MOVIE | Interface.mov

If you want to learn more about the Final Cut Pro interface and watch it in action, be sure to watch the **Interface.mov** located inside the **movies** folder on the **FCP HD HOT** DVD.

All windows float, meaning you can drag them anywhere on your computer screen, resize them, park them on the Dock, even make them disappear—though it is very tough to edit your project when some windows are missing.

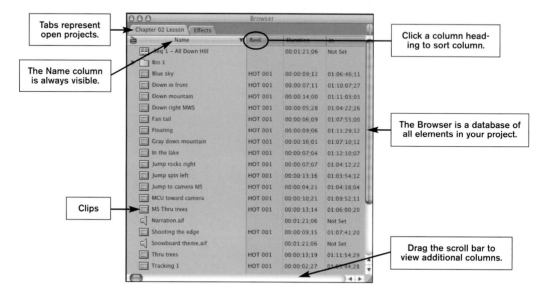

Tabs represent open projects.

The Name column is always visible.

Clips

Click a column heading to sort column.

The Browser is a database of all elements in your project.

Drag the scroll bar to view additional columns.

The **Browser** is a list of all the elements you can access for your project. Think of this as a database, showing you everything you need to know about all the different clips, graphics, music files, and sequences in your project. (The files in this example are the ones you'll be using in Chapter 4, *"Build Your Story."*)

NOTE | Definitions

Project: This is the master file that Final Cut Pro creates to store all the information needed to edit your video—*except* the actual media itself.

Media files: These are the actual audio and video elements, recorded on videotape, that get transferred to your computer's hard disk for editing and output. All media files created by Final Cut are stored as QuickTime movies.

Clips: References stored within Final Cut to the actual media files stored on your hard disk. Clips stored in Final Cut are simply pointers that "point" to the media files. Although it seems like you are editing your actual media files, in fact, you are simply arranging these small pointer files. The benefit to this approach is that your project files remain small, allowing you to edit huge projects easily.

Sequence: When you edit in Final Cut, you are editing a sequence of clips that start at the beginning and go to the end. Some projects have only one sequence; others have dozens. There is no real limit to the number of sequences you can store in Final Cut.

Tabs provide access to different functions and controls.

The Viewer is your preview window.

Playhead window

Transport controls

Shuttle bar

Jog wheel

Editing and marking controls

The **Viewer** window is where you preview and modify your clips, transitions, filters, and effects. It has the following sections, starting at the top:

- Window tabs to select specific window functions
- Timecode and window display controls
- Video frame or audio waveform display
- Playhead window
- Playback controls
- Editing and marking controls (left side)
- Recent clips and Generator pop-up menus (right side)

Each open sequence has its own tab.

The Canvas is your "program" window. This shows what your sequence looks like.

Transport controls

Shuttle bar

Jog wheel

Editing controls

The **Canvas** window displays your final program. Its layout is almost identical to the Viewer window, but its function is different. The Viewer helps you decide how to edit your clips or create your effects. The Canvas shows you the final results. In fact, the Canvas window works in tandem with the Timeline to give you two different views of your project.

Viewer

Canvas

The Canvas window layout is almost identical to the Viewer, except for the names of the tabs at the top and the controls in the bottom corners of each window. The great benefit to this is that once you know how to operate one window, you know how to operate both. And, in fact, it's even better than that, because there are several other specialized windows that also involve video control–Log & Capture, Trim Edit, and Edit to Tape–that look and act just like the Canvas and Viewer. This consistency of interface is one of the great strengths of Final Cut and helps make learning it a lot easier.

Video tracks

Open Sequence tab

Timeline controls

Audio tracks

Move the slider to navigate through your sequence.

The **Timeline** window is where you assemble all your clips into a final program. Clips are laid out from left to right, with the start of your program beginning on the left. The Timeline has four major sections:

- Video tracks, on top, in blue
- Audio tracks, on the bottom, in green
- Track controls, on the left side
- Timeline controls, on the bottom

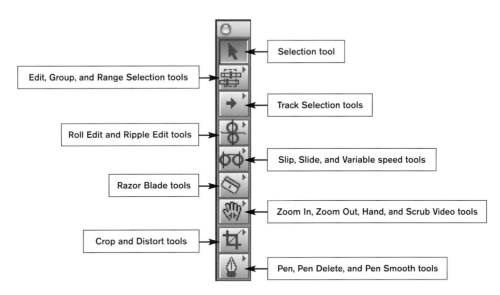

In addition to these four main windows, two floating palettes have a principal role in Final Cut. The first is the **Tool palette**, which contains the editing, sizing, and trimming tools. You'll start working with this in Chapter 5, *"Organize Your Story."*

The other floating palette holds the **Audio Meters**. You'll learn more about these in Chapter 7, *"Audio— The Secret to a Great Picture."*

Now that you've been introduced to the interface, it's time to take a closer look at each of these windows. Since you'll be spending a lot of time with them, you might as well be friends.

Editing Flow in Final Cut Pro

There's a basic system to how Final Cut encourages you to edit:

1. Load a clip from the Browser into the Viewer.

2. Set the In and the Out for the clip.

3. Edit the clip from the Viewer into the Timeline.

4. View the finished result in the Canvas.

Although there are lots of different ways you can accomplish each step, these four steps lie at the core of all your editing. You'll perform them dozens, even hundreds, of times in each project.

You may recognize these steps as a subset of the nine-step editing workflow you learned about in Chapter 1. That's because even though many shows may not need any special effects or animation, they each need their clips strung together in the right order, then viewed to make sure everything looks right.

I. _____Explore the Browser

In this exercise, you'll learn what the Browser is, how to organize column headings, how to create a new storage bin, and how to use clip labels.

NOTE | How to Open Lesson Files

The lesson and media files you installed in the Introduction chapter are used throughout this book.

There are two ways to open lesson files.

Method 1

1. Open Final Cut Pro.

2. Choose **File > Open** (or press **Cmd+O**).

3. Open the boot disk (the one in the top-right corner of your Mac's screen—often called **Macintosh HD**, but not always).

4. Open the **FCP Projects** folder.

5. Open the **FCP Hot files** folder

6. Open the **Lessons** folder.

7. Select the project file you want to open, for example **Chapter 02 Lesson**.

8. Click **Open**.

Method 2

1. From the **Finder**, open the boot disk.

2. Locate and open the **FCP Projects** folder.

3. Open the **FCP HOT files** folder

4. Open the **Lessons** folder.

5. Double-click the project file you want to open, for example **Chapter 02 Lesson**.

You can select whichever of these two methods is most convenient for you to use.

After you've opened a lesson file, you can easily find it again by choosing **File > Open Recent** from within Final Cut and selecting the file you want to reopen.

If you want to go back to the original project before you started making changes (or go back to the last time you saved the project), choose **File > Revert**. Click **OK** to agree to losing all changes.

---

1. Open **Chapter 02 Lesson**.

*If you already have the file open, choose **File > Revert** (and click **Yes** to agree to lose all changes) to reopen the project to the condition it was in the last time it was saved.*

*This is the Browser. (Notice that the window is labeled at the top in its title bar.) The Browser acts like a database tracking all the elements of your project. It contains 52 columns of information (called **metadata**, or data about data) on each of the items loaded into it. Thirty-six columns are initially visible in the Browser, the other 16 are hidden, but accessible if you know where to look.*

On the left side of the Browser are icons that indicate the form of each element stored in the Browser.

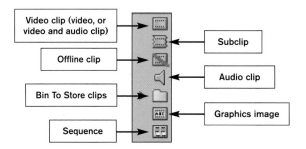

The seven Browser icons indicate the following:

- *A video clip, which can be video-only or video and audio (see Chapter 3, "Gather Your Media")*

- *A subclip, which is a special form of a normal clip (see Chapter 6, "Trim Your Story")*

- *An offline clip (see Chapter 3, "Gather Your Media")*

- *A bin (or storage folder) (see Chapter 4, "Build Your Story")*

- *An audio clip with audio only (such as a sound effect or music file) (see Chapter 7, "Audio–The Secret to a Great Picture")*

• *Imported graphics file, such as a scanned image (see Chapter 9, "Text, Titles and Graphics")*

• *Timeline sequence (see Chapter 4, "Build Your Story")*

You'll work with all of these during this book.

2. For now, grab the window sizing tab in the lower-right corner of the **Browser** and drag it down and to the right to make the Browser bigger.

Notice, as you do so, all the additional columns of information that appear. Scroll around them using the horizontal scroll bar at the bottom of the Browser.

NOTE | Revealing the Hidden Secrets of the Browser

There are 36 columns of information displayed by default in the Browser, with another 16 columns of less-used information initially hidden. To display a hidden column, **Ctrl+click** any column heading *except* the Name column, and choose one of the columns in the shortcut menu to display it in the Browser.

To hide a column, **Ctrl+click** any column heading *except* the Name column and choose **Hide Column**. However, even though the column is hidden, Final Cut still keeps track of the information it contains.

Click and drag column header to move it

3. Reorder the columns in the **Browser** by clicking a column header and dragging it to a new location. In this case, use the horizontal scroll bars and scroll right until you find the **Reel** column, about two-thirds across the Browser.

4. Click and drag the **Reel** column to the right, until it is next to the **Name** column.

NOTE | Reel Names and Numbers

As you will learn, reel numbers are essential to harnessing the power of Final Cut because they allow you to find and recapture clips if you ever need to reedit a project in the future. For this reason, I always move the Reel column from the far right where it's buried in the Browser, all the way to the left, next to the clip name column, so I can easily see it.

Chapter 3, "*Gather Your Media*," covers working with reel names in more detail.

Ascending sort on clip name

Descending sort on clip name

5. Click the column header to alphabetically sort a column. (Notice the downward-pointing arrow.) To do a reverse sort, click the header again. (Notice that the arrow direction now points up.)

Sort first by Reel ID, then by clip name.

6. It is often useful to sort on two columns at once. To do this, click the first column header (the primary sort), then hold the **Shift** key and click the second column (the secondary sort). For instance, click first on the **Reel** column to sort all clips by reel name, then **Shift+click** the **Name** column to sort clips alphabetically by reel.

To switch from sorting on two columns to sorting using only one column, click any column head that isn't one of the sorting columns. For instance, if you are primarily sorting on Reel, and secondarily on Name, clicking the Name header will toggle between ascending and descending sorts by clip name. Clicking the Duration column header (or any header that isn't the Reel or Name column) will re-sort the Browser by only that column.

7. Bins in the Browser are used just like folders in the Finder; to help you organize, store, and locate clips. There are three ways to create a new bin in the **Browser**:

• Choose **File > New > Bin**.

• **Ctrl+click** in the light-gray area of the **Name** column and choose **New Bin** from the shortcut menu.

• Click in the **Browser** to make it active, then press **Cmd+B**.

NOTE | How to Tell if a Window Is Selected

You can tell if a window is selected by looking at the color of the title bar at the top of a window.

Selected windows have a light-gray title bar with a subtle, rounded, 3-D look.

Unselected windows have a dark-gray title bar, with a flat look.

8. Change the name of any bin or clip by double-clicking it, then typing in a new name.

WARNING | Clip Names and Media Files

Changing a clip name does *not* change the name of the media file to which that clip points. If you plan to recapture the media for a project, for instance to convert from a low-resolution offline edit to a high-resolution online edit, try not to change your clip names. Keeping file names consistent minimizes confusion in matching clips.

However, if you are working at your final resolution (i.e., DV) and don't plan to recapture media, renaming clips in the Browser will not cause any problems.

NOTE | Tips on Naming Bins

I use bins to keep similar things together: music files, sound effects, all answers from one interview guest, all B-roll, and so on. Generally, I try to keep the top level of the Browser pretty well organized and not have hundreds of files to scroll through.

For most projects, I find myself creating a similar series of bins:

- Interviews
- B-roll
- Music
- Graphics
- Sound Effects

Final Cut allows you to nest (which means to put something inside something else) bins up to eight levels deep. However, I've found that FCP has trouble if you get more than five or six bin levels deep (meaning a bin stored in a bin stored in a bin, and so on). Since there is no limit to the number of bins you can create at a single level, and you can store hundreds of clips in a single bin, I've not found this five- to six-level restriction a significant limit.

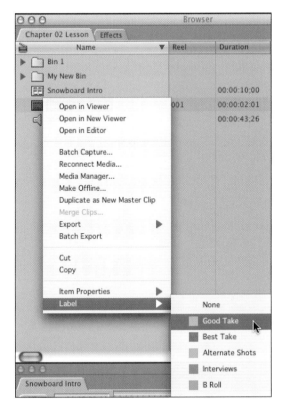

9. You can also use labels to help organize your bins and clips. To apply a label, **Ctrl+click** a clip in the **Browser**, drag down the resulting shortcut menu to the bottom, choose **Label**, then slide across and select one of the five label choices. (There's also a label column in the **Browser** that you can use, but this is faster.) Notice how, when you label a clip, it changes color. You'll learn later in this chapter how you can change the text of a label.

10. If you are done exploring for the moment, choose **File > Close Project** and don't save changes. Otherwise, leave Final Cut open to take a look around the **Viewer**.

2. _____Explore the Viewer

In this exercise, you will learn what the Viewer is, how it works, and how to navigate around in it.

The Viewer is your preview window. In it, you'll set Ins and Outs, modify transitions, adjust filters and effects, enter type, and create animations. Not, however, all in this lesson! Still, the Viewer is a highly flexible device that gives you plenty of control over your program.

NOTE | Larry's First Interface Rule of Final Cut Pro

Thinking about the Viewer brings to mind the first of my two interface rules for Final Cut Pro:

Select something, then do something to it.

Although this may not be as deep as "I think, therefore I am," it *is* the underlying method Final Cut uses to determine what you want to do. You select a clip and edit it to the Timeline. You select a clip and delete it. You select an edit point and add a transition. You select an audio clip and apply a filter. And so on.

NOTE | The Great "Mouse vs. Keyboard" Debate

I will confess right here near the beginning that I am a huge keyboard shortcuts fan; which is why you'll find at the end of each chapter a summary of relevant keyboard shortcuts for that chapter.

On the other hand, I work with a very talented editor who does everything with the mouse. In fact, Ed does everything he can to avoid touching the keyboard.

Fortunately, Final Cut is not so partisan. It doesn't particularly care if you edit using just the keyboard, just the mouse, or some combination of both. There are over 600 menu commands in Final Cut Pro. You can access them using menus, program them into keyboard shortcuts, or create individual mouse button shortcuts (which you'll learn how to do later in this chapter).

My goal is to show you the options, then let you pick the one that works best for you.

Clip duration

Timecode position of playhead

Playhead

Start of clip

End of clip

This is the Viewer window, with the Video tab selected. Although there's a lot of depth here, for right now, you'll concentrate on general layout and navigation.

1. Start by opening **Chapter 02 Lesson**, if it isn't already open.

*If you already have it open, choose **File > Revert** (and click **OK** to accept losing all changes) to reopen the project to the condition it was in the last time it was saved.*

2. Look for the **MCU to camera** clip in the **Browser**. Load it into the **Viewer** by double-clicking it.

NOTE | Three Ways to Load a Clip into the Viewer

In order to view a clip or set Ins and Outs, you need to load it into the Viewer. Because loading clips is something you'll do hundreds of times in a project, Final Cut makes it easy by providing three ways to load a clip into the Viewer:

• Double-click the clip name in the **Browser**.

• Click the clip name in the **Browser**, then press **Return**.

• Drag the clip from the **Browser** to the image section of the **Viewer**.

I've used all three, but I tend to be a double-clicker.

NOTE | Larry's Second Interface Rule of Final Cut Pro

Loading a clip into the Viewer reminds me of my second interface rule for Final Cut:

Double-click something to load it into the Viewer.

As you've just seen, double-clicking the name of a clip loads it from the Browser into the Viewer. Double-clicking also can do the following:

• Load clips from the Timeline into the Viewer (see Chapter 4, "*Build Your Story*")

• Load edit points into the Trim Edit window (see Chapter 6, "*Trim Your Story*")

• Load transitions into the Transition Editor (see Chapter 8, "*Transitions—Making Change Beautiful*")

The reason the Viewer is so important is that you use it to make changes to a clip—whether it's something as simple as resetting an In or an Out, or as complex as modifying a filter, the Viewer, and the tabs it contains.

The lower portion of the Viewer window contains the playback controls for a clip, which consist of the following:

Playhead: *The vertical black line with the yellow triangle on top is called the playhead, and it represents the width of a single frame. The frame the playhead is parked on, or playing over, or scrolling across, is shown in the image section of the Viewer. By sliding the playhead back and forth in the white horizontal space at the bottom of the clip (remember, clips can be video, audio, or both), you can view the entire contents of the clip.*

The look and operation of the playhead is identical in the Viewer, the Canvas, and the Timeline. The key point is that the vertical black line represents the frame being displayed in the window.

Media limits: *The thin black vertical line at the left and right edges of the playhead scroll space represent the absolute beginning and ending of the clip loaded into the Viewer, These are called the clip's media limits. You'll discover the importance of these in Chapter 6, "Trim Your Story," and Chapter 8, "Transitions—Making Change Beautiful."*

Shuttle bar: The shuttle bar allows you to quickly scroll back and forth in your clip. The farther you move the bar from the center, the faster you go in that direction.

Jog wheel: The jog wheel allows you to slowly move the playhead through a clip. You move it by dragging it left or right.

Playback buttons: The playback buttons provide a series of specialized button shortcuts for playing the clip in the Viewer. The center button plays a clip from the location of the playhead. When a clip is playing, this button converts to a Stop button. You can also play a clip by pressing the spacebar. When a clip is playing the spacebar also stops it. The other buttons will be discussed more in Chapter 4, "Build Your Story."

3. Experiment with moving around in a clip:

- Press the spacebar to play and stop the clip.

- Grab the playhead with the mouse and drag it around.

- Slide the shuttle bar to the left and right to fast forward and rewind through a clip.

- Turn the jog wheel to learn how to move a clip in slow motion.

4. Experiment with the five buttons just below the image of the clip to see what they do:

- Click the center button (the right-pointing arrow) to play a clip.

- Click it again to stop the playback.

- Click the leftmost button to jump to the beginning of a clip.

- Click the rightmost button to jump to the end of a clip.

• Click the second button from the left to play a clip from beginning to end. (You will learn about a more powerful function of this button in Chapter 4, "*Build Your Story*," when you see it also allows you to play a clip from the In to the Out.)

• Click the second button from the right to play a clip starting a few seconds before the playhead and ending a few seconds after the playhead. (You'll learn how to change the length of this pre-roll and post-roll in Chapter 4.)

But there are even more powerful tools you can use to play clips.

NOTE | Power Playback: The J-K-L Keys

In addition to the buttons and controls built in to the Viewer, there are three power keys that I use all the time. These are the J, K, and L keys. They have a variety of functions, depending upon how many times you press each key, as the following table illustrates:

J, K, and L Playback Control Keys

Press	What Happens
L	The clip plays forward from the location of the playhead.
K	The clip stops.
J	The clip plays backward from the location of the playhead.
L+L (press L twice)	The clip plays forward at double speed from the playhead.
L+L+L	The clip plays forward at 4x speed from the playhead.
J+J	The clip plays backward at double speed from the playhead.
J+J+J	The clip plays backward at 4x speed from the playhead.
K+L (hold down both)	The clip plays forward at about one-third normal speed from the playhead.
K+J (hold down both)	The clip plays backward at about one-third normal speed from the playhead.

I use the J, K, and L keys all the time. In fact, I almost never use the shuttle bar or jog wheel. Between the mouse and the J, K, and L keys, I have all the speed and control I need.

Notice the two boxes at the top-left and top-right corners of the Viewer window. These are placed to display and enter timecode. The left box displays the duration of the clip loaded in the Viewer. The right box displays the location of the playhead in timecode. You'll work with these boxes extensively in Chapter 4, "Build Your Story."

5. Grab the playhead and slide it around. Notice how the timecode in the upper-right display changes as you move the playhead.

6. Now, put the playhead in the middle of the clip. Double-click in the box in the top-right corner to select everything in it.

7. Press the **+** key on your keypad or keyboard. If you are using a PowerBook, you'll need to press a special function key to access the keypad keys.

Now, type **30** and press **Enter**.

See how the playhead jumped forward a full second?

8. Press the **–** key on your keypad or keyboard. Type **45** and press **Enter**.

See how the playhead jumped backward a second and a half?

This capability to jump around in a clip is due to Final Cut using timecode to keep track of every frame of video. And you'll learn about timecode next.

9. That's it for the moment. If you want to stop, choose **File > Close Project** and *don't* save your changes. Otherwise, leave everything right where it is and go on to the next section.

What Is Timecode?

Timecode is one of the core concepts at the foundation of all professional video editing. In this section, you'll learn what timecode is, how to read it, and how to use it in Final Cut.

Timecode is a label that uniquely identifies each frame of video in your production. In fact, when you record or play back a videotape, you are actually recording, or playing back, more than just audio and video. You are also recording timecode. Each frame of video, and its corresponding audio, is assigned a unique, sequential timecode label.

Final Cut reads that timecode and uses it to make sure all your clips and edits are exactly where you want them.

Timecode consists of eight numbers, grouped in pairs and separated by colons or semicolons. The first pair of numbers (01) represent the hour—in this example, hour 1. There are 24 hours of timecode, starting at hour 00 and ending at hour 23. In a DV environment, all recordings start at hour 00. In a professional environment, timecode can be preset. One of the tricks professional camerapeople often use is to change the timecode hour to reflect the number of tapes being shot. Thus, the first tape would be set to hour 1, the second to hour 2, and so on. This helps keep track of tapes and shots during the editing process.

The second pair of numbers (23) represents minutes. There are 60 minutes of timecode, starting at 00 and ending with 59. When the 60th minute arrives, the minutes reset to 0 and the hours increase by 1.

The third pair of numbers (15) represents seconds. There are 60 seconds of timecode, starting at 00 and running through 59. When the 60th second arrives, the seconds reset to 0 and the minutes increase by 1.

The fourth pair of numbers (08) represents frames. There are three principal frame rates: 24, 25, and 30 frames per second. Frames are displayed from 0 to 23, or 24, or 29, depending upon frame rate. Then, the frame number resets to 0.

Who Uses What Frame Rate?	
Frame Rate	**Used Where**
30 frames per second	NTSC video—North America and Japan
25 frames per second	PAL video—Rest of the world
24 frames per second	Film, most high-definition video, a few DV cameras

Final Cut can edit any of these three frame rates. However, only one frame rate can be selected per sequence. You need to create different sequences for each frame rate you want to edit. A project can contain multiple sequences, each with different frame rates, as needed.

NOTE | The Power of Timecode

The power of timecode is that, since every frame has its own unique identifying number, every frame can be precisely located and displayed. This makes it possible to do frame-accurate edits.

In Final Cut, a clip is identified by both its reel name and its timecode, which is why keeping the reel names accurate is so important.

Timecode is a label that identifies each frame (the way that "Fred" and "Ginger" uniquely identify two dancers). There are two types of timecode: **drop-frame** and **non-drop-frame**. The difference between the two is that drop-frame timecode is used when you want to represent real time, whereas non-drop-frame timecode gives every frame a perfectly sequential number.

All DV footage uses drop-frame timecode; professional formats can select between the two. Final Cut also has the capability to select between the two. Which should you choose? If you are shooting DV footage, stay with drop-frame timecode.

In a professional environment, non-drop-frame time code is used in film, commercial, DVD, and animation work. Drop-frame timecode is used in any program that will be broadcast, cablecast, or any situation where knowing exactly how long a sequence runs in real time is important.

Because timecode is a number, Final Cut uses it to make calculations regarding clip location, duration, playhead placement, and edit points. That's why you are able to move the playhead by simply typing an "offset timecode." What you are saying to Final Cut is, "Please move the playhead forward (+) or backward (−) the number of frames I type next."

In the example at the end of the preceding exercise, we moved the playhead forward 30 frames and backward 45 frames. Remember, there are 30 frames of video in every second of time for NTSC video.

3. ——————————**Explore the Timeline**

In this exercise, you'll learn the basic operation of the Timeline and how clips are laid out in the Timeline, and discover the similarities between how the Viewer and Timeline play back clips.

The Timeline and the Canvas are, essentially, two views of the same thing. The Timeline allows you to organize your clips from start to finish, whereas the Canvas displays the video under the Timeline playhead. You need both to be able to edit and view your program.

1. Start by opening **Chapter 02 Lesson**, if it isn't already open.

*If you already have it open, choose **File > Revert** (and click **OK** to agree to lose all changes) to reopen the project to the condition it was in the last time it was saved.*

Notice that when you open this project, a sequence automatically opens into the Timeline. The Timeline is the window that contains sequences of edited clips. You can have as many sequences open as you like—in all cases, though, they are displayed in the Timeline.

> ## NOTE | Sequences Take Memory
>
> Although Final Cut allows you to open as many sequences into the Timeline as you want, the more sequences you open, the more memory they will take. For this reason, I make it a habit to keep the number of open sequences to a minimum. Sequences in the Browser take almost no memory, but memory *is* allocated when they are opened in the Timeline.

The Timeline is divided into four main sections: video tracks and audio tracks that contain clips, track controls, and Timeline controls.

The audio and video clips section of the Timeline is divided into two halves, separated by the double-gray line in the center: the top half contains video clips, displayed in blue, and the bottom half displays audio clips, displayed in green.

*Each horizontal line of clips is called a **track**. Final Cut allows you to create sequences containing up to 99 tracks of video and 99 tracks of audio. In general, you stack clips vertically when you want more than one image (or sound) on the screen at one time. You lay clips out horizontally when you want one shot followed by another. The shot on the left goes first.*

NOTE | Turn Audio Waveforms Off for Better Performance

Although the Timeline in this exercise shows audio waveforms on, you'll get better performance from Final Cut Pro by turning waveforms off because when they are on, the computer needs to allocate CPU resources to calculate them. Especially if you are using a slower computer, turning waveforms off will make a big difference in how quickly Final Cut responds.

To turn waveforms off, press **Option+Cmd+W**, or click the small right-pointing arrow in the bottom left section of the **Timeline**, then uncheck **Show Audio Waveforms**.

Playhead

Notice that the playhead in the Timeline is similar to, but much bigger than, the playhead in the Viewer. However, its function is identical. The thin, black, vertical line stretching down from the yellow triangle of the playhead represents the frame currently displayed in the Canvas.

2. To play the playhead, press the **spacebar**. To stop, press the **spacebar** again. The **J**, **K**, and **L** keys also work. Everything you learned about how to play clips in the Viewer also applies here in the Timeline!

Go to In button

Go to Out button

Play button

Since the Canvas and Timeline are essentially two different views of the same edited program, you can also use the buttons on the Canvas to control the playhead in the Timeline.

3. Click the **Play** button in the lower center of the **Canvas**. Watch what happens to the playhead in the Timeline.

4. Click the **Go to In** button and watch what happens. The playhead jumps to the beginning of your sequence.

5. Click the **Go to Out** button and watch what happens. The playhead jumps to the end of your sequence.

6. Click the second button from the right (**Play Around Current Frame**) and watch what happens. The playhead jumps back a few seconds, plays, then stops a few seconds after the point where playback started. Again, just like the buttons in the Viewer.

*You'll learn ways to use the **Play In to Out** button (second from left) in Chapter 4, "Build Your Story."*

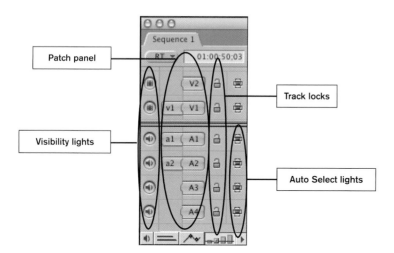

On the left side of the Timeline are the track controls. The green visibility indicators are all lit by default. Turning off the visibility indicator for a track makes a video track invisible or an audio track inaudible. You'll work with these more in Chapter 7, "Audio—The Secret to a Great Picture," and Chapter 10, "Motion Effects."

7. Put your playhead in the middle of a clip. Click the green **visibility indicator** next to the **V1** patch panel. Notice that your **Canvas** has gone black because all your video clips on the **V1** track are now invisible.

8. Turn off the green **visibility indicators** for all audio tracks and play a portion of your sequence. Notice that now all the audio has become silent.

9. Turn on all **visibility indicators** by clicking them so they glow green.

The patch panel controls how audio is routed from the Viewer to the Timeline. You will learn more about this in Chapter 7, "Audio—The Secret to a Great Picture."

The track locks are off by default. Turning a lock on makes it impossible to make changes to a track, including repositioning a clip. You'll learn more about them in Chapter 6, "Trim Your Story."

The Auto Select buttons are on by default. Turning them off, or on, controls track and range selection, as well as copy and paste. You'll learn more about them in Chapter 5, "Organize Your Story."

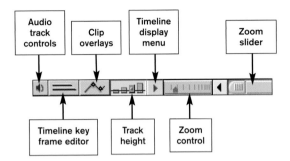

10. At the bottom left of the **Timeline** are the **Timeline** controls. Click one of the four bars in the "bar chart" and notice how the height of the tracks changes.

11. Click the small right-pointing triangle to display the pop-up menu for the **Timeline**. You've already used this to turn off, or on, the display of audio waveforms. Turn on, or off, the other four options in the top section of the menu and watch what happens.

12. Click one of the bottom four choices (Reduced, Small, Medium, and Large). Notice that choosing one of these is exactly the same as clicking the blue/gray bar chart icons immediately to the left of this menu.

13. Next, grab the horizontal track **Zoom** slider and slide it back and forth. Notice how it repositions the **Timeline**.

14. Now, grab either end of the **Zoom** slider (I tend to call this the "mad popsicle stick") and change the size of the slider bar. Notice, as you do so, how the horizontal scale of the **Timeline** changes.

15. If you want to stop, choose **File > Close Project** and don't save your changes. If you are ready to tackle the next stage, leave the project file open.

NOTE | Which Should You Use: Zoom Control or Zoom Slider?

By dragging the middle of the Zoom slider from left to right and back again, you can easily get from one side of a large sequence to another. It can also be used to quickly change the scale of the Timeline, by grabbing one of the tabs at either end and dragging. However, zooming using the Zoom slider changes the scale of the Timeline without any respect to the playhead.

This means you can zoom in such a fashion that the playhead will totally disappear off the edge of the screen. When this happens, look in the Zoom slider track and you'll see a small, thin, almost invisible purple line. Click it and the Timeline will automatically jump to the current location of the playhead.

Zooming by using the horizontal Zoom slider, however, automatically centers the playhead in the Timeline, then changes the scale. For me, using the Zoom slider, rather than the Zoom control, helps keep me from losing the playhead (which is the principal reason I call the Zoom control the "mad popsicle stick").

Well, um, this is not *totally* true. I love keyboard shortcuts. So, if you want to know the truth, when I want to zoom in or out on the Timeline, I *could* press Cmd+ + (that's the Cmd key and the plus key) to zoom in, or Cmd+ − (Cmd and the hyphen key) to zoom out.

But, uh, if you demand absolute honesty, I don't really use any of these. I use the Zoom tool. I wasn't going to mention this until later, but, well, you force me to reveal another secret.

To access the **Zoom** tool, either click the **magnifying glass** in the **Tool** palette and select the **Zoom** tool with a plus (**+**) sign in it, or press the letter **Z** once. To zoom out, select the second **Zoom** tool, the one with a minus (**−**) sign in it, or press the letter **Z** twice. Then, drag the **Zoom** tool around the portion of the **Timeline** you want to enlarge (or shrink).

Even faster, press the letter **Z** once, to select the **Zoom In** tool, then hold down the **Option** key to switch to the **Zoom Out** tool.

Like I said, Final Cut has lots and lots of different ways to do the same thing.

Explore the Canvas

By now, you know almost everything you need to know to get started using the Canvas. (Not, however, everything about the Canvas there is to know.) In this exercise, you'll review what you've learned about playing video in the Viewer, then you'll explore the Fit to Window and View pop-up menus.

Remember, the Canvas is simply another view of the Timeline. The Timeline shows the organization of your program on a clip-by-clip basis. The Canvas provides you a way to view it.

1. Start by opening **Chapter 02 Lesson**, if it isn't already open.

*If you already have it open, choose **File > Revert** (and click **OK** to agree to lose all changes) to reopen the project to the condition it was in the last time it was saved.*

Each open sequence has its own tab.

The Canvas is where you see what your sequence looks like.

Transport controls

Shuttle bar

Editing controls

Jog wheel

2. Notice that the **Canvas** window looks pretty darn near identical to the **Viewer** window. Spend a minute reassuring yourself that the spacebar; J, K, and L keys; shuttle bar; and jog wheel work exactly the same as in the **Viewer**. Because they do.

3. Drag the **playhead** in the **Canvas** and notice that the **Timeline** playhead moves exactly in sync with the **Canvas**. Move the **playhead** in the **Timeline**. Notice that the **playhead** moves in the **Canvas**. As I said, these are two views of the same thing—your sequence.

Can't find the playhead? Remember, it's the thin vertical black line with the yellow triangle on top that you first met when you explored the Viewer and the Timeline.

Window Scaling menu

Window View menu

Playhead sync

Now, time to move on to something new. At the top of both the Canvas and Viewer windows are three small pop-up menus, which are identical for both windows.

The left-hand Window Scaling pop-up menu controls the scaling (or size) of the image inside the Canvas window. (Remember, this same menu also appears in the Viewer, so everything you learn here applies to the Viewer, too.)

---

4. Experiment by selecting different zoom sizes and watch what happens to the picture. Be sure to always leave **Show as Sq. Pixels** checked.

*Generally, the best practice is to always display your images using the **Fit to Window** option. The additional scale options in this menu are very useful when you are creating effects and animation, so you'll revisit these concepts in Chapter 10, "Motion Effects."*

---

5. If you want to stop, choose **File > Close Project** and don't save your changes. If you are ready to plunge forward, leave the project file open.

NOTE | Pay Attention to This Sneaky Trick

If you, in a fit of wild enthusiasm, zoom into your image so that vertical or horizontal scroll bars appear and then try to play your movie, Final Cut will attempt to display your video to the computer monitor in real time in this zoomed-in mode. However, what FCP will *not* do is display your video to an external NTSC monitor or FireWire device. So, if you are busily editing and all of a sudden your external monitor stops working, it's probably because you zoomed into either the Canvas or Viewer windows.

Which brings me to my second favorite keyboard shortcut. It's one that solves this problem: **Shift+Z**. It's called **Fit to Window**, and it automatically scales the video in the Canvas, or the Viewer, or the clips in the Timeline to fit into whatever the active window is. I use this keyboard shortcut constantly.

The second Playhead Sync pop-up menu, in the middle, adjusts playhead sync. This provides some very handy power features, which will be discussed in Chapter 6, "Trim Your Story." However, for editing, leave this off.

The third menu, all the way to the right, is the Window View pop-up menu. This controls how images in the window are displayed. For editing, using the defaults is the best choice. (The defaults have the first line in each of the four menu sections checked.) You'll learn more about using this menu throughout the rest of this book, especially in Chapters 9, 10, and 11.

Power Tools—Specialized Windows You'll Learn About Later

Although the windows discussed in this chapter are the principal windows in Final Cut, there are a whole variety of other windows that you'll learn about later, as shown in the following table.

Other Windows in Final Cut Pro

Window Name	Function	Chapter Discussed
Video Scopes	Check color and video levels	Chapter 3
Log & Capture	Control and capture clips	Chapter 3
Storyboard editing	Edit clips using thumbnails	Chapter 4
Tool palette	Trimming and editing tools	Chapter 6
Trim Edit	Precision, on-the-fly editing	Chapter 6
Audio Meters	Measure audio levels	Chapter 7
Audio Mixer	Combine and control audio tracks	Chapter 7
Voice Over tool	Record narration directly into FCP	Chapter 7
Transition Editor	Modify transitions	Chapter 8
QuickView	View effects without rendering	Chapter 10
Frame Viewer	Simultaneously compare frames	Chapter 11
Media Manager	Copy, move, and convert clips	Appendix

5. _____Customize Final Cut Pro

In this exercise, you'll learn how to customize Final Cut Pro. The best tools, I've discovered, disappear as you learn how to use them. Thus, with practice, you stop worrying about how to hold the hammer, and instead concentrate on hitting the nail. You pay attention to your driving, not to how the spark plugs work.

This is also true for Final Cut Pro. As you get familiar with how it works, you'll pay less attention to the software and more to bringing the ideas in your mind out into your project. One of the ways Final Cut makes this possible is through some truly extensive customization. This exercise explains how it works.

1. Start by opening **Chapter 02 Lesson**, if it isn't already open.

If you already have it open, choose **File > Revert** *(and click* **OK** *to agree to lose all changes) to reopen the project to the condition it was in the last time it was saved.*

2. Click the **Browser** to make it active.

3. Change the size of the window (or any active window) by grabbing the resize tab in the lower-right corner of any window and dragging the window to whatever size you want.

4. However, it's more efficient, and a lot more fun, to put your cursor on the black dividing line between any two (or three) windows (notice the shape of your cursor) and drag them all as a group.

5. Best of all, once you have a window layout you like, store it by holding down the **Option** key and choosing **Window > Arrange > Set Custom Layout 1** (or **Set Custom Layout 2**). These layouts are stored in your Preferences files. It's easy to change them by creating a new layout, then using this same procedure to save the new layout in place of the old.

*This brings me to my third favorite keyboard shortcut: **Ctrl+U**. This shortcut automatically resets all your windows to a default layout—something I find very useful because I constantly rearrange windows when I'm editing.*

*Even better, when you save a window layout using this Option key method, you can toggle between the default layout and your new custom layout by pressing **Ctrl+U** and **Shift+U**.*

6. To save a window layout permanently to disk, arrange the windows to your liking, then choose **Window > Arrange > Save Window Layout.**

7. In the dialog box that appears, give your layout a name and save it. By using the default location, Final Cut will display the first five of your saved layout files in the **Window > Arrange** menu.

Auto-Aspect Layout *means that if you move that layout to a different monitor, using a different screen resolution, the layout will automatically scale to fit the new monitor size.*

> **NOTE | Customizing to Memory vs. Saving to Disk**
>
> Final Cut will remember all the customization settings in effect when you quit the program. So that when you restart the program, everything opens up just as you left it.
>
> Very cool.
>
> However, Final Cut does this by storing your layouts in its Preference files. And, as you'll read in the Appendix, sometimes you need to delete the Preference files in order to solve an instability problem with Final Cut. In that case, all your carefully constructed customization settings will be lost.
>
> To prevent this, get in the habit of saving important customization settings to disk. (This exercise will show you how.) That way, when you need to delete Preference files, (and notice I said "when," not "if") restoring customization settings is as easy as choosing **Window > Arrange > Restore Window Layout**.

8. You've already learned how to customize the **Browser** by dragging columns to different locations. Try it now. Grab the divider between **Browser** column headings and slide it from left to right to change the width of a column.

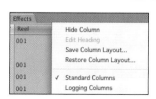

9. Two default column layouts are built into the Browser: **Standard Columns** and **Logging Columns**. Toggle between them by **Ctrl+clicking** any column header, except **Name**, and choosing the one you want to use. Watch how the number, order, and layout of the columns in the **Browser** change.

10. You can also hide columns you don't want, or show columns you do, by **Ctrl+clicking** any column heading, except **Name**, and choosing either **Hide Column** or the name of the column you want to show.

NOTE | A Fast Way to Move Columns

A trick to quickly move a column is to hide it where it is, then **Ctrl+click** the column header where you want it to move to. Your new column will appear to the **left** of the column you Ctrl+clicked.

---

11. Again, Final Cut will remember your columns just the way you left them. However, to make your layouts permanent, save them by **Ctrl+clicking** any column header, except, you know, the **Name** column, and choose **Save Custom Layout**.

12. To recall a saved layout, **Ctrl+click** any header and choose **Restore Column Layout**. Notice that saved layouts automatically appear in this contextual pop-up menu.

13. Remember, a while back, when you applied a label to a clip, I mentioned that you can customize the text for the label? To do so, choose **Final Cut Pro > User Preferences**.

14. In the **User Preferences** dialog box, click the **Labels** tab.

15. In the **Labels** window, you can't change the ugly colors. But you can change the label text to anything you want, by simply selecting the text in the field you want to change and typing in your new label text. Click **OK** to save your changes.

NOTE | There Are FOUR Ways to Apply Labels to a Clip (Whew!)

Method 1

Select a clip. Choose **Modify > Label** and select the label you want to apply to a clip. This is the only method that works on clips in both the **Browser** and the **Timeline**.

Method 2

Ctrl+click a clip in the **Browser.** Select the label from the shortcut menu.

Method 3

Ctrl+click in the **Label** column in the **Browser** on the line for the clip you want to change.

Method 4

Use the keyboard shortcuts—**Option+Cmd+1** (the first label, **None**) through **Option+Cmd+6** (the last label, **B Roll**).

You can even customize the Timeline in terms of track height and a series of attributes. You've already learned how to use the small bar graph to set the track height for all tracks.

16. However, you can also adjust the height of individual tracks by clicking the small gray line between tracks. Hold the **Option** key and drag to adjust the height of all audio or all video tracks. Hold the **Shift** key and drag to adjust the height of all tracks.

17. Click the small right-pointing arrow next to the track height bar chart, and a pop-up menu appears where you can choose Timeline attributes. The bottom four menu choices duplicate the gray bar chart to adjust track height. The purpose of the top five choices are illustrated in the table on the next page.

18. Now, though, choose **Save Track Layout** to save your **Timeline** settings. Previously saved layouts also appear on this menu. Choose **Restore Track Layout** to load a previously saved layout back into the **Timeline**.

Timeline Attributes	
Attribute	**What It Does**
Show Video Filmstrips	Toggles between displaying video clips as picture and file name, and a series of pictures.
Show Audio Waveforms	Toggles audio waveform display on or off.
Show Through Edits	Indicates when you've made an edit where there is no change in video, audio, or timecode. In other words, it's a cut invisible to the viewer. This is often done to start or end an effect.
Show Duplicate Frames	Used when editing film to indicate if you've used the same shot more than once.
Show Clip Labels	After all the work you've done to create custom labels, this will prevent them from being displayed on the Timeline. (Labels are always displayed in the Browser.) Labels are often used to minimize confusion when editing a complex project.
Save... Restore	Saves and restores Timeline layouts to disk.
Reduced... Large	Duplicates the function of the track height bar graph.

One of the most powerful customization features of Final Cut is the capability to modify the keyboard layout.

19. Choose **Tools > Keyboard Layout > Customize** to display the **Default Keyboard Layout**.

20. In this case, you will learn to map one of my favorite keyboard shortcuts (**Fit to Window**) to a different key combination, **Ctrl+0** (zero). To do this, first click the **Lock** icon in the lower-left corner to unlock the keyboard; this allows you to make changes.

21. Next, type **fit** in the data entry box in the top-right corner. (Or, if you know the menu it is located in, twirl down the menu list on the right-hand side of this dialog box to display the menu choice you want to map to a particular keystroke.)

Notice that every menu command containing the letters "fit" is now displayed. There are four of them.

22. Click the **ctrl** modifier key tab to assign this particular command to a specific combination of modifier and keyboard keys. Clicking the tab itself brings it to the front and makes it active. Again, in our case, we want to map the **Fit to Window** command to **Ctrl+0** (zero).

23. Now, grab the **Fit to Window** command from the right side of the window, and drag it on top of the number **0** on the keyboard display.

*Ta-DA! That's it. You have now mapped the **Fit to Window** command to a new key combination. Notice that both the old and new keystrokes are listed in the command list on the right of the name of the command.*

24. To delete a command from a key combination, be sure the keyboard is unlocked (remember that lock icon in the lower-left corner?), then drag the icon for the command you want to remove off the key.

Poof! It's gone.

25. You can export a customized keyboard layout to use on another computer by choosing **Tools > Keyboard Layout > Export**. To change your layout from the default to something else, choose **Tools > Keyboard Layout > Import**.

An excellent editor who I work with hates using the keyboard. He does everything with the mouse. So, Ed was rather put out with all the keyboard customization—until I showed him how to create mouse button bars, which converts menu commands into buttons.

26. To convert menu commands to buttons, choose **Tools > Button List**.

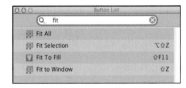

27. Then, just as you did in finding a command to customize into a keyboard shortcut, type the first few letters of the command you want to convert into a button.

To convert a command to a button, drag it from the button list into a button bar. Button bars are located in the top-right corner of each of the four main windows. You can reorganize buttons in the bar by dragging them to their new locations.

28. Drag the command **Fit To Window** into the button bar at the top-right corner of the **Timeline**. Voilà! Instant button shortcut.

In fact, all four windows have button bars that expand to fill the dark gray area at the top of each window. If you fill the entire space with buttons, the button bar prevents you from adding more buttons.

29. And here's my favorite part. If you want to delete a button, simply grab it and drag it out of the bar. Poof! It disappears in a puff of smoke. (Ah, I love that part!)

30. If you **Ctrl+click** a button in any button bar, you can color it, add a spacer, save the button bar to a disk file, or load a different button bar from disk. What you can't do with buttons is rename them, or add something that isn't a menu (like a clip or favorite transition) to the button bar. My suggestion is that if you intend to use buttons, save them to disk—just in case.

31. It's time to end this chapter. Choose **File > Close Project** and don't save changes. If you are done using Final Cut for a while, choose **Final Cut Pro HD > Quit Final Cut Pro HD**. Otherwise, go on to Chapter 3, "*Gather Your Media*."

Helpful Keyboard Shortcuts	
Shortcut	**Function**
Option+Cmd+D	Show, or hide, the Dock
Cmd+O	Open a Final Cut Project File
Cmd+1	Show, or hide, the Viewer
Cmd+2	Show, or hide, the Canvas
Cmd+3	Show, or hide, the Timeline
Cmd+4	Show, or hide, the Browser
Option+Cmd+W	Show, or hide, audio waveforms in the Timeline
Double-click a clip name	Load a clip from the Browser (or Timeline) into the Viewer
Type a letter	Selects clip name starting with that letter in the Browser
Option+Cmd+1	Removes a label from a clip in Browser or Timeline
Option+Cmd+2 through 6	Assigns a label to a clip in Browser or Timeline
Spacebar	Plays, or stops, a clip in the Viewer, Canvas, or Timeline
J, JJ, JJJ	Plays a clip in reverse at normal, 2x, and 4x speed
K	Stops clip playback
L, LL, LLL	Plays a clip forward in normal, 2x, and 4x speed
K+L (hold down both)	Plays a clip forward at about one-third normal speed
K+J (hold down both)	Plays a clip backward at about one-third normal speed
A	Selects the Arrow tool from the Tool palette
Z	Selects the Zoom In tool from the Tool palette
ZZ	Selects the Zoom Out tool from the Tool palette, or just press Option while using the Zoom In tool to convert it to the Zoom Out tool
Shift+Z	Fit to Window (my third favorite keyboard shortcut)
Ctrl+U	Resets all windows to their default sizes and positions (my second favorite shortcut)
Shift+U	Resets all windows to the layout you saved as Custom Layout 1
Option+drag gray bar	Changes height of all audio or all video tracks
Shift+drag gray bar	Changes height of all tracks

Summary

This chapter covered a lot of territory in providing an overview of the Final Cut interface, along with ways you can customize it to make it more efficient. During the rest of this book, you'll discover additional depths in this interface, along with more shortcuts and power tools.

3

Gather Your Media

| Introduction | About Video Formats | Getting Ready to Capture |
| Exploring the Log and Capture Screen |
| Logging and Capturing Media | Reconnecting Media |
| Tools for Power Users |

No Lesson Files

FCP HD HOT DVD

In this chapter, you will learn how to capture media into Final Cut Pro HD.

Capturing is the process of converting the information stored on your videotapes into something the computer can read. And, whether you are capturing DV, VHS, Betacam SP, or High Definition, the process of capturing media using Final Cut is exactly the same.

And, as usual, Final Cut gives you a variety of ways to capture media. This chapter shows you the options.

The Capture Process

This chapter, even more so than Chapter 2, is an exercise in using your imagination. Why? Because the video you capture from your projects on your system won't match the illustrations in this book. So it's hard to write a step-by-step tutorial unless I ship you the same videotape I'm using to create this chapter.

Sadly, I can't ship a videotape with each copy of the book, because it doesn't fit in the binding. So, I'll just show you how to capture and make sure you understand how the whole process works.

Here are the basic steps:

1. Get organized.

2. Set up Final Cut to capture your media.

3. Determine what you want to capture.

4. Capture it.

Chapter 1, "*Get Organized*," got you organized, with a naming and filing system you can use in real life.

Chapter 2, "*Understanding the Final Cut Pro Interface*," gave you an orientation to the Final Cut interface, so you can find your way around the application.

Now, the next step is to get Final Cut ready to capture media. The good news is that Final Cut is automatically configured during installation to work with DV video. So, if DV is your medium, you don't need to do a lot more to prepare.

About Video Formats

I tend to be persnickety about terminology because, goodness knows, there's a lot of it, both in computers and video. So, if you're going to impress people with your ability to talk in jargon, at least use it correctly! Nothing makes me feel like I'm talking to a flake faster than hearing them spout off using words totally out of context.

So, to improve your status in life, here are some key terms you need to understand:

Capturing: The process of converting the information stored on your videotapes into a QuickTime file that Final Cut can read. This "information" includes the video, audio, timecode, and metadata (the data that describes your media) that is recorded on your tapes.

Importing: Bringing information that is already in digital form into Final Cut. For example, all the files I included on the DVD have already been captured, so if you want to bring them into one of your projects, you would only need to import them. The difference between capturing and importing is that a captured file needs to be converted before Final Cut can use it.

FireWire: FireWire is a communications protocol; it is not a video format. FireWire is simply how two devices, such as a computer and hard disk, or computer and video camera, communicate. It's like two people deciding they will both speak French so they can understand each other. If one were speaking English and the other German, they would not be able to understand each other. FireWire is a high-speed protocol for communication.

DV, or Digital Video: As I use it, DV means the collection of all video formats that include MiniDV, DVCPRO-25, and DVCAM. Technical purists will argue that Betacam SX and DigiBeta are also digital formats and, although that is true, for the purposes of this book, I'm going to use the term "DV" to mean these three video formats.

The reason for lumping MiniDV, DVCAM, and DVCPRO-25 together is that, given the same camera, lens. lighting, and subject matter, the image quality and data rate of all three are the same. They record their data to tape differently, but image and compression is identical. Consequently, they are easy to lump into one collective term, "DV."

Video images in DV are significantly compressed in order to keep their file sizes and data rates small, but the video image quality remains high. The data rate for DV video is about 3.75 megabytes per second (MB/s).

SD, or Standard Definition: As I use it, SD is a higher quality video signal than DV. Generally, SD video comes from DVCPRO-50, Betacam SX, Betacam SP, and DigiBetacam. In order to capture SD video, you generally need to use a capture card, which is a device to convert this higher quality video into a format Final Cut can read.

Although the quality of SD images is, generally, better than DV, the data rate for SD ranges from 7.5 MB/s all the way to 27 MB/s.

HD, or High Definition: HD is the new darling of video production. Its images are spectacular, but so are its file sizes. HD video comes from a variety of sources, but fits into one of several file types: DVCPRO-HD (DVCPRO-100), 1080p, 1080i, 720p, or 720i.

HD video file sizes range from roughly the size of SD to 44 times larger than DV. In fact, the largest HD image file has a data rate of almost 160 MB/s!

Frame rate: The speed, measured in frames per second, that your video plays back. There are, essentially, three playback rates: 24 fps, 25 fps, and 30 fps. And, in general, film and some HD use 24, PAL uses 25, and NTSC and other HD formats use 30. (Purists would argue that there are additional frame rates, such as 29.97 and 23.98. They are correct, but for now I'm ignoring them.)

Reel: A name or number given to each reel of videotape to uniquely identify it to Final Cut Pro. I am passionate about using Reel IDs and will explain why later in this chapter.

Data Rates and File Sizes		
Video Format	Approx. Data Rate (MB/per second)	Size of 1 Hour of Video
DV (MiniDV, DVCAM, DVCPRO-25)	3.75	12 GB
DVCPRO-50	7.5	24 GB
DVCPRO-HD	15	48 GB
8-bit uncompressed (Betacam SP)	20.2	72 GB
10-bit uncompressed (DigiBetacam)	27	97 GB
HD (1080p)	160	576 GB

The key point behind these specs is that even though the video formats change, Final Cut remains the same. So, whether you are cutting DV footage or a major motion picture, the process of capturing, editing, and outputting remains the same.

NOTE | Why External Hard Disks Are Necessary

A single, external hard disk is fast enough to capture and play back video for DV and DVCPRO-50. However, for all other video, a RAID provides faster performance and greater storage.

Final Cut Pro HD has developed some special software optimized for handling DVCPRO-HD files. Because of this, you are able to edit DVCPRO-HD files on a single, external hard disk, but you will get more real-time effects and greater storage using a RAID.

I. ——————Getting Ready to Capture

Your entire project takes its organizational, technical, and quality cues from how you capture your video. Although you can always change where files are stored or change their file names, it's a *whole* lot easier to spend a few extra minutes at the beginning of a project getting your system set up properly, rather than spending days later in your project trying to convert everything into the proper format.

In this exercise, you'll learn how to set key Final Cut preferences.

1. Open Final Cut Pro. Although you don't need to open a project file for this exercise, if no project is open, choose **File > New Project**.

Final Cut has four main preference screens:

- *Easy Setup*
- *Audio/Video Preferences*
- *System Settings*
- *User Preferences*

Let's take a quick look through all of them, to make sure your system is ready to capture.

2. Choose **Final Cut Pro HD > Easy Setup**.

The Easy Setup dialog gives you a single, simple location to set all your audio and video preferences for DV or any other format.

3. Click the **Setup For** menu. Choose the video format you want to use for this project. If you are in North America, choose **DV-NTSC**; elsewhere, the **DV-PAL** option is the best choice.

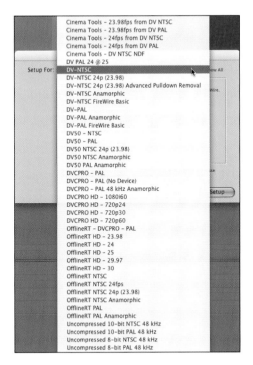

However, Final Cut can handle a whole lot more video formats than just those eight. Click the **Show All** check box, then reselect the **Setup For** menu. Forty-two different video formats are available, and capture card vendors provide even more.

Generally, my recommendation is to match the setup for your project with the video format of your camera.

When you select an Easy Setup, Final Cut uses that choice to set a vast range of technical preference settings, which affect sequences, media capture, video deck control, and video and audio playback.

4. Choose **Final Cut Pro HD > Audio/Video Settings**.

The Audio/Video Settings dialog illustrates the five major areas controlled via Easy Setup.

5. Click the **Video Playback** menu. This controls where you see the video playback from Final Cut. If you intend to have your camera or deck connected to the computer, set this to **Apple FireWire NTSC** (for North America) or **Apple FireWire PAL** (for outside North America). If you don't intend to have a deck or camera connected, be sure to set this to **None**.

6. Click the **Audio Playback** menu. This controls where you hear the audio playback from Final Cut. If you have your speakers connected to your camera or deck, set this to **FireWire DV**; otherwise, set it to **Built-in Audio**.

NOTE | Monitoring Audio and Video

It is important to monitor your audio and video from the same place. If you are watching your video on your computer screen, set your audio to **Built-In Audio**. If you are watching your video on a monitor connected to your camera or deck, set audio playback to **FireWire DV**.

If you listen to your audio on the computer and watch it on a monitor connected to your camera or deck (or vice versa), the audio and video will be 4 to 8 frames out of sync. (That is, their lips are moving earlier or later than when you hear the sound.)

Apple simplified this in FCP HD by adding a new menu to the **View** menu. Now the last choice is **Audio Playback**. To minimize your headaches, leave this set to **Audio Follows Video**.

As an additional note, if you change your video playback settings, or connect a new device, choose **View > Refresh A/V Devices** (or press **Option+F12**) so that FCP will recognize the change.

7. From the **Audio/Video Settings > Summary** screen, click the **Sequence Presets** tab. This illustrates the large number of presets and settings that Final Cut uses to make your video look great.

> ## WARNING | Don't Mess with the Presets!
>
> It is entirely possible to change only one setting file and Final Cut will stop working. If you don't know what you are doing, please be very, VERY careful in changing these. I spend a lot of my consulting time traveling to various clients and resetting settings changed by an overly inquisitive editor. My accountant likes these trips.
>
> If you are shooting and editing DV, there is no reason to change these presets—except if you are shooting Anamorphic DV (see the Appendix for more information on this format).

8. Click **Cancel** to close the **Audio/Video Settings** window.

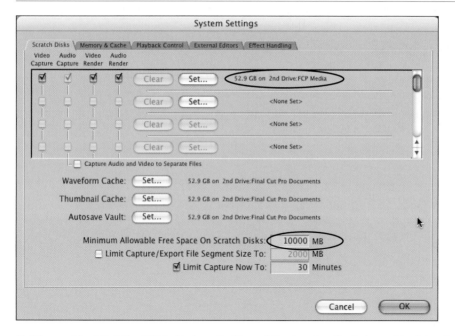

9. Choose **Final Cut Pro HD > System Settings**. We already talked about this dialog in Chapter 1, "*Get Organized.*" However, before the start of every project, I open it and make sure all my settings are correct. This is a good habit for you to get into as well.

10. Verify that your scratch disk points to the **FCP Media** file on your second hard drive. Make sure you have at least 5 percent of your hard drive's total space reserved as **Minimum Allowable Free Space.**

11. Here's a power user tip: Click the **Memory & Cache** tab. If you intend to use a lot of still images in your projects *and* you have more than 768 MB of RAM in your computer, increase the **Still Cache** so that it is at least 100%. If you have lots of RAM in your computer, this will probably be set to more than 100% already, in which case, the default setting of **10%** is OK. Giving more memory to managing stills helps Final Cut improve its performance.

12. Click **OK** to accept the changes you made to **System Settings**.

13. Choose **Final Cut Pro HD > User Preferences**.

*This **General** screen changed in Final Cut Pro HD. It's now divided into two screens (**General** and **Editing**) and a few more options have been added. The settings shown here are how I set up my system, which is changed somewhat from the defaults.*

14. If you are looking for a quick tip, change your settings to match mine in the screen on the previous page.

Changing the levels of Undo requires more than 512 MB of RAM; however, if you have sufficient memory increasing the Undo levels gives you more opportunities to backtrack from a series of editing mistakes.

The **AutoSave Vault** is a backup system. You should still save your project files, as you would do normally. This is an insurance policy to protect against disaster, not a means for you to avoid saving your projects.

The Autosave Vault is an automatic backup system built into Final Cut to help make sure you don't accidentally lose a project. **Save a Copy Every** is a timer, which saves a new version of your project file in the Autosave Vault folder inside the FCP Media folder on your second hard drive. Fifteen minutes is, for me, a nice balance between safety and constantly waiting for FCP to save my project. (You change the location of where the Autosave Vault saves files using the **System Settings > Scratch Disks** dialog.)

Keep at Most tells Final Cut how many backup copies of your project you want to keep. In this case, when the twenty-first version is saved, the first version is erased. This makes sure your hard disk doesn't fill up with backup project files.

Maximum Of tells Final Cut how many projects should be backed up. I don't work on that many projects at one time, so, in this case, when the sixteenth project is backed up, all the backup files from the oldest project are erased. If you are editing lots of projects at once, you should increase this number.

The **Auto Render** settings tell Final Cut that when the computer is idle, in this case, for 15 minutes, to go ahead and render all open sequences. This means that if I am called into a meeting, or on the phone, Final Cut will get to work and render my effects so I don't have to wait for rendering later. You'll learn more about rendering in Chapter 8, "*Transitions—Making Change Beautiful.*"

| Make New Clip |
| Abort Capture |
| Warn After Capture |

Additionally, I want to point out that this screen contains the menu setting for what to do on a timecode break. Timecode breaks are the bane of our existence. In the past, when Final Cut Pro tripped over a timecode break, it would just stop the capture and stand there, pouting. Now, instead, Final Cut gives you three choices when it senses a timecode break:

Make a New Clip: FCP closes the current clip it is recording to disk, creates a new file, gives it a new reel number (by incrementing the old reel number by one), creates a new file name (by incrementing the old file name by one), recues the tape as close to the timecode break as possible, and starts capturing the new clip, starting about 3 seconds after the break. Best of all, this is all done automatically.

Abort Capture: Here, Final Cut stops immediately after it senses a break and waits for instructions from you. Nothing gets recorded to the disk.

Warn After Capture: *Final Cut captures the clip with the bad timecode, then warns you after it's finished recording the clip that the captured clip will probably be unusable.*

If you are capturing from a DV tape, my recommendation is to select the first option, which is the default. However, if you are capturing from an uncontrolled deck (such as VHS), or capturing a live feed (such as from a camera), the third option is a better choice.

15. Click the **Editing** tab. This screen is new in FCP HD. Again, as long as we are here, change your settings to match mine. You'll learn more about what these settings do in Chapter 4, "*Build Your Story.*"

16. Click **OK** when you are done making changes.

17. One last point. There are two options in the **File** menu that relate to the User Preferences dialog: **Revert Project** and **Restore Project**.

Revert Project cancels your current project, though giving you the ability to save your changes, and loads the last version of the project that you saved to disk.

Restore Project cancels your current project, though giving you the ability to save your changes, and opens a dialog listing all the different versions of the project saved in the Autosave Vault, sorted from most recent at the top to oldest at the bottom.

18. You are now done with this exercise. If you are done using Final Cut, choose **Final Cut Pro HD > Quit**; otherwise, choose **File > Close Project** and don't save changes.

2. _____Exploring the Log and Capture Screen

I probably get more questions from my students about capturing than any other two subjects in Final Cut Pro. In this exercise and demo, you'll explore the Log and Capture screen, discover how Final Cut captures audio, and hear my final rant on reel numbers.

NOTE | Logging

First, though, a definition of "logging." Logging is the process of describing each shot you plan to capture. Generally, this involves recording the timecode for the start and end of a shot, the reel it is on, a description of what is in the shot, and whether it is any good or not. Final Cut simplifies this process, but logging is just about everyone's least favorite editing activity.

Sadly, it is also indispensable.

---

1. Open Final Cut Pro. Then, choose **File > New Project** and create a new empty project.

---

2. Choose **File > Log and Capture (Cmd+8)**.

The Log and Capture window is divided into two sections:

• The left side contains a preview window, timecode entry boxes, and machine controls.

• The right side contains three tabs, the first of which is the data entry fields for logging a clip.

This is the bottom of the image preview window. The machine controls are exactly like those in the Viewer and Canvas, which you learned how to use in Chapter 2, "Understanding the Final Cut Pro Interface." The machine control message panel in the lower center of the screen, here showing **VTR OK**, indicates whether Final Cut can communicate with your camera or deck.

The timecode boxes in each of the four corners are discussed later in this exercise.

Machine Control Messages	
Message	**Meaning**
VTR OK	This means that Final Cut is able to control your deck or camera. Generally, when you are using FireWire, this message also means that FCP is also able to see audio, video, and timecode.
	When using RS-422 signals to communicate with your deck, which is very common in SD and HD editing, this message means that Final Cut has machine control. You should not assume that Final Cut can also see audio or video.
VTR in Local	You need to set your Local/Remote switch on the deck to Remote for Final Cut to control the deck or camera.
Tape not threaded	There's no videotape in your deck.
No communication	Final Cut is not able to communicate with the deck for deck control. This message is always displayed when using Capture Now to capture from a noncontrollable device, such as a VHS deck or live camera.

The right side of the Log and Capture window is where you log clips (the top half) or capture clips (the bottom panel).

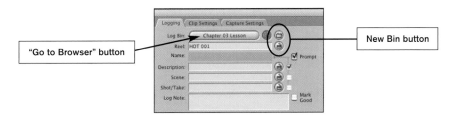

"Go to Browser" button

New Bin button

*Clicking the long oval, labeled **Untitled Project 1** automatically takes you to the Browser for the current project.*

*Clicking the **New Bin** button creates a new bin in the Browser for you to store your clips.*

NOTE | Set Logging Bin

Unless you tell Final Cut otherwise, all your newly logged clips go into the Browser at the top level, that is, outside any bins.

However, if you want to automatically have Final Cut store all your newly logged clips into a bin, select the bin you want the clips stored in and choose **File > Set Logging Bin**.

Notice when you do that the little "logging slate" icon moves from the top-left corner of the Browser, down next to the bin you selected as your logging bin. This slate icon indicates where all newly logged clips are stored: either the default setting of the Browser at large, or next to a specific bin.

Just below the **Log Bin** section is the **Name** section, where you enter the **Reel** name or number, along with naming the clip.

> ### NOTE | A Rant on Reel Numbers and Names
>
> If you never, ever, not even once, plan to reuse any of your projects or media, you can skip to the next section. On the other hand, if you are like the rest of us, you're always reusing projects, in which case, this is important.
>
> When you log a clip, Final Cut records the reel number along with the rest of the logging information. When you capture a clip, Final Cut records the reel number into the media file itself, which is stored on your hard disk, and into the clip information tracked by the Browser. This means that if you ever use the same clip in more than one project, the reel information follows right along with it.
>
> Why is this important? Because when it comes time to recapture a project, either because you want to convert it to higher quality, or you want to reedit an old project, Final Cut uses the reel numbers to locate the source reels of your clips.
>
> If all your reel numbers start with "001," the default for Final Cut, how will you, or Final Cut, know which tape a piece of media came from? Right. You won't. And Final Cut won't. Which means you'll need to go through every one of your tapes to find the one you need.
>
> And that is just plain stupid. Whenever you put a new tape into your deck to capture into Final Cut, enter its reel number into the Reel data field and let Final Cut track it, automatically.
>
> By the way, reel numbers can contain letters, numbers, spaces, and underscores. Avoid punctuation. Keep them short.
>
> Whew. OK—I'm done now.

The check box next to **Prompt** means that Final Cut will ask you to confirm the clip name before it saves it to the Browser.

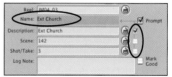

The **Description, Scene**, and **Shot/Take** fields are simply text fields you use to name your clip. Final Cut combines what you enter here to form the clip name, based on the check boxes to the right of each field.

For instance, in the left screen shot, all three check boxes are checked, so the **Name** field combines all three fields into one name, with each field separated by an underscore.

In the center screen shot, the first and third check boxes are checked, so the **Name** combines only the first and third fields.

In the right screen shot, only the first check box is checked, so the **Name** uses only the contents of the first field.

This automation helps make naming clips easier.

The **Capture** controls, at the bottom of the right side, are explained a little later in this chapter, during the capture demo.

There are three tabs at the top-right side of the Log and Capture window. Clicking the second tab, **Clip Settings**, displays this screen.

When you are capturing DV, none of the top settings are active, because DV is a purely digital transfer. These controls become active only when you are using a capture card to bring in analog video (such as a VHS, live camera, or Betacam SP).

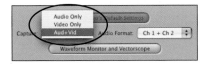

However, the menus in the middle are *important. The left menu controls whether you are capturing audio only, video only, or audio and video. My recommendation is to always capture both. You can always discard audio or video you don't need during the editing process. Going back to recapture it later is possible (because you kept track of your reel numbers, remember?), but it is time-consuming.*

The right menu is surprisingly important, because it can trap the unwary (like it did to me a few weeks ago).

NOTE | How Final Cut Handles Audio Capture

Final Cut *always* and *only* captures two channels of audio. This is really important to keep in mind. If you need to bring in more than two channels of audio, you'll need to do it in groups of two channels at a time.

Second, Final Cut does not like audio recorded at LP speed on your tape, so be sure all your cameras are set to SP speed.

Third, when you are working with DV material, transported over FireWire, you don't have any level (volume) control during capture. This means Final Cut captures your audio exactly as it is on the tape. If you need to make changes, you'll do so during the editing process.

Audio Capture Settings and What They Mean	
Setting	**Translation into English**
Ch 1 + Ch 2	Captures your audio as dual mono. That is, the two audio channels are brought in separately (not mixed), with both channels panned to the center. This is the preferred setting for most audio transfers.
Ch 1 (L)	Takes the audio from camera channel 1 (the left channel), duplicates it to both channel 1 and channel 2, then captures both channels. Both channels are panned center.

continues on next page

Audio Capture Settings and What They Mean *continued*	
Setting	**Translation into English**
Ch 2 (R)	Takes the audio from camera channel 2 (the right channel), duplicates it to both channel 1 and channel 2, then captures both channels. Both channels are panned center.
Stereo	Captures your audio as a stereo pair. That is, the two audio channels are brought in separately (not mixed), with channel 1 panned to the extreme left and channel 2 panned to the extreme right.
	This is the preferred setting for capturing audio when you need to maintain a sense of left and right in the captured audio.
Mono Mix	Combines the audio from camera channel 1 and camera channel 2 into a single mono mix, then duplicates that mix to both channels and captures both.
	I really don't recommend this setting. When you combine multiple tracks, you can get bizarre phase cancellation and weird volume changes, and generally drive yourself nuts. (I'm speaking from painful experience here.)

There's one other section on this tab to look at—**Waveform Monitor and Vectorscope**.

Wave Form Monitor

Vectorscope

The Waveform monitor (left picture) shows the gray-scale shading in your picture from black, at the bottom, to white, at the top.

The Vectorscope (right picture) shows the color in your picture, from all shades of gray at the center, to highly saturated colors radiating out toward the edges.

If you are capturing DV, you can ignore the scopes during capture, because DV is simply transferring the digital signal from the tape to your computer. All video adjustment settings are turned off.

If you are capturing analog tape, scopes are important in properly setting up your images. Chapter 9, "Text, Titles, and Graphics," covers scopes in more detail.

*The third tab, **Capture Settings**, allows you to change device control, capture settings, and scratch disks. These are simply shortcuts to preference windows you've already learned; its just that Apple has provided you a quick way to access them from the Log and Capture window.*

Generally, when capturing DV, once you have these set, you won't need to change them.

3. Close the **Log and Capture** window. This exercise is done. If you are done using Final Cut for now, choose **Final Cut Pro HD > Quit**; otherwise, choose **File > Close Project** and don't save changes.

 MOVIE | Capture.mov

If you want to watch capturing in action, check out **Capture.mov** in the **movies** folder of the **FCP HD HOT** DVD bound into the back of this book.

3. ——————————Logging and Capturing Media

In this exercise and demo, you'll learn how to mark clips, name clips, determine the best way to capture them, and then capture the media.

Keep in mind that since you and I are working with different tapes, our screens won't match. However, the process of capturing is identical, regardless of the content.

For the media in this exercise, I am working with snowboarding footage shot by Standard Films, of Lake Tahoe, Nevada. The footage was first shot on Super 16 film, telecined to Betacam SP, then converted to DVCAM for use in this book.

1. Open Final Cut Pro. Although you don't need to open a project file for this exercise, if no project is open, choose **File > New Project**.

2. Open the **Log and Capture** window (Cmd+8).

3. Put a tape in your deck or camera. (OK, stop laughing. You must admit, it is pretty hard to capture a tape when you forgot to put it in your deck.)

NOTE | Deck vs. Camera

I tend to use the term "deck" because that's what I work with most often. If you are serious about your editing, and can afford it, a videotape deck makes a great deal of sense. It decreases wear and tear on your camera, it has a more rugged tape transport, it allows you to permanently connect your video monitor and speakers to something that doesn't keep moving around all the time, and it frees up your camera for shooting.

So, from here on out, I'll use the term "deck" to include both camera and deck.

Notice that when you put the tape in your deck, the message at the bottom of the **Log and Capture** window changes from **Not Threaded** to **VTR OK**.

4. Enter the reel number for that tape in the **Reel** field. (After all the preaching I've done on this point, don't let me down now.)

NOTE | Definitions

Scrub a clip: To view a clip in Log and Capture, Viewer, or Canvas by dragging the playhead.

Marking a clip: To view a clip to set an In (where it starts) and an Out (where it ends) using timecode.

Logging a clip: Giving a clip that you've marked a name and storing it in the Browser.

Capture Now: Capturing a clip immediately, without first assigning an In or an Out.

Log and Capture: Capturing a clip after you first assigned a name and given it an In and an Out.

Talking head: The audio and video of the person being interviewed.

B-roll: Pictures of what the person being interviewed is talking about, used for illustration.

SOT: Sound on tape. Video with audio, generally meaning a person talking.

Natural sound: Sounds from the environment, not from someone being interviewed, such as the sound of machinery being used, an audience applauding, or animals in the field, which are included with B-roll video to provide a greater sense of realism.

NOTE | Log and Capture vs. Capture Now

There's a lot of heated debate about which is better, Log and Capture or Capture Now. Each has its benefits, and as usual, Final Cut supports both. You get to pick.

Log and Capture. The benefit to Log and Capture is that you look at all your tape before you capture it and make decisions on what you want to capture. This means that you don't waste disk space, or time, capturing footage you won't use; for example, the 20-minute shot of the cameraman's foot as he walks from one location to another when he forgot to turn off the Record button.

The logging side of the Log and Capture window is specifically designed to make logging as painless as possible.

The disadvantage to Log and Capture is that you have to look at all your tape and start making decisions before you capture anything. This takes a lot of time and thought.

I am a huge fan of Log and Capture, but I will confess I hate to log my tapes. It takes time, and it forces me to start making editing decisions very early in the process.

Capture Now. The benefit to Capture Now is that you click one button, **Capture Now**, and Final Cut starts immediately recording whatever you play from your deck onto your hard drive. This means that you can capture huge quantities of media, without having to watch them first.

continues on next page

NOTE | Log and Capture vs. Capture Now *continued*

Capture Now is a favorite of assistant editors in Hollywood whose job description is to capture material so that the editors can decide what they want to cut.

It is also a favorite of people who shoot DV material, because of the capability of Final Cut to flag the start of each scene where the Record button was pressed, which can be a great help in figuring out what you want to edit. (This process of marking DV Starts and Stops is discussed later in this chapter.)

The disadvantage to Capture Now is that you are capturing *huge* data files, most of which you won't use. If disk space is at a premium, this is not an ideal way to work.

One other point. Several versions of Final Cut 4.x have a bug that causes material captured using Capture Now to drift out of sync if you are capturing more than, say, 15 minutes of material at a time. If this happens to you, I recommend you log all your clips (meaning to set a timecode In and Out), even for long clips, and using the Log and Capture, or Capture Clip, features, instead of Capture Now. Capturing a clip under timecode control solves this problem.

This first example shows you how to capture a clip using logging techniques. Later in this exercise, you'll learn how to capture a clip using Capture Now.

There are six machine control buttons (from left to right):

- *Rewind*

- *Play from the In to the Out*

- *Stop*

- *Play*

- *Play Around Playhead, which plays from a few seconds before the current playhead location to a few seconds afterward (you set this timing in the Editing tab of **User Preferences**)*

- *Fast Forward*

---

5. In the **Log and Capture** window, use the machine controls, or the navigation controls you learned in Chapter 2, "*Understanding the Final Cut Pro Interface*" (the J, K, and L keys, spacebar, jog wheel, or shuttle bar), to play your tape until you find the beginning of the shot you want to use.

---

6. Press the **I** key to set an **In**, or click the **Set In** button in the lower-left corner of the window. The timecode for your **In** now appears in the In field.

---

7. Play your tape until you find the end of the shot.

---

8. Press the **O** key to set an **Out**, or click the **Set Out** button in the lower-right corner of the window. The timecode for your **Out** now appears in the **Out** field.

Duration of shot

Notice that Final Cut automatically calculates the duration of your shot and displays it in the upper-left corner of the window.

Timecode position of deck

The box in the upper-right corner displays the current timecode location of the deck.

Reel ID

Prompt for file name check box

Clip naming fields

9. Give your clip a name by entering it into the **Name** fields you learned about in the last exercise. (Notice that a unique reel ID has been assigned to this clip.)

Generally, when I am editing an interview with B-roll, I start all interview clip names with the last name of the person being interviewed, and all B-roll shots with the letter "B." This makes it easer for me to find the shots I need later.

Logs clip for later capture

Captures group of previously logged clips

Captures currently marked clip

Captures clip without setting In or Out

10. Click **Clip** in the **Capture** box. Final Cut cues up the deck to the proper spot and captures the clip. Once the clip is captured, Final Cut gives it the name you assigned in the logging window and displays it in the Browser. This is the easiest way to capture a clip when all you need is one clip.

11. Ta-DA! You've captured your very first clip. (Well, at least, the very first clip using this book.) Double-click the clip in the **Browser** to load it into the **Viewer**, then scrub it to see how great it looks!

Leave the Log and Capture window open. Although it is not a good idea to leave the Log and Capture window open while you are editing, for now, you can leave the window open to view this clip in the Viewer.

12. When you are done viewing the clip, click once on the **Log and Capture** window to bring it to the front. Notice, when you do that the clip name in the logging section of the **Capture** window has a number after it, or, if it ended with a number, that number has been increased by one. This is Final Cut's way to help you name your clips.

NOTE | Clip Names Must Be Unique

The name you give a clip is used in two places: one is the Browser, the other is the name of the actual media file recorded on your hard disk. For this reason, all of your clip names *must* be unique and not contain any characters prohibited by the operating system—such as colons, semicolons, question marks, exclamation points, and other punctuation.

This is why Final Cut adds, or increments, a number at the end of a clip name. It wants to make sure that all clip, and media file, names are unique.

---

13. Repeat Steps 5 through 9 to mark and log a second clip.

14. This time, click the **Log Clip** button.

15. A dialog pops up (assuming the **Prompt** check box is checked on the main logging screen) asking you to confirm the clip name and allowing you to add a descriptive comment and a check box indicating if the clip is any good. All of this information is also displayed in various columns in the **Browser**.

*If the **Prompt** check box is not checked, the clip is recorded directly to the **Browser** using whatever name is currently entered in the **Name** field, and the confirmation dialog is not displayed.*

Notice that the Browser clip has a red line through the icon. This indicates that the Browser has all the information it needs to capture the clip, but the media file itself either doesn't exist or needs to be reconnected. You'll learn about reconnection in Exercise 5. You'll learn about how to capture this clip in a few steps.

16. Repeat Steps 5 through 9 to select a third clip, then, click **Log Clip** to load it into the **Browser**. Do this again until you have a series of clips that are ready to capture. (A clip is ready to capture if it is listed in the **Browser** with a red line through its icon.)

17. Select all the clips you want to capture (all the clips with red lines through them). Then, choose **File > Batch Capture**.

18. In the **Batch Capture** screen, I strongly recommend checking **Add Handles**. Handles are extra video before the **In** and after the **Out**, which you use a *lot* during editing. You'll find handles extremely helpful in trimming shots, adding transitions and just giving you room to change your mind as you put your show together. Generally, I put 2-second handles on all clips I capture.

Notice how Final Cut prompts you to make sure the right tape is in the deck. If you had selected clips from more than one tape, Final Cut will group them by tape, then prompt you to put in each tape as Final Cut needs it for capture.

This is one reason I am such a firm believer in using reel IDs.

19. Once you verify the tape in the deck is correct, click **Continue**.

Sigh…this is my favorite part of editing. Final Cut now goes off and captures every clip that you've selected, while you put your feet up and sip a cup of tea. You monitor progress by viewing the Capture window.

20. When Final Cut is done capturing, up pops another screen reporting completion, or requesting a new tape. Click **Finished**.

*Final Cut removes the red lines from each icon, meaning that each clip in the **Browser** is linked to its media file on your hard disk.*

*You've now captured individual clips, using the **Clip** button, and a range of clips by logging them first, then capturing them all as a batch.*

*There is no limit to the number of clips you can capture at one time in batch mode. You can capture clips from multiple reels during the same batch capture. And once a clip is in the **Browser**, you can drag it into whatever bin you want to help keep your clips organized.*

21. There is no reason to save this project. Your clips have been saved to the hard disk, and in Chapter 5, "*Organize Your Story,*" you'll learn how to import them into a new project. If you are done using Final Cut, for now, choose **Final Cut Pro HD > Quit**; otherwise, choose **File > Close Project** and don't save changes.

Using Capture Now

In this exercise, you'll learn how to capture clips using Capture Now, discover clip markers, and use the automated tools in Final Cut to indicate the start of scenes on DV tapes. In many ways, Capture Now is easier than logging, because you don't need to make as many decisions at the outset.

1. Open Final Cut Pro, if it isn't already open. There are no project files you need for this exercise.

2. Open the **Log and Capture** window.

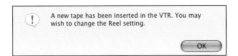

3. Insert a tape into your deck for capture. Be sure to enter its reel number into the **Reel** field. A dialog pops up to remind you.

4. Using either the controls on your deck, or the navigation controls in the **Log and Capture** window, cue the tape so you are a few seconds before the shot you want to capture.

5. Press the **spacebar** to start playing the tape (or press **Play** on your deck).

6. Once your tape is playing, click the **Capture Now** button.

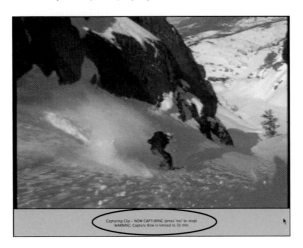

*The **Capture** screen appears, showing the clip you are capturing.*

7. When you reach the end of the clip you want to capture, press the **Esc** key.

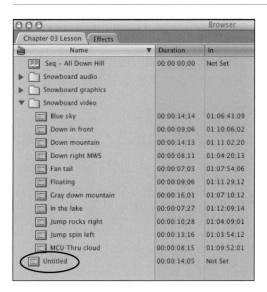

8. Notice that once you are done capturing, the clip appears in the **Browser** with a name already assigned. If there is no name in the **Name** field of the **Log and Capture** window, it will be named **Untitled**; otherwise, FCP gives the clip the name entered in the **Name** field.

NOTE | Wow! Why Not Use Capture Now All the Time?

Well, you can.

Log and Capture is more precise, Capture Now is easier. However, you can't use Batch Capture with Capture Now. That means that you need to stay at your computer to capture every clip.

Also, there's a problem with Capture Now in current versions of Final Cut in that if you capture long sections (say longer than 15 minutes) of tape, there's a good chance audio and video will drift out of sync.

To prevent this, set an In at the beginning of the tape you want to capture and set an Out at the end. Then, capture it using either Batch Capture, if you have a lot of shots to capture, or Capture Clip, if you have only one shot. Even if you are capturing long passages, capturing using time-code keeps your clips in sync.

WARNING | Renaming Clips

Generally, if you are using Capture Now, you will probably want to rename the clips in the Browser after they've been captured to change the default names to something you'd rather use.

Be careful here. Renaming a clip in the Browser does *not* rename the media file on your hard disk. This means that even though you name the clip, "WS My House," in the Browser, the media file on your hard disk retains its original name, which might be something like, "Untitled 23."

This is another reason I like Log and Capture versus Capture Now.

NOTE | DV Start/Stop Detection Is a Great Benefit

One of the great benefits to shooting DV footage is using Start/Stop Detection. When you shoot DV footage, every time you press the Record button, an indicator gets recorded invisibly on the tape, saying that the Record button was pressed here.

Once you capture a clip, you can use Final Cut's **DV Start/Stop Detect** to locate those record points.

Select the clip you want to mark for record points. Choose **Mark > DV Start/Stop Detect**.

Final Cut puts markers into the selected clip showing where the Record button was pressed during production. (You'll learn more about markers in Chapter 5, "*Organize Your Story*.")

continues on next page

NOTE | DV Start/Stop Detection Is a Great Benefit *continued*

If you double-click the clip icon to load it into the Viewer, you'll see these markers in the white bar along with the Playhead. A clip marker is pink, until the Playhead is parked on top of it, when it turns yellow.

Clip markers have two colors: yellow for selected markers and pink for unselected markers. The name of the marker is displayed at the bottom of the screen. To change the name of a marker, place the **playhead** on top of a marker, so it changes color, and press **M**.

You'll learn much more about markers and DV Start/Stop Detection in Exercises 6 and 7 of Chapter 5.

9. This concludes the exercise on using Capture Now. Choose **File > Close Project** and don't save changes. Your media files are stored on your hard disk and are imported into FCP in Chapter 5, *"Organize Your Story."* If you are done using Final Cut for now, choose **Final Cut Pro HD > Quit**.

 MOVIE | Reconnect.mov—Reconnecting Media

If you want to see an example of how to reconnect media, play the **Reconnect.mov** in the **movies** folder of the **FCP HD HOT** DVD.

————————**Demo—Reconnecting Media**

In this exercise, you'll learn why media needs to be reconnected and discover how to reconnect it. Final Cut stores the path name—the name of every folder between the name of your computer down to each individual media file—with each media clip. This makes sure that Final Cut knows exactly where every file is stored. The problem with this approach is that if you move a media file or, more commonly, rename any of the folders in which those media clips are stored, Final Cut loses track of the file. Reconnecting is not necessary all the time. But, if media is missing, this is the only option that puts things back in order.

Because Final Cut can't find the source media, it puts a red line through the clip name in the Browser, saying, "Help, I can't find the file."

This is where the organizing you did in Chapter 1 starts to pay off.

Remember the **FCP Media** folder you created in Chapter 1, *"Get Organized"*? Well, when you pointed your scratch disk to that folder, Final Cut created either three or six folders inside it, depending on how you set the rest of your preferences.

All captured media is stored inside the **Capture Scratch** folder.

In the **Capture Scratch** folder, you'll see that Final Cut has created folders for every project you've created. (Again, your folders will be different from mine.) To see all the video I captured for this chapter of the book, I just have to look inside the **Chapter 03 Lesson** folder.

Using this system keeps everything clean and organized—provided you name and save your projects before you start capturing media.

Now that you know where Final Cut stores media files (inside the folders named after project files and stored inside **Capture Scratch**), it becomes easy to reconnect lost files.

1. When you have missing media, the next time you restart Final Cut an **Offline Files** dialog appears, asking your help in locating these missing files. Click **Reconnect**.

2. In the **Reconnect Options** window that appears, make sure **Offline** is checked and click **OK**. (If the preceding dialog says render files are missing, I've found it far easier to re-render missing files than to try to reconnect existing render files. You'll learn more about render files in Chapter 8, "*Transitions– Making Change Beautiful*.")

The **Reconnect** window appears. Final Cut attempts to find the missing file by looking for the name of a missing media file on your hard disk that matches the name of the file in the **Browser** (as long as the **Matched Name Only** check box is checked).

If it finds the file, it highlights it in the top-right side of the dialog.

*If it doesn't find the file, you have the option to track it down and select it yourself, or click the **Skip File** button in the lower left. This tells Final Cut to skip over this file and try to locate the next missing file.*

3. Click **Skip Remaining Files**, if you want FCP to stop looking for all remaining missing files.

4. If the files are gone permanently, and you want Final Cut to stop pestering you with this **Offline Files** dialog, click **Forget Files: Movie**.

6. ——————Importing Media

Not all the media you'll use in your project needs to be captured. For instance, scans, graphics, music, sound effects, animation...anything that is already digital doesn't have to be captured. All you need to do to load it into the Browser is import it.

In this exercise, you'll learn how to import video clips, graphics, and audio files into Final Cut. Plus, you'll learn what sizes to create graphics so they can look their best.

1. Start Final Cut Pro if it isn't running already. If you have an open project, choose **File > Close Project**. You don't need to save changes.

2. Create a new project by choosing **File > New Project**. You will only use this for this exercise, so you don't need to save it.

3. Start by importing just one file. Choose **File > Import > Files**. Navigate to the **HOT DVD files/Media/Snowboard** folder.

4. Select **Thru trees** and click **Choose**. Notice that the file, which had already been captured, is now listed in the **Browser**.

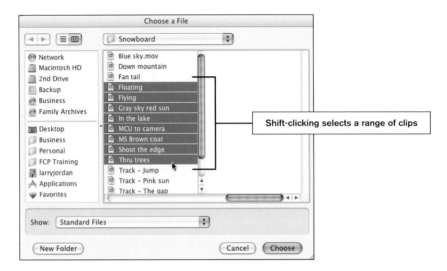

5. Choose **File > Import > Files**. Navigate to the **HOT DVD files/Media/Snowboard** folder and select **Floating**. Then, hold down the **Shift** key and click **Thru trees**. Notice how all files between these two files are also selected. Click **Choose**, and all selected files now appear in the **Browser**.

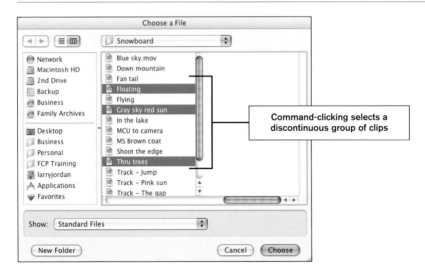

6. Choose **File > Import > Files**. Navigate to the **HOT DVD files/Media/Snowboard** folder and select **Floating**. Hold down the **Cmd** key and click **Gray sky red sun**. Then, still holding down the **Cmd** key, click **Thru trees**. Notice how only the files you **Cmd+clicked** are selected. Click **Choose**, and all selected files now appear in the **Browser**. And, in fact, even though it's the same media file on your hard disk, Final Cut treats it like an entirely separate file, so you see two copies of **Floating**, **Gray sky red sun**, and **Thru trees** in the **Browser**.

7. However, there's a better way to bring in a lot of files. Choose **File > Import > Folder**. Navigate to the **HOT DVD files.Media/Snowboard** folder and select it.

8. Now, all the files in that folder are imported and put into a bin in the **Browser** with the same name as the folder. This is a great way to mimic inside Final Cut the way you have your files organized in your computer.

Chapter 9, "Text, Titles, and Graphics," goes into all the details you need to know to create video graphics. For now, you need to know only how to import them into your Final Cut project. There are two types of graphics: single-layer images (such as scans) and multilayer (such as Photoshop PSD files).

9. With either type of graphics, though, the process is the same. Choose **File > Import > Files** and navigate to **HOT DVD files/Media/Graphics/Canoe.tif** and click **Choose**.

(By the way, TIFF is an excellent format to use for single-layer graphics. Final Cut supports others, but I've never had a problem with TIFF.)

This hundred-year-old photograph is from a series on turn-of-the-last-century clothing. Notice that it has a default duration of 10:00.

10. The default duration for imported graphics is 10:00. You can change it to whatever length you want by choosing **Final Cut Pro HD > User Preferences** and clicking the **Editing** tab. Set the **Still/Freeze Duration** to whatever length you'd like; I have mine set to **5:00**.

---

11. Importing a layered Photoshop document is the same, but the results are different. Again, choose **File > Import > Files**, navigate to **HOT DVD files/Media/Graphics/Snowboard Title.psd**, and click **Choose**.

Scans display a graphics icon

Layered Photoshop files import as a sequence

*Notice that it came in, not as a graphic file, as **Canoe.tif** did, but, instead, as a sequence.*

*The great benefit to importing a layered Photoshop file is that all the layers are maintained, along with their alpha channels (transparency information). In Chapter 9, you'll learn how Final Cut works with LiveType projects to create some amazing animated text. However, whether it's a scanned image, Photoshop file, or LiveType project, you import them all exactly the same way—**File > Import > Files**.*

When it comes time to import music, or sound effects files, there are a couple of rules to keep in mind. Final Cut can mix 44.1K and 48K sample rates on the same Timeline. (If you don't know what a sample rate is, you'll learn about it in Chapter 7, "Audio–The Secret to a Great Picture.")

However, try to avoid 32K sample rate audio files, which is often the default audio setting on some low-end consumer cameras. Switch the audio setting to 16-bit, or 48K (depending on the menu) to avoid audio problems in Final Cut.

Another problem to avoid is using MP3 or AAC files inside Final Cut. Both MP3 and AAC files are significantly compressed, and do not play back well–at all! You'll hear this in detail in Chapter 7.

12. However, the process of importing audio is the same as all other formats. Choose **File > Import > Files**. (When you've learned more about how to use Final Cut, import these two versions of the same audio file and compare the quality of an AIF to an MP3.)

13. That ends this exercise. Choose **Final Cut Pro HD > Quit** and don't save changes. You'll be working with all of these files later in the book.

NOTE | Cheap Importing Tricks

It wouldn't be Final Cut if there weren't some tricks you can use for importing. Here are two tips that speed up importing:

- **Ctrl+click** in the gray area of the **Name** column in the **Browser** and choose **Import > Files**.

- Move some windows around within Final Cut so you can see the **Desktop** underneath FCP. Locate a file or folder that has something you want to import and drag it directly from the **Finder** into the **Browser**.

Both of these tricks making importing faster and easier. Keep in mind, and this is *really* important, that you are *not* importing any *media* into Final Cut. You are only creating a pointer inside Final Cut that *points* to where this media is stored on your computer. If you move this file, you'll need to reconnect it. If you delete it from the hard disk, it's gone.

Tools for the Power User

Striping Tapes

Timecode breaks are the bane of an editor's existence, especially when working with tapes shot by amateur photographers.

When a DV camera starts to record video, it looks to see if the portion of the tape over which it is parked has timecode on it. If it does, the camera matches the timecode and starts recording. If it doesn't, it starts new timecode at 00:00:00:00. If this occurs in the middle of a tape, this is called a "timecode break." To prevent these breaks, you can record timecode for the entire length of the tape. This is called "striping the tape," or "black and coding" a tape. In all cases, it totally solves the problem of timecode breaks during video recording.

Final Cut provides a facility to record audio and video black with continuous timecode on your tapes using the **Edit to Tape** function. Although using Edit to Tape to output your videos is discussed thoroughly in Chapter 12, "*Output Your Project*," using Edit to Tape to "black and code" your tapes is a good thing to learn now.

To start, choose **File > Edit to Tape**.

This is the **Edit to Tape** screen. For now, you can ignore all of it, except…

…this tiny little widget in the top center of the screen. It looks like a squashed centipede. Click it.

This pop-up in this dialog enables you to select what kind of video black you want to feed to the deck. In virtually all cases, **Current Settings** works just fine.

On high-end decks, a second dialog appears, allowing you to enter a starting timecode. Generally, all DV decks start at timecode hour 0 and use drop-frame timecode. Higher-end decks allow you to specify the starting timecode (often 00:58:20:00) and whether the timecode is drop-frame or non-drop-frame.

A final warning dialog appears, alerting you that you are about to totally, completely, and irretrievably erase the tape in your deck. Once you click **OK**, Final Cut erases the tape by recording audio, video black, and continuous timecode on the tape.

Unfortunately, it does this in real time, so come back in an hour, rewind your tape, and you're ready to go.

Changing Reel Numbers

During the first three chapters, I've made a big deal about properly recording reel numbers. However, sometimes, the wrong reel number gets entered into a clip. Sigh…accidents happen.

Often, this is due to Final Cut using a default reel ID of 001. If you don't make a point of changing the reel when you put in a new tape, you'll end up with the Browser showing a whole lot of clips—all from reel 001.

Fortunately, Final Cut provides three different ways to change reel numbers:

Remember, back in Chapter 2, "*Understanding the Final Cut Pro Interface*," when you learned how to rearrange Browser columns by dragging the column header? Well, one of the clips I captured has the wrong reel number. (I, um, forgot to change it.) So, go to the **Browser**, scroll way over to the far-right column, locate the **Reel** column, and drag the **Reel** column header left, next to the **Name** column.

One way to change the reel number is to double-click the reel number. It highlights and allows you to change it. This is the only way to enter a totally new reel number.

The second way to change a reel number is to **Ctrl+click** it. The shortcut menu that appears allows you to select from a list of all the different reel numbers currently in use in your project.

The third way to change a reel number is to use the **Edit > Item Properties > Logging Info** window. However, the first two ways are easier.

Whichever way you choose, this dialog appears, warning you that you are about to change the actual media file on your hard disk. Click **OK**, and the reel number is permanently changed—both in the **Browser** and in the media file on the hard disk itself.

Keyboard Shortcuts Used in This Chapter	
Shortcut	**What It Does**
Cmd+8	Opens the Log and Capture window
I	Sets an In
O	Sets an Out
F2	Opens the Log Clip window (use after setting an In and Out)
Shift+I	Shuttles the videotape deck to the In
Shift+O	Shuttles the videotape deck to the Out
M	Places a Marker in a clip in the Viewer
Shift+M	Goes to the next downstream marker
Option+M	Goes to the next upstream marker
Ctrl+Q	Opens the Easy Setup preference window
Option+Cmd+Q	Opens the Audio/Video Preferences window
Shift+Q	Opens the System Settings window
Option+Q	Opens the User Preferences window
Esc	Cancels any open dialog, as well as Capture Now
Option+F12	Reconnects with the audio/video device (camera or deck)
Enter (keypad)	Accepts the default (glowing blue) button in any dialog

Summary

This chapter has covered everything you need to know about capturing media, whether you are using Capture Now, or Logging before Capturing. And, I can say with relief, all the hard organizational work is over. Starting with the next chapter, you'll dive right into editing.

And you'll start by creating a 30-second snowboarding commercial.

4

Build Your Story

Introduction	Creating and Saving a New Project
Viewing Clips	Setting Ins and Outs	Building the Timeline
Three-Point Editing	Browser Power Tips

Chapter 04 Lesson

FCP HD HOT DVD

I really wanted to call this chapter, "The Ins and Outs of Ins and Outs," because it is.

These next four chapters present the heart and soul of editing in Final Cut Pro. The next three are on editing techniques, and the next one focuses on (amplifies?) audio.

This chapter teaches you how to create and save a new project file, how to select and view clips in the Viewer, set Ins and Outs, and edit these clips into the Timeline.

The Story Is the Heart of Your Video

Any video worth watching has a story at its core. Whether your video is corporate training, a wedding, a commercial, or a documentary, telling your story effectively is essential to keeping the attention of your audience.

The mantra for these chapters is, "Editing is the process of getting rid of everything that isn't relevant to telling your story." Sometimes that selection process is easy, like dumping a blurry image. Sometimes it's painful, like trashing a beautiful tracking shot that took several hours to get, but isn't ultimately relevant to the video you are editing.

Now that you are comfortable with the FCP interface and have gathered your media, it's time to put Final Cut to work and start editing.

I. —————————Creating and Saving a New Project

In this exercise, you'll learn how to create and save a new project, create a new sequence, and learn tips on protecting your projects from disaster.

1. Start by opening Final Cut, if it isn't already running. If it is running, close any open projects by choosing **File > Close Project**. (Saving changes is not necessary.)

2. Choose **File > New Project**, or press **Shift+Cmd+N**.

3. Final Cut automatically creates an empty project and puts a new sequence into the **Browser** and opens it into the **Timeline**.

NOTE | Sequence

A **sequence** is where you edit your clips. A program can consist of a single sequence, or many sequences. Just as the Browser holds clips, the Timeline holds sequences—sometimes just one, other times, lots and lots. Because the Timeline can hold more than one sequence, Final Cut makes it easy to copy clips from one sequence to another.

---

4. Now, before you do anything else—*save* your new project. Choose **File > Save Project As**. In the **Save** dialog, navigate to the **FCP Projects** folder you created during setup, at the beginning of this book.

5. Click **New Folder**, in the bottom-left corner, and create a folder called **FCP HOT Book Projects**, inside the **FCP Projects** folder. You use this folder for all the projects you create in this book.

6. Name your project **My Chapter 4 Project**, and click **Save**.

NOTE | Why Save a Project Now?

Saving a project as soon as you create it is a good strategy, for three reasons:

- The Autosave Vault can't begin creating backups of your project until you save and name it. (The Autosave Vault was presented in Chapter 3.)

- Capturing video for a named project means all the video goes into a folder with the same name as the project. Captured video from untitled projects goes into an "Untitled" folder.

- Saving and naming your project now means that future saves are only a keystroke away (Cmd+S).

7. Create a new bin for your project by choosing **File > New > Bin** (**Cmd+B**). The new bin appears in your **Browser**.

8. Double-click the words **Bin 1**, and name it **Video Clips**. Press **Return**, or click somewhere else to deselect the name.

---

9. As practice in creating a new sequence, create a second sequence for your project by choosing **File > New > Sequence (Cmd+N)**. Leave it named **Sequence 2**.

10. Next, make a copy of this sequence by **Ctrl+clicking** the sequence name in the **Browser** and choosing **Duplicate Sequence** from the shortcut menu.

*Duplicating a sequence is very useful if you have an edited sequence that you like, but want to continue experimenting to see if you can improve it. Duplicate a sequence in the Browser by **Ctrl+clicking** the sequence name and selecting **Duplicate**. This makes an exact copy of the sequence, which you can then change, while still leaving the original sequence intact, in case your great new idea doesn't pan out.*

11. In this case, you don't need these sequences, so select both **Sequence 2** and **Sequence 2 Copy** by dragging a rectangle around them, then delete both of them by pressing the **Delete** key.

12. Save your project by choosing **File > Save** (**Cmd+S**). Then, close this project (**File > Close Project**)—you won't need it for the next exercise. If you are done working for the moment, choose **Final Cut Pro HD > Quit**; otherwise, leave FCP running.

NOTE | Protecting Your Projects

Once you've started working on your project, it's a good idea to protect it from disasters. Here's a tip I recommend to my clients:

If I'm working on a project that will take longer than a day or two to edit, at the end of every couple of days, I choose **File > Save Project As** (or press **Shift+Cmd+S**) and save it under a new name. Generally, I just give it a new version number at the end, such as "My Project v2," "My Project v3," and so on.

The reason for using **Save As**, instead of duplicating the project in the **Finder**, is that during the **Save As** process, Final Cut straightens out any potential technical problems that may exist with the file. This tends to make project files open and close faster, and have fewer errors during editing. Then, the next time I edit the project, I make sure to open the new version.

2. —————————Viewing and Marking Clips

In this exercise, you'll learn how to view thumbnails in the Browser, open clips in the Viewer, and set Ins and Outs for your clips.

Why is setting Ins and Outs so important? Because you always capture more footage than you need. Setting an In and Out allows you to select exactly the portion of the clip that best meets the need of your story at that point in time.

In other words, this is all about giving you the control you need to precisely tell your story.

NOTE | Marking Terms

Media Start: The first frame of the media file stored on your hard disk.

Media End: The last frame of the media file stored on your hard disk.

In: The timecode location where a shot starts. If no In is set, the Media Start becomes the In.

Out: The timecode location where a shot ends. If no Out is set, the Media End becomes the Out.

Marking: Opening a clip in the Viewer and setting the In and/or Out prior to editing it into the Timeline. Marking is generally done in the Viewer, though it can also be done in the Timeline.

Trimming: The process of adjusting the In and Out of a clip, or series of clips, to improve the flow of an edited sequence. Trimming is generally done in the Timeline.

---

1. Open Final Cut, if it isn't already running. Notice, when you do, that it automatically opens the project you were working on when you last quit. If it opens a project file, choose **File > Close Project** to close it.

---

2. Choose **File > Open** and open **Chapter 04 Lesson**. It's in the **FCP Projects > FCP HOT files > Lessons** folder you created at the beginning of this book.

---

3. Double-click **Sequence 1** and rename it to " **Seq – Snowboard Start**," with a space as the first character, preceding the name. Because the Browser automatically sorts clips and sequences by file name, starting all your sequences with a space means they appear at the top of the **Browser**, making them very easy to find.

What you are about to create is a 30-second commercial for a snowboard company, called **Board Feet**. *So, the first thing you need to do in starting a new project is to save it and give it a name.*

4. Choose **File > Save Project As**.

5. Save this in your **FCP HOT Book Projects** folder with the name of **Board Feet**.

Now that you've saved your project, start looking for your opening shot. The Browser provides a handy way to view and play thumbnails of all your clips.

6. Click the **Browser**, **Ctrl+click** the **Duration** column header, and choose **Show Thumbnail** from the shortcut menu.

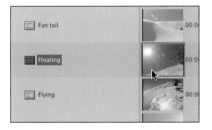

7. Thumbnails of all your clips appear to the left of the **Duration** column. Put your mouse in the middle of the **Floating** clip. Click and drag inside the thumbnail from left to right. Watch, as you do, how the clip plays in the thumbnail.

8. The still image you see as a thumbnail is called the clip's **poster frame** (the still image that represents the clip). It defaults to the first frame of the clip, but you can reset it by dragging the thumbnail to the frame you want to set as the new poster frame, then hold down the **Control** key and let go of the mouse.

9. To hide thumbnails, **Ctrl+click** the **Thumbnail** column header and choose **Hide Column** from the shortcut menu.

10. In order to set the **In** and **Out** for a clip, you need to move it to the **Viewer**. There are three ways you can do this:

- Grab a clip in the **Browser** and drag it into the **Viewer**.

- Double-click the icon of a clip in the **Browser** to load it into the **Viewer**.

- Highlight a clip in the **Browser** and press **Return**.

Pick a favorite method (I, personally, am a big fan of double-clicking) and load the clip named **Track – Pink Sun** into the **Viewer**.

11. When the clip first loads, the sprocket holes on the left side of the image indicate you are at the start of the media for that clip. (If the sprocket holes are not showing, press the **Home** key.) Press the **End** key to jump to the end of the clip. The sprocket holes on the right indicate you are at the end of the clip.

---

12. In Chapter 2, "*Understanding the Final Cut Pro Interface*," you learned about how to navigate a clip using the spacebar to start and stop, or the J, K, and L keys, or grabbing the playhead with the mouse and dragging it, or using the shuttle bar, or moving the jog wheel. So many choices!

Scrub through this clip using each of these techniques till you are comfortable moving around in a clip.

If you look in the top-left corner of the **Viewer***, you'll see that the duration of this shot is* **15:27** *(15 seconds and 27 frames). This is too long for the opening shot, so you need to set a different starting point. This starting point is called the "In."*

---

13. To set the **In**, move the **playhead** forward a few seconds until the fan of snow behind the board starts to appear. This is at timecode **1:02:13:21**.

14. Now, click the **Mark In** button to set the **In** (or press the letter **I**).

In indicator

In marker

Media start

*Notice the **In** indicator in the top-left corner of the screen? Also, a smaller version of the same indicator, called the **In** marker, is now located next to the playhead. This In tells Final Cut where you want your shot to start.*

15. If you don't see the **In** indicator in the image, be sure that **Show Overlays** is turned on from the **View** pop-up menu at the top of the **Viewer**.

16. If you want to change the **In**, simply grab it with the arrow cursor and move it. As you do, the picture in the **Viewer** changes as the **In** moves to reflect the change in the starting point. When you are happy with its new position, stop dragging.

*Now you need to determine where the shot ends, which is called the **Out**. Make the duration long enough so you can add opening titles when graphics are discussed later, in Chapter 9, "Text, Titles, and Graphics."*

17. Move forward a few seconds until the snowboarder seems swallowed by the cloud of snow. This is around timecode **1:02:19:23**.

18. Click the **Mark Out** button (or press the letter **O**). Notice the **Out** indicator appears in the top-right corner of the image.

Out marker

19. As well, Final Cut automatically calculated the **duration** of your shot as **6:03** (6 seconds and 3 frames). And, the **Out** marker moved right next to the **playhead**.

20. Finally, you can watch your newly marked shot by clicking the **Play In to Out** button (or press **Shift+**) to make sure it looks OK.

Congratulations! You've loaded and marked your first clip!

I spent a lot of time covering this procedure because setting Ins and Outs is essential to editing. You'll do it hundreds of times in a project. And the two Notes that follow provide even more shortcuts you can use to make this whole process even faster and easier.

21. Since this is the last step in this exercise, choose **File > Save** (or press **Cmd+S**). It's a good habit to save your work frequently.

NOTE | Changing your Mind

If you decide you don't like your In or Out, use these keyboard shortcuts to get rid of them:

Option+I   Clears the In

Option+O   Clears the Out

Option+X   Clears both the In and the Out

NOTE | Using Timecode to Mark Clips

Because marking clips is so essential, Final Cut allows you to use timecode to help set your Out.

Say you want to create a shot that's a specific length (for instance, 3:15). Set your In as you would normally.

Then, double-click the **duration** field at the top left of the **Viewer** window to select it and enter the **duration** of your shot (again, **3:15**). Final Cut automatically sets the Out point exactly 3:15 from the In.

I use this technique a lot, especially for titles, stills, and shots that need to hit a fixed musical beat.

3. —————————Building the Timeline

In this exercise, you'll start building your first sequence of clips to create your commercial. You'll continue practicing loading clips into the Viewer and marking them. Then, you'll learn 10 different ways to edit your clips to the Timeline—and a couple of ways to avoid!

1. If the last exercise is still open, great. If not, open **Board Feet** from your **FCP HOT Book Projects** folder.

2. Load **Track – Pink Sun** into the **Viewer** and set the **In** and **Out** as described in the previous lesson. Your clip should have a **duration** of **6:03**.

3. In the **Browser**, double-click the **Seq – Snowboard Start** sequence to open it in the **Timeline**. You know it's open because a tab appears in the top-left corner of the **Timeline** containing the name of the sequence. Be sure the **playhead** is at the beginning of the sequence. You can move it there quickly by pressing the **Home** key.

4. Click in the center of the **Viewer** and drag the clip over to the **Canvas** window. As you drag near the right edge of the **Canvas**, a pop-up overlay menu appears. Drag your clip on top of the pink **Overwrite** rectangle and let go.

Your clip has now been edited to the Timeline at the location of the playhead. Since there is no sound with this clip, only the video has been added to the Timeline. You'll start working with audio in Chapter 7, "Audio—The Secret to a Great Picture."

Notice that the playhead automatically moved to the end of the clip. When there is no In or Out set in the Timeline (something you'll learn about in Exercise 4, later in this chapter), the Timeline playhead acts as the In. All clips edited from the Viewer are automatically placed at the position of the play-head in the Timeline.

Shot duration

Playhead location

5. Now select and mark a second clip by loading **Blue sky** into the **Viewer**. Move the **playhead** and set the **In** at **1:00:03:11**—just before he slides off the cliff. Then, move the **playhead** and set the **Out** at **1:00:07:10**. If your **duration** is **4:00**, you've done this correctly.

6. This time, click the **red Overwrite button** at the lower left of the **Canvas**. (The red Overwrite button does the exact same thing as the Overwrite overlay you used for the last clip. It's a different interface—a button—but the same result.) Your clip has been edited to the **Timeline** at the location of the **playhead**. And, again, the **playhead** moves to the end of the clip to get ready to position the next edit.

7. Time to add a third clip. Load **Track – The gap** into the **Viewer**. Set the **In** about 5 seconds in, where his legs are covered in a cloud of snow. The timecode is **01:02:33:03**. Set the **duration** to **3:26**.

8. Now, drag the clip from the **Viewer** and place it on top of the **red Overwrite button** in the lower-left corner of the **Canvas**. Again, the clip is edited to the **Timeline**, and the **playhead** moves position.

9. Load the fourth clip, **Down the Mountain**, into the **Viewer** and drag the **playhead** a few seconds in, to where he straightens out to head downhill. (The **In** is **1:00:15:03** with a **duration** of **10:13**.)

Here's the fourth way to edit a clip to the ***Timeline:*** *Press the* ***F10*** *key.*

NOTE | If Your Screen Suddenly Goes Crazy...

It's not your fault. When Apple released OS X 10.3, they created a new feature called **Exposé**. Exposé is a very useful tool in that, when your screen is covered with lots of different windows from different applications, Exposé will scale and move all these windows so that you can see them all and pick the one you want. I use it a lot. The problem is that FCP and Exposé use the same keystrokes. Since I use the F10 key combination all the time in FCP (because, for me, it's the fastest way to edit), I've changed my Exposé settings so they don't interfere with Final Cut.

Here's how.

Click the **Blue Apple** at the top-left corner of your Mac, drag down and choose **System Preferences**.

Click the **Exposé** icon.

continues on next page

NOTE | If Your Screen Suddenly Goes Crazy... *continued*

While holding down the **Control** key, click the **All Windows** pop-up menu and choose **^F9**. This changes the Exposé keystroke from **F9** to **Ctrl+F9**.

Do the same for **Application windows** and **Desktop**.

Note the Control icon (the caret symbol) in front of each function key

When you've made these changes, quit System Preferences.

Now, your screen will no longer go crazy when you try to edit a clip to the Timeline using the function keys.

10. Finally, let's add a last shot as payoff to the commercial. Load **In the Lake** into the **Viewer**. Set the **In** where he is just about to take off from the jump. Set the **Out** to where he's trying to keep from drowning. (The In is **01:01:06:18** with a **duration** of **6:23**.)

11. This time, drag the clip from the **Viewer** to the end of the clips in the **Timeline**. Watch for the cursor to turn to a downward-pointing arrow, then let go. The clip is added to the end of the **Timeline**.

NOTE | Five Ways to Edit to the Timeline

You've now learned five ways to edit a clip to the Timeline, four of them automated:

- Drag the clip from the **Viewer** to the overlay window in the **Canvas**.

- Drag the clip from the **Viewer** to the **red Overwrite button** in the **Canvas**.

- Click the **red Overwrite button**.

- Press the **F10** key.

- Drag the clip from the **Viewer** to the **Timeline**. When the cursor turns to a downward-pointing arrow, let go.

The first four automatically put the clip at the location of the Timeline Playhead. I find using these automated tools, especially while building my main story track, makes my editing faster and more accurate.

However, I find that using the "drag-to-the-Timeline" approach works well when I am spotting in sound effects or creating composites. In other words, I use dragging to the Timeline only in special situations.

> ## NOTE | Defining Overwrite Edits vs. Insert Edits
>
> You've just spent a fair amount of time learning how to create an Overwrite edit. An Overwrite edit drops a clip to the Timeline and replaces any video it lands upon.
>
> There is a second kind of edit, called an **Insert** edit. This takes the clip on the Viewer, edits it to the Timeline at the point of the playhead, and pushes all the clips from that location downstream, or later in the Timeline.
>
> An Insert edit is very useful when you want to sandwich a shot between two shots that are already on the Timeline, as you'll see next.

Hmm...There's a problem. I just realized that the beginning of the sequence has two wide shots in a row. This would look better if you put in a different angle between the first and second shots.

12. To do this, load **Fan Tail** into the **Viewer**. Set the **In** to **1:00:28:11** and the **duration** to **4:05**.

13. Move the **playhead** to the end of the first clip. The fastest way to do this is to use the **up** and **down** arrow keys on your keyboard, but you can also drag the **playhead** with your mouse until it seems to "lock" into position between the two clips.

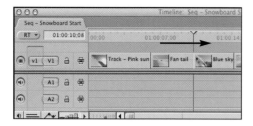

14. Drag the clip from the **Viewer** over to the yellow overlay rectangle in the **Canvas** labeled **Insert**. Notice how the clip is placed where the **playhead** was located, and all the clips, starting with **Blue sky**, were shoved down further on the **Timeline**. This new clip was "inserted" into the middle of the sequence.

15. Keep this project open. You'll come right back to it in the next exercise. Save your work by pressing **Cmd+S**.

NOTE | Five Ways to Do an Insert Edit

Just as there are five ways to perform an Overwrite edit, there are also five ways to create an Insert edit. In all cases, you start by setting the In and the Out for the clip in the Viewer.

- Drag the clip from the **Viewer** to the **Insert** option of the overlay window in the **Canvas**.

- Drag the clip from the **Viewer** to the **yellow Insert button** in the lower-left corner of the **Canvas**.

- Click the **yellow Insert button** in the lower-left corner of the **Canvas**.

- Press the **F9** key.

- Drag the clip from the **Viewer** to the **Timeline**. When the cursor turns into a right-pointing arrow, let go.

Note brown border with hollow inside icon for Insert edit

Note solid icon for Overwrite edit

What determines if the cursor is a down-pointing or right-pointing arrow when you drag to the Timeline? The thin, light gray horizontal line in the middle of the video track. If the cursor is above the line, the arrow points right and creates an Insert edit. If the cursor is below the gray line, the arrow points down and creates an Overwrite edit.

MOVIE | editing.mov

If you want to see these 10 editing techniques in action, watch the movie named **Editing.mov** inside the **movies** folder on the **FCP HD HOT** DVD. This movie illustrates how to mark clips, the differences between Overwrite and Insert edits, and all the different ways to move a clip from the Viewer to the Timeline.

NOTE | Don't Drag Clips from the Browser

Although this may seem tempting, it is generally not a good idea to drag a clip directly from the Browser to the Timeline. There are four reasons for this:

• You can't set an In or Out on the clip. Ins or Outs are only set in the Viewer or Timeline.

• You can't use the automated tools to control clip placement, such as using the F10 key or the Overwrite overlay to send a clip to the exact position of the playhead.

• Moving a clip manually means once you move it to the Timeline, you still need to trim it, which creates potential Timeline gaps and positioning errors.

• You can't easily view a clip in the Browser to make sure it's the right one. Yes, you can use thumbnails, but those are often far too small to see what's actually in the shot.

It is faster, more accurate, and easier to get into the habit of loading a clip into the Viewer, set the In and Out, and use your favorite automated technique to drop the clip exactly where you want it to go on the Timeline.

4. _____Three-Point Editing

The techniques you learned in the last exercise assumed that you only needed to set the In or the Out on the clip in the Viewer. However, there are times where setting an In or Out on the Timeline can bail you out of a tough situation.

In point of fact, in order to make an edit, Final Cut needs to know three of four timecode coordinates—the In or Out of the clip in the Viewer and the In or Out of the Timeline—which is why this technique is called **three-point editing**.

Normally, you would set the In and Out for the clip in the Viewer as the first two points, and use the Timeline Playhead for the third reference.

However, there are times when you need more precision on the Timeline than that.

1. If the project from the last exercise is not open, open **Board Feet** from your **FCP HOT Book Projects** folder.

2. Start with a simple example. Create a new sequence and call it "**Seq – 3-point.**" (Note the leading space in the name.) Double-click it to load it into the **Timeline**. Notice you now have two sequence tabs open in the **Timeline**.

It's OK to have more than one sequence open in the Timeline at once. However, if you have less than 1 GB of RAM in your computer, performance improves if you limit the number of opened sequences in the Timeline. Sequences in the Browser use virtually no memory, so you can store as many sequences there as you want.

This is why I had you leave the sequence from the last exercise open. It's time now to learn how to close a sequence that's open in the Timeline.

3. Ctrl+click the tab of the sequence you wish to close and choose **Close Tab** from the shortcut menu. The sequence is removed from the **Timeline**, but still accessible from the **Browser**. Double-click it to open it back into the **Timeline**.

4. Load the clip **Track – The gap** into the **Viewer**. Set an **In** 2 seconds after the start of the clip. Set the **duration** to **5:00** (**In: 1:02:29:08**, **duration: 5:00**).

---

5. Now, move the **playhead** in the **Timeline** to **1:00:02:00**. The fastest way to do this is to double-click in the timecode box in the upper-left corner of the **Timeline** and type in the numbers. Be sure to use colons to separate the numbers.

See how the playhead immediately jumped to the timecode you entered?

---

6. Now, press **I** to set an **In**. Next, move the **playhead** 3 seconds later in the **Timeline**. The easiest way to do this is to press the **+** key on the keypad or keyboard, type **300**, and press **Return**. (Note you didn't use any periods or commas—more on this later.)

See how the playhead jumped to the new location? You combine + or – with timecode entered from the keypad to move the playhead—in the Timeline, Viewer, or Canvas.

---

7. Press **O** to set an **Out**.

---

8. Finally, just to make this challenging, slide the **playhead** so it's before the **In**; the exact amount doesn't matter.

Here's what you've done. You marked a 5-second clip in the Viewer. Then, you set a 3-second duration in the Timeline. Finally, you moved the playhead to a location outside the In and Out on the Timeline.

When you perform this edit, what do you think will happen? Will the edit start at the playhead or at the Timeline In? Will the edit duration be 3 seconds or 5 seconds?

9. To find out, drag the clip from the **Viewer** onto the **Overwrite** overlay in the **Canvas**.

Ah-HA! The clip started at the Timeline In and ended at the Timeline Out. In other words:

- *Setting an In on the Timeline overrides the position of the playhead in determining where a clip starts when edited from the Viewer.*

- *Setting a duration on the Timeline overrides the duration set in the Viewer.*

Now that you know how Final Cut uses the Ins and the Outs on the Timeline, here's another interesting technique you can use to back-time a clip.

Back-timing *means you determine where you want to a clip to end, and Final Cut calculates where it needs to start. Here's an example.*

10. Again, using the **Seq – 3-point**, load the **Thru trees** clip into the **Viewer**. Go to timecode **1:02:01:16** and set an **Out**. (Right, I said set an **Out**.)

11. Now, press the minus (–) key on the keypad, type **400**, and press **Return**. The **playhead** in the **Viewer** moves back 4 seconds. Set an **In** (**01:12:03:12**). You should have a clip **duration** of **4:01**.

12. On the **Timeline**, move your **playhead** to **1:00:10:00**, either by entering the number into the time-code box or sliding the **playhead**. Set an **Out**. Don't set an **In** on the **Timeline**.

13. Now, drag the clip from the **Viewer** on top of the **red Overwrite button** in the lower-left corner of the **Canvas** and watch what happens.

The 4-second clip in the Viewer was moved to the Timeline so that the Out of the clip in the Viewer matched the Out set in the Timeline.

I use this technique frequently when I want to have the end of a video clip match a sound cue or when I need more control over where a clip ends on the Timeline than where it begins.

14. Save your work, but keep this project open. You'll need it once more before this chapter is done.

NOTE | Timecode Shortcuts

This last exercise illustrated how you can use timecode to move the playhead in the Viewer and Timeline (and Canvas, too, for that matter). In fact, Final Cut tries to bend over backwards in making it easy to enter timecode.

For instance, the following numbers on each row are equivalent for NTSC video:

1:00:00:00	1000000	1...	
3:00	300	3.	90
1:00:02:15	1000215	1..2.15	1...75

Here's the translation:

- You can substitute a period in place of two zeros for minutes, seconds, or frames.

- Colons are optional; you can leave them out.

- Type a one- or two-digit number and Final Cut assumes you mean frames. So 15 = 15 frames, 30 = 1:00, 45 = 1:15, and 75 = 2:15.

- Type a three- or four-digit number and Final Cut assumes you mean seconds and frames. So, 115 = 1:15, 1200 = 12:00, 2445 = 25:15 (that was tricky), and 9999 = 1:42:09. (OK, I haven't really used that last one, but I was curious, so I checked.)

- Type a five- or six-digit number and Final Cut assumes you mean minutes, seconds and frames.

You can use these techniques to set durations, move the playhead, or, as you'll see later, move clips and even edit points.

Timecode is very cool and makes video editing much faster and more precise. (For PAL video, the concept is the same, but the numbers are different, because PAL plays 25 frames per second, whereas NTSC plays 30.)

5. ——————————**Browser Power Tips**

One more quick exercise, this one on harnessing the built-in database power of the Browser to find clips.

1. If the project from the last exercise is not open, open **Board Feet** from your **FCP HOT Book Projects** folder.

The easiest way to think of the Browser is that it is a database, listing all the elements you can access in your project. Sometimes, though, a project has so many elements, it's hard to find the one you are looking for.

That's where the Find command comes in.

2. Click once in the **Browser** to select it. Choose **Edit > Find** (**Cmd+F**).

3. In the **Find** dialog box, type **Flying** and click **Find Next**.

4. The **Flying** clip is highlighted in the **Browser**. You can find clips based on an entry in any column or a specific column. To find another clip that meets the same criteria, press **Cmd+G**.

5. But it gets better. This time, choose **Edit > Find**, type **track** into the data entry box, then click **Find All**.

Lists all clips or
sequences containing
the word "track"

6. This time, every clip that meets your search criteria is displayed in the **Find Results** dialog box, including sequences that contain clips whose name includes "track."

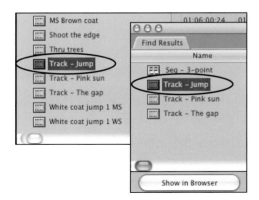

7. Click a clip name in the **Find Results** dialog box to display that clip in the **Browser**.

This next tip is one of my personal favorites.

8. Select **Seq – Snowboard Start**. Choose **Edit > Find**.

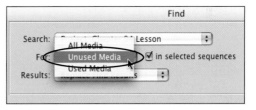

9. Delete any text in the **Any Column Contains** entry box in the lower-right corner, then choose **Unused Media** from the **For** pop-up menu, and click **Find All**.

All clips that are *not* used in selected sequence

Every clip in the Browser that is not in your selected sequence (or sequences) is displayed in the Find Results dialog box. Finding unused media is a great help when you are desperate to find a shot you haven't used yet.

A word of caution, however. If you have a clip that runs, say, 30 minutes and you use 5 seconds of it, the entire clip is flagged as used. For me, this is another great reason to log your clips and capture them in shorter pieces, rather than capturing an entire tape to disk.

10. Well, that's it for this chapter. Save your work and quit Final Cut if you are going to take a break for a while.

Summary

You've just learned the technical core of editing with Final Cut. Although there's lots still to learn about how you can make your productions fancier, the techniques you've learned here are the bread-and-butter of every production you will ever edit.

And, although the clips you've been working with are video only, every technique in this chapter works the same whether you are editing video, audio, or both.

Helpful Keyboard Shortcuts

Shortcut	Function
Shift+Cmd+N	Creates a new project
Cmd+N	Creates a new sequence in the Browser
Cmd+B	Creates a new bin in the Browser
Cmd+S	Saves the current project
Shift+Cmd+S	Saves the current project using a different name
Option+Cmd+S	Saves all open projects
I	Sets an In (Viewer, Timeline, or Canvas)
Shift+I	Moves the playhead to the In
Option+I	Clears the In
O	Sets an Out (Viewer, Timeline, or Canvas)
Shift+O	Moves the playhead to the Out
Option+O	Clears the Out
X	Sets an In and Out simultaneously for the clip the playhead is parked in (Timeline only)
Option+X	Clears both the In and the Out
\	Plays a few seconds before and after the playhead
Shift+\	Plays from the marked In to the marked Out
Up arrow	Moves playhead to the In of the preceding clip
Down arrow	Moves playhead to the In of the following clip
Cmd+F	Opens the Find dialog box
Cmd+G	Finds the next clip that meets your search criteria

5

Organize Your Story

Selecting Clips	Deleting Clips	Moving Clips
Match Frame Edit	Replace Edit	Fit-to-Fill Edit
Storyboard Editing	More About Markers
Working with Subclips

Chapter 05 Lesson

FCP HD HOT DVD

Repeat after me: "Editing is the process of getting rid of everything that isn't relevant to my story." Make this your editing mantra, because it is the heart of all editing.

In Chapter 3, "*Gather Your Media*," you got rid of all the footage that wasn't worth digitizing. In Chapter 4, "*Build Your Story*," you got rid of all the footage that wasn't worth putting into the sequence. In this chapter, you'll learn techniques to select, move, and delete the clips in your sequence that aren't worth keeping. Finally, in Chapter 6, "*Trim Your Story*," you'll learn how to trim your edits—to get rid of all the frames that make your edits less than perfect.

I. —————————Navigating the Timeline and Selecting Clips

The number one interface rule for Final Cut is, "select something, then do something to it." Since there is a lot you can do to your clips, it makes sense to spend a few minutes now to learn all the different ways to select them.

1. If Final Cut is not running, start it and open **Chapter 05 Lesson**. It's in the **FCP Projects/ FCP HOT files** folder you created at the beginning of this book. Double-click **Seq- Snowboard Start** to open it. This is a modified version of the commercial you started to create in Chapter 4, *"Build Your Story."* I added four shots to the end of it, so the running time is now 59:17; well over the ultimate limit of 30 seconds.

2. Save this project as **Board Feet v2** in your **FCP HOT Book Projects** folder. Why "v2"? Because this the second version of the commercial, and in case you don't like your modifications, you can easily go back to the previous version.

3. Take a minute to play the sequence to get familiar with the new shots on it.

So, how did you play the sequence? Did you use the spacebar? The J, K, and L keys? Scroll using the playhead? Everything you learned in the last chapter about navigating a clip in the Viewer also applies to the Timeline.

Plus, in the Timeline you have even more navigation options. With the Timeline window selected, press the up and down arrow keys. See how the playhead jumps from clip to clip? This is a very fast way to move precisely through the Timeline.

Final Cut is an "inclusive" editor, which means that the playhead always shows the frame it is parked on. Here, I've zoomed in on the Timeline. See the dark bar starting at the playhead and spreading to the right in the screen shot above? This dark bar represents the frame currently displayed in the Canvas. It occupies a certain amount of time on the Timeline because each video frame is one-thirtieth of a second long.

It is also important to note that when you use the up and down arrow keys, FCP always moves the playhead to the In of the previous or next clip, never the Out. You'll work with this more in Chapter 6, "Trim Your Story."

4. There are two other keyboard navigation tips you'll find yourself using frequently:

- Press the **left** or **right** arrow keys to move earlier or later one frame at a time.

- Hold down the **Shift** key and press the **left** or **right** arrows to move earlier or later one second at a time.

Now that you are a wizard at navigation, it is time to learn how to select clips so you can get your Timeline organized.

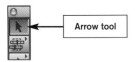

Arrow tool

5. Click the **Arrow** tool in the **Tool** palette or, what I find much faster, press the **A** key.

6. Click the **Blue sky** clip.

Instant selection. Darn, that was easy! Naturally, this barely scratches the surface.

7. With **Blue sky** selected, hold down the **Shift** key and click **In the lake**.

See how the Shift key allows you to select a range of clips?

Click in gray area to deselect

8. To deselect a clip, or range of clips, click in the dark gray area above your video tracks but below the timecode indicator bar; or below the last audio track and above the scroll bar. You will find yourself continuously selecting and deselecting clips within Final Cut.

Selection rectangle

9. Here's a faster way to select a range of clips: using the **Arrow** tool, drag a rectangle around the clips. For instance, drag a rectangle around the first three clips in this sequence.

10. There are also three selection tools that can help you select clips:

Edit Selection Tool – g

Group Selection Tool – gg

Range Selection Tool – ggg

• **Edit Selection** tool (selects edit points across multiple tracks–Chapter 10)

• **Group Selection** tool (essentially mimics the Arrow tool)

• **Range Selection** tool

In this case, select the third tool: the **Range Selection** tool, or press **GGG**.

Range selection

11. Using the **Range Selection** tool, drag from the end of **Down Mountain** into **In the Lake**. The precise coordinates don't matter. Notice that you've selected portions of two different clips. You'll learn how to apply these selection techniques next.

12. This ends this exercise in selecting clips. Next you'll see how you can use these selection techniques to determine which clips to delete. If you want to take a break, quit Final Cut. Don't save any changes. Otherwise, leave everything open for the next exercise.

2.————————Deleting Clips

In this exercise, you will learn a variety of ways to delete clips and gaps from the Timeline. Remember, "you select something, then you do something to it."

1. Open **Chapter 05 Lesson**, if it isn't already open. And load **Seq – Snowboard start** into the **Timeline**.

2. Click **Blue sky** to select it. Press the **Delete** key. Poof. (Remember, the **Delete** key is the one that says "Delete" at the top of the keyboard, not "del" next to the **End** key.)

3. OK. Maybe that was too easy. Get the clip back by pressing **Cmd+Z** to undo the deletion. But deleting dozens of clips is the same as deleting one: Select what you want to delete, and press the **Delete** key.

Selection rectangle

4. Again, select the first three clips by dragging a rectangle around them, then press the **Delete** key. (You could choose **Sequence > Lift**, but…why? Life is too short.)

*Notice the gap that removing these clips has left? Sometimes you want the gap. Sometimes you don't. Removing clips and leaving a gap is called a **lift**. Removing clips and pulling up all downstream clips so that there is no gap is called a **ripple delete**, because its effect ripples through the rest of the sequence.*

5. Again, press **Cmd+Z** (or choose **Edit > Undo**) to bring those three clips back.

To perform a ripple delete, select a clip in the middle of the sequence; for instance, **Down mountain**, and press **Shift+Delete**. (Again, you could choose **Sequence > Ripple Delete**, but, really, do you actually have that much time?)

Instead of pressing **Shift+Delete**, you could also press the **del** key, next to the **End** key.

6. There are three more selection techniques to illustrate. Select the **Range Selection** tool you learned about in the last exercise, select the end of **White coat jump WS**, and select the beginning of **White coat jump MS**. Then, press the **Delete** key.

Notice that the selected area disappears and leaves a gap.

7. Press **Cmd+Z** (or choose **Edit > Undo**) to undo that last deletion. This time, press **Shift+Delete** and watch how the selected area disappears, along with the gap.

This gap-closing technique is very helpful in quickly trimming between clips.

The following is another technique that, although I rarely use it for deleting clips, I use a lot with the power editing techniques I show you in Exercise 4.

8. Choose **File > Revert** to load the last saved version back from disk.

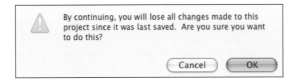

When you revert a file, you lose all the changes you've made since you last saved the project. However, sometimes, I make so many changes to a sequence that just don't work out, it is faster to revert back to a saved version than to try to restore everything using undo.

In this case, reverting makes it easy to get all the original clips back that were deleted earlier in this exercise.

9. Now, position the **playhead** in the **Timeline** to timecode **01:00:23:00** and press **I** to set an **In**.

10. Notice that, just as in the **Viewer**, an **In** appears on the **Timeline**. And, unlike the **Viewer**, the **Timeline** highlights to show which clips are affected by the **In**.

11. Next, drag the **playhead** forward to **01:00:26:00**, and press **O** to set an **Out**.

You could, if you prefer, use the Marking tools in the Canvas to set the In and Out, because the Canvas is just another view of the Timeline. The same tools work in both places. However, you can't use the marking tools in the Viewer, because those tools have no effect on clips in the Timeline, only clips in the Viewer.

Regardless of how you set the In and Out, when you are done your Timeline now has a highlighted section marked by an In and Out.

Look up to the top-left corner of the Canvas. The duration of this Timeline shot is 3:01. Why the extra frame? Because, as you learned in the last exercise, Final Cut is an inclusive editor, which means that it always includes the frame the playhead is parked on. From 23:00 to 26:00 is 3 seconds and 1 frame:

- 23:00 – 23:29   (30 frames = one second)
- 24:00 – 24:29   (30 frames = one second)
- 25:00 – 25:29   (30 frames = one second)
- 26:00   (the extra frame)

12. Now, after all this effort setting the In and Out, press the **Delete** key, and the section bounded by the In and Out disappears. This is called a **Lift Delete**. Or, press **Shift+Delete** to make the highlighted section disappear *and* close the gap. This is called a **Ripple Delete**. (By the way, the **Delete** key is the key just above the **Return** key that has the word **Delete** written on it. The **del** key, which I call the "Forward Delete" key, is not the same as the **Delete** key.)

One more deletion technique to cover—finding and deleting gaps in the Timeline—and you are done with this lesson.

*Gaps creep into the Timeline when clips are dragged down from the Viewer, or the playhead is in the wrong position when you apply an automated tool. A **gap** is defined as a horizontal space between all tracks in the Timeline.*

Timeline gap

13. For instance, scroll down the **Timeline** and look immediately after the **In the lake** clip. There's a small gap in the **Timeline** between these two clips.

14. Such a small gap. Wouldn't it be nice to see it more easily? Well, you can—with the **Zoom** tool. Select the first **Zoom** tool in the **Tool** palette (or press the letter **Z**.)

15. Draw across the area you want to enlarge and let go of the mouse.

The Timeline zooms in so you can see the gap a whole lot better.

16. If you zoomed in too far, you can zoom out by selecting the **Zoom Out** tool, or by pressing **ZZ**, or, what's easiest for me, **Option+clicking** where you want to zoom out using the **Zoom In** tool.

17. In any case, click once in the gap to highlight it, then press the **Delete** key, and the gap is closed.

NOTE | When Deleting Gaps Doesn't Work

If you are trying to close a gap in a video track, but the audio is continuous underneath, Final Cut will not delete the video gap because, in most cases, this would throw the audio out of sync with the video. You can solve this problem by locking all your audio tracks by clicking the little padlock icons at the far left of each track (or pressing **Shift+F5**). Once all your audio tracks are locked, you can easily delete the video gap. (This process also works in reverse for deleting audio gaps, by locking all video tracks [**Shift+F4**].)

You'll learn more about locking tracks in Chapter 7, "*Audio—The Secret to a Great Picture.*"

18. Final Cut can help you find gaps in your Timeline. Choose **Mark > Next > Gap** (**Shift+G**) or **Mark > Previous > Gap** (**Option+G**).

This jumps the playhead to the next (or previous) gap in the Timeline.

Another way to delete a gap is to leave the playhead positioned at the beginning of the gap...

19. ...then choose **Sequence > Close Gap**, or press **Ctrl+G**.

Track gap

*However, not all gaps are across all tracks. Sometimes a gap in a video (or audio) track is covered by other video or audio clips on other tracks. This gap in a single track is called a **track gap**.*

There's a special command in Final Cut you can use to find these gaps.

20. For this command to work, select a track by **Option+clicking** its **Auto Select** button. This selects a specific track by turning off all other **Auto Select** buttons except the one for the track you want to select. (You'll learn more about **Auto Select** buttons in the next exercise.)

21. Next, choose **Mark > Next > Track Gap** (or press **Shift+G**).

This technique finds gaps in tracks, even when they are covered by other video or audio clips. Once you've found a gap, you can then decide whether you want to delete it or not.

22. Well, that ends this exercise on deletion. Next, you'll learn how to harness selecting and deleting clips, along with some new techniques to get your Timeline into shape for final trimming.

If you are done for a while, quit Final Cut and don't *save changes. If you are going immediately into the next exercise,* **File > Revert** *this lesson back to the last saved version on disk.*

3. ——————————Moving Clips

In this exercise, you'll learn techniques to move clips around on the Timeline, as well as an explanation of the "infamous" cut and paste.

1. To get started, open **Board Feet v2**, if it isn't open already.

*In looking at this sequence again, I realized it would look better if the clip **MCU to camera** moved up to be shot number three in the sequence. Also, the first shot, **Track – red sun**, needs to be deleted and replaced with **Gray sky red sun**.*

There are several ways to move clips, but one of the easiest is to create multiple tracks and shuffle clips around until you are happy.

2. There are at least four ways to create new tracks in a sequence. Here's the first: choose **Sequence > Insert Tracks**.

3. From the dialog that appears, indicate how many tracks you want to add. In this case, add one video track and click **OK**. A new video track appears in the sequence, labeled **V2**.

The benefit to using this approach is you can easily add any number of audio and/or video tracks at the same time.

4. Here's a second, and faster, approach. **Ctrl+click** in the gray area above the video tracks, and below the timecode bar, and choose **Add Track** from the shortcut menu to add a new video track. Or, **Ctrl+click** below the audio tracks and above the zoom bar at the bottom, and choose **Add Track** from the shortcut menu to add a new audio track. Either way, a new track appears in the **Timeline**.

5. This technique, though, is my favorite. Simply drag a clip, in this case **MCU to camera**, where you want the track to appear, and Final Cut creates a track to hold the clip. (I use this technique a lot!)

6. However you decide to create an additional video (or audio) track, move the clip **MCU to camera**, onto **V2** and slide it back so it starts at the same time as the current third clip in the sequence, **Blue sky**.

7. Now, click **Blue sky** to select it. Then, hold down the **Shift** key and click **White coat jump MS** to select the range of clips that needs to move to make room for the new clip.

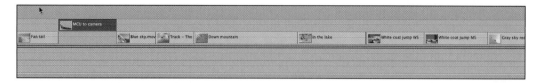

8. Grab all the selected clips and drag them right until they fill the hole on the far right of the **Timeline**. Deselect them.

9. Grab the **MCU to camera** clip on **V2** and drag it down into its new position. Or, as I prefer to do, hold the **Option** key and press the **down** arrow to move a clip down a track. (Oh, yes. **Option+up arrow** moves a clip *up* a track. And using the **Option+up/down arrow** technique is the fourth way to create a new track.)

NOTE | Clip Collisions

If you get an error message saying, "Clip collision on…," it means that the action you want to take is blocked by another clip. In the case of moving a clip using **Option+down arrow**, it means that the gap you are trying to move the clip into is smaller than the clip itself. Zoom closer and make sure that there's enough room in the gap for your clip to fit.

Final Cut works hard to prevent you from accidentally erasing media.

---

*However, there's a much easier way to move clips. Apple calls it a **swap edit**. I prefer to call it a **move edit**, because nothing actually "swaps."*

10. File > Revert this sequence to go back to the beginning.

11. Click **MCU to camera** to select it. Then, grab it with the mouse and start dragging it, still on **V1**, toward its new position. Notice the cursor looks like a downward-pointing arrow.

12. While still dragging the clip (and this is important), hold down the **Option** key. Notice the cursor has changed shape to a curved downward-pointing arrow.

13. Drag the clip into place, then, in this order, let go of the mouse, then let go of the **Option** key.

Everything reshuffles. The clip is in its new position, all other clips move down, and the gap left by the clip you moved is filled. All at the same time.

(If you have snapping turned on, it is easier to align the clip by its edit points. If snapping is off, it is easier to drop the clip into the middle of another clip. If you don't know what snapping is, you'll learn about it in the next chapter.)

This technique works in both directions. Try it until you are comfortable with it. I also use this a lot, too.

There's one more technique still to cover for moving clips: copy and paste. Apple has received a lot of complaints about how this works—mainly because they change it with each iteration of the program. It worked one way in FCP 4.0.x. Then, it changed with FCP 4.1.x. And it changed, again, in FCP HD.

Sigh. Here's how it works...at least, for now.

14. Select the clip **Gray sky red sun** at the end of the **Timeline**. You are going to move it to the front of the sequence.

15. Choose **Edit > Cut**, or press **Cmd+X**, to cut it to the clipboard and remove it from the **Timeline**.

16. Press the **Home** key to move the playhead to the beginning of the sequence. Then, press **Cmd+V** (or choose **Edit > Paste**). The clip appears at the location of the playhead as an **Overwrite** edit.

*Hmmm…this **Overwrite** edit chops into the second shot. Bad idea. Undo this edit (**Cmd+Z** or **Edit > Undo**).*

NOTE | Setting Undo Levels

The default number of undo levels in Final Cut Pro is 10. However, you can easily change this in **Final Cut Pro HD > User Preferences**.

When the **User Preferences** window opens, change the **Levels of Undo** to suit your style. I set mine to **25**. You can pick any number from 1 to 99; however, higher undo levels require significant additional RAM in your computer.

---

17. With the **playhead** still at the start of the sequence, choose **Edit > Paste Insert**, or press **Shift+V**.

Now the clip appears at the playhead as an Insert edit, pushing everything else down. Much better.

---

18. Click **Track – red sun** to select it and press **Shift+Delete** to remove the clip and the gap.

---

19. And that wraps up this exercise. Save your work. Quit Final Cut if you want to stop. Otherwise, leave everything open for the next exercise.

NOTE | Copy, Paste, and Auto Select

That copy/paste example didn't seem particularly painful, but using copy/paste used to be much worse. Here's the logic behind how Final Cut currently does a copy/paste.

Track inactive

Track active

The Auto Select buttons determine if a track is "selected," or active. If the button is lit (dark), as it is for V1, the track is active. If the button is off (hollow center), as it is for V2, the track is inactive.

There isn't enough room to discuss all the different ways that Auto Select affects Final Cut behavior; at last count it was well over 12, but in the case of copy/paste, it works like this:

If you copy a clip on any track, it will paste to the same track, at the location of the playhead, *unless* you click an Auto Select button *after* moving a clip to the clipboard. In that case, FCP will paste the clip to the lowest numbered track whose Auto Select button is lit.

See? Simple.

If all your video is on one track, this won't be a problem. However, if you start doing multitrack composites, you'll need to pay attention to the Auto Select buttons.

4. _____Power Editing Techniques

In this exercise, you'll learn three power techniques to help you get your Timeline organized: finding the match frame of a shot on the Timeline, doing a Replace edit, and changing the speed of a clip using a Fit to Fill edit. Although you may not use these techniques frequently, knowing they exist can bail you out of some tight editing situations.

1. If it isn't open already, open **Board Feet v2**.

The **match frame** technique allows you to find the original clip of a shot in the Timeline.

2. Put the **playhead** in the middle of **MCU to camera**. It should be the third shot in the Timeline, around **1:00:14:00**.

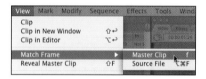

3. Choose **View > Match Frame > Match Clip** (or press the letter **F**).

Viewer ← → Canvas

Notice that Final Cut immediately loaded the source clip from the Browser into the Viewer, matched the In and Out from the clip on the Timeline, and positioned the playhead in the Viewer to exactly match the location of the playhead in the Timeline.

*This is because clips in the Timeline are **affiliate clips** to the **master clip** located in the Browser. Although there is only one master for each clip, there can be many affiliate clips to that master.*

NOTE | Recognizing a Browser Clip from a Timeline Clip

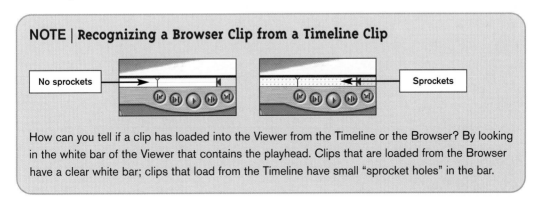

How can you tell if a clip has loaded into the Viewer from the Timeline or the Browser? By looking in the white bar of the Viewer that contains the playhead. Clips that are loaded from the Browser have a clear white bar; clips that load from the Timeline have small "sprocket holes" in the bar.

How is this match frame technique useful? Well, for instance, if you make an edit that is video-only, then later discover that you need to add the audio from the shot, using match frame makes this easy. One keystroke and you have the source clip loaded and marked in the Viewer, ready to edit.

4. Also, if you want to find the source clip in the **Browser**, rather than load it into the **Viewer**, choose **View > Reveal Master Clip** (or press **Shift+F**).

Final Cut highlights the name of the source clip in the Browser.

NOTE | Finding a Shot in the Timeline

I'd finished writing this chapter when I discovered a way to use match frame to find a specific shot in the Timeline by using a clip from the Browser as a reference. Here's how it works.

1. Open a clip from the **Browser** into the **Viewer**.

2. Move the **playhead** in the **Viewer** until you find the specific frame you want to find in the **Timeline**.

3. Press the **F** key.

If that frame exists in the currently selected sequence in the Timeline, the Timeline playhead will jump immediately to that frame and display it in the Canvas. If you haven't used that specific frame in the Timeline, the computer will beep, and the Timeline playhead won't move.

This procedure looks for specific frames. If you use a frame that is close to the shot your playhead is parked on, but not that *specific* frame, Final Cut won't find it.

The **Replace edit** technique enables you to replace one clip with another. What makes this tip special is that you don't need to set an In or an Out. This technique works best when you are trying to line up shots based on a frame in the middle of a clip, rather than at either end.

5. Put your Timeline **playhead** in the middle of **Blue sky**, where the snowboarder is in midflight (timecode: **1:00:18:00**).

What you are going to do is replace the wide shot of this jump with a closer shot. But, to keep the overall pacing consistent, you need to match where he is in midair, rather than from the start of the clip. You can only do this with a Replace edit.

6. Choose the **Browser** and open **MS brown coat** into the Viewer. Scroll until you see him start his jump (timecode: **1:01:33:04**). You don't need to set any **Ins** or **Outs** in the Viewer. The **Replace** edit doesn't need them.

7. Now, drag the clip from the **Viewer** to the **Canvas** and drop it on top of the **Replace** overlay (press **F12**).

Final Cut instantly replaces the old shot with the new shot—keeping the same duration and Timeline location—and puts the frame under the playhead in the Viewer (where the boarder was just starting his jump) under the playhead in the Timeline.

8. Play this new section of the sequence.

I use Replace edits whenever I need to match action in the middle of the shot. The basic rule is the Replace edit ignores Ins and Outs in the Viewer and lines up the edit based on the position of the playhead. Experiment with this technique by putting the Timeline playhead at the beginning and end of a clip and watch the resulting edits.

*There's one more technique in this exercise: the **Fit to Fill** edit. This specialized edit changes the speed of an incoming clip to match the duration set by the In and Out on the Timeline.*

9. Go to the second clip, **Fan tail**, and put the **playhead** anywhere in the middle of the clip. Press **X** to set an **In** and an **Out** for the clip.

This, in itself, is a really fast way to mark a clip on the Timeline.

Notice that the duration of the Timeline edit is 4:01. What you are going to do is replace this shot with a longer clip, which you will speed up to emphasize just how fast these snowboarders are going. (It will work nicely contrasted with the slow motion of the first, opening clip.)

10. Open **Shoot the edge** and find the spot just after he lands from a short jump. Set the **In** (timecode: **1:01:42:26**). Set the **Out** just after he disappears (duration: **6:09**). Again, notice that this shot is about 50 percent longer than the duration of the edit on the **Timeline**.

11. Drag the clip from the **Viewer** to the **Fit to Fill** overlay in the **Canvas** and drop it.

12. Notice that **Shoot the edge** is edited to the **Timeline** with a green render bar over it. Play the clip and see that it is, indeed, faster than normal speed. The green bar indicates that a speed change has been applied to the clip, which Final Cut is able to play in real time. If the bar was red, you would first need to render it. (More on rendering in Chapter 8, *"Transitions—Making Change Beautiful,"* and Chapter 11, *"Filters and Keying."*)

13. That wraps up this exercise. Save your changes, and leave Final Cut open for the next exercise.

 MOVIE | Organize.mov

It may be easier to understand how these techniques work by watching them in action. To do so, watch the movie named **Organize.mov** inside the **movies** folder on the **FCP HD HOT** DVD. This movie illustrates many of the techniques covered in this chapter.

5. —————————Storyboard Editing

When I first saw this next technique, I thought it was pretty silly—until I showed it to some wedding photographers who told me it was an incredible timesaver for the kinds of projects they do. Their opinion has since been reinforced by other editors I've spoken with, which simply goes to show that everyone learns from everyone else—including me.

Final Cut has an additional way you can edit clips in the Browser: the **Storyboard edit**. Here's how it works.

1. Open **Chapter 05 Lesson** or **Board Feet v2**, whichever is easier, and create a new sequence. Name it " **Seq - Storyboard**." (Notice the initial space.) Double-click it to load it into the **Timeline** as an empty sequence.

2. Ctrl+click in the gray area of the **Name** column and choose **View as Large Icons** from the shortcut menu.

The Browser converts into a digital "light table," allowing you to view all your clips at once.

This is a great way to lay out photo montages, animated storyboards, or any other sequence of shots where seeing multiple clips at once is helpful.

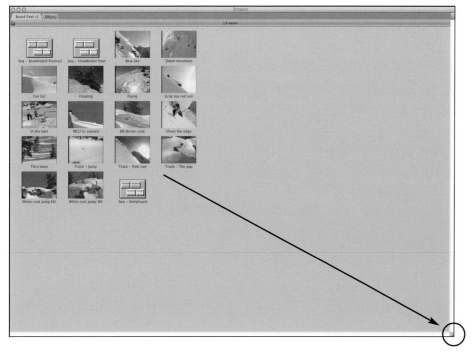

3. Grab the size tab in the lower-right corner of the Browser and drag to make the **Browser** bigger. You'll be moving clips into the blank area on the right.

4. Using the **Arrow** tool, grab clips and lay them into a grid. The top-left image will be the first in the sequence, then going across the row, then down until the last shot is reached. Reorganize your shots as much as you wish.

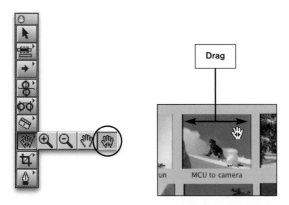

5. To view the thumbnail, select the second **Hand** tool (press **HH**) from the **Tool** palette and drag it over the thumbnail you want to view. (If the **Browser** is active, pressing **HH** doesn't select the **Hand** tool; instead, it jumps down to the next clip that starts with the letter H. To select the **Hand** tool with the keyboard, click the **Timeline** to make it active, then press **HH**. Once the **Hand** tool is selected, you can use it in the **Browser** with no problems.)

6. If you want to see a shot in the **Viewer** to set a specific **In** or **Out**, double-click it.

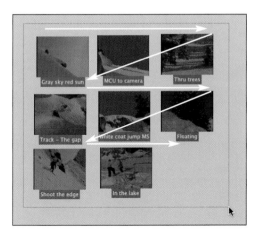

7. When you are happy with the order of your clips, use the **Arrow** tool and move all the clips you want to edit to the **Timeline** by dragging a rectangle around them.

Final Cut organizes the clips starting in the top-left corner, moving right along the top row, then down along the next row, and the next, until it reaches the end at the bottom right.

8. Drag the selected clips to the **Overwrite** overlay in the **Canvas**.

Poof! All your clips are edited into the Timeline, in the order selected, without any gaps. An instantly completed sequence. (Though we haven't talked about transitions yet, if you drag your clips from the Browser to the Overwrite with Transition overlay, they will be edited to the Timeline using the default transition between all clips. You'll learn about transitions in Chapter 8, "Transitions–Making Change Beautiful.")

9. You are done with this exercise. You can close this project and save your changes. Quit Final Cut if you want to take a break. However, there are two more exercises to go through before the end of this chapter.

6. _____More on Markers

In this exercise, you will learn more about **markers**. Markers were first introduced in Chapter 3, "*Gather Your Media*." In this exercise, you will learn that there are two types of markers: **clip** and **Timeline**. Plus, you'll learn how to use markers to indicate music beats, create subclips, add DVD chapter markers and, oh, golly, all kinds of neat stuff.

First, though, a quick note. A marker is like the "yellow sticky note" of Final Cut Pro. In and of itself, it doesn't do anything. It just sits there, like a sticky note, reminding you of something you don't want to forget.

1. Open **Seq – Markers** in the **Chapter 05 Lesson** project. Then, double-click **Track – Pink sun** to load it into the **Viewer.**

2. Move the **playhead** to **01:02:13:04**. Then, with the playhead stopped, press the **M** key to create a marker—the yellow object that appears beneath the **playhead**.

The name of the marker appears at the bottom of the Viewer window. This type of marker is called a clip marker because it is located inside a clip.

3. To change the name of the marker, be sure the **playhead** is parked on top of it, and press **M** again. The **Edit Marker** dialog appears.

4. Click once in the **Name** field and change the name of the marker to **Skier and Sun**, then click **OK**. See how the new name appears in the **Viewer** window?

5. Set another two markers in this clip, one at **01:02:17:00** and the other at **01:02:22:28**. (There's no magic in these numbers, so feel free to set your markers anywhere in this clip.)

Notice, when the playhead is on top of a marker, it is colored yellow. The normal color of a clip marker is pink.

6. To move between markers, press **Option+M** to go to the previous marker and **Shift+M** to go to the next marker. This is a very handy keyboard shortcut which I use a lot. You can also choose **Mark > Previous > Marker** or **Mark > Next > Marker**, but there never seems to be enough time to use the menu.

7. Using the **Shift** and **Option** keys, go to the last marker in the clip. To delete a marker, press **M** and click the **Delete** button in the **Edit Marker** dialog or choose **Mark > Markers > Delete**, or press **Cmd+`**. (The ` key is immediately above the **Tab** key.) The **playhead** must always be positioned on top of a marker to edit or delete it. Delete the second marker, so that there is only one marker in the clip—the first one, which you named **Skier and Sun**.

Clip markers are very useful when you want to mark, say, the beat of a music clip, or the location of a sound effect or explosion. The best part about using clip markers is that they travel with the clip.

8. With **Seq – Markers** open in the **Timeline** and the **playhead** positioned at the beginning of the sequence, edit the clip **Track – Pink sun** into the **Timeline**.

9. Grab the clip and drag it.

Notice that as you move the clip, the marker moves with it. And, the shape of the marker sprouts a long, thin line out the top, allowing you to align the marker more easily with other elements in the Timeline.

10. Leaving this clip selected, move the **playhead** so that it is not on the marker and press **Option+M** or **Shift+M**.

Just as in the Viewer, the playhead moves to the location of the marker, and the name of the marker shows up in the Canvas, when the Timeline playhead is parked directly on the marker.

11. You can also set clip markers in the **Timeline**. With the clip still selected, move the **playhead** to a location where there isn't a marker and press **M**. Again, a new marker appears in the clip at the location of the **playhead**.

Important note: In order to set a clip marker, the clip must be selected and the playhead must be at the location you want the marker to appear.

12. Deselect this clip. Now press **Option+M** and **Shift+M**. The **playhead** doesn't move.

This illustrates the biggest weakness of a clip marker. Unless the clip is selected, the playhead doesn't know where the marker is.

Consequently, although I use clip markers, I don't use them a lot—only to flag the start of a sound or visual effect that I want to remember later. The markers I use all the time are similar to clip markers, but they're located in the Timeline itself. I call them, appropriately, Timeline markers.

13. To set a **Timeline** marker, be sure nothing is selected in the **Timeline**, then move the **playhead** to, say, **01:00:04:00** in the **Timeline**. Press **M** to set the marker and **M** again to open the **Edit Marker** dialog.

You set, edit, delete, and move to a Timeline marker exactly the way you do with a clip marker. The big advantage to using Timeline markers is that you don't have to have a clip selected to be able to move to them.

14. Set three more markers, one at **01:00:08:00**, **01:00:12:00**, and one at the end of the clip, **01:00:15:27**. (Again, you can set markers anywhere—that's one of their great strengths.) Practice using **Shift+M** and **Option+M** to move between markers.

15. You can remove one marker, or you can remove all markers, but you can't select and remove a group of markers. To remove all the markers in a clip, double-click the clip to load it into the **Viewer**, and choose **Mark > Markers > Delete All**, or press **Ctrl+`**.

16. Move to the first marker in the **Timeline**. Press **M** to open the **Edit Marker** dialog, then change the name to **My Marker 1**, and add **This is my first Timeline marker** to the **Description**. Notice that both the name and description are now visible in the **Canvas**.

17. If the marker name and description are not visible, be sure that **Show Overlays** is turned on in the **View** pop-up menu of the **Canvas**. If marker names don't show up in the **Viewer**, be sure **Show Overlays** is turned on there, as well.

The following are three other useful marker tricks that I want to share before the end of this exercise:

18. Ctrl+click with the **Arrow** tool in the timecode strip of the **Timeline**. At the bottom of the shortcut menu is a list of all your **Timeline** markers. Select the marker you want to jump to, and the **playhead** moves there instantly.

I use this navigation technique constantly to move to specific points in the Timeline, such as the start of an act, or a clip that needs further attention.

19. Move to a marker and press **M** to open the **Marker** dialog box. There are three large buttons in the lower half:

- **Add Chapter Marker** adds a special marker that indicates the start of a DVD chapter. When you export your project, which you'll learn about in Chapter 12, "*Output Your Project*," this marker can be read by iDVD, DVD Studio Pro, or Compressor and turned into a DVD chapter marker. The advantage to setting chapter markers inside Final Cut is that they are frame-accurate, unlike setting chapter markers in the DVD programs themselves.

- **Add Compression Marker** is used as a flag to force Compressor to set an "I" frame at a particular frame to improve the compression of a particularly active transition or scene. In general, I don't use these—the default GOP settings for Compressor are fine for my work.

- **Add Scoring Marker** adds a special marker that is displayed inside Soundtrack to help you flag particular sections of your video within Soundtrack.

20. You can move a marker by positioning the **playhead** to the right of a marker and place it on the frame you want the marker to move to. Then choose **Mark > Markers > Reposition**, or press **Shift+`**, and the marker jumps to the **playhead**.

While this is cool, sort of, it's not that useful. Markers move only to the right, never to the left. So, if you want to move a marker earlier in the Timeline, open the Edit Marker dialog box and type in the new timecode location for the marker.

21. Finally, Timeline markers do have one limitation. They don't move when you move clips on the **Timeline**. For instance, grab the clip **Track – Red Sun** and move it. Notice that the **Timeline** markers don't move.

Generally, this isn't a big deal. However, there is no way to link a marker on the Timeline to a clip so that if the clip moves, the Timeline marker moves with it.

22. That ends this exercise on markers. You don't need to save your work; you won't be coming back to this sequence again.

7.————————**Creating Subclips**

In this exercise, you'll learn what a subclip is, how to create a subclip, how to use DV Start/Stop Detect to identify scenes on your tape, and a clever technique, using markers and subclips, that makes working with long sections of footage a lot easier.

1. To get started, open **Chapter 05 Project** and load **Seq – Markers** to the **Timeline**. The sequence may be empty, which is perfectly OK. Double-click **MS Brown coat** to load it from the **Browser** to the **Viewer**. If there are any **Ins** or **Outs**, delete them (press **Option+X**). Notice that the clip has a total duration of **13:01**.

Imagine that this clip, instead of being 13 seconds long, is actually 13 minutes long. Further, imagine that you want to work only with a small portion of the clip, and you want to pull multiple shots from that small section. One technique that works really well is to turn just the portion of the clip you want into a subclip. A subclip acts like it's a real, stand-alone clip. But, in point of fact, it's just "pointing" into a small section of the much larger media file on your hard disk.

Subclips make working with large files much easier, without requiring any changes to your master media files or even any additional disk space for new media.

2. Using the **MS Brown coat** in the **Viewer**, set an **In** at **01:01:30:24**. Then, set an **Out** at **01:01:39:15**. Notice that the clip has a new duration of **8:22**. So far, this is nothing new.

3. Choose **Modify > Make Subclip** and watch what happens. The shot in the **Viewer** remains unchanged. But, in the **Browser** a new icon appears with the name **MS Brown coat Subclip**.

4. Double-click this new subclip and look at it in the **Viewer**. Notice that where the **Out** was is now the end of the clip, indicated by the sprocket holes on the right edge.

What you've done is create a new version of this clip, where the old In and Out have been replaced by the new clip's Media Start and Media End. It's as though you had just captured this clip directly from tape. But you didn't; you just pointed to the original media file and created a new clip from it— not by duplicating the actual media files, but by creating a new pointer file that just points to a small section of the media file.

Subclips are a great way to make large, lengthy media files usable within Final Cut.

5. You edit with subclips exactly as you would a regular clip. Set an **In** and **Out**, and edit it to the **Timeline**. Trim it. Move it around. It acts just like a regular clip. With one added feature: Double-click the subclip to load it back into the **Viewer**. Then, choose **Modify > Remove Subclip Limits**.

The Viewer goes black, indicating the subclip is no longer a separate entity from the master clip it came from.

6. Double-click **MS Brown coat Subclip** in the **Browser** to load it back into the **Viewer**. With the subclip limits removed, this clip is an exact duplicate of **MS Brown coat**.

7. That ends this exercise, so you can close this project. You don't need to save your work; you won't be coming back to this sequence.

There's another really useful feature of Final Cut Pro that involves a combination of markers and subclips. But to use it, you need to understand DV Start/Stop Detect.

NOTE | Using DV Start/Stop Detect

When you are shooting DV video, every time you press the Record button, your camera records a special, invisible signal on the tape saying, essentially, "Hey! Somebody pushed the Record button!!" (Or, you know, something reasonably close to that, anyway.)

These record flags, as they are called, are transferred when you capture your DV footage into Final Cut as part of the metadata that's transferred along with the audio, video, and timecode. (Metadata is data that describes other data, similar to the way you would use words like height, weight, and hair color to describe a person.) These record flags, by the way, exist only in DV. If you are capturing SD or HD footage, this technique won't work.

When you run **Mark > DV Start/Stop Detect**, you are telling Final Cut to put a clip marker in the clip everywhere it finds one of those record flags. When this process is done, a marker indicates every time you pushed the record button on your camera during production.

I don't have any long clips with record flags, so rather than create an exercise, I'll just show you how this works, so you can practice on your own tapes. For the sake of this explanation, pretend that **MS Brown coat** is a long DV clip with record flags indicating the start of multiple different shots.

To run DV Start/Stop Detect, load the clip into the **Viewer**. Then, choose **Mark > DV Start/Stop Detect**. In just a few seconds, your entire tape is scanned and every record flag has a marker.

continues on next page

NOTE | Using DV Start/Stop Detect *continued*

Notice, also, that in the **Browser**, a small, right-pointing triangle now indicates that the **MS Brown coat** clip has markers. Twirl down the triangle to view the list of markers.

Here's the neat part: Create a new bin in the **Browser** and name it, say, **MS Brown subclips**. Then, *drag* just the markers from **MS Brown coat** in the **Browser** into the **MS Brown subclips** folder.

Twirl open the folder. Every marker has been converted into a subclip that starts at the marker and ends the frame before the next marker. In other words, you've just created subclips that start when the Record button was pushed and end the frame before the Record button was pushed, again. You've just divided your whole video in separate scenes, where each subclip is a scene.

This is a very powerful way to locate and organize your shots—all using markers, subclips, and DV Start/Stop Detect.

You can test this for yourself by capturing a long tape, containing multiple shots, into Final Cut, loading it into the **Viewer**, and running **Mark > DV Start/Stop Detect**.

Very cool. Very fast. Very slick.

Helpful Keyboard Shortcuts

Shortcut	Function
Up arrow	Moves playhead back to In of previous clip
Down arrow	Moves playhead forward to In of next clip
Shift+Left arrow	Moves playhead back 1 second
Shift+Right arrow	Moves playhead forward 1 second
Left arrow	Moves playhead back one frame
Right arrow	Moves playhead forward one frame
A	Selects the Arrow tool
Z	Selects the Zoom In tool
ZZ	Selects the Zoom Out tool
Option+click with Zoom tool	Zooms in opposite direction
Shift+click a clip	Selects a range of clips in the sequence
G	Selects the Edit Selection tool
GG	Selects the Group Selection tool
GGG	Selects the Range Selection tool
Cmd+Z	Undos a change
Shift+Cmd+Z	Redos an Undo
Delete	Deletes a selected clip(s) and leaves a gap
Shift+Delete	Deletes a selected clip(s) and removes the gap
Shift+G	Moves playhead to next gap in Timeline
Option+G	Moves playhead to previous gap in Timeline
Option+drag clip	Creates a new video or audio track
Cmd+X	Cuts selected clip(s) to the clipboard
Cmd+C	Copies selected clip(s) to the clipboard
Cmd+V	Creates an Overwrite edit at the playhead from the clipboard

continues on next page

Shortcut	Function
Helpful Keyboard Shortcuts *continued*	
Shift+V	Creates an Insert edit at the playhead from the clipboard
F	Opens a match frame clip in the Viewer to match the Timeline (or vice versa)
Shift+F	Displays the source clip in the Browser for the clip in the Timeline that contains the playhead
X	Marks an In and an Out for the clip on the Timeline that contains the playhead
Option+X	Removes both the In and the Out
HH	Selects the scrolling Hand tool—used for viewing thumbnails
M	Creates a marker at the position of playhead
MM	Opens Edit Marker dialog (playhead must be sitting on top of marker)
Shift+M	Goes to next marker
Option+M	Goes to previous marker
Cmd+`	Deletes a marker
Shift+`	Repositions marker (moves downstream only)
Ctrl+`	Deletes all markers
Cmd+U	Creates subclip based on In and Out of a clip

Summary

In this chapter, you learned how to reorganize and replace clips on the Timeline, all with the goal of telling your story as concisely and powerfully as possible. The last step in the initial story-building process is to look at each edit point and trim it to make it as tight and perfect and invisible as possible. That's next.

6

Trim Your Story

Introduction	Understanding Handles
General Trimming Tools	One-Sided Trimming Tools
Two-Sided Trimming Tools	Trimming with Timecode
Two-Track Editing	Trim Edit Window

Chapter 06 Lesson

FCP HD HOT DVD

Chapters 4 and 6 are at the heart of editing with Final Cut Pro HD. In Chapter 4, *"Build Your Story,"* you learned how to select clips and edit them to the Timeline. In this chapter, you will learn how to trim your edit points to perfection.

Although there is lots more still to cover, this chapter (along with Chapter 4) will give you the skills and confidence to edit anything.

What Is Trimming?

Trimming is the process of removing, or adding, frames to the beginning and end of your shots so that the edits flow naturally, maintaining your story, without calling attention to your editing. This is because the best editing is invisible. Your viewer should get absorbed into your story and not be thinking, "Wow! Killer cuts!"

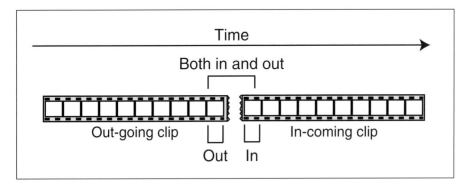

An edit point has three "sides" that can be adjusted:

- The Out of the outgoing clip

- The In of the incoming clip

- The In and the Out simultaneously

To select an edit point, click it with the **Arrow** tool, or press **V** to jump the **playhead** to the nearest edit point. You can toggle between the three sides of an edit point by pressing **U**.

In this chapter, you will learn, first, about general-purpose trimming tools, then tools that trim just one side of an edit, then tools that trim both sides of an edit. This chapter concludes with exercises in how to trim using timecode and using the Trim Edit window.

 MOVIE | Trimming.mov

If you want to see examples of trimming in action, watch the movie **Trimming.mov** in the **movies** folder on the **FCP HD HOT** DVD.

NOTE | The Importance of Having Handles

A clip with handles before the In and after the Out

A clip with no handles

Understanding and using handles is critical to successful editing. **Handles** are defined as extra media between the Media Start and the In and, again, between the Out and Media End. The reason these are so important is because when you trim an In by moving it earlier, you are actually using frames located in the handle. If you started your shot at the exact beginning of the media, there would be no extra frames you could use to move the In earlier.

In Chapter 2, "*Understanding the Final Cut Pro Interface*," you learned about Media Start and Media End. These vertical line indicators at the beginning and end of your clip show the start and end of the media file stored on your hard disk. The goal in capturing media is to capture a few extra seconds before and after your clip so that you have some additional footage to work with in adjusting exactly where your edits and transitions occur. This extra footage is called the "handle."

Without handles, you can't add transitions, extend shots, or start an In sooner or an Out later. Making sure you capture your media with handles is just really, really important.

I. ———————————General Trimming Tools

There are two general-purpose trimming tools: the **Arrow** tool and the **Razor Blade**. Both are more flexible than you might think, as you'll discover in this lesson.

1. Open **Chapter 06 Lesson**. This is a slightly modified version of what you were working on in the last chapter.

2. Duplicate **Seq – Snowboard start** by **Ctrl+clicking** the sequence title and choosing **Duplicate** from the shortcut menu.

The reason for duplicating a sequence is that it allows you to make changes to a sequence without running the risk of messing up the work you've already done.

3. Name this newly duplicated sequence " **Seq – Trimmed 30**". Again, note the use of the leading space in the name to make sure it sorts to the top of the **Browser**.

The video in this sequence currently runs over 55 seconds. Your goal is to get it down to exactly 30 seconds, ready for broadcast. To do this, you need to trim all your edits.

4. Click the **Arrow** tool (or press **A**), grab the **In** of the first clip, **Gray sky red sun**, and drag it to the right to timecode **1:00:02:24** in the **Timeline**. Notice how the yellow tooltip shows you in real time how much you are trimming? When you reach **2:24**, stop dragging and let go of the mouse.

5. The advantage of using the **Arrow** tool is that it is easy. Just grab the edge of a clip where the cursor turns to a double-pointing arrow and click and drag. The disadvantage to using the **Arrow** tool is that it always leaves gaps. So, to get rid of this gap, click in the gap to select it and press **Shift+Delete**. The gap is removed and all downstream clips are moved up (to the left).

Good. You are now 2:24 closer to reaching your goal of a 30-second commercial.

Arrow Tool Summary	
Key command	A
Advantages	Easy to use.
	Tool readily available.
Disadvantages	Moving a clip's edge always leaves gaps.
	Can't move an In earlier when blocked by preceding clip.
	Can't move an Out later when blocked by following clip.
	Only moves one side of an edit, not both.
Tool options	Holding down Option key turns Arrow into Pen tool.
Impact on sequence	No change in the duration of the sequence.

*Next, the end of the **Gray sky red sun** clip runs too long. This time, instead of using the Arrow tool to trim it, you'll use the Razor Blade tool to cut the cllip.*

6. Drag the **playhead** until the snowboarder seems about to be swallowed by the plume of snow (timecode **01:00:03:04** in the **Timeline**).

There are actually two different timecodes associated with this shot: the timecode of the shot in the Timeline (01:00:03:04), and the timecode of the original shot (which you can't see at this point).

7. However, seeing the timecode of the source tape is often helpful in trimming. To turn the display of the source timecode on, go to the **Canvas** window, click the third pop-up menu, and choose **Show Timecode Overlays**. Be sure **Show Overlays** is also turned on.

The numbers at the bottom of the screen show the timecode of the source video and audio clips at the position of the playhead in the Timeline. In this case, the playhead is at timecode 1:00:59:26 of the source clip located on track V1. This timecode on the clip is called "Source Timecode."

8. Click the **Razor Blade** tool (or press **B**) to select the single-bladed tool.

9. Click the **Razor Blade** where the **playhead** runs over the clip. The clip is cut, but the excess footage still remains on the **Timeline**.

10. Select the **Arrow** tool (or press **A**), click the excess footage to the right of the **playhead** to select it, then delete it by pressing **Shift+Delete** to remove the clip and close the gap.

11. When you delete the excess footage, the **playhead** displays the first frame of the second clip. To make sure you cut the first clip at the correct spot, press the **left** arrow key to back up one frame. Your **Canvas** should look similar to this screen shot at timecode **1:00:59:25**.

The Razor Blade always cuts just before the frame the Razor Blade tool clicks on, which, in this case, is the frame under the playhead. In other words, if you click the Razor Blade on frame 26, the cut occurs between frame 25 and frame 26.

Razor Blade Tool Summary	
Key command	B
Advantages	Cuts clips anywhere in Timeline.
Disadvantages	Difficult to align with playhead unless snapping turned on.
	Removing cut footage is a multistep process.
	When cutting, removes the frame under the Blade tool.
Tool options	Multitrack razor blade (RR) cuts all tracks simultaneously.
	Holding down Shift key toggles between single and multitrack Blade tool.
Impact on sequence	No change in the duration of the sequence by cutting a clip.
Secret keystroke	Ctrl+V cuts all clips at playhead without using Blade tool.

12. To see the results of your changes so far, click once in the **Timeline** and press **Shift+Z**. This fits the entire sequence into the **Timeline** window. I use this keyboard shortcut *constantly*.

13. That ends this exploration of trimming using the general-purpose tools of the **Arrow** and the **Razor Blade**. Save your work, but leave this exercise open—you'll need it next.

NOTE | The Red Bow Tie

When you first cut a clip, a small red bow tie appears. This icon indicates a **Through edit**—a cut in a clip where there is no change in the timecode, no change in the video, and no change in the audio. In other words, to the Viewer, this edit point is invisible.

In this chapter, you are using the Razor Blade tool to cut and remove unwanted portions of a clip. In later chapters, you'll use the Razor Blade tool to cut a clip so you can apply an effect to one part of a clip, without affecting other parts.

If seeing little red bow ties in your Timeline drives you nuts, you can turn off their display (but not their existence) by clicking the small, right-pointing arrow at the bottom of the **Timeline** and deselecting **Show Through Edits**.

By the way, to delete a **Through edit**, thereby reconnecting the entire clip, just select the **Through edit**, and press **Delete**.

NOTE | What Is Snapping?

Have you noticed when you move the playhead or a clip, it wants to "jump" to the end or beginning of a clip whenever it gets close? This is due to snapping.

Whenever the playhead, or a clip, gets within 15 frames of the edge of another clip, snapping jumps the two of them together.

Snapping is a truly wonderful feature when you are building and organizing clips on the Timeline, because it helps you align clips so that the end of one clip touches the next, with no flash of black. Snapping also quickly positions the playhead to the beginning or end of a clip.

However, for trimming, snapping is a pain in the neck. Why? Because almost all the trims you make are just a few frames here, a few frames there. And snapping keeps interfering.

Fortunately, there are three quick ways to toggle snapping on or off:

- Choose **Sequence** > **Snapping**.

Snapping turned off

- Click the **Snapping** button in the top-right corner of the **Timeline**. Green is "on," and gray is "off."

- Press **N**. This is my favorite, because using this keyboard shortcut allows you to turn snapping on, or off, in the middle of dragging a clip. The menu and button don't allow this flexibility.

Snapping, by the way, works for both audio and video clips on all tracks. With snapping turned on, whenever a clip or the playhead gets within 15 frames of any edit point of any clip on any track, snapping jumps them so they align.

You'll see examples of how to use snapping throughout the rest of this book, just not in the rest of this chapter.

_____One-Sided Trimming

In this exercise, and for the rest of this chapter, you'll work with tools designed specifically for trimming. I don't use these tools all the time, but when I need them, they are very handy. In this exercise, you'll learn about a one-sided trimming tool called the **Ripple** tool and a way to change the duration of a clip on the Timeline.

One-sided trimming means to adjust _just_ the In or just the Out of an edit point. The Arrow tool is a good example of a one-sided trimmer. The problem with using the Arrow tool for all your trimming is that, when a clip is surrounded by other clips, the Arrow tool can't make an In start sooner, only later. Also, the Arrow tool can't make an Out run later, only sooner. The Ripple tool solves this problem.

> **1.** Open **Chapter 06 Lesson**, if it isn't open already. Load the sequence **Seq – Trimmed 30**, which you created in Exercise 1, into the **Timeline**.

> **2.** Before you start trimming, make sure snapping is turned off (press **N**).

> **3.** Select the **Ripple** tool from the **Tool** palette—it's the one with a single roller—or press **RR**.
>
> _The Ripple tool allows you to change an In or an Out in ways you can't with the Arrow tool._

> **4.** For example, click the **In** of **Shoot the edge** and drag it to the _left_.
>
> _Notice the yellow tooltip that appears, showing you how much the shot is altered. Also, the dark brown box (wireframe) that represents the size of the clip grows larger as you move the In earlier._
>
> _When working with Timecode, negative numbers mean something is moving earlier, to the left, on the Timeline. Positive numbers mean something is moving later on the Timeline. In this case, the In has moved 18 frames earlier, making the clip 18 frames longer. It's longer because you didn't change the Out for that clip when you changed the In._

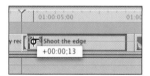

5. Using the **Ripple** tool, drag the **In** to the *right* until the tooltip says you've moved the **In 13** frames later (**+13**).

Notice how the brown wireframe gets shorter as you move the In later. This may look like you are adjusting both the In and the Out. You aren't. You are simply making the whole clip shorter or longer, by adjusting where the In starts.

Look up into the Canvas. As you move the Ripple tool, two small pictures appear.

The left picture shows the Out of the outgoing clip. The right picture shows the In of the incoming clip. As you move the mouse, the right picture changes, showing you the results of moving the In. This is a very helpful visual reminder of how you are changing the edit point and allows you to visualize the best place to cut between these two shots.

6. Watch what happens when you move the **Ripple** tool **+13** and let go of the mouse. See how the **Shoot the Edge** clip is automatically shortened, the gap is removed, and all the clips later in the sequence are moved up to fill the gap?

This is the big benefit of using the Ripple tool to trim frames; either adding them or removing them. In both cases, it does not leave a gap in the Timeline.

The displayed source timecode of your new In appears in the Canvas as 1:01:43:09.

Ripple Tool Summary	
Key command	RR
Advantages	Trims one side of an edit longer or shorter without leaving gaps. Can be used for video-only, audio-only, or video and audio clips.
Disadvantages	Trimming just the video or just the audio of a linked clip will cause the clip to go out of sync.
Tool options	Holding down the Shift key toggles between Ripple and Roll tool. (You'll learn about the Roll tool in the next exercise.)
Impact on sequence	Rippling always changes the duration of the sequence.

There's another "tool" that can be used for trimming. In writing this chapter, I realized that I use this technique a lot, but never considered it a trimming tool—mainly because it isn't a tool—it's the Duration dialog.

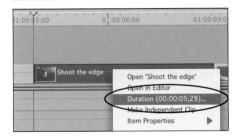

7. Select the **Arrow** tool, then **Ctrl+click** on the **Shoot the edge** clip. Notice that the third line down in the contextual menu displays the duration of the clip.

8. You need to change this duration to **4:29**. To do so, select **Shoot the edge** and choose **Modify > Duration** (or press **Ctrl+D**).

The Duration dialog appears with the current duration (5:29) of the clip preset.

9. Change the **Duration** to **4:29** and click **OK**.

*The Out of **Shoot the edge** is instantly shortened and all the downstream clips are automatically moved up to the left. I use this technique a lot to change the length of titles, graphics, still frames, and shots that don't have any significant movement in them, such as wide shots.*

10. Now you need to trim up the rest of the clips in this sequence. Using all the tools you've learned so far, make the following changes to these clips:

Actions to Clips in the Sequence	
Clip	**Action**
MCU to camera	Set duration to **3:05.**
Blue sky	Delete the clip—leave a gap in the **Timeline.**
Down mountain	Move this clip ahead of **Track the gap**, and start it at **01:00:15:01** on the **Timeline.** The starting source timecode of the clip is **1:00:15:03** and its duration is **5:27**.
Track the gap	Starts on the **Timeline** at **1:00:20:28** at source timecode **1:02:33:03** with a duration of **3:26.**
In the lake	Starts on the **Timeline** at **1:00:24:24** at source timecode **1:01:06:18** with a duration of **5:06.**
White coat jump MS	Leave as is.
White coat jump WS	Leave as is.

11. When you are done, your sequence should match **Seq – First Trim** with a timecode of **1:00:42:07** when you press the **End** key to jump to the end of the sequence.

12. This completes this exercise. Save your work, but leave everything open. You aren't done yet. Your commercial still runs over 12 seconds long.

NOTE | Ripple Delete

There is one other one-sided trimming function that you learned about in the last chapter. Although you don't need to cover it, again, in detail, I want to mention it here for the sake of completeness: the **Ripple Delete**.

Selecting a clip and pressing **Delete**, or choosing **Sequence > Lift**, deletes the clip and leaves a gap. Deleting a clip does not change the duration of the sequence. This is called a **Lift edit**.

Selecting a clip and pressing **Shift+Delete**, or choosing **Sequence > Ripple Delete**, deletes the clip, removes the gap, and pulls up all the clips to the right (downstream) of the gap. Ripple deleting always changes the duration of the sequence.

Which brings me around to why the Ripple tool and the Ripple Delete are both called "Ripple;" both of them create results that "ripple" through the rest of the sequence.

NOTE | When Rippling Doesn't Work

Rippling works great when you are trimming a video-only clip, an audio-only clip, or a clip with video and audio linked together.

Where it doesn't work is when you want to trim just the video, or just the audio, of a linked clip. In this case, one of two things will happen:

Out-of-sync flag

Your audio and video will go out of sync, indicated by the red flags.

continues on next page

NOTE | When Rippling Doesn't Work *continued*

Or, you'll get an error message saying "Clip Collision."

You'll learn how to deal with sync issues in Chapter 7, *"Audio—The Secret to a Great Picture,"* including a *much* better way to trim a linked clip.

However, to solve the "Clip Collision" message, you need to "lock" the tracks you *don't* want to change.

For instance, if you want to adjust a video edit point, and you know you won't force any of your audio tracks out of sync, you can lock your audio tracks. Locking a track tells Final Cut to ignore it when making changes to other tracks. In fact, locking a track is a good way to prevent yourself from making changes to a track, because as long as it is locked, you can't make any changes to that track either.

To lock a track, click the small **padlock** at the left side of the **Timeline.**

A locked track has diagonal lines running through all the clips on the track. An unlocked track, which is the default, has no diagonal lines.

To unlock a track, click the **padlock** icon again.

---

3. —————————**Two-Sided Trimming**

In this exercise, you'll learn about tools that adjust both the In and the Out simultaneously: the Roll, Slip, and Slide tools.

The **Roll** tool allows you to move both sides of the edit point simultaneously.

The **Slip** tool allows you to change the content of a clip while keeping its duration and location in the Timeline unchanged.

The **Slide** tool allows you to change the location of a clip in the Timeline, in relation to the clip before it and after it, while keeping its content and duration unchanged.

1. Start by opening **Chapter 06 Lesson**, if it isn't already open. Then, if you did all the work in the last exercise, open the **Seq – Trimmed 30** sequence. If not, open the **Seq – First trim** sequence.

2. Move the **playhead** so it is between the first and second clips. This step, which is optional, helps you remember which edit you are working on.

3. In the **Tool** palette, click the **Roll** tool (or press **R**).

The Roll tool icon has two rollers, implying that it is changing two sides of the edit at once.

4. Click the **Roll** tool on the edit point containing the **playhead**.

What you are going to do is to tweak the placement of the edit point to improve the flow between two shots by simultaneously changing both the In and the Out.

5. Drag the **Roll** tool to the left. Notice the changing numbers in the tooltip.

6. Now, drag the **Roll** tool to the right. Watch the tooltip and the two images in the **Canvas**. The left picture shows the changes to the **Out** of the outgoing clip. The right picture shows the changes to the **In** of the incoming clip. Stop when your numbers match those in the screen shot.

7. Let go of the mouse and press the **** (backslash) key.

The backslash is a fast way to preview the location of the playhead, which is why I had you position the playhead at the edit point in Step 2. The default setting is for playback to start 5 seconds before the playhead and end 2 seconds after.

NOTE | Changing Playback Preview Settings

The settings for Playback Preview are set in **Final Cut Pro HD > User Preferences**.

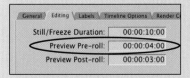

The default settings are 5:00 pre-roll and 2:00 post-roll. I prefer **4:00** and **3:00**. You can set them however you like in the **Final Cut Pro HD > User Preferences > Editing tab**.

Roll trims are excellent when the action in both shots matches, and you are just trying to find the best place to make the cut.

Roll Tool Summary	
Key command	R
Advantages	Trims both sides of an edit point simultaneously.
	Can be used for video-only, audio-only, or video and audio clips.
Disadvantages	Moves the edit point exactly the same amount for each clip, though in opposite directions.
Tool options	Holding down the Shift key toggles between the Ripple and Roll tools.
Impact on sequence	Rolling never changes the duration of the sequence.

The next trim tool you will learn is the Slip tool. This is often a tricky tool to get your mind around because it is not initially intuitive.

8. Put the **playhead** between the first and second shots and play the second clip. Notice how the snowboarder doesn't get completely out of frame before he skis into the third shot?

What you are going to do is keep the second clip the same length and at the same location in the Timeline, but change the content of the shot itself, by simultaneously changing the In and the Out of the second shot.

9. Select the **Slip** tool from the **Tool** palette (or press **S**).

10. Click in the middle of **Shoot the edge** and drag slowly left and right.

11. Watch the **Canvas** images to see your changes. The left image shows the changing **In**, the right image shows the changing **Out**, both from **Shoot the edge**. See how you are changing the content of the shot, without changing the duration or its location on the **Timeline**?

Drag to the left until the tooltip says **–:24** and the snowboarder is just leaving the frame in the **Out** image.

12. Press **** (backslash) and preview the edit.

Hmmm…something doesn't feel right. The cut feels "jumpy."

13. Grab the **Slip** tool and slip the clip back two frames (**-:02** in the tooltip).

14. Preview the edit again. Much better! For some reason, many edits flow better when you don't perfectly match the action, but take out a few frames between the end of the first shot and the start of the second to slightly speed the action.

Slip Tool Summary	
Key command	S
Advantages	Changes the content of a shot (by simultaneously shifting the In and the Out of a clip in the same direction) without affecting its duration or location on the Timeline.
Disadvantages	Hard to understand conceptually.
	Only slips one clip at a time.
Tool options	Holding down the Shift key toggles between the Slip and Arrow tools.
Impact on sequence	Slipping never changes the duration of the sequence.

The Slide tool is, essentially, the opposite of the Slip tool. The Slide tool maintains the current duration and content of a clip, but slides it along the Timeline by simultaneously adjusting the Out of the preceding clip and the In of the following clip in the same direction. It's a concept that has been known to drive strong men to drink.

15. Select the **Slide** tool from the **Tool** palette (or press **SS**).

16. Click in the middle of **Track – The gap** and drag left and right. Watch as the location of the clip shifts on the **Timeline**. Drag the clip to the left and you'll discover a point where you can't drag it anymore. This is because you have run out of handles on the **In the lake** clip. Without handles, you can't slide the clip any further.

17. Slide the clip to the left nine frames (**–:09**) until the snowboarder in the right image, the **In**, disappears from the frame, but not his shadow. The images in the **Canvas** represent the changing **Out** of the outgoing clip on the left, and the changing **In** of the incoming clip on the right.

18. Let go and preview the edit. Giving a little more time to the last shot helps to pay off the joke of him skiing into the lake (showcasing, I guess, a new approach to water skiing).

Slide Tool Summary	
Key command	SS
Advantages	Trims the Out of the preceding clip and the In of the following clip simultaneously so that the clip in the middle changes location on the Timeline.
	Can be used for video-only, audio-only, or video and audio clips.
Disadvantages	Can't completely cover up the preceding or following clip.
	Total clip movement is limited by handles.
	Can't jump over a clip.
Tool options	Holding down the Shift key toggles between the Slide and Arrow tools.
Impact on sequence	Sliding never changes the duration of the sequence.

19. This ends the exercise. Save your work. But keep everything open because even with all this trimming, your commercial is still heavy (um, TV-speak for "way the heck too long"). In the next exercise you'll finally bring it into time.

An Alternate Way to Edit

In this exercise, you'll learn an alternate way to edit that is especially useful in documentaries and other "talking head" programs—editing using multiple tracks.

NOTE | How Final Cut Handles Multiple Tracks

Final Cut allows up to 99 tracks of video and 99 tracks of audio in each sequence. There are so many that track count is, essentially, unlimited. The highest number of video tracks I've ever used was 32 and, in a different project, I used 21 audio tracks.

Final Cut reads video tracks from the top to the bottom. That is, it displays video on V99 on top of V98 on top of V97 down to V1. Further, if video on a higher-numbered track is full-screen and fully opaque, it totally blocks any video below it. Since you won't be learning about how to change opacity or image size until Chapters 9 and 10, any video that you put on a higher-numbered track now will totally block any underlying clips.

You can take advantage of this in your editing. If I am doing dramatic work, I try to keep all my clips on one track. It makes trimming and editing easier. If I am editing a documentary, corporate training, or news story, I often put my video on two tracks: V1 and V2.

This exercise shows you how.

---

1. Start by opening **Chapter 06 Project**, if it isn't already open. Then, if you did all the work in the last exercise, open the **Seq – Trimmed 30** sequence. If not, open the **Seq – Second trim** sequence.

---

2. Add a second video track by **Ctrl+clicking** in the gray area above the **V1** track and choosing **Add Track** from the shortcut menu.

---

3. By the way, you can delete a track, whether there are clips on it or not, by **Ctrl+clicking** between the track label (V1, V2, and so on) and the **padlock** icon and choosing **Delete Track** from the shortcut menu.

---

4. Drag **White coat jump WS** up to **V2**. Then, drag **White coat jump MS** up to **V2**.

5. Turn snapping on for this next move, then turn it back off when you are done. (Remember, the easiest way to do this is to press **N**, to toggle snapping.)

Drag

6. Grab both clips on **V2** and drag them until the first clip, **White coat jump WS**, lines up with the end of **MCU to camera**. Because snapping is on, you'll see two triangles at the edit point indicating that the ends of the clips line up.

7. Play the sequence.

The playhead starts out by playing the clips on V1. When it reaches the clips on V2, FCP jumps up and plays them. Then, for the period of time that the clip on V2 covers the clip on V1, Final Cut continues to play just V2 video. Only when V2 is empty is the video on V1 displayed.

Drag

8. Next, use the **Arrow** tool to drag the **Out** of the second clip back until it ends at source timecode **01:02:49:12**. Notice, as you do so, that the image and timecode for the **Out** you are dragging show up in the **Canvas**.

9. Play the sequence again and you'll see that **White coat jump WS** and **White coat jump MS** are two different angles of the same jump. What you are going to do is use what you've learned about trimming to figure out the best place to cut between these two shots.

10. Select the **Ripple** tool and drag the **Out** of the first clip back.

Hmmm…What's wrong? Why a clip collision? Because there is video on track V1, and Final Cut doesn't know whether to pull it up with the ripple or leave it alone. When FCP is uncertain, it prevents you from doing a trim.

11. To fix this problem, recall what you learned earlier about locking tracks and lock **V1**.

12. Using the **Ripple** tool, drag the **Out** of **White coat jump WS** back until you reach timecode **01:02:56:03**. Again, the **Out** and **In** are displayed in the **Canvas**.

Play the sequence. Cool—but he jumps twice. This is not ideal. In fact, it's considered an editing faux pas. You need to fix it.

13. This time, unlock track **V1** and select the **Arrow** tool. Why? Just to give you a different way to do a trim.

14. Drag the **In** of the second clip, **White coat jumps MS**, to the right to tighten the shot until you reach timecode **1:02:45:16**. Delete the gap by clicking in it and pressing **Shift+Delete**.

Oops! Deleting the gap moved video on *both* **V1** and **V2**. Undo.

Again, the objective is to delete the gap on **V2**. However, pressing **Shift+Delete** deleted the gap across *all* tracks. So, either remove the gap on **V2** by locking **V1**, then using **Shift+Delete** to delete the gap, or grab the second clip on **V2** with the **Arrow** tool and drag it next to the clip on **V1**. Again, turning on snapping will help with the alignment.

15. Preview the edit by pressing \ (backslash). Then, unlock **V1**.

Sigh...It looks simple when you trim edits this way, but I will confess that when I was writing this exercise, figuring out the best place to put that edit took me about 30 minutes. To give you an example of the difference in feeling that results from where an edit hits, select the edit point in the middle of his jump with the Roll tool. Roll the edit point around and watch what a difference a change in timing makes.

16. Ta-da! Your commercial is done for time. Press the **End** key and notice the timecode: **1:00:30:00**.

In the next chapter, you'll add music. In Chapter 8, "Transitions–Making Change Beautiful," you'll add a couple of flashy transitions. Chapter 9, "Text, Titles, and Graphics," shows you how to add opening and closing text. And, finally, Chapter 11, "Filters and Keying," adds some interesting effects.

But, in terms of editing, you are done.

17. Save your work. You can keep Final Cut open for the next exercise, but you'll be using a different sequence.

You'll see more examples of using two video tracks for editing in Chapter 7, "Audio–The Secret to a Great Picture."

5. ——————Trimming with Timecode

In this exercise, you'll discover some power trimming techniques that can significantly improve the speed and precision of your trims.

You'll learn how to select edits using just the keyboard, how to harness timecode or the keyboard to make edit adjustments, and how to perform a high-speed editing technique to do a Roll edit, called the Extend edit.

On a personal note, although all the tools illustrated earlier in this chapter are important, the techniques in this exercise are the ones I use every day to get my work done.

1. Open **Chapter 06 Lesson** and load **Seq – 3 Clips** to the **Timeline**. This is a simple three-clip sequence that you will use to experiment with these techniques.

2. Drag your **playhead** to timecode **1:00:05:00**. Took you a while, didn't it?

3. Now, press **Home**, then click in the timecode box at the top-left corner of the **Timeline** and type **1.0.05.0**, then press **Return**.

Notice that you don't need to enter double zeros, just one. And periods, instead of colons. This is a much faster way to move the playhead, when you know where you are going.

4. You already know how to use the **up** and **down** arrow keys to jump between clips. Now, press **V**. The **playhead** jumps to the nearest edit and selects it.

5. Now, press the **up** and **down** arrow keys. See how the playhead not only moves between clips, but also selects the edit it lands on?

Both sides selected

In selected

Out selected

6. Watch this: with an edit selected, press **U**. This selects one side of an edit, specifically the **In**. Press **U** again. Now the **Out** is selected. Press **U** a third time. Both sides of the edit are selected.

7. Here's the cool part. Press **U** until only one side of the edit is selected. Now, use the **up** and **down** arrow keys to move between clips and watch what happens. Right! The playhead jumps to the next edit and selects it in the exact same way it selected the edit point it just left.

This is a really fast way to quickly trim a number of different clips.

8. Here's why. Go to the edit point between the first and second clip. Press **U**, until the **In** is selected. Be sure the **Arrow** tool is selected.

9. Now, press the period key (.) and watch the **In** trim to the right one frame. You are doing a **Ripple** edit, using the keyboard.

10. Press the comma key (,) and watch the **In** trim to the left, also by a frame.

11. Press **U** until both sides of the edit are selected. Now, press the comma and period keys and watch the location of the edit shift. You are doing a **Roll** edit, totally under keyboard control!

12. But wait! There's more. Continue to keep both sides of this edit point selected. Press the **plus** key (**+**) on the keypad or the keyboard. Next, type **15** and press **Return**. The edit point just moved 15 frames downstream, to the right.

By the way, using the keys on the keypad used to be the only way to enter timecode offsets, which is what these are called. In Final Cut Pro HD, you can use either the keyboard or the keypad.

13. Press the **minus** (**-**) key. Type **20** and press **Return**. The edit point shifts to the left.

OK, truth be told, while you do *need to press the minus key, you don't really need to press the plus key. Final Cut assumes a positive number, unless you tell it otherwise. But I like typing the plus key because it reminds me which direction I want the edit point to move.*

14. Next, press **U** until only the **Out** is selected. Press the **minus** key, then type **20**, then press **Return**. You instantly trimmed the **Out** by 20 frames.

For me, this is an amazing timesaver. Using only the keyboard and timecode, you can ripple or roll any edit point in your sequence—up to the limit of your handles. (You do remember about handles, right?)

15. Click the last clip, **Track - Jump**, to select it. Press **Option+up arrow** to move it to track **V2**. Make sure the clip remains selected.

16. Now, press the **minus** key, type **60** and press **Return**. The entire clip moves left 60 frames. Press the **plus** key, type **20** and press **Return**. The entire clip moves right 20 frames.

17. One more thing to try. Grab the clip on **V2** and bring it back down to **V1** so that it edits tightly to the end of the **Fan tail** clip (meaning no gaps).

18. Next, make sure no clips or edit points are selected. Move the **playhead** out somewhere near the middle of the sequence; the exact location doesn't matter. Now, press the **plus** key, type **25**, press **Return** and watch the **playhead** move a relative amount.

Earlier in this exercise you moved the playhead to an absolute timecode location: 01:00:05:00. Here you told it to move 25 frames downstream from wherever it is at that moment, and it moved.

These timecode keyboard shortcuts make editing fly. Using timecode offsets, you can move the play-head, clips, groups of clips, or edit points, as long as they are selected and they have room on the Timeline to move. Oh, yes—and as long as the edit points have handles.

There's one more technique to cover in this exercise: the Extend edit, which is my favorite edit. It's a Roll edit on steroids, which, um, have not yet been banned by the World Editing Federation.

19. Select the edit point between clips 2 and 3.

Amount edit point needs to move

20. Put your **playhead** at **1:00:10:10** and press **E**. The edit point jumps to match the position of the **playhead**.

NOTE | The Power of the Extend Edit

There are three situations where I find the Extend edit really useful:

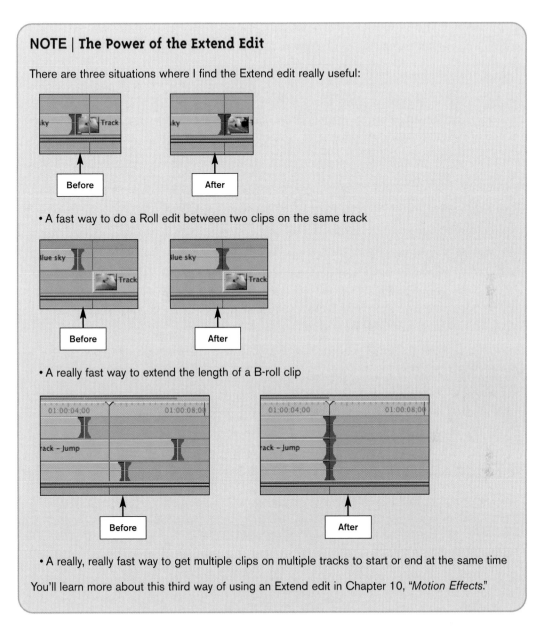

• A fast way to do a Roll edit between two clips on the same track

• A really fast way to extend the length of a B-roll clip

• A really, really fast way to get multiple clips on multiple tracks to start or end at the same time

You'll learn more about this third way of using an Extend edit in Chapter 10, *"Motion Effects."*

21. That wraps up this exercise on power trimming tools. Quit Final Cut if you are done; otherwise keep everything open for the last exercise in this chapter. If you are quitting, you don't need to save your work.

Trim Edit Window

OK. Here's another confession. I am such a keyboard shortcuts junkie that I thought the Trim Edit window was more pain that it was worth. Then, two things happened: Apple added an incredible improvement in Final Cut 4, and I heard Walter Murch (a multiple-Oscar-winning editor) give a talk on how he edits using Final Cut Pro. Suddenly, the Trim Edit window made a whole lot more sense. In this exercise, you'll learn how to use it and understand what makes it a unique editing tool within Final Cut.

1. If it isn't already open, start Final Cut, open **Chapter 06 Lesson**, and load **Seq – 3 clips** to the **Timeline**.

Since this is a tutorial for you to learn a technique, you won't need to use more than three clips.

The Trim Edit window has three big benefits not easily available by editing on the Timeline:
  • *It allows you to adjust your Ins and Outs in real time, while the video is playing.*
  • *It allows you to see your edits in a larger window.*
  • *It allows you quick access to a variety of precise controls to trim your edits.*

2. Double-click the edit point between clips 1 and 2 to open the **Trim Edit** window (or select the edit point and press **Cmd+7**).

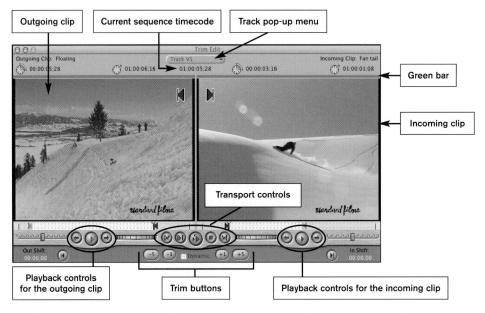

The Trim Edit window opens with each window the exact size of the Canvas. If you want the Trim Edit window to be bigger, make your Canvas window bigger before opening the Trim Edit window.

There are six main sections to the Trim Edit window:

- *The outgoing clip window on the left*
- *The incoming clip window on the right*
- *Playback controls for the Out on the lower left*
- *Playback controls for the In on the lower right*
- *Edit point controls at the bottom middle*
- *Green bars that indicate what type of trim is being performed at the top*

The Trim Edit window is designed, as its name indicates, to trim edits. There are three types of trims you can do in this window:

- *Rolls (the default setting when the window opens)*
- *Ripples*
- *Slips*

3. At the bottom of each image are the playback controls. Although the shuttle bar and jog wheel are similar to other windows, the arrow controls are different. Click the left-pointing arrow to go back one frame. Click the right-pointing arrow to go forward a frame. Click the center arrow to play the clip from the position of the **playhead** at normal speed.

In all cases, clicking these arrows does not change the placement of the In or the Out.

4. The green bars at the top indicate what type of trim is being performed. Click inside the right window (the incoming clip). Notice that your cursor turns into the **Ripple** tool pointing to the right, and the green bar over the right window lights up. This indicates that you are making a **Ripple** edit on the incoming clip.

5. Click inside the left window (the outgoing clip). Your cursor turns into the **Ripple** tool pointing to the left, and the green bar over the left window lights up. This indicates you are making a **Ripple** edit on the outgoing clip.

Roll edit

6. Click the vertical bar separating the two windows. Both bars light up, which means you are now doing a **Roll** edit to both clips.

These two buttons cannot be modified.

Trim backward buttons

Trim forward buttons

7. At the bottom center of the window are the trim buttons. Click the vertical bar to set the **Trim Edit** window to a **Roll** edit, then click the **−5** button.

You just rolled the edit point back five frames, as indicated by the Out Shift and In Shift indicators in each of the corners. These provide a running total of all your edit point changes.

8. Click the **+5** button to get back to where you started. You can trim in multiple frames or single frames, depending upon which button you click.

Roll   Ripple out   Ripple in

9. Another way to make changes is to put your cursor on top of the **Out** (or the **In**).

If both green bars are lit, dragging the **Out** (or **In**) left or right makes a **Roll** edit.

If the left green bar is lit, dragging the **Out** makes a **Ripple** edit on the **Out**.

If the right green bar is lit, dragging the **In** makes a **Ripple** edit on the **In**.

In all cases, the results of your changes show up in the indicators in the corners.

Out   In

10. Just above the trim buttons are the playback controls.

Click the far-left button to go to the previous edit point.

Click the far-right button to go to the following edit point.

Click the second-left button to play from the **In** to the **Out** and stop (**Shift+**).

Click the middle button to preview the edit and repeat it (**spacebar**).

Click the second-right button to stop playback.

---

11. Here's where the magic of the Trim Edit window appears. Click the **Dynamic** check box to turn it on. (It is off by default.)

---

12. Now, follow these instructions exactly (in fact, read these before you do it):

a. With both windows in the **Trim Edit** window selected, that is, they have a green bar over them, press **J** to play backward for a few seconds.

b. Press the **spacebar** to stop.

c. Press **L** to play forward.

d. Watch the left window. When the snowboarder comes in for a landing, press **K** to stop playback. At the instant you pressed **K**, the **In** and the **Out** were rolled to match the position of the playhead.

Using the J, K, and L keys, you can watch and set your edit points in real time. Use J and L to play the edit. Every time you press K, the edit points are updated.

If you are doing a Roll, both the In and the Out update.

If you are doing a Ripple, only the side being rippled is updated

You've known how to use the J, K, and L keys for a while. The magic of the Trim Edit window is that, with the Dynamic check box checked, you are able to use the J, K, and L keys to adjust your edit points in real time. It is this combination of precision, using trim buttons and dragging, using real-time trimming, and utilizing the J, K, and L keys that makes the Trim Edit window so useful.

---

13. Take a minute to experiment with different trims, both **Ripples** and **Rolls**, and watch how using the **J**, **K**, and **L** keys work.

Here are some tips to keep in mind:

- *Using the spacebar to stop playback does not change the edit point.*
- *Using the spacebar to start playback and the K key to stop does not change the edit point.*
- *Using the J, K, and L keys in the Timeline does not change the edit point.*
- *Only using the J, K, and L keys in the Trim Edit window resets the edit point—provided the Dynamic check box is checked. Otherwise, no real-time update occurs.*
- *You can change edit points playing forward or backward.*
- *You can play forward in slow motion by holding down the K and L keys simultaneously.*

> • *You can play backward in slow motion by holding down the K and J keys simultaneously.*

> • *Edit points change when you press the K key, alone.*

I don't use the Trim Edit window for every edit. But when I need to see how an edit looks in real time and make tweaks quickly, the Trim Edit window is my first choice.

14. This ends this exercise and chapter. You don't need to save your work from this exercise. Feel free to quit Final Cut and take a break, because we are moving on to something totally different—audio.

NOTE | Setting Trim Edit Preferences

There are two preference settings that affect how the Trim Edit window works. Their location changed in Final Cut Pro HD, you can find them in the Final Cut Pro HD > User Preferences > Editing tab.

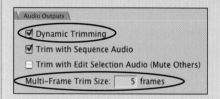

The Dynamic Trimming check box, which is off by default, controls whether the Dynamic check box is turned on when the Trim Edit window opens. If the Dynamic Trimming check box is *off*, the Trim Edit window opens with the Dynamic check box unchecked. If it is *on*, the Trim Edit window opens with the Dynamic check box on.

The Multi-Frame Trim Size setting allows you to change the default trim setting in the small ovals at the bottom center of the Trim Edit window from 5 frames (the default) to any number between 1 and 99 (I like setting mine at 6. Why? Because, for some reason, trimming in multiples of three frames works best for me.)

Summary

One-sided trimming tools *always* change the duration of a sequence. Two-sided tools do not. And, because trimming is such an integral part of editing, Final Cut provides lots of options for trimming your clips.

Helpful Keyboard Shortcuts

Shortcut	Function
V	Moves playhead to nearest edit point and selects it
U	Toggles between the three sides of an edit: In, Out, or both
Shift+Z	Depending on which window is selected, scales video in Viewer or Canvas to fit into the window, or scales sequence to fit entirely in Timeline window
A	Selects Arrow tool
Option+click with Arrow tool	Turns Arrow into Pen tool
B	Selects the Razor Blade tool (single-track)
BB	Selects the Razor Blade tool (multitrack)
Shift+click with Razor Blade tool	Toggles between single- and multitrack mode
Z	Selects the Zoom In tool
ZZ	Selects the Zoom Out tool
Option+click with Zoom	Toggles between Zoom In and Zoom Out tools
R	Selects the Roll tool
RR	Selects the Ripple tool
S	Selects the Slip tool
SS	Selects the Slide tool
N	Toggles snapping on or off
Ctrl+D	Opens Duration dialog for clip or transition on Timeline
Shift+F4	Locks all video tracks
Shift+F5	Locks all audio tracks
\	Plays a clip or sequence from a few seconds before the current location of the playhead to a few seconds after
Shift+\	Plays a clip from the In to the Out
Option+up arrow	Moves selected clip, or clips, up a track
Option+down arrow	Moves selected clip, or clips, down a track
Comma	Moves selected clip or edit point back one frame
Period	Moves selected clip or edit point ahead one frame
Cmd+7	Opens the Trim Edit window

7

Audio—The Secret to a Great Picture

The Workflow of Editing Audio	Editing Audio to the Timeline
Trimming Audio	Setting Audio Levels	Adding Music and Effects
Converting Audio	Narration and the Voice-Over Tool	Mixing Audio

Chapter 07 Lesson 1
Chapter 07 Lesson 2

FCP HD HOT DVD

Editing audio for video could fill an entire book just on its own. In many productions, the audio (what people say) is far more important than the visuals (how they look). Yet, far too often, audio is virtually ignored during the production process.

In this chapter, you will learn a basic audio editing workflow, how to edit and trim audio clips, set basic audio levels, add music and effects, then mix everything together so it sounds great.

Still, for all the audio tools, flexibility, and power that Final Cut provides, keep in mind that in the end, it all comes down to your ears. Be an active listener. Concentrate on building a "sound picture" in your mind using your audio track. Because the better your audio sounds, the better your picture looks.

The Workflow of Editing Audio

Editing audio goes hand-in-hand with editing video. In fact, as you'll see in these exercises, when you have clips with synced audio and video, you edit both the audio and video at the same time.

However, there are many, many times when you want to adjust the timing of the audio differently from the video. Or use one transition for video and another for audio. Or add music and effects to your sequence.

For all these reasons, I've found it helpful to follow a workflow for editing audio, similar to what you learned in Chapter 1, "*Get Organized*," for Final Cut itself. This audio workflow consists of five steps:

1. Edit the audio to the Timeline.

2. Trim the audio.

3. Add transitions.

4. Add effects.

5. Mix.

The exercises in this chapter directly follow this editing workflow, with the exception of audio transitions, which are covered in the next chapter, so you can learn a *process* for editing, as well as specific techniques.

The Math of Audio

But, first, you need to understand some of the math behind the audio. Why? Because, when it comes to audio, what you don't know can make your life really unpleasant.

You've probably tossed around terms like "48K," "44.1K," "32K," or "8-bit," "16-bit," even "24-bit." But, what do those terms mean? When I ask my students, I either get "quality," or some seriously blank looks.

But understanding what these terms mean has a direct impact on your audio—especially when, as a marketing ploy, many DV cameras ship from the factory with the wrong audio settings for digital editing.

So, sharpen your pencil and grab an extra cup of coffee. This stuff is important and won't take long to read.

Frequency 101

In order to understand digital audio, you first need to understand "normal" audio.

All audio is analog—variations in air pressure that cause your eardrum, or a microphone diaphragm, to vibrate. Those vibrations are translated by our brain, or the mic, into electrical signals, which can then be heard or recorded.

The "normal" range of human hearing is 20 to 20,000 cycles per second. This is called the *frequency response* of human hearing. However, human hearing changes with age. As people get older, they tend to lose the ability to hear higher frequencies. A middle-aged man, for instance, can only hear frequencies up to 12,000 to 14,000 cycles. Women tend to lose high-frequency hearing more slowly than men.

A deep pipe on an organ, or bass guitar, is in the 60 to 100 cycle range. Much below that, and you'll feel the vibration, but not hear the tone.

Human speech is in the range of 300 to 3,500 cycles per second, with some sounds, like "S" and "F," going a bit higher.

Orchestral triangles are in the 8,000 to 12,000 range.

Why is this important? Because if you want to emphasize the loudness of a ship's horn (which I did in a recent video for a cruise line), you can either increase the volume for the entire clip (which raises the overall noise) or just increase the frequencies for the horn (which makes it louder, without affecting anything else). You'll learn how to do this later in Chapter 11, *"Filters and Keying."*

Sample Rate

The first set of terms, "48K, 44.1K, and 32K," all have to do with the frequency response of a digital audio clip.

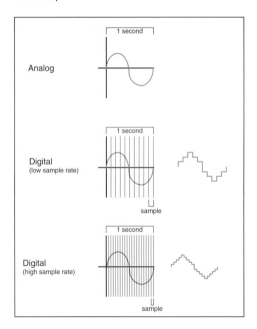

By its very nature, analog signals are infinitely variable, like the smooth curve of the sine wave in this illustration. And, although we can deal with analog signals perfectly well, a computer can't. It needs to convert these infinite changes into discrete numbers that it can store and process.

This conversion is called *quantizing*, and it works like this: The computer "listens" to an incoming audio signal and, every so often, records the average level of the sound it "hears." If those digital samples are far apart, as in the second illustration, only a very rough digital image of that sound is recorded. However, if those samples are very close together, as in the third example above, then a much more accurate picture of the sound is recorded.

The sample rate is the measure of how many digital samples are recorded by the computer. The higher the number of samples per second, the more accurate the picture of the sound is captured by the computer.

According to the Nyquist Theorem, the frequency response (or range of frequencies a clip contains) of a digital audio signal is equal to half its sample rate. Thus, a 32K sample rate contains a range of frequencies from 20 to 16,000 cycles. A 48K sample rate ranges from 20 to 24,000.

Final Cut does not like editing 32K audio files. It works much better on 44.1K and 48K sample rates. However, many inexpensive digital cameras are set to 32K sample rates for weird marketing reasons. So, make sure the production crew sets the audio sample rate on the camera to 48K (the digital standard). This is often listed in camera menus as 16-bit. Converting files from 32K to 48K after shooting never improves quality and should be avoided.

Dynamic Range

The second set of numbers, "8-bit, 16-bit, and 24-bit," all have to do with dynamic range, the amount of difference between the softest and loudest sound in a clip.

But where did the word "bit" come from? Not surprisingly, it came from the computer. A bit is the smallest amount of information the computer can record. Since all computer numbers are recorded in binary ones and zeros, an 8-bit audio file means that all its different volumes are represented by a series of numbers that range from 0 to 255—or 256 different values. Why 256 values? Because 256 is equal to 2 to the 8th power, where 8 represents the bit-depth of the audio file. The standard for CDs, 16-bit audio, has 65,536 discrete volume settings (2 to the 16th power).

This means that an 8-bit sound with a level of 1 is very, very, *very* soft. A sound with a level of 255 is as loud as it can get; because in an 8-bit environment no loudness number can be greater than 255. If your audio track gets too loud, so that the combined signal is greater than 255 (shown as 0 dB on the Audio Meter), your audio gets clipped and parts of the signal are thrown away.

As a warning, Final Cut lights these two small clips lights to tell you your audio is too "hot," or loud.

Why is this important? Because audio mixing is additive. As you add more tracks, the additional signals increase the overall volume, which makes it very easy for those levels to get too high. Then, because the computer does not have any more numbers to use to represent this extra loudness, it throws that excess audio away, leaving flat-top waveforms where audio should be.

This missing signal creates digital distortion. Little computer bits, flying out of your computer, landing higgledy-piggledy on the floor. Homeless. (Well, OK, maybe they don't really fly out of your computer. But digital distortion sounds *awful*, and if you output it to tape, there is no technology on the planet that can fix your audio to make it sound good.)

So, watch your Audio Meters! Be very, very careful those clip lights don't light. Not once. Not even flicker.

Dynamic Range Table			
Bit Depth	**# of Levels**	**Dynamic Range**	**Common Use**
8-bit	256	0–96 dB	Internet, Broadcast TV
16-bit	65,536	0–124 dB	CD-ROM & Digital Video
24-bit	16,777,216	0-143 dB	Theatrical films
Human hearing	N/A	0–120 dB	Life

Final Cut can handle either .WAV or .AIFF files, 8- or 16-bit depth, with sample rates from 8 to 48 kHz.

MOVIE | Audio.mov

For audio tutorials illustrating this chapter, check out **Audio.mov** in the **movies** folder on the **FCP HD HOT** DVD. This audio tutorial shows you how to set audio levels and use the audio mixer within Final Cut.

I. ————————Building the Audio Story

In this exercise, you will learn how to read audio waveforms, how to add audio to the Timeline, and how to trim clips based on the audio.

In this chapter, you will work with news footage from CNN ImageSource showing the 1999 preparations for Hurricane Irene in Florida to create a promo for an upcoming documentary on hurricanes. The editing techniques presented here are especially useful in documentaries, education, training, or whenever you have to illustrate what someone is talking about.

1. Open **Chapter 07 Lesson 1**. It's in your **FCP Projects** folder. Double-click **Seq – Talking Heads start** to load it into the **Timeline**.

Save this project under a new name (**File > Save As**). Call it **Hurricane**, and save it in your **FCP Projects** folder.

NOTE | Talking Head

Talking head is an old newsroom term that refers to video showing a close-up of the person talking. *B-roll* is an even older film term that refers to pictures that are used to illustrate what the talking head is talking about. You work with both in this exercise.

2. Open the bin named **Heads**, and double-click the clip **Bush – Major threat** to load it into the **Viewer**. Notice that a new tab appears at the top: **Stereo (a1a2)**. Click it to display the audio associated with this clip.

Final Cut displays audio as a "waveform." A waveform shows the volume of the audio. Where the waveform is thin, the audio is quiet. Where the waveform is thick, the audio is loud. Although a waveform doesn't indicate either the quality or the frequency of the sound, being able to read a waveform is really, really helpful in editing audio.

Here, for example, right at the beginning, are the words, "The major threat from Hurricane Irene..." Human speech is "bursty," meaning that there is always a slight pause between words. This makes it possible to edit audio by looking to see where phrases begin and end.

3. Now, move the **playhead** to just before he starts to speak and set an **In**. Press the **spacebar** and notice that he starts speaking immediately.

Hmmm, a bit *too* immediately, actually. Move your **playhead** back to the **In** and move it to the left about six frames and reset the **In**. Play this again.

See how much better this sounds? This brief pause gives the start of your sequence a little room for your audience to see the visual before the audio starts. Also, later, it will give you room to add a brief audio fade-in to make the start sound more natural. (Your new In, by the way, should be at timecode **01:00:00:05.***)*

4. Edit this clip to the **Timeline** by dragging the clip from the **Viewer** to the **Overwrite** overlay in the **Canvas**, or by using one of the other automated tools you learned about in Chapter 4, "*Build Your Story.*"

This is one of the great strengths of Final Cut. Whether you are editing video, audio, or audio and video, all the tools work exactly the same. So, everything you learned about editing clips to the Timeline, organizing them once they are on the Timeline, and trimming your clips to remove the parts you don't need still apply when you add audio into your sequence.

5. Play the end of the clip on the **Timeline**. Notice the "um" at the end? Trim this. You can do this several ways, but, remember, for trimming, *always* turn off snapping (press **N**). Otherwise, snapping keeps jumping you to the nearest edit point.

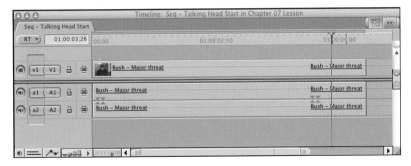

6. First you need to find out where the **Out** needs to be set, so grab the **playhead**, back it up before the end of the clip, and play it. Stop the clip when he says, "rainfall" (timecode: **01:00:03:26**).

7. Often, when editing audio, turning on audio waveforms in the **Timeline** is helpful. You can do this by pressing **Option+Cmd+W** or…

…clicking the small right-pointing arrow in the lower-left corner of the **Timeline** and turning on **Show Audio Waveforms**.

Keep in mind, however, that there is a performance hit in Final Cut when you have audio waveforms on. So, keep them off when you are editing video, and your system will perform faster.

8. Now you have several choices for trimming the end of the clip:

- Turn on snapping, grab the end of the clip, and drag it to the **playhead**.

- Turn on snapping, select the **Razor Blade**, cut the clip at the **playhead**, and delete the unused portion on the right.

- Turn on snapping, select the **Ripple** tool, and ripple the end of the clip to the **playhead**.

- Press **Ctrl+V** to cut the clip at the **playhead** and delete the unused portion.

Pick one of these methods and delete the excess audio and video.

9. Double-click **Bush – Emergency** to load it into the **Viewer**. This time, you'll set both the **In** and the **Out** in the **Viewer**, so you won't need to trim it on the **Timeline**.

Click the **Stereo (a1a2)** audio tab, and find the beginning of the audio, where he says, "Uh, yesterday…." Set your **In** three frames before he starts speaking (**01:00:14:03**).

Again, you are giving a little breathing room to the clip to make the audio sound more natural and less "clipped."

10. Go to the end of the clip, where he says, "…across the state." Using the arrow tools can help find the exact end of the audio. Again, add three more frames and set the **Out** (**01:00:23:10**).

Using one of the automated tools, edit this clip to the **Timeline**. If you have problems editing using one of the automated tools, be sure you don't have an **In** or **Out** set on the **Timeline** (press **Option+X**). Play the two clips and watch the video.

Image at Out   Edit point   Image at In

Did you see where he "jumped" when the edit point went through? This sudden video shift is called a "jump cut," and these, also, are considered bad editing and need to be fixed.

There are two ways to conceal a jump cut:

- *Put a different shot between the two shots.*
- *Put video on top of the two shots to cover it.*

In this lesson, you'll learn how to do both.

---

11. Using the **Up Arrow** tool, move the **playhead** between these two clips (**01:00:14:03**).

---

12. Double-click **Devanas – Big story** to load it into the **Viewer**. Set the **In** and the **Out** to the beginning and the end of his sound bite. (This term comes from radio news where a "sound bite" is a short clip of someone talking, in this case, Mr. Devanas. It is a "small bite of sound.") Your timecode points should be close to an **In** of **01:00:05:10** and an **Out** of **01:00:13:20**.

Try, if you can, to cut out the "uh" at the beginning of the sound bite, which will make it sound better.

Edit this clip to the **Timeline**, so that it fits between the first two clips. You'll need to use an **Insert** edit.

---

13. Now, position your **playhead** to the end of the sequence and add the remaining four sound bites to the sequence. Use the order in the following table. You should be able to listen to each clip and decide where to set the **In** and the **Out**, but, if you want to check yourself, the table lists the **In** and **Out** for each clip.

<table>
<tr><th colspan="3" align="center">Building the Sound Bites</th></tr>
<tr><th>Clip Name</th><th>Source timecode In</th><th>Source timecode Out</th></tr>
<tr><td>Bush – Major threat</td><td>01:00:00:05</td><td>01:00:04:00</td></tr>
<tr><td>Devanas – Big story</td><td>01:00:05:10</td><td>01:00:13:20</td></tr>
<tr><td>Bush – Emergency</td><td>01:00:14:03</td><td>01:00:23:10</td></tr>
<tr><td>Easley – Get safe*</td><td>00:01:05:17</td><td>00:01:16:24</td></tr>
<tr><td>Myers – Flooding</td><td>00:12:19:28</td><td>00:12:25:21</td></tr>
<tr><td>Jerrill – Big threat</td><td>00:21:37:09</td><td>00:21:46:18</td></tr>
<tr><td>Woman – We're safe</td><td>00:54:46:08</td><td>00:54:48:26</td></tr>
</table>

*The politically astute reader undoubtedly noticed that former Gov. Easley has nothing whatever to do with Hurricane Irene in Florida, since he is the former governor of North Carolina, and is talking about a different hurricane. Two liberties were taken in selecting video for this chapter. The first is pretending Gov. Easley had something to do with Hurricane Irene, when he didn't. The second is using B-roll from a variety of hurricanes. My reasoning is that the purpose of this chapter is to teach you how to edit with audio, not to teach you the ethics of editing. You may delete his clip if it bothers you.

14. When you are done, your sequence should look like **Seq – Talking Heads finished**, and end at **01:00:50:16**.

15. In looking at this sequence one more time, I realized that the second Bush clip is too long. Using the **Ripple** tool, trim it back so that it ends when he says, "…of emergency in Florida" (**01:00:17:15** on the **Timeline**).

Now, your whole sequence should end at **01:00:46:16** in the **Timeline**.

16. Another idea to experiment with is using the **Move** (or **Swap**) edit you learned about in Chapter 5, "*Trim Your Story*." Shuffle the clips around to see if it improves the clarity of the story.

The key point to this exercise is that the editing tools you've already learned work exactly the same way when you are editing audio. It's just that now, when you are building an audio-driven story, you need to make your edits based on what's being said in the audio, not the visuals in the video.

17. In the next exercise, you'll learn how to add B-roll to illustrate what the speakers are talking about. For now, though, save your work. You'll be using this exact same sequence in the next exercise.

NOTE | Audio Scrubbing

Audio scrubbing is a quick way to review audio while you are editing.

You turn audio scrubbing on (or off) in the **View** menu, or by pressing **Shift+S**. When it's on, dragging the playhead across clips in the **Timeline**, **Viewer**, or **Canvas** allows you to hear snippets of the audio. When scrubbing is off, dragging the **playhead** is silent.

NOTE | The Benefits of Two-Track Editing

When I'm editing dramatic material, I tend to keep the video to one track because it helps me to see the pacing of a scene.

However, when I'm editing anything that's a talking head with B-roll, two-track video editing is far easier. First, because moving B-roll clips is as easy as dragging them from one spot to another on the V2 track, this means I don't have to mess with the trimming tools. Second, I can see where all my jump cuts are in v1. Once I overwrite the v1 video, all my jump cuts are covered. Third, using two tracks of video makes it easier for me to checkerboard my audio clips, which you'll learn about in Exercise 5. Finally, keeping my talking heads on v1 makes it easier to see where I need to put my lower-third supers and IDs, because I can see where the shots change. (You'll learn about text and titles in Chapter 9, "*Text, Titles, and Graphics*.")

You can, of course, edit your pieces any way you like. However, this is a system that works well for me.

2. ——————————Adding B-Roll for Illustration

In this exercise, you'll learn how to use a second video track to provide B-roll coverage for a talking head, how to do a split edit, how to use the Timeline patch panel, and some basic approaches to laying out your audio tracks in a sequence.

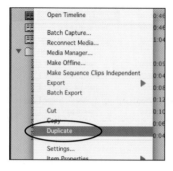

1. Open the **Hurricane** project, if it isn't open already. Then, **Ctrl+click Seq – Talking Head finished** in **Browser** and choose **Duplicate** from the shortcut menu. This makes a copy of the sequence so you can make changes without damaging the original sequence. Name the new sequence **Seq – B-roll added**.

First, in this style of editing, you are going to keep your talking head video on v1 and add additional video to v2. I call this multitrack editing.

2. So, you need to add one more video track and two more audio tracks. There are several ways to do this, but when you are adding multiple tracks, the fastest is to choose **Sequence > Insert Tracks** and fill in the two dialogs.

Next, in order to use the automated tools for editing a clip from the Viewer to the Timeline, you need to change the settings in the patch panel, on the left side of the Timeline.

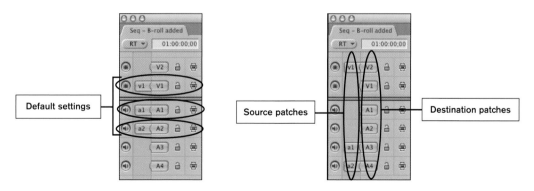

3. The default settings work fine, when all your video is on **V1** and your audio is on **A1** and **A2**. However, in this case, you want to put your B-roll video on **V2** and the natural sounds from it on **A3** and **A4**.

To do this move the **v1** on the *left* side up to match **V2** on the *right* side. This means that the video from the **Viewer** (which comes into the patch panel from the left on **v1**) goes out to the **Timeline** using the **V2** patch. (If you wanted to put the video on **V3** on the **Timeline**, you'd move the left **v1** patch up to **V3**, thus connecting the **Viewer** on the left to the **Timeline** on the right.)

Similarly, you need to move the audio patches so that the audio from the **Viewer** (which, again, comes in from the left on **a1** and **a2**) goes out to the **Timeline** on **A3** and **A4**.

In brief, the patch panel controls how signals are routed from the Viewer to the Timeline.

NOTE | The Patch Panel

The patch panel tells Final Cut how to route the audio and video from the Viewer to the Timeline when you use the automated editing tools (such as dragging to the Canvas overlay, pressing F10, or clicking the red button). The patch panel is "smart," meaning that it knows what type of clip is in the Viewer and adjusts itself accordingly.

Normally, the default settings are fine—but not when you want to put video or audio on other tracks. The patch panel is also highly useful when you want to do an audio-only or video-only edit with a clip that contains both audio and video.

continues on next page

NOTE | The Patch Panel *continued*

Video only

Here, a video-only clip is loaded into the Viewer, and only the v1 patch is available on the Viewer side of the patch panel.

Audio only

Here, a dual-channel audio-only clip is loaded into the Viewer, and only the a1 and a2 patches are available.

A1 only

Here, a mono audio file is loaded into the Viewer, and only the a1 patch is available. These are all straightforward examples. The next three are more interesting.

Audio and video

This is an audio and video clip, loaded into the Timeline. All three signals (v1, a1, and a2) are patched through to the Timeline.

continues on next page

NOTE | The Patch Panel *continued*

Video, no audio

Here's the same clip, but only the video is connected. See that small gap between the two audio patches on the left and right? You create that gap by clicking the a1 or a2 patches on the left. When you click them, Final Cut disconnects the signal. In this case, only the video is passed from the Viewer to the Timeline.

Audio, no video

Here's the opposite situation. There's a clip with audio and video in the Viewer, but the patch panel is allowing only the audio to go through. See that small gap between v1 on the left (the Viewer) and v1 on the right (the Timeline)? This tells Final Cut to block the video but let the audio go through.

Whenever you use an automated editing tool to move a clip from the Viewer to the Timeline, it always passes through the patch panel.

4. Move the **playhead** to where the speaker in the first clip says, "…from Hurricane Irene…" (**01:00:02:01**) and set an **In**. You are going to establish who is speaking, but then almost immediately cover them with footage about the hurricane.

5. Open the B-roll bin and double-click the clip **B – sandbags CU** to load it into the **Viewer**.

Notice how all the B-roll shots start with "B"? That helps me in sorting B-roll video from interviews. Feel free to steal my idea and use it yourself.

6. Set an **In** at the beginning of the clip. Set a duration of **2:00**. Once you have the clip marked, press **F10** to edit it to the **Timeline**.

Notice how Final Cut automatically puts the video on V2 and the audio on A3 and A4? This is why you use the patch panel in combination with the playhead—they give you precise control over where clips get placed. And, as you've come to expect when editing video, the playhead automatically moves to the end of the clip, positioning itself for the next edit.

NOTE | How Final Cut "Reads" Video Tracks

Clips laid out horizontally on the Timeline play one after the other. Clips stacked vertically play at the same time.

Final Cut has a rule for reading stacked video tracks: The video on the higher numbered track covers the video on the lower numbered track. Thus, V2 totally blocks video on V1.

However, there's an addition to this rule: Video on higher tracks blocks video on lower tracks, *provided the video on the higher track is 100 percent opaque and 100 percent full-screen.* Changing those settings is the whole idea behind compositing and motion effects. You will learn about these rules in Chapter 10, *"Motion Effects."*

---

7. OK. Now that you've got the first B-roll shot in the sequence, the following table shows the rest of the clips and the timecode at which they start. Given what you know, you should be able to easily edit these to the **Timeline**.

To make it easier to edit, all the rest of the B-roll clips are trimmed, so you don't need to set **Ins** or **Outs**.

B-Roll Clip Order		
Clip Name	**Timeline Start**	**Duration**
B – sandbags WS	01:00:04:01	4:11
B – board carry	01:00:08:12	3:04
B – board saw	01:00:11:16	3:06
B – board drill	01:00:14:22	2:07
B – storm trees L	01:00:16:19	3:00
B – storm trees R	01:00:19:29	2:22
B – storm road	01:00:22:21	2:29
B – storm light	01:00:25:20	4:06
B – storm waves	01:00:29:26	3:01
B – storm trees	01:00:32:27	2:19
B – storm boats	01:00:35:16	3:14
B – storm police	01:00:39:00	3:01
B – storm flooding	01:00:42:01	4:14

Perfect. Except, um, the B-roll ends one frame sooner than the video on v1. This causes a flash frame at the end of the sequence. Here's a quick trick to fix it. Remember the Extend edit you learned about in Chapter 6, "Trim Your Story"? It is ideally suited to getting video on multiple tracks to end at the same time.

8. Select the **Zoom** tool (press **Z**) and zoom into the end of the sequence until you can see a difference between the ending of the shots on **V1** and **V2**.

9. Move the **playhead** so that it is sitting on the **Out** of **V2**. Then, select the **Arrow** tool, hold down the **Command** key and click to select the edit points on all tracks.

10. Press the letter **E**, and watch as all six tracks instantly line up with the position of the **playhead**. No muss. No fuss. And no flash frames.

11. That's a lot to cover in one exercise. In the next exercise, you'll learn how to trim the audio without touching the video. But, for now, save your work and take a break.

3. ————————Trimming Audio While Staying in Sync

In this exercise, you'll learn how to trim audio separately from video, while still keeping everything in sync.

1. If it isn't already, open the project **Hurricane**, and double-click **Seq – B-roll added** to load it into the **Timeline**.

2. Position the **playhead** so it is at the start of the B-roll. Then, zoom in so that the first clip (also called the *A-roll clip*) and the two B-roll clips fill the **Timeline**. (A quick way to have a selection fill the **Timeline** window is to select what you want to zoom in on, then press **Shift+Option+Z**.) Be sure you can see all six tracks.

3. Play the beginning of the sequence. Hear how the audio level and energy drop after the first B-roll clip?

What you are going to do in this exercise is remove the audio from the second B-roll clip, and extend the audio from the first clip to cover both B-roll clips.

4. Go to the upper-right corner of the **Timeline** and click the **Link** button to deselect it (gray).

5. Now, grab the video from the first B-roll clip and drag it to the left a few frames. (You may want to turn off snapping before trying to move the clip.)

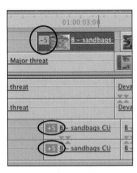

See those red flags? It means you've just moved the video of this clip out of sync!

NOTE | A Rant on the Link Button

This Link button drives me absolutely nuts! *Why* would anyone put a button on the Timeline that, when you use it, almost assuredly allows you to get your clips out of sync?!?

I grant that, in certain instances, being able to control linking is necessary. But it is *not* necessary on the Timeline as a button. This thing is bad and needs to be destroyed!

First, click the button to turn it back on (green).

Then, grab the Link button from the **Timeline** button bar, drag it out and let go. *Poof!* It's gone and good riddance. If you really need to mess with linking, you can select it in the **Modify** menu.

But this button is just stupid!

…Oh, what is linking, you ask? A linked clip is one where the audio and video are locked in sync, or *linked*.

continues on next page

6. There's an extra-secret way of moving one side (meaning the video side or the audio side) of a linked clip without getting everything out of sync. But, first, you need to get your video clip back in sync. However, because linking is on, whenever you click one side of a clip, the whole clip gets selected.

So, deselect everything. Then, hold down the **Option** key and click the out-of-sync video clip to select it. Then, with just the video clip selected, **Ctrl+click** the red sync flag and choose **Move Into Sync** from the shortcut menu. (Be sure to click only the red flag, not the edit point or elsewhere in the clip.)

The Option key is the secret. You can use it to get rid of one side of a linked clip, or trim just a video In, or change an audio Out. Whenever you need to work with just one side of a clip, the Option key makes it possible. Like now.

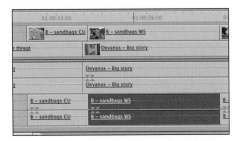

7. Hold down the **Option** key and click once to select the audio for the second B-roll clip.

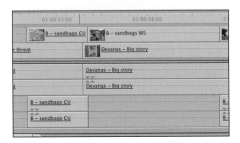

8. Delete the selected audio and leave a gap.

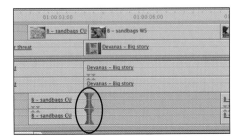

9. Next, hold down the **Option** key and select the audio **Out** of the first B-roll clip.

10. Now, while still holding down the **Option** key, drag the **Out** all the way to the right to fill the gap.

11. Play the first part of the sequence.

Hear how the B-roll audio carries the energy and excitement of the first B-roll clip through the second B-roll clip?

 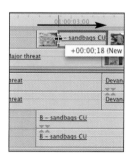

12. This is such an incredibly important technique that I want you to discover one more way you can use this. As additional practice, **Option+click** the video **In** of the first B-roll clip. Drag it to the right.

See how you can move the edit point of a clip, yet the audio and video elements of the clip stay in sync? Using the Option key to drag an edit point or select one side of a clip is far, FAR better than using the Link button.

NOTE | Split Edits

Split edits are where the video and the audio edit occur at different times. There are two types of split edits: an *L-edit* and a *J-edit*.

An L-edit is one where the audio edit occurs later than the video edit. It's called an L-edit because the shape of the end of the outgoing clip looks like the letter L.

The easiest way to create an L-edit is to **Option+click** the audio (or video) edit point with the **Roll** tool, then **Option+drag** the edit point with the **Roll** tool to where you want it to go.

continues on next page

NOTE | Split Edits *continued*

A J-edit is one where the audio edit occurs earlier than the video edit. It's called a J-edit because the shape of the end of the outgoing clip looks like the letter J.

The easiest way to create a J-edit is to **Option+click** the audio (or video) edit point with the **Roll** tool, then **Option+drag** the edit point with the **Roll** tool to where you want it to go. In fact, the process of creating a J-edit is identical to creating an L-edit. The only difference is the direction you drag the edit point.

Split edits are used constantly, whenever you want to see one thing and hear another.

13. That ends this exercise. Save your work, but keep everything handy. You're going to use this same exercise again.

NOTE | When Should You Use the Link Command?

I don't like the Link button, because it gets too many people into trouble. But the **Link** command (**Cmd+L**) is very useful—in certain situations.

As you've probably surmised, I don't recommend unlinking a clip when you can use the **Option** key instead.

However, a good use of the Link command is when you have two different clips, and you want to connect them; for instance, a video-only clip and an audio-only sound effect.

Linking them together tells Final Cut that it should treat these two clips as being "in sync." That way, whenever you move one side of the clip—the video, for example—the sound effect follows.

To link a clip, align the two clips so that the sound and video play together with the right timing. Then, select both clips and choose **Modify > Link**. Both clip names become underlined and for the rest of that **Timeline**, they move together.

There's also a reason to *unlink* a clip. Say you want to use the audio from a clip several times in a sequence. (For example, it could be traffic noise you want to use as background.) Unlinking the audio from the video makes it easy to move the audio around as its own separate clip; because you never want to use the video, maintaining sync is irrelevant.

4. ——————————Setting Audio Levels

In this exercise, you will learn the difference between a stereo and dual-mono audio file, how to read the Audio Meters, and how to set proper audio levels. You'll also get an introduction to keyframes.

NOTE | Stereo vs. Dual-Mono Audio files

In Chapter 3, "*Gather Your Media*," you learned about the different audio capture settings. There are really only two that are important: stereo and dual-mono.

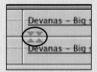

A stereo file has both channels linked for sync (their clip name is underlined) and with a little green bow tie between the clips. Channel 1 is panned all the way to the left, and Channel 2 is panned all the way to the right. Stereo is the correct file choice when you care about the spatial relationship of the sound, that is, whether it is on the left, right, or center.

You can easily convert between a stereo file and dual-mono by selecting the audio clip and choosing **Modify > Stereo Pair**, or pressing **Option+L**. There is no loss in quality by turning stereo linking on or off.

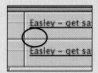

A dual-mono file has both channels linked for sync, but without the green bow tie. This means that both channels are panned to the center. Dual-mono is the default setting for audio capture and is used when the spatial relationship of the sound is not important, for example, in an interview.

---

1. Open **Hurricane**, if it isn't already open. Then, double-click **Seq – B-roll added** to load it into the **Timeline**.

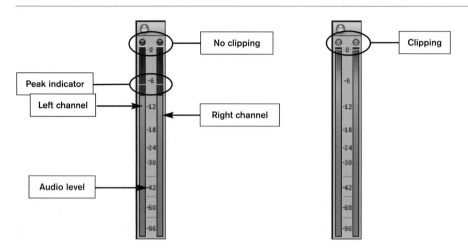

2. Play the sequence and watch the **Audio Meter**. Notice that the audio levels bounce between **−6** and **−12 dB**, with a little yellow bar floating over the top of the green meters. The yellow bar is called the peak indicator. This shows you the level of your loudest sound over the last 3 seconds. The green bars indicate the sound level of your left and right audio channels.

The peak indicator is handy because it is often hard to see the levels of the green bars since they are bouncing so much.

By default, all odd-numbered channels are assigned to the left channel, and all even-numbered channels are assigned to the right channel.

As the audio gets louder, the green bars get taller. When the audio is too loud, even for an instant, the red clip lights light. It is critical that you adjust your audio levels so that the clip lights never light.

Generally, for dialogue, you want your meters to bounce between −6 and −12. They can go higher than this occasionally, but this is a good range for average levels. Running your audio at this level allows you plenty of headroom for loud sounds and sudden changes in volume. Set your volume (called "audio gain") much lower than this and it is hard to hear what is being said.

There are at least four ways to set audio levels for a clip, plus two more when you learn about the Audio Mixer. Which one is best? Whichever one helps you get your work done.

Devanas waveform

3. Double-click the **Devanas** clip to load it into the **Viewer**. Play the clip. Notice how the audio levels are low, between **−12** and **−18**? These levels need to be increased so the speaker's audio is between **−6** and **−12**.

Volume level slider

Level box

4. One way to change the level of a clip in the **Viewer** is to slide the audio level slider left and right until the audio level is where you want it. In this case, drag the **Level** slider to the right until the audio level is bouncing between **−6** and **−12**.

5. Another way to change the level in the **Viewer** is to click in the **Level** box to the right of the **Level** slider and type a number. In this case, increasing the level to **5** brings the volume up appropriately. Every clip is different; the key is to make decisions by watching the meters.

6. A third way to change the level of a clip in the **Viewer** is to grab the red horizontal lines running through the middle of each waveform and drag them up (to increase the audio level) or down (to decrease the level). (These horizontal lines are also affectionately called *rubber bands*.)

Try this and see how, as you move these rubber bands, the Level slider moves, and the number inside the level box changes.

These are all great tips to know. However, I don't use any of them, because there is an easier way.

7. Click the button at the bottom left of the **Timeline** that looks like a mountain range. This toggles on (or off) clip overlays. See the red rubber bands in the audio clips? You can easily set audio levels of clips directly in the **Timeline** by adjusting these bands. (These lines get their name, rubber bands, for their flexibility, which you'll understand better as you start to set keyframes a little later in this chapter.)

These volume rubber bands exist in both the Timeline and the Viewer. They work the same way. You can use whichever is the easiest for your method of working.

8. Play each of the clips in the **Timeline** and set the levels so that the meters are bouncing between **−6** and **−12**. When you play the sequence now, all the voices should sound about the same, in terms of volume.

What do you mean, you can't hear the voices because the B-roll audio is too loud? Oh, yeah. You should probably fix that.

9. On the extreme left side of the **Timeline** are green visibility indicators. When these lights are lit, you can see the contents of a video track, or hear the contents of an audio track. Turn the visibility indicator off for audio tracks **a3** and **a4**, and you'll be able to hear the voices a *lot* better.

NOTE | Clip Enable vs. Visibility Indicators

Turning off visibility indicators deletes render files for the entire track. For audio, this isn't a big deal. Audio render files don't take long to rebuild. However, as you'll learn in Chapter 9, "*Text, Titles, and Graphics*," video render files are a different story. Many times, you won't want to delete all your video render files because they take so long to calculate.

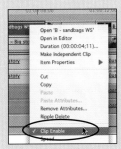

Instead of using the visibility indicators, another way to turn off a clip is to **Ctrl+click** it and deselect **Clip Enable** (or press **Option+B**). This makes a clip invisible for video, or inaudible for audio, without deleting render files for the entire track. However, it *does* delete the render files associated with that clip. Still, this is often far better than having to redo all your render files for the entire sequence.

NOTE | An Alternative to Visibility Indicators

New in FCP HD is an audio alternative to the track visibility indicators—audio solo and mute controls.

Click the small speaker icon in the lower-left corner of the **Timeline**.

This turns on the audio **Mute** and **Solo** buttons. To silence an audio track, click the **Mute** button, on the left. To silence all tracks, except one, click the **Solo** button, on the right. You can mute or solo multiple tracks, so you can listen to exactly the tracks in your sequence you want to hear.

The benefit to using the Mute and Solo buttons is that neither destroys render files, unlike the visibility indicators.

These same controls are also available in the Audio Mixer, which you'll learn about in Exercise 7.

10. Turn the visibility indicators on for **A3** and **A4** and off for **A1** and **A2**, because you now need to adjust the audio levels of the B-roll. Better yet, turn on all visibility indicators and turn on the **Solo** buttons for **A3** and **A4**.

The Solo button automatically mutes A1 and A2 and allows A3 and A4 to play.

---

11. Go to the last B-roll clip, **B – storm flood**, and play it. First, bring the audio level up a bit so you can hear it better.

Hmmm…the truck is going from the left to the right, but the audio stays center. Panning the audio from left to right as the truck moves would improve this effect.

---

12. Double-click the clip to load it into the **Viewer**. Click the audio tab (**Mono a1**) to display the wave-form. In case you raised the audio all the way up, as I did, bring the audio level down to, say, **2**. (Note, this is a positive 2, not a negative 2.)

Now, this truck clip, unlike the other clips, has only one audio track: a mono track which is panned to the center. And the audio waveform is so small as to be almost invisible. Sigh. Not all audio is great quality.

Pan slider

13. Drag the **Pan** slider up and down and watch the dark-purple line in the center of the waveform window move. This purple line indicates the pan of this clip from left to right.

Simply dragging the pan to a new position doesn't give you the effect you want, because dragging the line moves the sound to the left, or right, and parks it there. You want it to change over time. Change requires keyframes.

NOTE | Definition: Keyframe

Understanding keyframes is one of the critical concepts necessary to getting the most out of Final Cut Pro HD. They rank right up there with timecode and handles.

A keyframe is a specific setting of a specific parameter at a specific point in time. Keyframes are required if you want something to change over time, such as the pan or volume of a clip, or any kind of animation. For example, to change the pan of this truck, you need to indicate where the sound starts, on the left, and where it ends, on the right. You do this with keyframes.

In this example, you will set two keyframes: one on the left when the truck drives in and one on the right when the truck drives out. Final Cut will calculate all the settings in-between to make your effect happen.

14. Drag the **Pan** slider until you can see the purple line clearly, somewhere in the middle of the window. Select the **Arrow** tool and hold down the **Option** key so that it turns into the **Pen** tool (or just select the **Pen** tool) and click near the end of the line to set a keyframe. Drag this keyframe up near the top of the waveform window.

To repeat, you create keyframes by **Option+clicking** with the **Arrow** tool or clicking with the **Pen** tool.

Final Cut, unlike virtually every audio program I've ever used, puts the left pan on the bottom and the right pan on the top.

15. Next, drag the **Pan** slider down to **−1** (the default setting) and watch the angle of the line change.

What you've done is set two keyframes—one at the beginning of the clip, using the Pan slider, that puts the sound on the extreme left, and one at the end of the clip, using the Pen tool, that puts the sound on the extreme right.

Because the two locations are different, the sound moves from side to side during the playing of the clip.

16. Increase the volume level of the clip to **12** (all the way up) and play the clip. (The technical term for volume level is "gain.")

Hear how the truck now sounds like it's moving from left to right? Final Cut automatically calculated all the intermediate steps so that the sound moves smoothly from one side of the screen to the other. This technique is used all the time to have sound effects reinforce movement on the screen.

Every audio clip, both mono and stereo, has pan controls. Feel free to experiment with other clips.

Pan Settings		
Setting	**What It Means in Mono**	**What It Means in Stereo**
−1	Clip panned left	Normal stereo effect
0	Clip panned center	Clip panned mono
1	Clip panned right	Reversed stereo (left goes right and right goes left)

17. You'll be working a *lot* with keyframes for the rest of this book. However, for now, take a break. Save your work. Next you'll be working with music and effects.

NOTE | A Faster Way to Check Audio Levels

Here's a very fast way to check the audio levels of a clip to see if they are too hot.

1. Double-click a clip to load it into the **Viewer**.

2. Choose **Mark > Audio Peaks > Mark**.

Final Cut will quickly check the entire file and put a clip marker everywhere it finds an audio level that is too hot.

This is the fastest way to check a clip for audio hot spots, much better than playing the entire clip.

To get rid of these markers, choose **Mark > Audio Peaks > Clear**.

5. ————————Adding Music or Effects

Music often provides the emotion of a scene. In other cases, music is what drives a scene. In still other cases, effects are what make a particular scene sound believable, or comically unbelievable. In all cases, adding music and effects can significantly enhance a project.

In this exercise, you will learn about track layout and checkerboarding audio clips, how to add music and sound effects, and how to convert audio files for use with Final Cut.

1. Open **Hurricane**, if it isn't already open. Then, double-click **Seq – B-roll added** to load it into the **Timeline**.

2. Look at the **Timeline**. See how the audio tracks are organized? This is called the **track layout**.

Now, audio, unlike video, doesn't care which track is on top, because there is no concept of one track "blocking" another. Rather, sounds are principally perceived based on volume; louder sounds are closer, softer sounds are further away. However, I've also found that the way you organize your tracks makes a difference in mixing and in understanding what you did when you return to a project after a long absence.

NOTE | Laying Out Your Audio Tracks

You can lay out your audio tracks in any order. But I strongly suggest you follow a plan. If you don't have your own a plan, the following table outlines one you can use.

Sample Track Layout	
Audio Track	**Content**
1 and 2	Sync sound from V1 (talking heads or key actors)
3 and 4	Sync sound from V2 B-roll
5, 6, 7, and 8	Sound effects and other wild (not synced to video) sounds
9 and 10	Music track
11 and 12	Music track

The two music tracks allow you to fade out one piece of music at a different rate than the second music clip fades in.

Leaving multiple tracks free for effects allows you to group and organize your effects in a way that makes sense to you and your project.

This process of putting different types of audio, sync sound, effects, and music on different tracks is called *checkerboarding*, because it resembles a checkerboard. A major motion picture takes this concept to extremes, where audio is scattered across dozens of tracks—often over 100. In this case, though, I just want you to think about how putting related audio on related tracks can help in organizing your project.

Obviously, not all Final Cut projects need as many as 12 tracks, though a few may use more. For instance, this project uses only six. The goal is to approach your audio layout logically so that when you go to reedit an old project, you don't need to spend time figuring out where you put stuff.

Plus, there is no penalty for leaving black space on tracks—audio track gaps don't take any memory or storage.

Because all our B-roll has audio, we don't need to add any special audio effects. However, if you wanted to emphasize the strength of the storm you could add more wind howling effects, or distant sirens, or...well, anything your imagination suggests, actually.

In this case, we want to add some music to emphasize the emotional response we want viewers to have with the story.

3. To do this, drag **Hurricane.aif** from the **Music** bin in the **Browser** down to below track **A4** in the **Timeline**.

Notice that Final Cut automatically creates two tracks to hold it. Why two tracks? Because the audio clip is stereo, which means it has two audio tracks in it—one for the left channel and one for the right. All tracks you capture from your camera will also have two tracks, as will most music and sound effects. However, as you'll see, not all sounds require two tracks.

Later in this chapter, you'll worry about setting levels for all this audio. For right now, the job is to get everything in the right place—both on the right track and at the right time.

Notice, also, that I had you drag the clip from the Browser to the Timeline. This is because the length of the music has already been trimmed to match the length of the story. Although I strongly recommend you use the Viewer to preview all your Timeline elements, there's nothing that prevents you from dragging a clip from the Browser to the Timeline.

4. And that's it. A nice, simple exercise. Final Cut makes adding music and effects to a sequence very easy. Simply preview it, set any necessary **Ins** and **Outs**, then put it on the **Timeline**—either by dragging, or, preferably, by using the automated tools.

Save your work. But read the next note before you take a break. It will help you prevent future audio problems. Then, you can close this project, because the next exercise uses a different project file.

NOTE | Converting Audio Files

Although Final Cut can handle a wide range of audio files, it likes 44.1K and 48K sample rates the best. You can combine both rates on the same Timeline without needing to render.

Audio Formats

Where things get tricky is in audio formats. Final Cut likes AIF and WAV files. From my experience, I've had the best results using AIF files. Noticeably absent from this list are MP3 and AAC—the two audio formats most common over the Web and in iTunes. This omission is not an accident—Final Cut *hates* MP3 and AAC files.

They pop. They crackle. They sound flat-out terrible. In short, they need to be converted.

You can buy expensive audio software to handle this conversion, but, truth be told, you already have everything you need bundled with your Mac—it's called iTunes. Here's how to use iTunes to convert MP3 or AAC files into AIFs for Final Cut.

1. Open iTunes.

2. Choose **iTunes > Preferences**.

3. Click the **Importing** tab.

4. Choose **AIFF Encoder** from the **Import Using** pop-up menu.

5. Close the **Preferences** window.

6. Select the song, or songs, you want to convert. This assumes the song you want to convert is stored in iTunes.

continues on next page

NOTE | Converting Audio Files *continued*

To make sure you have the right format, **Ctrl+click** any iTunes column header and choose **Kind** from the shortcut menu. This displays the compression format for all the songs in your library.

7. Choose **Advanced > Convert to AIFF**.

iTunes converts your selected clips to AIFF and puts them in your iTunes folder. You can find them either by rooting around your iTunes folder or simply selecting the song title you converted in iTunes and dragging it to your desktop.

8. In either case, once you find the AIFF version of your song, drag it from iTunes to where you want to store it, import it into Final Cut (**Cmd+I**), and you're all set.

CD Audio

In OS 9, and earlier versions of Final Cut, converting CD audio into something FCP can read was, well, tricky.

In OS X, that is no longer the case. To convert any audio file on CD into something Final Cut can read, simply drag it from the CD into wherever you want it stored on your computer. The operating system converts it so that Final Cut can play it smoothly.

Important note: Never import an audio file directly from CD into Final Cut, for two reasons. First, that means the CD needs to be in your drive whenever you edit that project, and, second, CD players are not as fast as hard drives and, many times, that lack of speed can cause dropped frame issues. Always copy all media files to your hard disk for editing.

By the way, it goes without saying that you should have permission from the copyright holder to use any copyrighted materials. All the clips in this book have been licensed—which is often a time-consuming process. But licensing is far, far better than dealing with lawyers and facing potential civil and criminal penalties because you borrowed a clip you didn't have permission to use. If you didn't create it, then someone else owns it, and you'll need to request permission to use it in any project you create.

6. ——————Using the Voice Over Tool for Narration

In this exercise, you will learn how to record narration using the Voice Over tool. However, in order to record narration, you also need to have a microphone connected to your Mac. Since many readers won't have mics connected, this section has been written so you can work through the exercise, or simply look at the pictures. Either way, when you are done, you will understand how this tool works.

1. Open **Chapter 07 Lesson 2**, which is in the **FCP HOT files** lessons folder. This is the same project you completed at the end of Chapter 6, "*Trim Your Story.*" Double-click **Seq – Snowboard Final** to load it into the **Timeline**.

2. Put the **playhead** at the beginning of the sequence, if it isn't already there. What you are going to do is to record an introductory narration for the beginning of the snowboard commercial.

You don't need to be James Earl Jones to be successful as a narrator. Nor do you even have to like listening to your recorded voice. Of all the actors I've ever worked with, none have ever liked the sound of their voices. That isn't the point. The point is do other *people like listening to the sound of your voice?*

A narrator needs to be easy to understand at first hearing and seem interested in the material he or she is presenting. Most importantly, his or her voice should complement the emotional tenor of your project.

3. Because this is the intro, move the **playhead** to the edit point between the second and third shots and set an **Out**. This tells the **Voice Over** tool to stop recording when it hits the **Out**.

Size tab

4. Choose **Tools > Voice Over** to open the **Voice Over** tool. The tool opens in its own window, though when it does, it sizes itself to match the size of the **Viewer**, then parks on top of it. You can drag this **Voice Over** window wherever you want and resize it.

The lower half of the window allows you to set the following:

- *The Input and Source (which vary depending upon how your microphone is connected to your computer).*

- *The sample Rate (default is 44,100 Hz); I set mine to 48,000 to match the audio sample rate of my Final Cut Timeline.*

- *Gain, which controls how loud or soft your mic volume is. Again, try to get your narration to record around the −6 level.*

- *Offset, which allows you to adjust for the delay between the time you talk and the time it gets recorded. This, too, varies by computer and operating system version, though the default of 1 Frame is a good place to start.*

At the bottom of the window is the Volume, which adjusts headphone volume, and a check box to turn on, or off, audible countdown beeps. Turn these on if you are wearing headphones; turn these off if you are listening to a speaker.

These audio beeps count you down to zero during recording, so that you can time the narration to end on time.

5. The top half of the window shows you where the recorded narration will appear in Final Cut. (Voiceover narration is always placed on the **Timeline** in the track immediately *below* the last used track—in this case, **A2**.)

Plus, this is where you enter the name of the soon-to-be-recorded clip. In this case, type **Snowboard Intro**.

6. When everything is ready, click the **Record** button.

Orange means get ready

The Voice Over tool flashes orange in its status screen, counting down to when the recording starts.

7. During the recording, the **Voice Over** status window turns red, the **Timeline** plays, the **Audio Meter** bounces, and…

…as you get near the end, the status screen counts down the final 10 seconds.

If you are wearing headphones, turn on **Sound Cues**. In addition to flashing red and counting down to zero on the screen, you will hear beeps in your headset that count you down as well. When I do voiceover recording, I find myself concentrating on the script and the reading, and I don't have time to watch the screen for a countdown. These audible beeps are really helpful to me in bringing the reading in on time.

When the recording is complete, Final Cut records it to disk and drops it on the Timeline into the track below *the last used track.*

*Voiceover recordings are stored in memory during recording. When recording is complete, they are permanently saved into the **Capture Scratch** folder. If I am working on a machine with limited memory, I make it a point to keep my recordings short.*

Also, Voice Over tool recordings don't show up in the Browser unless you drag them from the Timeline to the Browser.

8. That's it for this exercise. If you recorded anything you want to keep, save your project. Otherwise, close this project because we are going back to the **Hurricane** project for the final exercise in this chapter.

7. ——————————**Mixing Your Project**

Now that you have assembled all your elements, sync sound, effects, music, and narration, it's time to mix them all together and make it sound right.

Cleve Landsberg, an Oscar-nominated sound editor, once wrote: "Sound is perceived emotionally, as well as intellectually. Each genre, such as comedy, action, or drama, demands its own approach and sound sensibilities."

There's no such thing as a perfect way to mix. But here are some techniques you can use to improve your own mixing skills. In this lesson, you'll learn how to use keyframes to control audio levels, and then discover how to use the Audio Mixer for real-time mixing.

1. Open **Hurricane**, if it isn't already open. Then, double-click **Seq – Ready to mix** to load it into the **Timeline**. This is a version of the documentary you've been working on earlier in this chapter. I've added room at the beginning for a title and additional shots at the end to bring it to 1 minute in length.

2. Take a minute and play this sequence. Listen to all the elements carefully.

You started the process of mixing this project in Exercise 4 when you listened to the talking head clips and set audio levels so the Audio Meters were bouncing between −6 and −12.

 Click

3. One way to automate your mix is to use keyframes. Keyframes provide a quick way to control audio levels. Zoom in to the front of the project and click the small gray-and-blue bar chart in the lower-left corner of the **Timeline** to expand the height of the tracks. What you need to do is start the music up full (that is, at full volume), then bring it down and under when the first speaker starts speaking.

This is a perfect opportunity to use keyframes.

4. Select the **Arrow** tool and **Option+click** near the start of **Hurricane.aif** on the red rubber band to set a keyframe for the start of the music. Drag the keyframe up until the tooltip says the keyframe is at **0 dB**.

The benefit to using the Option key with the Arrow tool is that it is a fast way to set keyframes. However, you can't get exactly to the edit point of a clip, because the Arrow tool turns into a trimming tool. If you need to move closer to the edit point, either zoom in closer or select the **Pen** *tool (press* **P***). In this case, we don't need the keyframe right at the beginning of the edit.*

NOTE | When Is Zero Not Equal to Zero?

When you are comparing a zero reading on the Audio Meter with a zero level on the red rubber band for an audio clip, the two are not the same.

The Audio Meter shows an *absolute* reference to sound level (which is what "dB"—an abbreviation for decibels, a measure of sound loudness—measures).

When you drag an audio level rubber band up or down, the tooltip shows a *relative* reference to changes in sound level. 0 dB means that you are not changing the level of the audio from the level at which it was recorded. Positive numbers (which range from 0.1 to 12 in Final Cut) mean you are amplifying, or increasing, the loudness of the sound compared to the level at which it was recorded. Negative numbers (which range from −0.1 to −inf dB) mean you are attenuating, or decreasing, the loudness of the sound compared to the level at which it was recorded.

The Audio Meter shows the *absolute* audio level and cannot go above zero. The tooltip shows the *relative* change in level and can wander all over the map.

---

5. Set a second keyframe just before the first sound bite. (Keyframes are set in both track **A5** and **A6** because these two tracks are a linked stereo pair.) Add a third keyframe just after the first sound bite. Leave the second keyframe unchanged and drag the third keyframe down to around **−18 dB**.

---

6. Play the sequence. Hear how the music starts nice and loud, to get your attention, then ducks down so you can hear the speakers? Perfect.

Except, audio in Final Cut is all clip-based. This means that you need to go through every clip and set the level. This is only a 60-second project, but it has 25 sound files that need adjusting. There has to be an easier way!

---

7. There is an easier way—it's called the **Audio Mixer**. There are two ways to find it:

- Choose **Tools > Audio Mixer**.

- Choose **Window > Arrange > Audio Mixing**.

When you use the first choice, the Audio Mixer pops up at the same size as the Viewer. When you use the second choice (my personal favorite), all the windows get rearranged so the mixer has room to work. I like that.

Pick a method that works with your size monitor and select the Audio Mixer. (At the end of this exercise, on page 270, is a more detailed look at the Audio Mixer. Please refer to it if you need an orientation before continuing this exercise.)

OK. Now it's time to get this sequence mixed.

8. First, though, get rid of the keyframes you've already set in the music by double-clicking the music track to load it into the **Viewer**. Then, click the small red **X** in the circle. This removes all keyframes from a clip. (This is a very handy way to reset a clip back to its default setting and clear keyframes, not just for audio, but for any effect or filter that uses keyframes.)

9. Next, go to the top-right corner of the **Audio Mixer** and click this small, insignificant little button. It's *this* button that turns on the real power of the **Audio Mixer**.

10. Position your **playhead** at the beginning of the sequence and play the first few seconds to get a sense of when the first sound bite starts, relative to the music.

11. Now, again, reset the **playhead** to the beginning, but this time, put your mouse on the slider for **A5** and play the sequence. Just before you get to the start of the sound bite, drag the fader down to around **−18**.

Because A5 and A6 are linked as a stereo clip, both A5 and A6 faders move together. If there was no link, only the A5 fader would move.

12. After the speaker starts talking, stop playing and look at the music clip. The **Audio Mixer** added keyframes to the audio clip every time you moved the fader. Best of all, if there are too many keyframes, as there are here, you can remove them by **Option+clicking** them with the **Arrow** tool.

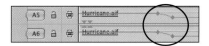

13. Remove all the extra keyframes until the start of your audio looks like this. (The audio level of the second keyframe is **−18 dB**.)

14. Jump forward to the end section where there is a break between speakers. Here the music needs to come up full, then duck down in time for the last speaker, the woman, to be heard.

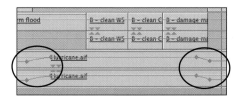

15. Again, using the **Audio Mixer**, play the sequence, set the level of the music, and trim your keyframes until it looks like this.

16. You can use the **Audio Mixer** to set the levels of not just one clip, but all the clips on a track. This technique is a whole lot faster than adjusting each clip individually.

If the **Record Keyframes** button is lit, every time you move a fader you'll set a keyframe. If the **Record Keyframes** button is not lit, every time you move a fader, you'll set the volume for the entire clip. In mixing, you'll toggle between these two options, depending upon whether you want to hear the audio change, or simply set a level for an entire clip.

For now, experiment with the **Audio Mixer** and mix down this entire sequence. The best way to do this is to mix one track, or linked pair of tracks, at a time. Remember to keep an eye on your levels. At *no* time should the clip lights blink; if they do, fix it.

17. Mixing is an art that takes practice. Whether you adjust individual clip levels or use the **Audio Mixer**, the ultimate judge of which method works best is how the sequence sounds. As always, practice makes perfect.

This ends this exercise. Save your work and quit Final Cut. In the next chapter, you will polish this sequence some more by putting in some audio transitions to smooth out the cuts between speakers.

A Quick Tour of the Audio Mixer

The Audio Mixer looks more complex than it really is. It actually isn't frightening once you understand it. On the far left is a list of all the audio tracks in your sequence. In the middle are the channel strips—one for each audio track. Each channel strip is identical to all the others, so once you know how one works, you know how they all work. On the far right is the master fader and a duplicate set of Audio Meters.

There are four areas of the mixer that can be explained quickly:

- *Master Fader*
- *Audio Meters*
- *View controls*
- *Pop-up menu*

First is the Master Fader which controls all the audio levels for your entire sequence. Here's the rule for the Master Fader: Don't touch it. Leave it at 0 and pretend it doesn't exist. If you have problems with your mix, fix it by adjusting individual tracks, not the master. Adjusting the master is a bad habit that will get you in trouble.

The Audio Meters, next to the Master Fader, correspond directly with the meters on the Audio Meter. Both zeros are equal. The Master Fader, though, shows how far over zero a particular sound has gone. If left unchanged, it will still distort. It will still sound bad on tape. But, at least now you know how far down you need to lower the volume to correct the clipping.

The View controls (across the top) allow you to display a subset of your audio tracks in the sequence. This is especially helpful when you have more audio tracks than you have room to display in the mixer.

Here's how this works:

1. Click the **2** button.

2. Unclick audio tracks **A3**, **A4**, **A5**, and **A6**. See how the number of tracks displayed in the mixer decreases?

3. Click the **3** button at the top.

4. Unclick the **A1** and **A2** tracks. See how **A1** and **A2** disappeared?

5. Click the **1** button. All your audio tracks are displayed in the Audio Mixer.

6. Click the **2** button. Only tracks A1 and A2 are displayed in the Audio Mixer.

7. Click the **3** button. Only tracks A3 through A6 are displayed in the Audio Mixer.

The pop-up menu in the top corner is best left set to **Auto**. This means that when you click the Viewer, the mixer shows you the audio tracks in the Viewer. When you select the Canvas or Timeline, the mixer shows you the tracks in the Timeline. However, you can force it to always show the Canvas or Viewer by selecting it in this pop-up menu.

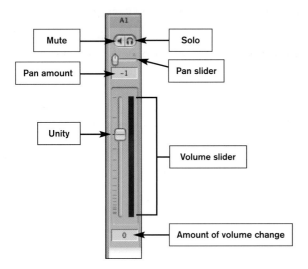

The heart and soul of the Audio Mixer is the channel strip. Every channel strip is identical in layout and operation. You change the level by sliding the large fader up and down. You change the pan by sliding the small fader from side to side. The numbers below each show the amount of change. Setting the level to the thick black line, labeled Unity above, means you are making no change to the audio level of a clip.

The Mute and Solo buttons are identical in look and operation to those you discovered earlier in the Timeline.

Summary

This chapter has covered a huge amount of material in a very short time. In this chapter, you started with audio editing and ended with mixing, with a whole lot of terminology and technique in the middle. Still to come are audio transitions in Chapter 8, "*Transitions—Making Change Beautiful*," and audio effects in Chapter 11, "*Filters and Keying*."

Helpful Keyboard Shortcuts

Shortcut	Function
N	Toggles snapping on and off
Shift+S	Toggles audio scrubbing on and off
Shift+Option+Z	Zooms selected clips to fill Timeline window
Shift+L	Toggles link selection (generally, a bad thing)
Cmd+L	Turns linking on and off (another dangerous thing)
Option+drag	(On edit point) Selects and moves either the audio or video side of a linked clip without allowing the clip to go out of sync (a much, much better thing)
Ctrl+click	(On red sync flag) Moves clip back into sync (menu choice)
Option+L	Toggles between making an audio clip stereo or dual-mono
Option+click Arrow tool	Toggles between Arrow and Pen tools
Option+click fader	(In Mixer) Resets the level and/or pan control to 0
Shift+Cmd+K	Toggles between recording and not recording keyframes in the Audio Mixer
Option+6	Displays Audio Mixer
Option+0	Displays the Voice Over tool
Option+Cmd+W	Toggles audio waveform display on and off in the Timeline
Option+W	Toggles clip overlays on and off
P	Selects the Pen tool to create and move keyframes
PP	Selects the Negative Pen tool to remove keyframes
Option+B	Makes a clip visible (enabled) or invisible (disabled)

Transitions—Making Change Beautiful

What's a Transition?	Creating an Audio Transition
Creating a Video Transition	Understanding Rendering
Another Way to Create a Transition	Creating a Default Transition
Creating a Favorite Transition	Creating a Gradient Wipe

Chapter 08 Lesson 1
Chapter 08 Lesson 2

FCP HD HOT DVD

A transition means a change… a change in scene, a change in level, a change in perspective, or content, or text, or… well, just about anything. A cut is a transition. But in this chapter you will see that "transition" means more than that. This chapter is all about how to make the transition from Shot 1 to Shot 2.

In this chapter, you will learn how to create audio and video transitions, how to edit a transition, and how to harness transitional power tools to create favorite and default transitions. You'll also learn about the importance of rendering,

"Everything Is a Transition"

A few years ago, an effects wizard told me that the secret to his success was in understanding that everything is a transition. And, the more I thought about it, the more I realized how true this is. Whether it's an actor walking across the screen, a camera panning across the scene, or a piece of animation, everything is always moving; going from one place to another.

In this chapter, you will learn how to add transitions to your edit points. Also with this chapter, you make a transition as well. You are moving out of hard-core editing, which is covered in the first half of the book, into how to make it prettier, which is the second half of the book.

And the best way to start is to segue into your first exercise.

I. —————————**Creating an Audio Transition**

All transitions are created in the Timeline. In this exercise, you will learn how to create an audio transition, then build on that knowledge by working on video transitions for the rest of the chapter.

1. Open **Chapter 08 Lesson 1** and double-click **Seq – Ready to mix** to load it into the **Timeline**. This is the same Hurricane project you were working on in Chapter 7, "*Audio—The Secret to a Great Picture*," but I removed the keyframes because using keyframes to create transitions is what the first part of this exercise is all about.

2. There are three ways to create a transition using the mouse, plus several more using keyboard shortcuts. Here's the first, which is a review from Chapter 7. Choose the **Zoom** tool (press **Z**) and zoom in on tracks **A5** and **A6**. Then, choose the **Pen** tool (press **P**) and set two keyframes at the beginning of the music.

(If you don't see the red "rubber bands," display them by clicking the **Clip Overlay** button in the lower-left corner of the **Timeline**. It's the icon that looks like a mountain.)

3. Then, using the **Pen** tool, drag the first keyframe down and to the edge of the clip. This brings the volume "rubber band" down so that the audio will fade in starting at the first keyframe and ending the fade at the second keyframe.

You've just created your first transition: a fade up from silence to full audio. Using keyframes is a very common way to create level changes. I use it all the time because it is reasonably fast and quite accurate.

4. However, there is more to learn, so double-click the music track to load it into the **Viewer**, then click the red **X** in a circle (the **Reset** button) to remove the keyframes to reset the clip to its beginning state.

5. Here's the second way to create a transition. Again, remember that transitions are created in the **Timeline**, so choose the **Arrow** tool (type **A**), and select the edit point in the Timeline where you want the transition to appear.

6. Now, choose **Effects > Audio Transitions > Cross Fade +3dB**. Immediately, a transition appears at the selected edit point.

This is the big benefit of using the Effects menu. You select an edit point, select a transition from the Effects menu, and the transition appears on the selected edit point.

7. Click in the center of the gray transition to select it, and press **Delete**.

*This is how you get rid of any transition—select it and press **Delete**. (Remember that first interface rule from Chapter 2: you select something, then you do something to it. That rule still applies, all these chapters later.)*

8. Here's the third way to create a transition. Using the **Arrow** tool, make sure nothing is selected on the **Timeline**. Then, go up to the **Browser** and click the **Effects** tab. This is a duplicate of all the effects available in the Effects menu, with one new benefit: you don't need to select the edit point before you pick your transition.

9. Twirl down the **Audio Transitions** folder, select **Cross Fade (+3 dB)** and drag it down on top of the first music edit point.

Poof! The transition is immediately applied to the edit point.

This is the really big benefit to pulling transitions from the Effects tab—you don't need to select the edit point first, you can just drag the transition to any edit point you want.

Which of these three ways of creating a transition is better? That's entirely your opinion. I use all three of these, constantly switching between them depending upon where I am and what I want to do.

One of the cool things about using a transition, as opposed to setting keyframes, is that it is easy to change the duration of the transition.

10. First, because you need to make a small adjustment, be sure to turn off snapping by clicking the **Snapping** button in the top-right corner of the **Timeline**, or pressing **N**. Using the **Arrow** tool, grab an edge of the transition and pull it to the right. See how the duration changes?

Drag this out until the new fade in duration is **2:00** (2 seconds).

It is not possible to use keyframes to create a dissolve between two audio clips—well, not with both clips on the same track, that is. But this is not a problem because it is far easier to create dissolves using the Effects menu and the Effects tab, as you are about to learn.

NOTE | What's the Difference Between a Cross Fade (0 dB) and Cross Fade (+3 dB)?

Unlike with video, there are only two audio transitions to choose from: 0 dB and +3 dB. What's the difference?

The **Cross Fade (0 dB)** option is called an *equal gain* cross fade. This transition fades the first clip down in a smooth straight line, while fading the second clip up, also linearly. Due to the physics of audio, this smooth fade makes the volume dip (get softer) in the middle of the dissolve.

The **Cross Fade (+3 dB)** option is called an *equal power* cross fade. Instead of fading the volume using a straight line, Final Cut fades the volume using a slight curve to bump the volume up a little bit in the middle of the transition. To the ear, this makes the cross-fade sound smooth.

My recommendation is to use the +3 dB cross fade. If it doesn't sound quite right to you, though, use the other transition. I use the +3 cross fade exclusively and am quite happy with it. This is also the default audio transition for FCP, as well.

11. Scroll up until you can see the first edit point between two clips on **A1** and **A2**. Because you are working on only these two tracks, turn on the **Solo** buttons for these two tracks on the far-left edge of the **Timeline**. Then, highlight the edit point.

(If the **Mute** and **Solo** buttons are not visible, display them by clicking the **Audio Controls** button in the lower-left corner of the **Timeline**.)

30-frame transition

12. Choose **Effects > Audio Transitions > Cross Fade (+3 dB)**. It appears on the selected edit point.

4-frame transition

13. Double-click the gray transition icon, and the **Duration** dialog opens. This is another way to change the duration of a transition. Many times, I've found it very useful to add a very short audio dissolve between two sound bites to smooth out the transition in background noise (called "room tone") between the two cuts.

For this reason, my favorite audio transition is four frames. Enter the number **4** and click **OK**. See how the edit point got smaller?

(By the way, you can get to the **Duration** dialog at any time, for both a clip or a transition, by **Ctrl+clicking** the clip and choosing **Duration** from the shortcut menu, or by selecting the clip, or transition, and pressing **Ctrl+D**.)

14. Play the first section of this piece with the first two tracks soloed. Can you hear how the transition makes the cut between the two voices sound less jarring? That's the point behind using this dissolve—it makes your audio sound smoother.

15. That's it for this introduction to transitions. For the rest of this chapter, you'll be working with video. Save your work and close this project.

NOTE | About Handles

Handles are critical to trimming and transitions—because if you don't have a little extra footage at the beginning and end of each shot, you can't trim, and you can't add a transition.

Why?

Because for the duration of the transition, whether it's a dissolve, wipe, or fabulous 3-D effect, there are two images on the screen at once. This means you need to have enough footage on the end of each clip for them to overlap for the duration of the transition.

For instance, a 30-frame dissolve, centered on the edit point, requires an extra 15 frames of video after the Out on the outgoing clip and 15 frames before the In of the incoming clip.

continues on next page

NOTE | About Handles *continued*

Although you can't tell by looking at a clip on the Timeline whether it has handles, it's easy to tell once you load a clip into the Viewer, Here are two examples:

| Handle | Handle | Handle | No handle |

The clip on the left (**Thru trees**) has plenty of video before the In and some video after the Out. This is enough handle for virtually any transition. The clip on the right (**MS Brown coat**), although having plenty of handle before the In, has no handle after the Out. Without a handle, you can't do a transition. (That is, unless you change the transition alignment to end at the edit point. You'll read about this next.)

Here's another example you can test on your own. In Chapter 7, "*Audio—The Secret to a Great Picture*," virtually all of the hurricane talking head footage has handles. None of the B-roll footage does. Which video (and audio) can you use for transitions?

Handles are just really, really important.

2. —————————Creating a Video Transition

In this exercise, you will build on what you just learned about audio transitions to explore the power of video transitions.

Consistency in how you do things (the Final Cut interface) is one of the great features of Final Cut Pro HD. Everything you've already learned about creating an audio transition also applies to a video transition. Also, although this chapter is about transitions, you'll learn later in this book that everything you've just learned about keyframes also applies to using keyframes for motion animation, filters, and effects.

1. Open **Chapter 08 Lesson 2**, and load **Seq – Snowboard final** to the **Timeline**. This is the same snowboard project you were working on in Chapter 7, *"Audio—The Secret to a Great Picture."*

2. You've been editing for a long time. Are you in a hurry to add a dissolve? OK, here it is, in two steps:

Select the edit point between the first two clips (timecode: **01:00:03:04**).

Press **Cmd+T**.

Poof. Instant dissolve. You've just applied the default transition, a 1-second cross-dissolve, to the selected edit point. (If you've changed your default transition, your default will appear instead of the cross dissolve. You will learn in Exercise 3 how to change the default transition.

That is, without a doubt, the fastest way to apply a dissolve to an edit point. But there's a lot more power available to you, if you can afford a few extra seconds.

3. Delete any transition by clicking slightly off center on the icon to select it, then press the **Delete** key.

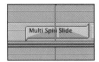

4. Select the edit point, and choose **Effects > Video Transitions > Slide > Multi-Spin Slide**. The Multi-Spin Slide edit appears at your edit point.

5. A fast way to change the duration of a transition is to grab the edge of the transition icon and drag it to the length you want. In this case, drag it shorter so that it is **20** frames long. (If you can't drag the edge of the transition, zoom into the Timeline a bit more.)

6. This next technique, though probably obvious to you, took me years to learn. Click the center of the edit point to select it. (You may need to zoom in on the transition for this to work.) Notice that the cursor turned into the **Roll** tool? Even though you have applied a transition to the edit point, you can still trim the edit using the trim tools you learned about in Chapter 6, "*Trim Your Story.*"

7. Turn off snapping (press **N**) and drag the edit point from side to side. Press **U** to select the three different sides of an edit.

You can roll or ripple the edit point as though the transition wasn't even there.

Gosh, I wish I knew this several years ago! Back then, when I needed to change an edit point, I'd remove the transition, correct the edit point, then reapply and adjust the transition. Trimming under the transition is just so much faster!

*As you might expect, Final Cut provides a number of ways to apply transitions. The benefit to using the **Effects** menu is that it automatically applies the transition to whatever edit point you have selected. This is especially handy if you want to apply the same transition to more than one clip at the same time.*

8. Here's an example. Scroll down until you see the two clips stacked on top of each other (timecode **01:00:11:08**). Click the lower edit point, then hold the **Command** key and click the upper edit point so that both are selected.

9. Choose **Effects > Video Transitions > Dissolves > Cross Dissolve**. Again, poof! Multiple transitions.

Final Cut will not allow you to select more than one edit point on a track. But if you had, say, five video tracks, you could select one edit point on each track and apply the same transition to all tracks all at once.

10. OK, undo that last double transition (press **Cmd+Z**) and go back to the first edit point again. It's between the first and second clips (timecode: **01:00:03:04**).

11. Select the **Multi-Spin Slide** transition by clicking it, slightly off center. Remember when, earlier, you changed its duration to 20 frames?

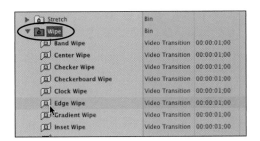

12. Go up to the **Browser** and click the **Effects** tab. Twirl down the **Video Transitions** folder. Twirl down the **Wipe** folder.

13. Select the **Edge Wipe** transition. Notice that it has a default length of **1:00** (1 second). Now, drag it from the **Effects** tab and place it on top of the existing **Multi-Spin Slide** transition. Notice that the new transition inherits all the timing and alignment characteristics of the old transition.

Another advantage of using the Effects tab to place transitions is that you can put a transition any-where on the Timeline, regardless of whether the edit point is selected or not.

I use both of these techniques regularly in my editing, plus one more, which you'll learn about a little later in this chapter.

14. Grab the edge of the transition and change the duration by dragging it shorter to a duration of **20** frames.

Transitions are remarkably flexible, if you know where to look. Here's where.

15. Double-click the transition to open it in the **Transition Editor**. Although the settings in the Editor vary by transition, this window contains the following sections:

- Transition duration and alignment
- Transition bar
- Transition settings

The transition bar shows you the location of the transition, which allows you to make changes to the transition or the edit point beneath it. The dark blue/gray bar indicates video displayed in the clip. The light blue/gray bar indicates clip handles, and the white bar indicates where there is no video.

16. Grab the edge of the transition and drag to change its duration.

17. You can also trim the edit point by using the trim tools. Click the playhead in the **Transition Editor** and drag to do a **Roll** edit.

Or, click the end of one of the dark gray video clip bars to do a **Ripple** edit.

At the top of the window, you can set the transition's duration and alignment, display a list of recent items, or grab the drag handle (the hand) and move the transition. (More on this in Exercise 4.)

The transition alignment buttons are very useful—especially when one of your clips doesn't have han-dles. Click the left-hand alignment button and watch the transition in the Timeline. This button aligns the transition so that it starts at the edit point.

18. Click the middle button. This aligns the transition so that the middle of the transition is at the edit point.

19. Click the right-hand button. This aligns the transition so that it ends at the edit point.

20. In the middle of the **Transition Editor** are all the transition settings, which you can use to alter the look of the transition. These settings vary depending upon which transition you are editing.

In the case of this **Edge** wipe, change your settings to match mine. (You can grab the hands of the clock and twist to change the **Angle** setting.) Press the **spacebar** to play the results of your work.

There are two very, very small buttons on this screen that you should notice: the **Reset** button (the tiny red **X** in a circle) and the **Change Direction** arrow just above it. Click the **Reset** button to reset all the transition settings to their default. Click the **Change Direction** arrow to change the direction of a wipe.

When you are done tweaking, change your settings back to match mine.

As you play the transition, the wipe travels in the same direction as the snowboarders (downhill to the right) and at about the same speed, making for an interesting transition between the two shots.

---

21. Feel free to add other transitions to the shots in this sequence. As you will learn, though, use wipes sparingly. A wipe, by definition, is designed to call attention to itself. If you've done your editing correctly, you don't want people watching your wipes, you want them watching your program.

Once you are done playing, sorry, intensively practicing this exercise, you can save your work (or not, depending). The remaining exercises in this chapter are a series of brief techniques you can use to make working with transitions more efficient.

 MOVIE | Transition.mov

For examples on using the Transition Editor, watch **Transition.mov** in the **movies** folder on the **FCP HD HOT** DVD included at the end of this book.

Understanding Rendering

Depending upon the speed of your computer, when you create a transition, you will see one of three colored bars at the top of the Timeline. These bars are called **render bars**. They indicate whether a transition or effect will play in real time or require rendering.

"Rendering" is simply a fancy word that means that the computer needs to calculate the effect you are creating before it can play it in real time. Many effects, such as dissolves, or motion effects, or some filters, can play perfectly in real time without needing to be rendered first. On the other hand, drop shadows and motion blurs always require rendering.

Although it seems like there's a whole rainbow of render bar colors, there are only three you really need to pay attention to: green, orange, and red.

Green render bars indicate that an effect or transition can be played in real time, without requiring rendering, until you are ready to output to tape.

Red render bars indicate that your computer is not fast enough to play the effect in real time. So, in order to see an effect that requires rendering, you need to do one of three things:

• Render the effect (**Sequence > Render All**, or **Sequence > Render Selection**).

• Press **Option+P** to play the clip as fast as the computer can calculate the effect from the position of the playhead, without first rendering the clip. (This is *my absolute favorite* keyboard shortcut.)

• Choose **Tools > QuickView**.

The QuickView window opens to the same size as the Viewer with a little timer at the bottom. What QuickView does is build a RAM preview of your effect; in other words, it calculates the effect and stores it temporarily into memory. Then, starting at the position of the playhead, it plays your effect forward for half the time indicated on the timer. Then, it backs up the full distance of the timer and plays the effect in real time in the small QuickView window.

The benefit to using QuickView is that, after the first time through calculating your effect, you'll see the effect in real time. The thing I don't like about it is that it requires me to put my playhead in the middle of the effect, then calculate how much time I need to see the effect. Plus, it won't play anything longer than 10 seconds.

For these reasons, I almost never use QuickView, but use **Option+P** all the time.

Top line Video render

01:00:06;00

01:00:06;00

Bottom line Audio render

If you look really closely at the render bar line, you'll notice it's divided into two sections. Video renders are indicated in the top half and audio renders in the bottom half. An audio render is required if the number of audio tracks (or effects) exceeds the computer's capability to play them simultaneously in real time.

You can set the number of real-time tracks your computer can play in **Final Cut Pro HD > User Settings > General**. (The **Audio Playback Quality** setting determines the quality of audio playback on the **Timeline**. The "Low" setting is a good choice. Audio quality will *always* be high for final output.) Generally, keep this track setting small, so that more of your CPU is reserved for processing video, rather than audio.

There's one more thing you need to understand about rendering and that's **Safe RT** versus **Unlimited RT**.

Apple has worked really hard to bring more real-time effects to Final Cut. Obviously, the more real-time effects, the less time you waste waiting for the computer to render. The thing is, see, there's real-time and "real-time."

You change the setting in the top-left corner of the **Timeline** by using the **RT** pop-up menu.

Safe RT plays all green bar renders in real time, exactly as it will output. (Well, "exactly," depending upon the video playback quality setting in your preferences.) If you always want to know what your effects will look like, set Final Cut to play using Safe RT (this is the default).

Unlimited RT give you more real-time effects by dropping calculation-intensive portions of the effect. For instance, drop shadows, motion blurs, feathered edges are all calculation-intensive effects. So, Final Cut does not display these in Unlimited RT, so that you can view the rest of the effect to decide if you like it. If you are doing an effects-intensive production, running in Unlimited RT can save you a ton of time in previewing your effects, because not all effects need to be perfect in order for you to decide if you like them. Effects that are playing in real time but not with all elements are indicated by an orange color in the render bar.

Most of my productions are not effects-heavy, so I run my system in Safe RT. However, this is purely personal preference because *all* effects will be fully rendered at the highest quality before outputting to tape.

3. ——————One More Way to Create a Transition

In this exercise, you'll learn one more way to create a transition—using keyframes. In this case, you will change the opacity of a clip to fade it from black to full screen.

Opacity is the measure of transparency of a clip. A clip with an opacity of 0% is completely transparent (invisible). A clip with an opacity of 100% is fully opaque. (You'll work more with opacity in Chapter 10, "*Motion Effects*.")

1. Open **Exercise 08 Lesson 2** and load **Seq – Keyframe** into the **Timeline**.

2. In the bottom left of the **Timeline**, click the third bar (it turns blue) to expand the vertical height of all tracks. Then, click the **Clip Overlays** button, next to it on the left, to turn on **Clip Overlays**.

You used this button in the last chapter to set audio volumes using the red rubber bands inside each clip. This time, you'll use it to set the video opacity for a clip.

This Timeline has been adjusted so that the small pictures at the beginning of a video clip are not displayed (Sequence > Settings > Timeline). This makes it easier to illustrate how to use keyframes to set a fade in/fade out.

3. Select the **Pen** tool (press **P**) and set a keyframe near the leading edit point of this clip.

4. Set a second keyframe about 1 second later. The exact time is not important.

5. Drag the first keyframe down until it reaches the bottom of the clip. The tooltip will show **0**. This sets the opacity of the first keyframe to **0** (fully transparent), while the second keyframe remains at **100**, which is fully opaque.

6. Play the clip and see how the clip fades in from black to full screen. Final Cut calculates all the transparency levels between the first keyframe and the second so that the clip fades in from black.

Where did this black at the beginning come from? The double-gray bar that separates the video from the audio acts as black (unlike other editors, which often force you to put a black clip next to a video clip whenever you want to fade to or from black). The rule is that this double-gray bar acts as black as long as there is a clip after it in the Timeline. When the end of all clips is reached (that is, there's no clip later in the Timeline), Final Cut no longer uses the double-gray bar as black, but instead stops playing the Timeline.

7. Set two more keyframes at the end of the clip and watch as the clip fades to black at the end.

Whew! Finally, an exercise that takes less than 10 steps! I use opacity settings a lot in animation and compositing. And, although I almost always use regular transitions for fade in/fade out, as you'll learn in Chapter 12, "Output Your Project," using a keyframe fade in/out has significant benefits when you are working with multiple levels of video. And this is the reason I mention it now—just to put all transition descriptions together in one place.

That's the end of this exercise. You can save your work if you want, but it isn't necessary. You won't be coming back to this sequence.

4. ——————————Changing the Default Transition

In this exercise, you'll learn how to change the default transition. You can only have one default video transition and one default audio transition. This exercise shows you how to change both of them. On my system, I set my default video transition to a 20-frame cross dissolve, and my default audio transition to a 4 frame +3dB cross fade.

1. Open **Exercise 08 Lesson 2** and load **Seq – Snowboard final** into the **Timeline**. You'll be working principally in the **Browser** for this exercise.

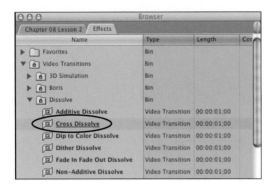

2. Go to the **Browser** and click the **Effects** tab, twirl down **Video Transitions**, then twirl down **Dissolves**. Assuming you haven't changed your default transition, **Cross Dissolve** should be underlined. (And, if you have changed your default transition, then skip ahead to the next exercise.)

See how the name ***Cross Dissolve*** *is underlined? This marks it as the default transition. In this case, you need to change the duration of the default transition from* ***1:00*** *(indicated in the* ***Length*** *column on the right) to* ***20*** *frames.*

3. Double-click the **Length** column to select it. Then, enter **20** for the new **Duration**. Press **Return** to make the change permanent.

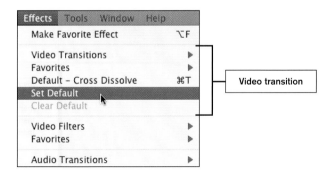

4. The last step is to save this as the new default. Select **Cross Dissolve** in the **Effects** tab, then click the **Effects** menu and choose **Video Transitions > Set Default**, and Final Cut will make this transition your new default transition. (Or, **Ctrl+click** the name of the transition and choose **Set Default** from the shortcut menu.)

The nice thing about default transitions is that you can apply them with a keystroke: **Cmd+T** applies the default video transition to any selected edit point or points.

If you wanted to make a different transition your default, simply select it, make any duration changes you need, go to the **Effects** menu, and choose **Set Default**.

In FCP 4.1.1 or earlier, you had to "Clear Default" before setting a new default. This extra step has been eliminated in FCP HD.

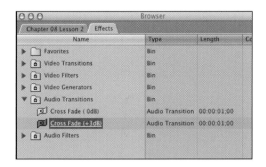

5. Changing the default audio transition is similar. In this case, twirl down **Audio Transitions** and select **Cross Fade (+3 dB)**.

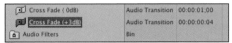

6. Change the **Duration** to **4** (for four frames) and press **Return**.

7. Select **Cross Fade (+3 dB)** and click the **Effects** menu, and choose **Audio Transitions > Set Default**. (Be sure you are in the **Audio Transitions** section.)

*Ta-da! That's it. Another "less-than-10-stepper." To apply the default audio transition, select an audio edit point and either use the **Effects** menu or press **Option+Cmd+T**.*

*You don't need to save your work; default audio and video transitions are saved automatically in your **Preferences** files.*

5. ——————Create a Favorite Transition

In this exercise, you'll learn how to take a transition you particularly like and turn it into a Favorite transition—and why you may not want to.

1. Open **Exercise 08 Lesson 2** and load **Seq – Snowboard final** into the **Timeline**. You'll be working principally in the **Browser** for this exercise.

2. You already know how to do most of this:

- Select an edit point.
- Apply a **Stretch > Cross Stretch** transition (or any transition that you like).
- Double-click the transition to load it into the **Viewer**.

3. Change your settings to match mine. (Not that mine are all that great, but, hey, it shows that you can create a customized favorite transition.)

4. See the small hand in the upper-right corner? It's called the **drag handle**. Grab it.

5. Drag the drag handle to the **Browser > Effects** tab and drop it on the **Favorites** folder. (OK, maybe I should have told you to locate this folder before you dragged the transition. Let go of the transition, click the Effects tab, locate the Favorites folder, and drag the transition into the folder again. Sorry.)

6. Twirl down the **Favorites** folder and see the **Cross Stretch** transition inside.

7. Go to the **Effects** menu. Choose **Favorites**, and see? There's your latest **Favorite** transition with a keyboard shortcut already assigned. This, too, is stored in your **Preferences** folder.

8. To apply a **Favorite** transition, either select your edit point, then choose **Effects > Video Transitions Favorites > [pick your transition]**, or drag it from the **Favorites** folder in the **Browser Effects** tab.

Wow! Eight steps. Very cool. You don't need to save your work; Favorites are saved automatically, also in the Preferences files.

NOTE | Preferences

Here's a quick heads-up on all this Preferences stuff. You can learn more about this in the Appendix, but the short answer is that one of the maintenance procedures you'll do fairly frequently with Final Cut is trash your Preferences files. (No, I won't tell you why now; otherwise, you won't read the Appendix.)

This means that anything that is stored *only* in Preferences files will be lost or reset when those files are trashed.

For this reason, I tend not to use Favorites (there are three: Transitions, Motions, and Effects), nor spend a lot of time obsessing over setting my default transition.

However, I expect the Preferences files to get a lot more stable over time, and these techniques are too good to ignore.

So, use them, but keep in mind that you'll need to redo your favorites every time you trash your Preferences.

6. ———————Bonus Transition: A Gradient Wipe

In this exercise, you'll learn an interesting effect that makes one image "melt" into another. Consider it a bonus for all the hard work you've been doing.

1. Open **Exercise 08 Lesson 2** and load **Seq – Snowboard final** into the **Timeline**. You'll be working principally in the **Browser** for this exercise.

2. If there's a transition between the first two clips, delete it.

3. Select the **Browser**, choose **File > Import > File** and import **Gradient.tif** from the **FCP HOT Projects > Media > Graphics** folder.

4. Double-click **Gradient.tif** to load it into the **Viewer**. Final Cut has a special wipe that uses the shading (gradient) of white to black for a wipe. It's called the **Gradient** wipe, and it's easier to understand when you see it than for me to explain it.

I started with a simple series of gradient bars in Photoshop and then twirled them, using a Photoshop filter. I then exported this as a TIF image. This is what you imported into Final Cut.

You can easily create your own gradient images; just remember to use shades of black and white.

5. Apply the **Video Transitions > Wipes > Gradient Wipe** transition to the first edit point. The default length of **1:00** is OK. You can use either the **Effects** menu or the **Effects** tab. The wipe is the same; the only thing that changes is how you apply it.

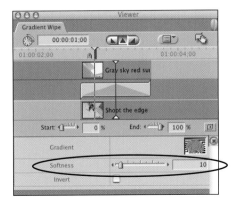

6. Double-click the transition to open it into the **Transition Editor**. If you feel adventurous, change the **Softness** setting to **10**.

7. Drag the **Gradient.tif** image from the **Browser** into the **graphics well** in the **Transition Editor**. This image will be what creates the wipe. Like I said, it's easier to see than to explain.

8. Your transition will require rendering. I used **Option+P** to view this transition without rendering, but you can use any of the three render options: **Sequence > Render Selection**, **Option+P**, or **Tools > QuickView**.

Voilá! A really cool, if somewhat "Batman-and-Robinish," gradient wipe. All in only 8 steps. You are getting really good.

9. Well, that's it for this chapter. Save whatever you want to save and quit Final Cut.

Summary

In this chapter, you've switched gears from editing into making your projects look beautiful. And, in so doing, you've learned many of the basic elements you'll be working with throughout the second half of the book: keyframes, renders, opacity, and transitions. In the next chapter, you'll work with text and graphics so you can really drive your message home.

Helpful Keyboard Shortcuts	
Shortcut	**Function**
Cmd+Z	Undos the last event (default setting tracks last 10 events)
P	Selects Pen tool to add keyframes
PP	Selects Negative Pen tool to remove keyframes
Option+P	Switches Pen tool into Negative Pen tool and vice versa
Option+8	Opens the QuickView window
Z	Selects Zoom tool
N	Toggle Snapping on and off
Ctrl+D	Opens the Duration dialog for selected clip or transition
Cmd+T	Applies default video transition to selected video edit point
Option+Cmd+T	Applies default audio transition to selected audio edit point
Cmd+R	Renders selection
Option+R	Renders everything
Option+P	Plays an effect that needs rendering as fast as it can be calculated, without first rendering the effect (my *favorite* keyboard shortcut)
Cmd+click	Select multiple edit points (one edit point per track)
Option+click	With Arrow tool to set keyframes if they don't exist, or delete keyframes if they do exist; click audio volume overlays (red rubber bands) or video overlays (black opacity lines)

9

Text, Titles, and Graphics

Creating a Main Title	Tips on Designing Video Graphics
Creating Lower-Third and Upper-Corner Titles	Graphic Math
Creating a Credit Roll	Understanding How to Read Scopes
Working with LiveType Projects
Working with Photoshop Multi-Layer Files

Chapter 09 Lesson 1
Chapter 09 Lesson 2

FCP HD HOT DVD

Text and graphics are often as important an element in telling your story as music, effects, or even B-roll. Identifying a speaker establishes his or her credibility. Showing a map of a historic battle is far better than a series of wide shots for establishing relationships.

In this chapter, you will learn how text and graphics for video are different from graphics for print or the computer screen (and they differ significantly!). You will learn how to create titles for your programs. You will also learn how to integrate LiveType and Photoshop graphics into your sequences.

─────────**Creating a Main Title**

In this exercise, you will learn how to create a full-screen title using Final Cut Pro HD's built-in
text generator.

1. Open **Chapter 09 Lesson 1**. You'll find it inside the **Lessons** folder on the **FCP HD HOT**
DVD included with this book. Double-click **Seq – Ready to Title** to load it into the **Timeline**.

*Notice at the beginning of the sequence there's a 5-second gap. This gap is where you will
put the opening title for this scene.*

2. Start by placing the **playhead** anywhere in this gap. This tells Final Cut where to locate
the text clip you are about to create.

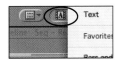

3. Click the small pop-up menu in the lower-right corner of the **Viewer** that has the letter "A"
inside it. This is the **Generator** menu. Scroll down and choose **Text > Text**.

NOTE | Text Clips

Moving a text clip to the Timeline is where most people have problems working with text in Final Cut. Because of this, let me first give you this three-step process so you understand it clearly. Then, you'll do it as part of this exercise:

Step 1: Put the **Timeline playhead** in the clip over which you want to superimpose your text. Click the **Generator** menu and choose the text you want to create.

Step 2: Before entering any text, drag the newly created text clip from the **Viewer** to the **Superimpose** overlay in the **Canvas** (or press **F12**).

Step 3: Immediately double-click the new text clip in the **Timeline** to load it back into the **Viewer**.

4. Before you enter any text, drag the new text clip from the **Viewer** to the **Canvas** and drop it on the **Superimpose** overlay.

*The text clip is immediately placed **above** the clip in which the **Timeline playhead** is located and trimmed so that they are both the exact same length. Notice, unlike with most other edits, you did not need to set an **In** or **Out**, or even move the **playhead** to the start of the clip. Final Cut calculates all that for you automatically. For those who demand exact technical precision, Final Cut looks for the lowest numbered track that contains a lit **Auto Select** button, then places the text clip in the next higher track, trimmed to match the lower clip for time and location. In most cases, this means your text super (TV jargon for a title "superimposed" over video) will appear on **V2**, timed to match the clip on **V1**.*

5. Next, double-click the text clip to load it back into the **Viewer**.

*The advantage to using this three-step process is that you not only automate the process of creating a text clip, placing it on the **Timeline** and trimming it to the correct length, but you also are able to see in the **Canvas** all the changes you make to the text clip because the **playhead** is already located in the middle of the new text clip.*

I use this technique, or a modification you'll learn in the next exercise, virtually every time I work with text.

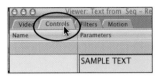

6. With the clip loaded into the **Viewer**, notice that a new tab (**Controls**) has appeared at the top. Click this tab to make adjustments to the contents and formatting of the text in this clip.

*The top half of the **Controls** window is where you enter text. The bottom half is where you control how it looks and where it is placed on the screen.*

7. Start by entering the title of this sequence: **Hurricane Irene 1999**. At the end of each word, press **Return** to insert a line break. This forces each word to appear on its own line of the screen.

Next, from the **Font** pop-up, choose the typeface **Impact**. (If **Impact** doesn't exist on your system, use **Arial Black**. However, by using **Arial Black**, you may need to adjust some of the formatting from that shown in these illustrations.)

*Another helpful technique to working with text and effects is to switch the **Canvas** from displaying only the video image to displaying the video image and wireframe. The wireframe allows you to make changes to the size and location of a video clip. Although you will work with this feature a lot in the next chapter, for now, it will be helpful in placing text on the screen.*

8. Go to the **Canvas** window. From the third small pop-up menu at the top, choose **Image+Wireframe**.

9. Next, change the font **Size** to **70** and adjust the **Tracking** to **1.5** and the **Leading** to **−5**.

Tracking is the spacing between characters. (Smaller numbers mean closer text.) Leading is the spacing between lines of text. (Smaller numbers mean closer lines.)

*Finally, you need to move the text so it centers properly on the screen. The best way to do this is to use the **Origin** control.*

10. Click once in the circle containing the crosshair to select it. Then, go to the **Canvas** and click where you want the center of the graphic to be located. **Continue holding the mouse** and drag to move the text around the **Canvas**. When you are happy with the location, let go of the mouse to position the text.

This technique of using the crosshair to set the position of text, graphics, or an effect is used a lot throughout the rest of this book.

NOTE | Using the Motion Tab to Set Font Size and Location

Some inexperienced FCP editors use the **Motion** tab, which you'll learn about in Chapter 10, "*Motion Effects*," to set font size and location. This is really not a good idea. First, moving text using the **Motion** tab makes it easy to unintentionally crop the edges of letters. Second, using the **Scale** command puts jagged edges on your text.

Use the **Controls** tab for all text sizing and placement. It always looks better.

---

*To precisely set the position of text or graphics, you can enter the coordinates directly into the **Origin**. The first number sets the horizontal position, the second sets the vertical.*

11. In this case, enter **0** in the first box to center the text horizontally and **−31** to move the text up a little bit.

NOTE | A Quick Word on Coordinates

Final Cut uses the coordinates **0,0** to represent the exact center of a frame of video. (Photoshop, on the other hand, uses **0,0** to represent the top-left corner of an image.)

The top-left corner for DV video is at coordinates **−360, −240**. The bottom-right corner for DV video is at coordinates **360, 240**.

To move an image to the left, type a negative number in the first box.

To move an image to the right, type a positive number in the first box.

To move an image up, type a negative number in the second box.

To move an image down, type a positive number in the second box.

In other words, up and left are negative, down and right are positive.

12. Finally, because this is the beginning of the sequence, you need to put a quick fade up on the beginning of the title and dissolve from the title to the first video. To do this, select the **In** of the title and apply a 20-frame **Cross Dissolve**.

---

13. One way to set the duration of a transition is to select it, and press **Ctrl+D**. Then enter the new duration into the **Duration** dialog.)

---

14. The **Out** of the text clip isn't long enough to support a dissolve. You need to extend it. A quick way to do this is to select the **Out** of the text clip and press the **+** key on either the keypad or keyboard. Then type **10** and press the **Return** key. This uses timecode to extend the **Out** 10 frames.

15. Finally, apply a 10-frame **Cross Dissolve** to the **Out**, and you are done. Save your work and quit Final Cut if you want to take a break. However, there is still more you can do with text, as you'll learn in the next exercise.

NOTE | Action Safe, Title Safe, and Full Screen

As you will soon discover, this chapter is filled with "Wouldn't it be nice if…?"

Well, in this case, wouldn't it be nice if all the elements in your program could go to the edge of the screen? Well, they can't, mainly because of the way television sets are manufactured and the way they age.

TVs, as you can imagine, are produced in huge quantities under a variety of conditions and quality control. Experience has taught that, essentially, every set loses some of the picture at the edge of the frame. This is because consumers want to see as big a picture as possible, and don't like seeing black around the edges. So the manufacturers zoom the picture slightly so it fills the screen. However, because this zooming in is not absolutely precise, some edges of the picture are often lost.

continues on next page

NOTE | Action Safe, Title Safe, and Full Screen *continued*

To compensate for this, Final Cut, and other professional video tools, draws a rectangle around the picture 5 percent in from each edge. This rectangle is called **Action Safe**. It is the area within which you need to keep all essential action; otherwise, some percentage of the TV sets out there will not be able to see it.

To compound matters, as TV sets age, their picture tubes zoom in, losing even more of the picture around the edge.

To compensate for this additional picture loss, Final Cut has a second rectangle, drawn 10 percent in from each edge, called **Title Safe**. When you are creating titles, company logos, sponsor phone numbers, or any other essential text information, be sure it entirely fits inside the **Title Safe** rectangle.

You toggle the display of these rectangles inside Final Cut by choosing **Show Title Safe** from the **View** menu or from the **View** pop-up menu in the **Canvas** (or **Viewer**).

NOTE | Tips on Designing Video Graphics

There isn't room, in a single book, to cover designing television graphics in the detail it deserves. So, rather than explain each of these in detail, here are some key guidelines you can use to improve the look of your graphics:

- All video, in all formats, worldwide, everywhere, all the time, period, is 72 dots per inch. Video is low-resolution. Printing is high-resolution. You cannot get the same look in video that you can create on your computer screen or a printer. Just accept this as a fact and move on.

- Avoid text with very thin lines in the font, like the bar in this "e." The bar disappears on video and makes the character impossible to read. This font does not work well at small point sizes. If you must use a font like this, make sure to set the text large on the screen.

- Avoid text that's so ornately scripted you have to look at the letter several times to figure out what it is. Your viewers don't have that much time. Even if you make the font really large, you won't see the smooth curves you expect, but lots of tiny little stair steps along the edges of each curved line.

- Avoid fonts with little "feet" or "bars" at the end of the characters, called *serifs*. These serifs often flicker and make the text hard to read.

- Avoid using any text in point sizes smaller than 24 point.

- Avoid using highly compressed or condensed fonts; they are too hard to read.

- Avoid using lines thinner than 4 pixels; they will flicker.

- Avoid using highly saturated colors. In Exercise 4, you'll learn how to use scopes to make sure your colors are safe.

- Avoid using pure white (more on this later). Again, in Exercise 4, you'll learn how to use the Waveform monitor to maintain good video levels.

- Basically, if someone who hasn't seen your design can't read it in less than 4 seconds, your design is too fancy. Figure out a way to make it simpler. Remember, video is *low*-resolution.

2. _____ Creating Lower-Third and Upper-Corner Titles

In this exercise, you'll learn how to create two more workhorse titles: the lower third and the upper corner. You will use many of the techniques you learned in the last exercise again in this exercise.

1. Open **Chapter 09 Lesson 1**. You'll find it inside the **Lessons** folder on the **FCP HD HOT** DVD included with this book. Double-click **Seq – Ready to Title** to load it into the **Timeline**. It should have all the graphics you've created so far during this chapter. If not, open, **Seq – Ready for lower third**.

2. Set an **In** on the **Timeline** at the start of Gov. Bush's statement. Set an **Out** just before the B-roll starts. (Remember, if you use the down arrow to find the start of the B-roll, you need to move **back** one frame to set the **Out**.)

3. Click the **Generator** menu and choose **Text > Lower 3rd**.

4. Add a new track (**V3**) by **Ctrl+clicking** in the gray area immediately above **V2** and choosing **Add Track** from the shortcut menu.

5. Because you want to edit this clip to the **Timeline** using the automated tools, connect the **v1 Source** in the patch panel to the **V3 Destination** by dragging up the patch connection.

6. Edit the lower-third text into the **Timeline** by clicking the red **Overwrite** button in the bottom-left corner of the **Canvas** (or pressing **F10**). Because of the way the patch panel is set, the clip appears at the location of the **playhead** on **V3**.

7. Because you want the lower-third super to dissolve in at the same rate that the title graphic is dissolving out, copy the transition at the end of the main title by **Option+dragging** it from the end of the main title to the beginning of the lower-third. (You don't need to worry about adding a transition at the end of the super because the super ends at a shot change.) Dragging the transition would simply move it. **Option-dragging** a transition makes a copy of the transition and moves it to the edit point you drop it on.

(If you can't Option-drag a transition, you probably have bad preferences files, which was a problem I ran into while writing this chapter. See Chapter 14, "*Additional Resources*," for instructions on how to delete and restore your preferences files.)

Now that the clip is in the **Timeline**, place the **playhead** in the middle of the clip and double-click it to load it into the **Viewer**.

8. Click the **Controls** tab.

This Controls window for a lower-third is different than the Controls window for full-screen text. This is a good example of how windows change to reflect different attributes of a clip, effect, or transition.

Essentially, this window has sets of controls for the first line of text, the second line, and a background effect.

9. Enter **Jeb Bush** into **Text 1**. Set the **Font** to **Arial Black** and the **Size** to **40** point.

10. Enter **Governor, Florida** into **Text 2**. Set the **Font** to **Arial** and the **Size** to **32** point.

11. Change the color of the second line by clicking the color chip for the second line of text and selecting a rich yellow color. Pick something a little back from the edge of the color circle.

12. You can save a color to reuse later, by dragging the color from the color bar at the top and dropping it into one of the color chips at the bottom. Since this color picker is a system-level utility, *any* application that opens this color selector is able to select the same color by clicking the small chip at the bottom.

The lower-third text clip has a background you can use to add additional visual variety to the clip. (Although I use this text format a lot, I sure wish it did more, truth be told.)

---

13. Choose **Bar** from the **Background** pop-up menu, and change the background color to brick red. This adds a thin red line behind the title.

There's one more setting you need to adjust, which I use for all my text: a drop shadow. Drop shadows make text much *more readable.*

---

14. To create a drop shadow click the **Motion** tab and check the **Drop Shadow** check box near the bottom of the window.

---

15. Adjust your shadow settings to match mine. (I've found these settings make for the most readable text: **Offset = 1.5**, **Angle = 135**, **Softness = 30**, and **Opacity = 90**.)

Drop shadows are essential in video. The image on the left has no shadow, although the image on the right does. While it may be hard to see in print, in video, drop shadows are highly effective and essential for making text readable.

You have one more quick task in this exercise, which is to add an upper-corner super to the first B-roll shot to identify it as historical footage (often called file footage*).*

16. Create a full-screen text clip, set its duration to **2** seconds, and edit it to the **Timeline** immediately after the lower-third super you just completed on **V3**. Double-click it in the **Timeline** to load it into the **Viewer**.

17. Enter **Florida**, press **Return** to create a line break, and then enter **1999**. Set the rest of the settings to match this screen. Use the same color yellow as the earlier super by clicking on the small yellow color chip at the bottom of the color picker. Then, drag it into position using the crosshairs or enter **285** for the horizontal position and **−170** for the vertical.

Graphics next to Title Safe

See how it lands nicely against the Title Safe gridline? Add a drop shadow and you're done.

18. Save your work. You'll be using this project again later. Quit Final Cut if you need to take a break. Otherwise, keep everything open for the next exercise.

NOTE | Graphic Math Anxiety, Part I—Square Pixels

Wouldn't it be nice if... video and computers displayed the same things the same way?

Well, they don't.

In fact, there are five principal ways computer video differs from television video. Some of these I have already discussed; the rest will be presented here:

- Computer video is progressive—it displays every horizontal line of pixels in order from top to bottom. Television video is interlaced—it displays all even-numbered lines, then all odd-numbered lines.

- Computers display a full-range of grayscale from pure black to pure white. Television video displays a more limited range of grayscale from "almost black" to "almost white."

- Computers display all colors as RGB values. Television video displays grayscale and color values using YUV, where Y is the grayscale value and U/V are the color values. YUV colors do not have the same range as RGB colors.

- Computers display all colors uncompressed, that is, each pixel is uniquely described using discrete red, green, and blue values. Television video, in order to squeeze more information onto a tape, compresses the color values using a variety of different compression schemes: 4:2:2, 4:3:1, and 4:1:1. This color compression further restricts the amount of color information contained in a video clip.

- And, finally, the key difference that drives editors the most nuts: computers display images using square pixels, whereas video displays images using rectangular pixels. This last point is the one I'll discuss first.

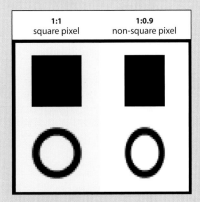

Computers display images as a series of square pixels. Video displays images as a series of rectangular pixels. This means that if you are creating graphics for video, you need to allow for this difference.

continues on next page

> ### NOTE | Graphic Math Anxiety, Part I—Square Pixels *continued*
>
> To make matters worse, Final Cut expects graphics in one size if they are a single layer, such as a scan of a photograph, and a different size if they are a multilayer Photoshop file (more on this later in this chapter). Rather than spend pages explaining this, here is a table you can use to make sure your graphics are the right size.
>
> By the way, there used to be a big brouhaha about whether to create your images in Photoshop, and then alter the image size in Photoshop before importing into Final Cut. My experience indicates you get the same result either way. So, keep it simple: create your graphic in Photoshop at the size indicated in the following table, save it, import it into Final Cut, and let Final Cut do any necessary resizing. The quality is fine.
>
> By the way (number 2), I use TIFFs as my preferred file format for single-layer images, and I use PSD (Photoshop documents) for multilayer images.
>
> By the way (number 3), Final Cut Pro HD changed the way it calculates pixel aspect ratios. The old numbers used to be 720 × 534 × 72. The table below is correct for FCP HD.

Graphic Image Sizes		
Video Format	**Single-Layer (TIFF)**	**Multilayer Photoshop (PSD)**
DV – NTSC	720 × 540 × 72	720 × 480 × 72
DV – NTSC (16x9)	853 × 480 × 72	720 × 480 × 72
DV & SD – PAL	768 × 576 × 72	720 × 576 × 72
DV & SD – PAL (16x9)	1024 × 576 × 72	720 × 576 × 72
601 – NTSC	720 × 547 × 72	720 × 486 × 72
601 – NTSC (16x9)	853 × 486 × 72	720 × 486 × 72
720i/p High Definition	N/A	1280 × 720 × 72
1080i/p High Definition	N/A	1920 × 1080 × 72

3. ——————————**Creating a Credit Roll**

In this exercise, you will create a simple credit roll for the end of the Hurricane sequence.

1. Open **Chapter 09 Lesson 1**. You'll find it inside the **Lessons** folder on the **FCP HD HOT** DVD included with this book. Double-click **Seq – Ready to Title** to load it into the **Timeline**. It should have all the graphics you've created so far during this chapter. If not, open **Seq – Ready for credits**.

2. Create a scrolling text clip by choosing **Text > Scrolling Text** from the **Generator** pop-up menu in the lower-right corner of the **Viewer**.

3. Go to the **Timeline** and put your **playhead** at the **In** of the fourth clip from the end, **B – clean WS**. Then, repatch the video so that **v1 Source** connects to **V2 Destination**.

4. Edit the text clip to the **Timeline**, then drag the **Out** with the **Arrow** tool so that the credits text covers the three clips prior to the final sound bite. Then, double-click it to load it into the **Viewer**.

5. Enter your credit list in the top half of the **Controls** panel. Put asterisks between the titles and names as a separator. Final Cut turns this into the correct spacing automatically using the **Gap Width** setting in the next step. You can change the font, size, and color as you like. In this case, use **Lucida Grande**, **32** point.

6. At the bottom of the **Controls** panel are some new settings:

Gap Width controls the size of the horizontal gap, indicated by the asterisk, between the title and the name.

Fade Size fades the text at the top and bottom of the screen. This is a percentage of the entire screen. Adding a slight fade makes the credit roll look nicer, to my way of thinking.

Direction controls which way the text scrolls.

Auto Kerning improves the spacing between letters. I always leave this on.

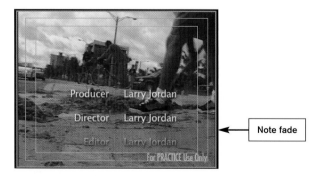

7. Add a drop shadow to your text and move your **playhead** near the middle of the clip to see what the credits look like. (Pretty darn nice, if you ask me!)

8. Save your work, and you're done. There's still more to come in the next exercise, so keep everything open.

NOTE | Graphic Math Anxiety, Part II—What Color Is White?

Wouldn't it be nice if... computers and video used the same white and black levels?

Well, they don't.

When you hear terms like "8-bit video" and "10-bit video," the bits refer to the number of levels between maximum black and maximum white. Eight-bit video has 256 discrete levels, and 10-bit video has 1,024 levels.

This means pure black on the computer has an RGB value of 0,0,0, and pure white on the computer has an RGB value of 255, 255, and 255.

The problem is that video doesn't have that great a range. In 8-bit video, video black in the U.S. is only 16 (as measured on the RGB scale) and video white is 235. To complicate matters, video is measured in IRE, where 7.5 IRE equals video black and 100 IRE equals video white.

continues on next page

NOTE | Graphic Math Anxiety, Part II—What Color Is White? *continued*

The reason you need to care is that you can create graphics on your computer that are too white. When they are broadcast, they visually distort and make the audio buzz. Not good. If you are creating professional-level video, this results in your tapes getting rejected for poor technical quality.

There is some good news, however. First, create all your graphics with black set to 0. Your capture card or DV deck handles the conversion to the proper level of black automatically.

With white settings, it isn't so easy, though Final Cut adds a preference to help. Choose **Sequence > Settings** (or press **Cmd+0**) and click the **Video Processing** tab.

Here's the rule: if you are outputting to DV or DVD, set this pop-up to **Super-White**. If you are outputting to a professional SD format, such as Betacam, set this pop-up to **White**.

What this menu tells Final Cut to do is "clamp," or automatically reduce, all imported graphics so that their white levels match the tape format to which you are recording. This setting affects only imported graphics, and not video, but, still, it's a great help. (You'll learn a way to clamp video white levels at the end of the next exercise.)

_____**Understanding Video Scopes**

In this video, you'll learn how to read the video scopes supplied with Final Cut, as well as when to use a Waveform monitor and when to use a Vectorscope.

1. Open **Chapter 09 Lesson 1**. You'll find it inside the **Lessons** folder on the **FCP HD HOT** DVD included with this book. Double-click **Seq – Ready to Title** to load it into the **Timeline**. It should have all the graphics you've created so far during this chapter. If not, open **Seq – Ready for credits**.

2. Position your **playhead** at **01:00:16:01**—the shot of the lady in the blue top holding a sheet of plywood.

3. Select the video scopes by choosing **Tools > Video Scopes**.

Final Cut has four video scopes: Waveform monitor, Vectorscope, RGB Parade, and Histogram.

These last two scopes, although helpful, are nowhere near as important as the first two. So, you will concentrate on the Waveform monitor and Vectorscope in this exercise.

4. Choose **Waveform** from the pop-up menu in the top-left corner of the **Video Scopes** window.

The Waveform monitor shows all the pixels in the picture in the Canvas, ranging from black, at the bottom, to white, at the top. Various shades of gray are in the middle. Pixels on the left edge of the Canvas are on the left edge of the Waveform and pixels on the right side of the Canvas are on the right side of the scope.

A properly exposed picture has pixel values that range from top to bottom. Images that look washed out are missing black levels. Images that are gray and dull are missing white levels.

Although you can't recognize specific images in the Waveform, you can recognize the various gray levels of shapes. For instance, it's easy to spot the highlights on her hat, the midtones of the plywood, and the darker shadows under the hedge.

5. Move the cursor inside the **Waveform** and watch as the yellow guidelines make it easy to measure the level of grayscale.

*The **Waveform** monitor is how you measure your video levels, which is why this scope is so important: video levels are "TV-safe" provided that white levels do not exceed 100% (100 IRE). The only time they can exceed 100% is if you are shooting, editing, and outputting to DV.*

*However, the **Waveform** monitor tells you nothing about color. For that, you need to open the Vectorscope.*

6. Choose **Vectorscope** from the pop-up menu.

The Vectorscope tells you everything about color and nothing about grayscale. In fact, all blacks, whites, and shades of gray are a single dot in the center of the scope. The Vectorscope displays color in two dimensions: hue is represented by the angle of the color, red is at the top left, magenta at the top right, green near the bottom left, and cyan near the bottom right. Saturation is represented by how far out from the middle the color is.

For instance, it is easy to see the colors in the picture by looking at where the pixels clump: the small jet of blue from her top, the red/yellow of the plywood, the green from the shrubbery, and a small jet of yellow from the tops of her gloves.

7. Move the cursor around the **Vectorscope** and watch as the yellow guidelines allow you to easily measure the distance and angle of a color.

The **Vectorscope** measures your color levels, which is why this scope is so important: color levels are "TV-safe" provided that they do not exceed a rectangle drawn to connect the tops of each of the six color boxes.

However, not all the boxes are the same distance from the center. Red and Cyan are the furthest out and allow the greatest color saturation. Yellow and Blue are the closest in and allow the least color saturation. It is very easy to create a graphic on the computer whose colors are well outside video color safe. The best way to tell is to use the **Vectorscope**.

If a color exceeds this "box," it will not play back safely on videotape or DVD. (The video distorts, or "tears," and often creates an audio buzz caused by how the video and audio signals are processed inside most TV sets.) You must correct any illegal colors before outputting.

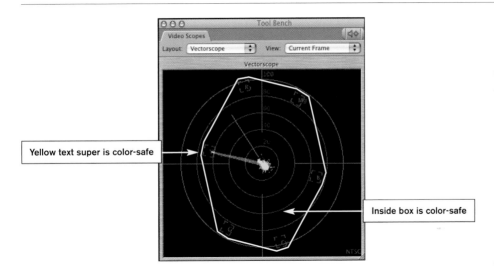

Yellow text super is color-safe

Inside box is color-safe

8. Remember in Exercise 2 when you created the yellow upper-corner graphic, and I told you to select a color near the edge of the color wheel? Put your **playhead** over the text clip and look at it on the **Vectorscope**.

If you got too close to the edge, your color would exceed the yellow color range. If this is the case, open the text clip in the **Viewer** and change the color of the super until the **Vectorscope** indicates it's OK. The yellow color in this screen shot has about the maximum saturation you can have without exceeding color limits.

9. That's it for this exercise. If you changed the color on your graphic, save your work. Otherwise, quit Final Cut if you need to take a break.

NOTE | Clamping Video Levels

Earlier in this chapter, you learned how to set the video rendering for a sequence to clamp (or reduce) white levels that were too high in imported graphics. There's also a filter you can use that does the same thing for video.

(Remember, if you are shooting, editing, *and* outputting all in DV, you don't need to worry about this.)

Chapter 11, *"Filters and Keying,"* talks about filters in detail, but this filter is important enough to discuss here. (You will learn how to apply filters in Chapter 11.)

White level extends into super-white

Here's a video test signal that is too white. Whites that are too white are called *super-white*. You can clamp this video level so that it doesn't exceed 100% by applying the **Broadcast Safe** filter (**Effects > Video Filters > Color Correction > Broadcast Safe**).

White is clamped at 100%

When this filter is applied, all the super-white levels are rolled down to 100%, although the remaining levels in the picture are not changed. You can use this filter whenever you need to control video levels for lots of different clips and don't want to color-correct each one.

NOTE | Title 3D

It's beyond the scope of this book to discuss Title 3D. Sigh… I just don't have enough pages to cover everything in Final Cut. (Some academic versions of Final Cut may not include the Title 3D plug-in. You can tell if you have it by going to the **Generator** menu, in the lower-right corner of the **Viewer**. If it is installed, it will be listed immediately below the **Text** menu option.)

However, this text and graphics plug-in is very helpful in creating titles where you need multiple

- Fonts
- Font sizes
- Font colors
- Shadows
- 3D text

You select it, like all other text, from the **Generator** menu by choosing **Title 3D**.

You edit text created in Title 3D by double-clicking the clip to load it into the **Viewer**, clicking the **Controls** tab, and double-clicking on the **Title 3D** icon.

Importing LiveType Projects

Final Cut Pro HD handles LiveType files differently than earlier versions of Final Cut did. In Chapter 3, *"Gather Your Media,"* you learned how to import. Although it's beyond the scope of this book to give you a proper introduction to LiveType, in this exercise, you'll work with an imported LiveType project. Plus, you'll learn a virtually secret way to edit LiveType files with a minimum of fuss.

1. Open **Chapter 09 Lesson 1**. You'll find it inside the **Lessons** folder on the **FCP HD HOT** DVD included with this book. Double-click **Seq − Ready to Title** to load it into the **Timeline**. It should have all the graphics you've created so far during this chapter. If not, open **Seq − LiveType**.

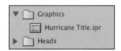

2. Twirl down the **Graphics** folder in the **Browser** and double-click **Hurricane Title.lpr** to load it into the **Viewer**. This is a LiveType project file.

With FCP HD, you no longer need to export your LiveType movie before bringing it into Final Cut. Now, all you need to do is create the LiveType project, save the project, and then import the project file into Final Cut. Final Cut does all the rendering inside itself.

This is much faster, and more flexible, as you will soon see.

Using LiveType, I've created an opening animation to go at the beginning of the Hurricane sequence.

3. In the **Timeline**, select and delete the opening title clip you created in Exercise 1.

4. Drag the **Hurricane Title** clip down from the **Viewer** and place it on **V2** of the **Timeline**, to replace the clip you just deleted.

Put a 20-frame **Cross Dissolve** at the beginning and a 10-frame **Cross Dissolve** at the end. (A fast way to create the ending dissolve is to **Option+drag** it from the **V3** clip to the end of the **V2** clip, since both dissolves are the same length.)

5. The red render bars at the top of the **Timeline** indicate that this title sequence, and the supers you put in immediately afterward, all need to render. Rendering means the computer is not fast enough to display them in real time, so it needs to calculate the effect before it plays it.

Deselect the **Hurricane Title** clip and choose **Sequence > Render All** (or press **Cmd+R**).

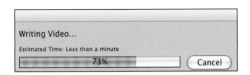

The render thermometer appears. Try to appear patient.

Ta-DA! Instant animated titles. (Well, virtually instant...)

But wait. Let's say you wanted to make a change to this LiveType file. Here's a really fast way to switch back and forth between Final Cut and LiveType to make changes to a file. (In fact, I used this a lot in creating this sequence.)

6. Choose **Final Cut Pro HD > System Settings** and click the **External Editors** tab. Click the **Set** button on the **LiveType Movie Files** line and, in the resulting dialog, navigate to the **Applications** folder and select the LiveType application. Click **Choose**.

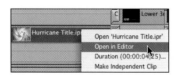

7. Now, go to the LiveType clip in the **Timeline** and **Ctrl+click** the clip and choose **Open in Editor** from the shortcut menu.

*Final Cut automatically opens LiveType and loads this project file into it. Then, after you make changes and save the file (saving the file is important), Final Cut loads the revised clip back into the **Timeline**.*

*No more **Media Offline** messages. This is a really fast way to make changes to a LiveType clip. It's called **round-tripping**.*

As you can also see in the External Editors tab screen shot above, I've also selected Adobe Photoshop for still image files and Bias Peak for audio files. I've found using external editors to be really, really helpful.

8. That's it. This sequence is done! Save your work and show your friends. The last exercise will work with the Snowboard project. Quit Final Cut if you need to take a break.

6. _____Working with Adobe Photoshop Graphics

In this exercise, you will learn how to work with an imported layered Photoshop graphics file and, more importantly, what makes a layered graphic especially useful in Final Cut. Plus, you'll learn how to change the default duration of all imported image files.

1. Open **Chapter 09 Lesson 2**. You'll find it inside the **Lessons** folder on the **FCP HD HOT** DVD included with this book. Double-click **Seq – Snowboard Final** to load it into the **Timeline**.

2. Blaine Albios created an opening Photoshop graphic specifically for you to use at the beginning of this sequence. I've already imported it, so go to the **Browser** and twirl down **Graphics**, then double-click **Snowboard Title** to load it into the **Viewer**.

*Whoops! What happened? It didn't load into the **Viewer**, it loaded directly into the **Timeline**! That's because imported Photoshop graphics that contain layers are treated as sequences, with each layer acting as a separate video track. Best of all, the alpha (transparency) channel information is retained by Final Cut.*

3. This time, drag the graphic from the **Browser** to the **Viewer** to load it into the **Viewer**.

4. You are going to replace the first shot in the sequence with this graphic, so **Ctrl+click** the first clip, **Gray sky red sun**, to read the duration on the third line: **3:04**. Then, delete the **Gray sky red sun** clip.

5. Now, go to the **Viewer** and change the duration of the graphic to **3:04**.

6. Drag the graphic from the **Viewer** into the space at the beginning of the **Timeline** where the first shot used to be.

7. Now, you *could* stop there. But, since this graphic came in layers, take advantage of an opportunity to create some simple animation to finish off this exercise.

Double-click the graphic to open it into the **Timeline** as a sequence.

8. Select the top three layers (**Board**, **Feet**, and **Swoop**), then type **+20** and press **Return**.

9. See how all three layers moved downstream **20** frames? Now select the top two layers and move them downstream another **20** frames. Then, move the top layer an additional **20** frames.

You should now have a staircase effect at the beginning of the graphic sequence.

10. Add a 20-frame dissolve to the beginning of each track.

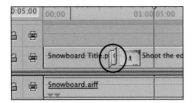

11. Click **Seq – Snowboard Final** on the **Timeline** to make it active. Add a 10-frame dissolve between the graphic and the first video shot. Render everything and play the sequence.

This technique is a very simple, but effective, way to create a feeling of animation for images like maps and complex drawings.

12. One other thing before you finish. All imported graphics default to a duration of **10:00** seconds. You can change this default setting by choosing **Final Cut Pro HD > User Preferences**, clicking the **Editing** tab, and changing the **Still/Freeze Duration** to whatever you like. I usually leave it at 10 seconds, unless I am importing an image sequence for animation, in which case I'll change this setting to one or two frames.

13. That's it. You're done. Save your work and take a break. Quit Final Cut–this wraps up this chapter.

Summary

In this chapter, you learned how to create text from within Final Cut, integrate LiveType animation, and create simple animation using Photoshop layered graphics. In the next chapter, you'll build on this foundation as you move further into effects and start creating motion and animation.

Helpful Keyboard Shortcuts	
Shortcut	**Function**
Ctrl+X	Creates a new full-screen text clip in the Viewer
F12	Superimposes a clip in the Viewer on the track immediately above the clip in which the Timeline playhead is located
Shift+Return	Places a line break after a text entry
W	Toggles the selected window (Canvas or Viewer) between displaying the Image, Image+Wireframe, or just Wireframe
Q	Toggles between selecting the Viewer and the Canvas
Option+9	Displays video scopes
Option+drag	(On a transition) Makes a copy of the transition onto another edit point
Cmd+R	Renders sequence, or whatever clips are selected
Cmd+0 (zero)	Opens Sequence Settings dialog

IO

Motion Effects

Tips to Creating Effective Effects	Creating a Picture-in-Picture
Using Wireframe Mode in the Canvas	Moving Images with Keyframes
Creating Favorite Motions	Moving Text with Keyframes
Creating Curved Motion Paths	Creating and Exporting a Still Frame
Creating Variable Speed Clips	Moving a Still Image

Chapter 10 Lesson

FCP HD HOT DVD

This chapter is about how to create motion effects inside Final Cut Pro to animate your projects. This chapter is part one of a two-part look at Final Cut effects.

In this chapter, you will learn how to use the Motion tab and keyframes to bring movement to your images. Making things move is often essential to creating a visually interesting program. Chapter 11, "*Filters and Keying*," rounds out this exploration of effects by showing you how to change the actual look of your video, or the sound of your audio, through the use of filters.

What Is a Motion Effect?

A motion effect is a special visual effect where an image, or text, changes its size, shape, opacity, or position during the course of the effect. Sometimes, just one image changes. Other times, many images are moving all over the place. It all depends upon the needs of your project.

Which brings to mind a quote from my favorite professor when I was studying television production in graduate school at the University of Wisconsin. Dr. Richard Lawson kept stressing: "Never make an aesthetic decision for technical reasons." Or, as I like to say, "Just because you can, doesn't mean you should."

Just because these effects exist doesn't mean you should use them. Many programs are produced without any special effects. But, for those times when you are editing a deadly dull show, and you are praying for something, anything, to move, it's nice to know that Final Cut can deliver the goods.

There are two types of motion effects: the first is where images don't change during an effect, and the second is where they do. The classic example of the first type is a newscaster with graphics over his or her shoulder. The size and placement of the graphic is preset and nothing changes position. This is the effect you'll create in the first exercise.

The second effect is where an image changes size, shape, opacity, or position during its time onscreen. Examples of this include virtually every commercial and music video on the air today. You'll create these type of effects starting with the second exercise.

Our eyes and brain are programmed to respond to movement. If something moves, our eyes move to it instinctively. As editors, we can use this to lead the viewer's eyes to the specific part of the screen we want them to watch.

NOTE | Programs Are Horizontal, Effects Are Vertical

So far, you have created programs that start on the left of the Timeline and finish on the right, one clip immediately following the other. In other words, everything is horizontal.

When you are working with effects, though, you start working vertically in the Timeline. In other words, to put multiple images on the screen at the same time, you stack them.

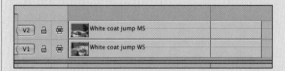

For instance, to put two images onscreen at the same time, you would stack two clips.

continues on next page

NOTE | Programs Are Horizontal, Effects Are Vertical *continued*

To put five images on the screen at the same time, stack five clips.

Final Cut reads video tracks from the top down. This means that the clip on the highest numbered track will totally block anything below it, provided it is 100% full screen and 100% opaque. You discovered this for yourself when you edited the B-roll of the hurricane footage in Chapter 7, "*Audio—The Secret to a Great Picture.*" Clips on higher numbered tracks are in front of clips on lower numbered tracks. Final Cut allows up to 99 video and 99 audio tracks.

So, in order for multiple images to be onscreen at once, in addition to stacking clips on multiple tracks, you also need to change the size, shape, position, or opacity of the clips on higher numbered tracks so the clips beneath them can be seen.

NOTE | Tips to Creating Effects

As you can probably imagine, entire books are devoted to creating effects. Still, here's a quick set of guidelines you can use to help make your effects work easier.

• Start by planning your effect—even if only for a minute in your head. Thinking about what you want to do helps to clarify how you want to go about doing it; especially in deciding what clip goes on what track.

• The best effects are short in length. The goal in creating an effect is to have your audience believe your effect is real. An effect is a failure if your audience turns to you and says, "Yep, by golly, *that* was really an effect!"

• I've found it faster to start at the end of a motion effect and construct it backwards. In other words, start where you want to end up.

• Finally, create your effect in small steps. This allows you to check things in process and fix them before they get out of control.

I. —————————**Creating a Picture-in-Picture Effect**

In this exercise, you will learn how to create a picture-in-picture effect showing two different angles of the same snowboard jump. To do this, you'll learn how to stack clips, use markers to indicate sync points, change the speed of a clip, and explore the Motion tab.

 MOVIE | Motion.mov

For tutorials illustrating this chapter, check out **Motion.mov**, located in the **movies** folder on the **FCP HD HOT** DVD. These tutorials show you how to create picture-in-picture effects, move images along a motion path, and create curved motion paths.

1. If Final Cut is not running, start it and open **Chapter 10 Lesson**. It's in the **FCP Projects/ FCP HOT files** folder you created at the beginning of this book. Double-click **Seq - Pix in Pix** to open it. Don't panic, this sequence is supposed to be empty. You'll soon add the content yourself.

2. Twirl down the **Clips** bin for Exercise 1 and double-click **White coat jump WS** to load it into the Viewer. (To save typing, I'll call this the **WS** clip.) Notice that I've added a marker, labeled **Sync point**, to the clip. Edit this clip, in its entirety, to **V1** on the **Timeline**. This shot is the wide shot. (And, just to clarify, when I say, "edit a clip," I mean for you to move a clip from the **Viewer** to the **Timeline**. In other words, edit it into its position on the **Timeline**.)

3. Before adding the next shot, you need to set another marker. Move the **playhead** down through the clip and watch for the point where the snowboarder crosses the track of another boarder.

4. Be sure the **WS** clip on **V1** is selected and press **M** to set a clip marker at the **playhead**. (The timecode of this marker is **01:00:07:02**.)

5. Next, double-click **White coat jump MS** to load it into the **Viewer**. Notice that I've added a marker to this clip, as well, labeled **Sync point**. I'll refer to this shot as **MS** because it is the medium-wide shot that will be shown inside the wide shot.

6. Go to the patch panel on the left side of the **Timeline** and drag the left-hand **v1** (the **Source**) up so it connects to (touches) the right-hand **V2** (the **Destination**). This patches the video from the **Viewer** (the left **v1**) to the **v2** track of the **Timeline**.

7. Move the **playhead** to the beginning of the **Timeline** and edit this clip to the **Timeline** by clicking the red **Overwrite** button in the lower-left corner of the **Canvas**. Notice that the clip markers traveled with each clip.

*These two shots are two angles of the same jump; one wide (**V1**) and the other medium-wide (**V2**). The point where he lands in each shot is indicated by the marker labeled **Sync point**. You will make the **MS** clip on the top track smaller and tucked into a corner of the wide shot so viewers can see both angles at once.*

8. Be sure snapping is turned on (press **N**) then select the bottom clip and position the **playhead** exactly on top of the first marker. (A fast way to do this is to press **Shift+M**, to move *right* to the next marker or **Option+M**, to move *left* to the next marker, depending upon the position of the **playhead**.)

9. Drag the top clip so that its first marker aligns with the **playhead** and the first marker of the **WS** clip. (The clip should move **2:04** down the **Timeline**, according to the tooltip.)

10. Select the top clip and slide the **Timeline playhead** down until the boarder crosses the same track you marked in the **WS** clip. (The timecode of this spot is **01:00:07:17**.) Be sure the top clip is selected and set a marker at the **playhead**.

Hmm… The two sets of markers don't line up. This is not good. In this case, I happen to know that the folks at Standard Films, who shot this sequence, filmed the top clip in slow motion. So, you need to slow down the bottom clip to match it.

11. Select the bottom clip (**WS**). Choose **Modify > Speed** and set the **Speed** to **75** percent. This slows down the bottom clip to 75 percent of its normal speed.

(By the way, if you want to reverse a clip, you use this same menu to do so. Simply click the **Reverse** check box, and your clip plays backwards, from **Out** to **In**.)

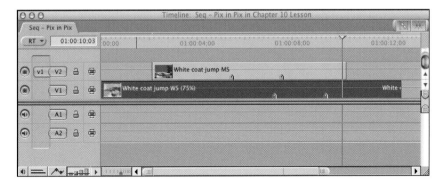

Oh, my goodness. Things just got worse! Now the bottom clip is much longer and none of the markers match.

This is normal. When you apply a constant speed change to a clip, it will always change duration based on the speed change. Clips that are slowed down get longer. Clips that are sped up get shorter. As well, the audio changes with the video. Slower video means deeper-pitched audio. Faster video means higher-pitched audio. (As you will see in Exercise 6, these rules are different when you make a variable speed change to a clip.)

12. Turn snapping on to help align the clips. Select the bottom clip and press **Option+M** to move the **playhead** to the first marker. Next, drag the top clip so the first two markers align, and you will see that the second markers now align as well. (If you are having problems getting your clips to align, double-click **Seq – Pix in pix (sync)** and use it instead.)

You have now matched the speed of both clips and aligned them so they are running in sync; that is, they are both showing the same portion of the jump at the same time. You are ready to create the picture-in-picture effect.

13. Double-click the **V2** clip to load it into the **Viewer**. Click the **Motion** tab to display the **Motion** menu. You'll be working a lot with this menu during this chapter, but for now, concentrate on the top portion, labeled **Basic Motion**.

There are four Basic Motions:

- ***Scale**, which controls the size of the image*

- ***Rotation**, which controls the rotation of the image*

- ***Center**, which controls the position of the image*

- ***Anchor Point**, which controls the point around which the image rotates*

The default settings are 100 percent size (full-screen), 0 degrees of rotation, centered in the middle of the screen, and rotating around the center of the image. Final Cut defines the Center coordinates of the center of the image as 0,0.

*You need to change two **View** settings in the **Canvas** in order to finish this effect. In the past, you've used the **Canvas** principally to review the results of changes you've made in the **Viewer** or **Timeline**. Now, you are going to use the **Canvas** to actually create some of your motion effects.*

14. From the **View** menu at the top of the **Canvas**, choose **Show Title Safe**. (You learned about Action Safe and Title Safe in Chapter 9, "*Text, Titles, and Graphics*.")

15. Go back to the same menu, and choose **Image+Wireframe**.

NOTE | Image, Image+Wireframe, and Wireframe Modes

The View menu in the Canvas and Viewer is a shortcut for the View menu itself, duplicating many of its menu choices in a more convenient location.

You learned about Title Safe and Action Safe in Chapter 9, "*Text, Titles, and Graphics*," but I want to explain the Image, Image+Wireframe, and Wireframe settings now.

When the Canvas is in **Image** mode, it simply displays whatever frame is under the playhead in the Timeline. When you are editing, this is the normal mode for the Canvas.

When you want to create motion effects, switching to **Image+Wireframe** allows you to manipulate the image in the Canvas as an object. As you will learn in Exercise 2, you can resize, move, rotate, crop, and distort images, all in the Canvas, without having to use the Motion tab in the Viewer at all. When I am doing compositing, which means combining two or more images to form a single, new image, I almost always use Image+Wireframe mode.

When I have a particularly complex effect that takes a long time to render, switching to **Wireframe** shows just the outline of an image, without filling in the image itself. This is a very fast way to watch how the shapes of images move during an effect, without needing to render first. In this exercise, switching to Wireframe mode won't help a lot, because, while the snowboarders are moving, the images that show the snowboarders are stationary. In Exercise 4, as you animate the movement of your clips, you'll get a better understanding of how helpful the Wireframe mode can be.

You can easily toggle between these three settings by selecting either the **Canvas** or the **Viewer**, then pressing **W**.

16. Click the **Motion** tab and change the size by typing **40** into the **Scale** text box, then pressing **Return**.

*The size of the **MS** clip is immediately reduced in size and centered in the screen.*

17. Using the **Arrow** tool, grab near, but *not* at, the center of the smaller image and drag it up and to the right until the edges of the image align with the top-right **Action Safe** corner.

18. Deselect all clips on the **Timeline** and play the sequence. Most motion effects are real time, so you shouldn't need to render this effect to see it.

Congratulations! Your very first motion effect.

19. Except... those black borders on the side of the small image are driving me nuts. So, double-click the top clip to load it into the **Viewer** and twirl down **Crop**.

Crop allows you to trim your image from the top, bottom, left, and right edges so that you can hide elements of your image. In this case, you want to eliminate the black borders.

20. In the **Crop** menu, drag the **Left** slider in a little until the left black border disappears. (A value of **3** should do it.) Then, drag the **Right** slider until the right black border disappears. (Again, a value of **3** should be fine, as well.)

Much better...

Except, well, now without that black border, the two images seem to blend into each other too much. You need to separate them.

21. Look further down in the **Motion** menu and choose **Drop Shadow**.

22. Ta-DA! Much better. Drop shadows always require rendering, so either render the sequence, or use my favorite keyboard shortcut–**Option+P**–to play the sequence without rendering.

Option+P plays an unrendered effect slightly slower than real time, but, then, you didn't need to wait for it to render either. I use Option+P constantly when I am building effects.

23. That's it for this exercise. Watch your sequence a couple more times to admire your handiwork, then save your project (**Cmd+S**). Quit Final Cut if you wish, but in the next exercise, you'll be using this project again.

2. _____ Working with Wireframe Mode in the Canvas

In this exercise, you'll learn how to alter the shape of an image using the Wireframe mode in the Canvas, plus discover a few little-known tips to make shape-shifting easier.

1. Open **Chapter 10 Lesson**, if it isn't already open. Double-click **Seq – Wireframe** to load it into the **Timeline**.

(You can use these techniques anywhere in the clip. However, if you want your screens to match mine, put your **playhead** on the marker contained in this sequence.)

2. Select the **Thru trees** clip. In order for these techniques to work, you must have the clip selected, and you must be working in the **Canvas**.

*The normal setting for the **Canvas** is to display all images as **Fit to Window**. This is the best way to display images while editing. However, when you are working on motion effects, you need to create some space around the edges of the image.*

3. In this case, choose **25%** from the **Image Scaling** pop-up menu (top-left menu in both the **Canvas** and **Viewer** windows).

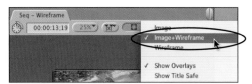

The gray area around the picture is outside the image area, but provides room for you to manipulate the image size and position. It's like a visual pasteboard—an area where you can position clips that you want to have enter or exit a frame. You'll work with this more in Exercise 3.

4. To allow you to directly manipulate the size and position of the image, choose **Image+Wireframe** from the **View** pop-up menu.

*With the clip selected on the **Timeline**, there is now a cyan border, with two diagonal white lines, around the image. And, if you look carefully, where the two diagonal lines cross, the number indicates the video track in which the clip is located.*

5. Press **A** to select the **Arrow** tool, then click one of the corners. (In this case, I used the top-right, but any corner will do.) While holding down the mouse, drag the corner and scale (resize) the image larger and smaller.

Scaling Shortcuts	
Shortcut	**What It Does**
Shift+drag corner with Arrow tool	Scales asymmetrically
Cmd+drag corner with Arrow tool	Scales and rotates at same time

6. Press **Cmd+Z** to undo that size change. With both the **Arrow** tool and the clip still selected, click *near* a corner and drag to rotate the image. (See how the shape of the cursor changes to a rotating, um, thingy?)

Rotation Shortcuts	
Shortcut	**What It Does**
Shift+drag *near* corner with Arrow tool	Constrains movement to 45-degree angles
Cmd+drag corner with Arrow tool	Scales and rotates at same time

7. Press **Cmd+Z** to undo that rotation change. With both the **Arrow** tool and the clip still selected, click near, but not *at*, the center of the image and drag to reposition the image on the screen.

In the case of this screen shot, I first made the image smaller, then dragged it up to the upper-right corner. This is another way to achieve the same effect you created using the Motion tab in Exercise 1.

Positioning Shortcut	
Shortcut	**What It Does**
Shift+drag position	Constrains movement to horizontal or vertical only

8. You don't need to keep undoing each of these moves, but I've found starting each move fresh helps make them easier to understand. So, press **Cmd+Z** and undo your positional changes. Remember, with Final Cut, you have multiple levels of undo, depending on how you set your **User Preferences** in Chapter 1, "*Get Organized*."

*There are two tools in the **Tool** palette that can help modify the shape of an image: **Crop** and **Distort**.*

9. Press **C** to select the **Crop** tool, then click a corner and drag to crop two sides of an image.

Crop Tool Shortcuts	
Shortcut	**What It Does**
Click+drag corner	Crops adjoining sides simultaneously
Click+drag edge	Crops one side
Shift+click+drag corner	Crops image and retains 4:3 aspect ratio
Cmd+drag edge	Crops opposite sides symmetrically
Cmd+drag corner	Crops all sides symmetrically

10. Undo, as usual, then press **D** to select the **Distort** tool. (I don't use this tool very often, but it creates a way cool effect when I do.)

The Distort tool allows you to put a forced perspective into your video, as though it was projecting on the side of a building, viewed from the side.

Using this tool, you can precisely control where each corner of your video is located, in a process called corner pinning. *Or just alter the overall shape of your clip. It is easier to see than to explain.*

11. Be sure the video clip is selected, then, in the **Canvas**, grab the bottom-left corner with the **Distort** tool and drag. See how the corner moves, distorting the rest of your clip? Undo that, then hold the **Shift** key and drag a corner again. See how the whole clip develops a forced perspective?

Distort Tool Shortcut	
Shortcut	**What It Does**
Shift+drag corner	Distorts all four corners symmetrically to create perspective

One last thing. Sometimes, an effect just isn't working and you want to reset everything back to the beginning. Here's a fast way to do it:

12. Double-click the clip to load it into the **Viewer**. Choose the **Motion** tab. Then, click the small, red, circled **X** for the parameter you want to reset. To reset all effects, click each of the seven circled **Xs** in the **Motion** tab.

*The red X is the **Reset** button. You will find it in all filters, motion effects, transitions, and audio wave-forms in the Viewer, and wherever other fine visual effects are sold.*

---

13. That's it for this exercise. In most exercises, I use numbers in the **Motion** tab so it's easier for your work to match mine. However, many times in real life, clicking and dragging a **Wireframe** is faster and works just as well. And now you know how to do it.

You're done with this exercise. Don't save your work. Quit Final Cut if you need to take a break. Otherwise, in the next exercise, you are going to make images fly.

NOTE | Fit to Window Menu

As you noticed, the Fit to Window menu allows you to zoom in or out on an image. You can also zoom using the Zoom tool (press **Z**). Keep in mind, however, that if you zoom in on an image, Final Cut will no longer display it in your external NTSC monitor.

So, if your external (meaning not your computer) monitor suddenly goes black, it's because you are zoomed in too far on an image in either the Canvas or Viewer.

To fix this, and get your image back, use one of these three steps:

• Choose **Fit to Window** from the pop-up menu.

• Click once in the offending window to select it and press **Shift+Z**.

• **Option+click** in the offending window with the **Zoom** tool to zoom back out.

A quick indicator that you are zoomed too far into a window is when you see scroll bars. If you see scroll bars, video to your external monitor will be turned off.

3. ――――――――**Moving Images with Keyframes**

In this exercise, you will learn how to move images around the frame using keyframes, and you'll learn how to create favorite motions. These techniques are used a lot in commercial work.

In this example, you are creating part of an opening title sequence where, during a long downhill run, a variety of images slide into and out of the frame. You can see the finished effect by playing **Seq – Keyframe finished**. (You may need to render this before it plays.)

> **1.** Open **Chapter 10 Lesson**, if it isn't open already. Double-click **Seq – Keyframe start** to load it into the Timeline.

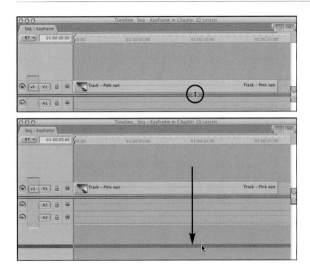

2. Because there will be a number of images onscreen at once, give yourself some room to work by dragging down the horizontal double bar in the middle of the **Timeline**.

3. Choose **Sequence > Insert Tracks** and add **4** new video tracks. Then, in the **Canvas**, turn on **Image+Wireframe** and **Show Title Safe**. These will help you to align the images. (If you've forgotten how to turn these on, refer back to the previous exercise.)

4. Start by opening the **Clips – Exercise 3** bin and loading **MCU to camera** into the **Viewer**. (Notice that I've already added the **In** and **Out** to set the duration to **5:00**, as well as two markers.)

5. Position your **playhead** at the beginning of the **Timeline** and edit the **MCU to camera** clip to **V2** in the **Timeline** (remember to use the patch panel). Then double-click the clip on **V2** to load it back into the **Viewer**. Click the **Motion** tab to select it and drag the **Viewer** wider so you can see the keyframe section on the right.

The light gray area in the keyframe section indicates the duration of the clip you are editing. Markers are pink and displayed at the top of the Motion tab.

NOTE | A Keyframe Review

Keyframes are essential to creating motion effects. Although they were introduced earlier in the book, here's a quick summary of what you need to know about keyframes, all in one place:

Definition: A keyframe is a specific setting of a specific parameter at a specific point in time.

Description: A keyframe is required whenever you want to make something move or change over time. They are very granular. In other words, a keyframe for one parameter (such as position) has no effect on a keyframe for a different parameter (such as color desaturation). In order for multiple things to happen at once, you need to add multiple keyframes. The minimum number of keyframes you need is two: one for the starting position and one for the ending position.

To create a keyframe: Option+click with the **Arrow** tool where a keyframe does not exist, click the **Keyframe** button, click with the **Pen** tool, or press **Ctrl+K.**

To go to a keyframe: Click the little left and right arrows on each side of the **Keyframe** button, press **Shift+K** (next keyframe), or press **Option+K** (previous keyframe).

To move a keyframe: Grab it with the mouse and drag it.

To delete a keyframe: Option+click the keyframe with the **Arrow** tool, click with the **Pen (minus)** tool, **Option+click** with the **Pen (plus)** tool, or place the **playhead** on the keyframe and click the **Keyframe** button.

6. First, change the **Scale** to **40**, and press **Return**, to shrink the image on **V2**.

7. Press the **Home** key to go to the beginning of the clip in the **Viewer**. Set a keyframe at the beginning of the clip by clicking the **Keyframe** button for **Center**.

8. Move the clip so that the lower-right corner of the clip is positioned on top of the lower-right corner of **Action Safe**. (If you can't move the clip, be sure **Image+Wireframe** is selected in the **Canvas** pop-up menu.)

9. As you move the clip, watch the coordinates change in the two **Center** boxes. You have positioned the clip correctly when the left box (showing the horizontal position) reads **180** and the right box (showing the vertical position) reads **120**.

Because you want everyone at home to see your animation, you must make sure to keep everything contained inside **Action Safe**. If this were a sponsor's logo or phone number, you should keep it inside **Title Safe**.

10. Because you were parked on a position keyframe when you moved the clip, the keyframe is auto-matically updated with the revised position of the clip.

Next, move **20** frames ahead, either by dragging the **playhead** or typing **+20**, and press **Return**. (You should be lined up with the marker.) Set a second keyframe for Center.

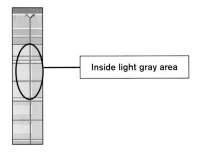

Inside light gray area

11. Move to the end of the clip (press **Shift+O**), or drag the **playhead**. Personally, I like using **Shift+O** because that way I know I am on the last frame of the clip. Many times, the **Viewer** is so small, it's hard to tell precisely where the **playhead** is positioned. (Notice that the **playhead** is just inside the lighter-gray area, which indicates the duration of the clip.)

Set another center keyframe. (This is the third.)

12. Move back from the end of the clip **30** frames. (Yup, you guessed it, type **-30** and press **Return**.) Set another center keyframe.

Your two interior keyframes should line up with the markers.

OK, you've sized and moved the clip into its final position onscreen and set four keyframes that will move it into and out of position. Now, you need to set the first and last keyframe so the clip will slide into frame at the beginning, and slide out of frame at the end.

NOTE | Is All This Precision Really Necessary?

The difference between a good effect and one that makes you cringe to watch is in the details. If all I wanted to do was move one clip around the screen, I wouldn't be this precise.

However, in this case, you are creating a master movement that will be copied to multiple clips that will chase each other across the screen. The only way this effect will be believable is to concentrate on getting the details right as you build the effect. In other words, yes, precisely aligning clips and setting keyframes exactly is pretty much standard.

Oh, and a little planning wouldn't hurt, either.

13. Zoom the Canvas back so the image size is **25%**. Use the Window Scaling pop-up menu. (A large computer monitor may allow you to work at **50%**. The results are the same.)

14. Position the **playhead** at the beginning of the clip. Hold down the **Shift** key and, with the **Arrow** tool selected, drag the clip to the right until the left edge of the clip touches the right side of the main image. In other words, you dragged it offscreen right (Center coordinates **500, 120**). You can type directly in the **Center** text boxes, if you need to correct your coordinates.

Holding down the Shift key makes sure the clip doesn't move vertically when you are dragging it.

15. Move the **playhead** so it is parked on the last keyframe. Hold down the **Shift** key and drag the clip to the left until it is offscreen left (Center coordinates **–500, 120**).

16. Since motion effects are real time, select the **Timeline** and position the **playhead** to the start of the sequence and play it.

Cool! The snowboard skids onto the screen in 20 frames. Glides for about 3 seconds, then dashes off in 30 frames—all while the background boarder is kicking up some huge fantails.

Now what you need to do is duplicate all that effort into four more clips. The good news is that Final Cut makes that process easy.

17. Select the **V2** clip on the **Timeline** and position the **playhead** over the last marker (press **Option+M**).

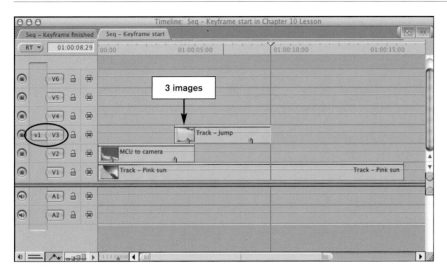

18. Double-click **Track – Jump** to load it into the **Viewer**. Adjust the patch panel so **v1** (**Source**) connects to **V3** (**Destination**). Do an **Overwrite** edit to edit the **Track – Jump** clip to the **Timeline** (F10).

You stacked the two clips because, for a brief period, you have three images on the screen at the same time (including the clip on V1). You shifted the V3 clip downstream because, although it uses the same movement as the V2 clip, that movement does not occur at the same time, but slightly later, than the clip on V2.

These two concepts, stacking and staggering, are used all the time in creating motion effects. The markers help to position the clips, and they help me remember what it is that I am doing.

19. On the **Timeline**, select **MCU to camera**, and choose **Edit > Copy** (or press **Cmd+C**). Select **Track – Jump** and choose **Edit > Paste Attributes** (or press **Option+V**).

Uncheck **Scale Attribute Times**, check **Basic Motion**, and click **OK**.

20. Play the sequence. Watch how all the position attributes of the first clip were copied into the second. This is looking better; the second clip almost pushes the first clip offscreen.

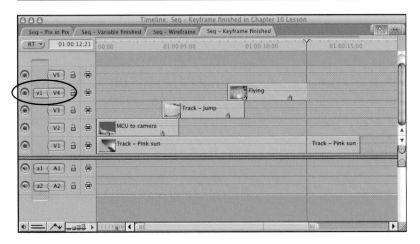

21. Double-click **Flying** to load it into the **Viewer**. Adjust the patch panel so **v1** (**Source**) connects to **V4** (**Destination**). Position the **playhead** to the last marker of the **V3** clip and do an **Overwrite** edit to put the **Flying** clip on the **Timeline** (**F10**).

22. This time, double-click **MCU to camera** and click the **Motion** tab to make it active. Choose **Effects > Make Favorite Motion**.

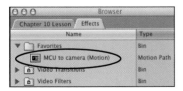

The motion path you created for **MCU to camera** *is saved to the* **Effects > Favorites** *folder of the* **Browser**, *available to you whenever you need it. Like, um, now.*

23. Select the **V4** clip (**Flying**) and choose **Effects > Motion Favorites > MCU to camera (Motion)**.

24. Play your sequence and watch how one clip chases the other off the screen.

NOTE | Paste Attributes vs. Favorite Motion

You've used two different ways to copy a motion from one clip to another: Paste Attributes and applying a Favorite Motion. Is there a difference? Yes, and they are significant.

Paste Attributes allows you to select which attributes you want to paste from the dialog. **Favorite Motion** pastes all motion attributes regardless.

Off by 2 Frames

More significant is the **Scale Attribute Times** option within Paste Attributes. Double-click **Flying** to load it into the **Viewer** and choose the **Motion** tab. Using the **Zoom** tool, zoom in on the second marker. See how the second set of keyframes doesn't line up precisely with the marker? They are early by two frames.

continues on next page

NOTE | Paste Attributes vs. Favorite Motion *continued*

This is because the **Flying** clip runs **4:21**, and all the other clips run **5:00**. Favorite Motion scales keyframe timing to match the length of the clip. In this case, it shortened the second set of keyframes by two frames and lengthened the third set of keyframes by a frame. Unless all your clips are the same length, using Favorite Motion isn't precise.

Favorite Motion *always* scales keyframe timing. Paste Attributes gives you the *option* of scaling keyframe timing.

Finally, Favorite Motions are stored as part of your preferences. When you trash your Final Cut preferences (and I said "when," not "if"), all your Favorite Motions will be lost.

For all these reasons, I use Paste Attributes almost exclusively.

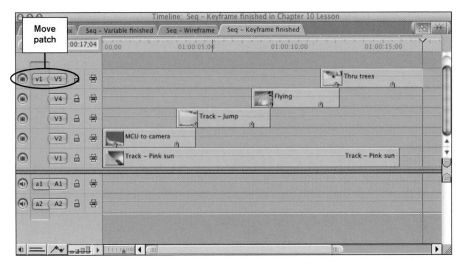

25. You have one last clip to add. Double-click **Thru trees** to load it into the **Viewer**. Adjust the patch panel so **V1** (**Source**) connects to **V5** (**Destination**). Position the **playhead** to the last marker of the **V4** clip and do an **Overwrite** edit to put the **Thru trees** clip on the **Timeline** (**F10**).

26. Again, select **MCU to camera**, copy it to the clipboard, select the **V5** clip, and choose **Edit >** **Paste Attributes** (or press **Option+V**). Uncheck **Scale Attribute Times**.

27. Play your sequence. You just need to trim up the end of the last shot, and the sequence is done.

28. Put the **playhead** at the end of the **V1** clip (press the **up arrow**). Select the ending edit point of **V5**, and press **E**. The edit point jumps to the position of the **playhead**. (See? I told you in Chapter 6, "*Trim Your Story*," there was a reason for learning this shortcut. I use it constantly when working with effects.)

---

29. Double-click the **V5** clip to load it into the **Viewer** and remove the last two keyframes so the image doesn't start to move at the end of the sequence, and you are done.

---

30. Play your sequence and compare it to **Seq – Keyframe finished**.

What do you mean, they don't match? Oh. Well, yeah, they don't. I adjusted the timing of the keyframes in Flying to match the other clips, cropped the left and right edges of each of the moving images, then added a drop shadow. But you learned how to do that in Exercise 1. Add them again here and the two sequences match.

---

31. Whew! Finished. That was a lot to cover. Save your work because you are going to use this project in the next lesson. Quit Final Cut if you need to take a break.

Cool Way to Fade to Black

The sequence you just finished is designed to cut to another shot, which is why everything ends so abruptly.

However, let's say you wanted to fade everything to black at the end. How would you do it?

Well, you could simply select the ending edit points for the clips on **V1** and **V5** and add a **Cross Fade** to black for each of them. But, what if you had lots more tracks? Is there an easier way? Well, depending upon how you define easier, the answer is *Yes*.

This process works best if you have lots of tracks, say more than four, that all need to fade at the same time.

1. In the **Viewer**, choose **Slug** from the **Generator** pop-up menu. ("Slug" is an old-fashioned word from the molten-lead printing days of the early 1900s that means "blank space." In Final Cut Pro HD, it means "audio and video black.")

2. Change the duration of the slug to **20** frames, or whatever length you want for your fade to black.

Note gap

3. Click the **a1** and **a2 Sources** on the patch panel to disconnect them.

4. Edit the slug to the **Timeline** so that it ends at the *end* of your sequence.

5. Turn on **Clip Overlays**.

6. **Option+click** with the **Arrow** tool to set keyframes at the beginning and end of the slug.

7. Drag the first keyframe all the way down, to make the slug transparent. The thin black line controls *clip opacity*. When the line is at the top, the clip is opaque. When the line is at the bottom, the clip is fully transparent. When the line is in the middle, the clip is varying amounts of translucent. You can use opacity keyframes to vary the translucency of any video clip.

8. Play the sequence. Instant fade to black. (Well, mostly instant.)

Again, if you only have one or two clips to fade, this second way is slower. If you have lots of clips to fade, this second way is much faster and much more flexible, because all you need to do to change the duration, or location, of a fade is change the length, or position, of the slug.

Moving Text with Keyframes

In this exercise, you will build on the movement skills you just learned and animate a simple text title to fly in as the images are moving along the bottom. Additionally, you will learn how to create a curved motion path for the text movement.

1. Open **Chapter 10 Lesson**, if it isn't open already. Double-click **Seq – Text start** to load it into the **Timeline**.

This sequence is identical to the one you just finished, except I deleted the last shot on V5, created a text clip on V6, and added some keyframes to the text clip—all using techniques you learned earlier in this chapter.

2. Double-click the text clip to load it into the **Viewer**. Choose the **Motion** tab and widen it so you can see the keyframe section. Slide the **Zoom** slider to the left to zoom in a little on the keyframe section so that you can easily see the keyframes that are already set.

3. Switch the Canvas to **25%** view (use the **Scaling** pop-up menu) and widen it to give you room to move the text clip around.

4. With the text clip selected and the **playhead** at the start of the clip, hold down the **Shift** key down (to constrain movement to only horizontal or vertical) and drag the clip to the right until the text disappears off the screen.

5. Put the **playhead** on the first marker of the text clip. Since the sequence needs rendering, rather than wait for rendering when you are only previewing the initial part of the effect, choose **Tools > QuickView**. This opens a window (the same size as the **Viewer**) that allows you to preview effects without rendering.

Use the default **Range** setting of **2** seconds and play your effect in the **QuickView** window.

NOTE | The QuickView Window

The QuickView window first temporarily builds your effect into memory (RAM). This means that the first time you play an effect in QuickView it will be slow, because Final Cut needs to calculate the effect and store it. QuickView always plays your effect as a loop, so starting with the second time through, since the effect is stored in memory, QuickView plays the effect in real time.

The QuickView window works a bit differently from other windows in that it always starts in the middle.

continues on next page

NOTE | The QuickView Window *continued*

See the Range slider at the bottom of the QuickView window? This slider allows you to select how long a clip you want to preview. The default is 2 seconds. The maximum is 10 seconds.

Say you have a 4-second duration selected on the Range slider. The QuickView window starts at the location of the playhead and plays for 2 seconds (half the time indicated on the Range slider). Then, it backs up to 2 seconds *before* the location of the playhead and plays for the full 4 seconds.

The great thing about the QuickView window is that you can see your effects in real time. But, because it always centers on the playhead location, I find it awkward to use, which is why I like **Option+P** more, because it *starts* at the playhead, rather than *centers* on the playhead.

For me, it's a matter of convenience. They both work great. Pick your favorite.

---

6. Now you need to set keyframe positions for the text to exit. Position the **playhead** on the last keyframe and drag the text clip down and left until it exits screen left (Center coordinates **−628, 215**). Play the ending of the sequence.

Hmmm…. It's OK, but not great. The text makes too straight a line, and travels right over the body of the snowboarder in the video clip. What you need to do is get the text to curve, so that it misses the snowboarder.

Position keyframe

Notice how Final Cut displays keyframes in the **Canvas** *as green dots? Knowing this is helpful in finding keyframes.*

7. Ctrl+click on the last (far left) keyframe and choose **Linear** from the shortcut menu. (It makes no difference if the **playhead** is on the frame or not. The important point is to click the correct green keyframe.)

*Two new blue dots now appear along the motion path. The one nearest the keyframe controls acceleration, the other one controls the shape of the curve. This keyframe provides Bezier curve control for the motion path. I call it the **Bezier controller**. The Bezier controller is always the outside dot and the acceleration controller is always the inside dot.*

8. Grab the furthest keyframe, the **Bezier** controller, and drag it down and to the right. See how the motion path converts from a straight line to a curve?

9. Next, move the **playhead** to the third keyframe. Your text image moves back to the center of the frame. (Positioning the **playhead** makes sure you are changing the correct keyframe, since there are two keyframes at this position.) **Ctrl+click** the keyframe and choose **Linear** from the shortcut menu.

10. Drag the **Bezier** controller down and to the right so you form a smooth curve for the motion path. Hmmm…. that's really hard to see.

11. Sometimes, its easier to adjust an image when you can't see it. Click the **View** pop-up menu and choose **Wireframe**.

This hides the image, but displays the wireframe. A wireframe shows the shape and position of an image without showing the image itself. Wireframes never require rendering, so previews are always in real time.

*Setting Bezier curves is an art, because you can't type in specific keyframe numbers. When the motion looks right to you, you are done. Here's the motion path I created for this sequence. You can view it in **Seq – Text finished**.*

12. There's a lot you can do with Bezier curves and motion paths, so feel free to experiment. At least now, you know where to click and what to do. Save your work. Quit Final Cut if you need a break.

In the next three exercises, you will learn several quick techniques that also relate to motion.

5.————————**Creating a Still Frame from a Clip**

In this short exercise, you will learn how to create a still frame and add it to the end of a clip to freeze movement. You will also learn the best way to export a still frame.

1. Open **Chapter 10 Lesson**, if it isn't open already. Double-click **Seq – Still frame start** to load it into the **Timeline**.

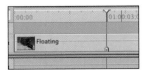

2. Position the **playhead** on the marker and choose **Modify > Make Freeze Frame** (which I never use) or press **Shift+N** (which I always use).

*Final Cut creates a still frame (or freeze frame, if you prefer) at the position of the **playhead** and loads it into the **Viewer**.*

3. The still frame appears in the **Viewer** with a default duration of **10:00**, which you can change by choosing **Final Cut Pro HD > User Preferences** and clicking the **Editing** tab.

4. Change the duration of the still frame in the **Viewer** to **3:00** for this example.

5. Without changing the position of the **playhead**, edit the still frame back to the **Timeline**– press **F10**, or click the red **Overwrite** button.

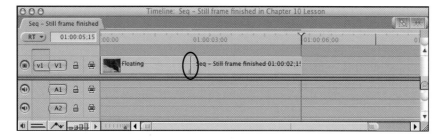

6. The still frame is edited back to the sequence at the position of the **playhead** using an **Overwrite** edit, so that the video flows smoothly up to the point of the freeze frame, then freezes. The middle of the **Floating** clip was covered (deleted) by the **Overwrite** edit. If there is any of the **Floating** clip left over at the end, delete it.

Done.

7. If you want to export this still frame from Final Cut so you can edit it in another program, here's how to do it: Start by loading the still frame into the **Viewer** and make sure the **Viewer** is selected.

8. Choose **File > Export > QuickTime Conversion**.

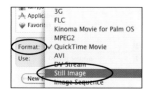

9. In the **Export** dialog, give your still frame a file name, then change the **Format** pop-up to **Still Image**.

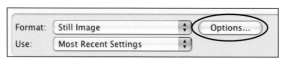

10. Although PNG is a good image format, and the default, I am old-school enough to prefer TIFF images. So, click the **Options** button, next to the **Format** button, and change the format from **PNG** to **TIFF**.

11. That's it. You can compare your still frame with mine in **Seq – Still frame finished**. Save your work, if you feel so inclined. Quit if you want to; otherwise, there are two more techniques to go.

6. ──────Running a Clip at Variable Speeds

In this exercise, you will learn how to create variable speed changes in a clip.

In Final Cut, there are several ways to create variable speed clips, including the **Time Remap** tool. I find all of them very confusing, complex, and difficult to teach. I learned this procedure from Ken Stone a while ago and found it clean, simple, and easy to understand—which is the reason I'm teaching it to you now.

1. Open **Chapter 10 Lesson**, if it isn't open already. Double-click **Seq – Variable start** to load it into the **Timeline**.

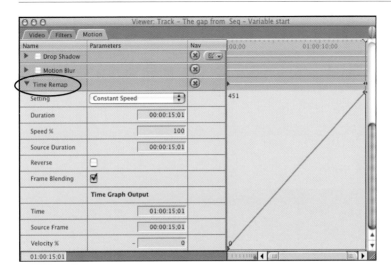

2. Double-click **Track – The gap** to load it into the **Viewer**. Click the **Motion** tab to make it active. Expand the width of the **Viewer** so you can see the keyframe section. Twirl down **Time Remap** so you can see the green diagonal line from beginning to end.

This green line represents the speed of your clip, with the two keyframes at the beginning and end representing the In and the Out of the clip.

NOTE | The Angle of the Time Remap Line

When it comes to changing the speed of a clip, the precise angle of the green line is not important. What is important is that the green line *has* an angle.

You change the speed of your clip by setting keyframes and changing the angle of this green line.

Angle Table	
Angle	**What It Does**
Equal to original line	Clip runs at normal speed
Less than original line	Clip runs slower than normal speed
Greater than original line	Clip runs faster than normal speed
Flat line	Clip freezes
Diagonal down-right	Clip runs in reverse, faster as the angle steepens

A few other notes:

• *A constant speed change* always *changes the duration of a clip; a variable speed change does not.*

• *A constant speed change* always *changes the audio; a variable speed change does not.*

• *And, finally, when you make a constant speed change to a clip, only those frames between the In and the Out are affected. When you make a variable speed change to a clip, all frames before or after the Out can be affected.*

3. Using the **Arrow** tool, **Option+click** where you want your speed changes to occur. Place four keyframes, equally spaced along the line.

Again, this is art, not science, so a little trial and error is necessary as you figure out the best place to put keyframes. In this exercise, where you put your keyframes is not important. In my classes, I tend to place them equally across the line, which makes illustrating my point easier.

4. Now, position your keyframes:

Drag the third keyframe down, slightly, so the angle of the line decreases.

Drag the fourth keyframe down, so that it forms a flat line compared to the third keyframe.

Drag the fifth keyframe down, so that it moves diagonally down and to the right.

5. Variable speed changes are played back in real time on most systems, so play your sequence and watch what happens as the angle of the line changes.

The first segment plays normally, the second slows down, the third stops, the fourth plays in reverse, and the final segment runs many times faster than full speed.

6. Adjust the angles and move the keyframes and watch the results. Then, set an **In** and **Out** and see what effect that has on where your clip starts and ends.

*Right. The **Out** had no effect. A variable speed change to a clip starts at the **In** and ignores the **Out** in order to give you the speed changes you request.*

*For instance, if you froze the first frame of a clip, the entire clip would consist of just the **In**.*

*If you ran the clip in reverse, the clip would start at the **In** and play backwards.*

*If you ran the clip forward at high speed, the clip would start at the **In** and play all the frames it needed, including those after the **Out**, in order to fulfill the duration of the clip.*

7. That ends this exercise. Save your work, if you wish. Quit Final Cut, if you need to take a break. There's one more exercise still to come: making moves on still images.

7. —————————Moving a Still Image

Ken Burns, in his PBS series "The Civil War," popularized a technique of moving still images around in the frame to heighten visual interest. In fact, iMovie created the "Ken Burns Effect" so beginning editors could do the same thing. Final Cut doesn't have a prebuilt filter for this kind of movement. On the other hand, using keyframes and Bezier curves, you can create the same effect with much more precision. This exercise shows you how.

In this example, you are going to do a simple move, starting in a lower corner, then tilt up and zoom in to a close-up. You'll also use an Ease-In, Ease-Out keyframe so that your image slows gently to a stop.

1. Open **Chapter 10 Lesson**, if it isn't open already. Double-click **Seq – Image start** to load it into the **Timeline**.

This sequence contains a still image that is larger than full-screen, which allows you to move around inside it, while still maintaining a high degree of image quality.

> ### NOTE | On Image Size
>
> Final Cut is designed to edit video, not large graphics or images. Although FCP has an internal limit of 4000 pixels × 4000 pixels, I've found it gets really grumpy if your images are much larger than 2000 × 2000.
>
> So, when you are scanning images for use in a video, pay close attention to the total pixel count. Video dots per inch (dpi) is always 72, so it isn't the dpi that matters; it's the total number of pixels.
>
> Remember, also, in your scanning calculations, that a full-screen 4:3 DV image of a still graphic is 720 × 540 × 72 (in FCP 4.1*x*, the sizes were 720 × 534 × 72).
>
> Image scanning tables can run dozens of pages, but the following table gives you a few numbers to start your thinking in the right direction. (This is for 4:3 DV video.)

Scanned Graphics Sizes

Image Size	What You Can Do
720 × 540 × 72	Full-screen, no movement
720 × 1080 × 72	Start full screen in bottom half, tilt up to top half
1440 × 540 × 72	Start full screen on one side, pan over to other side
1440 × 1080 × 72	Start in lower corner, pan and tilt up to opposite upper corner

2. Double-click the **Fred Kalbermatten.tiff** image clip to load it into the **Viewer**. Notice the duration of this clip is **5:00**. Click the **Motion** tab to make it active.

*The scale was set to **50%** when the picture was imported. This is because Final Cut always imports a still image so that the entire image is visible in the Viewer or Canvas. This particular image was scanned at 1440×1080, so that it fits perfectly in a 4:3 aspect ratio.*

3. Set the **Canvas** to **Image+Wireframe** (or select the **Canvas** and press **W** to toggle to the **Wireframe** mode).

4. Position the **playhead** at the beginning of the sequence. In the **Motion** tab of the **Viewer**, set a **Center** keyframe and a **Scale** keyframe.

5. Position the **playhead** at the end of the sequence and change the **Scale** to **100%**. *Don't* create any keyframes. Again, using the **Arrow** tool, drag the image in the **Canvas** until the snowboarder's body fills the frame. Notice that whenever you change a setting, Final Cut automatically set new keyframes for the appropriate motion control.

6. Play the sequence. It looks nice, but it would be even nicer if the final move gently slowed down and "landed" on the close-up. To do this, **Ctrl+click** the green keyframe that represents the final **Center** keyframe and select **Ease In/Ease Out**.

Play your sequence again. See how the motion gently slows down and stops. You can adjust this by dragging the inside control point closer to the keyframe (to speed this landing up) or further from the keyframe (to slow the landing down).

You may also notice that the image seems to "pop" when playback stops. This is because, during playback, Final Cut does not show the full resolution of the image in order to allow the CPU to create more real-time effects. Once playback stops, Final Cut displays the image at high-quality resolution, which makes the image seem to suddenly "pop" into focus.

Everything you've already learned about keyframes, Bezier control points, and curves also applies to moving graphics. The nice thing is that because they are larger than full-screen, you can move around inside them with no loss in quality—which is something you can't do with a video image.

*You can compare your version to mine by playing **Seq – Image finished**.*

7. That wraps up this chapter. Save your work, quit Final Cut, and take a break. You've earned it.

Helpful Keyboard Shortcuts	
Shortcut	**Function**
Cmd+J	Displays the Constant Speed change dialog
Q	Toggles between selecting the Viewer and the Canvas
W	Toggles the Canvas, or Viewer, between Image, Image+Wireframe, and Wireframe modes
M	Sets a marker
MM	Edits a Marker
	continues on next page

Helpful Keyboard Shortcuts *continued*	
Shortcut	**Function**
Option+P	Plays a sequence requiring rendering without first rendering it.
A	Selects the Arrow tool
C	Selects the Crop tool
D	Selects the Distort tool
Shift+drag corner with Arrow tool	(In Canvas) Scales a clip asymmetrically
Cmd+drag corner with Arrow tool	(In Canvas) Scales and rotates a clip simultaneously
Shift+drag corner with Crop tool	(In Canvas) Crops a clip while maintaining 4:3 aspect ratio
Cmd+drag corner with Crop tool	(In Canvas) Crops all sides of a clip simultaneously
Shift+drag corner with Distort tool	(In Canvas) Distorts all four corners to create perspective simultaneously
Shift+drag position with Arrow tool	(In Canvas) Constrains clip movement to horizontal or vertical
Shift+drag rotation with Arrow tool	(In Canvas) Constrains clip rotation to 45-degree increments
Ctrl+K	Adds a Motion keyframe
Shift+K	Goes to next keyframe
Option+K	Goes to previous keyframe
Shift+I	Goes to the In of a clip or Timeline
Shift+O	Goes to the Out of a clip or Timeline
Option+V	Pastes the attributes of one clip into a selected clip, or range of clips
Shift+N	Creates a still frame at the position of the playhead in either the Viewer or the Canvas

Summary

In this chapter, you've learned about motion effects: from changing the size of an image to creating keyframes and getting images and text to move around the screen. In the next chapter, you'll continue your exploration of effects by looking at filters and keying. And you'll start with a change of pace: creating an *audio* special effect.

11

Filters and Keying

| Using Audio Filters | Using Video Filters |

| Combining Multiple Filters | Keyframing Filters |

| Nesting Sequences | Explaining Color Space |

| Simple Color Correction | Creating Luma Keys |

| Creating Chroma Keys | Creating Travel Mattes |

Chapter 11 Lesson

FCP HD HOT DVD

Compositing is the process of combining two, or more, images to form a new image. One way to composite is using motion effects. Another is through filters and keying.

The difference between the motion effects you learned about in Chapter 10, "*Motion Effects*," and the filters covered in this chapter is that, in general, motion effects change the size, shape, opacity, and/or position of a video clip; filters change the actual look of the video, or sound of the audio.

In this chapter, you will learn how to use audio and video filters, discover a simple way to color-correct a scene with color problems, and practice combining multiple images using a variety of keying techniques.

MOVIES | Filters.mov

For tutorials illustrating this chapter, check out **Filters.mov**, located in the **movies** folder on the **FCP HD HOT** DVD. These tutorials show you how to create a telephone audio effect, apply and keyframe a filter, and perform a simple color correction.

NOTE | Frequency 201

You learned about audio frequencies in Chapter 7, "*Audio—The Secret to a Great Picture.*" Here is some additional information you need to make this next exercise appear less like magic.

Large rooms sound different than small rooms. It isn't that they are noisier, necessarily, but the echoes they create are different. A large room has wider, louder, more noticeable echoes than a small room.

In the first exercise, you will adjust the echoes created by a voice to make it sound like he is moving from a large room in the first half of the clip, into a small room in the second half. This effect could be enhanced further with the sound effect of a door closing and the speaker saying something like, "Come in here, we need to talk."

Human hearing ranges from 20 cycles per second (very, *very* low-pitched sounds) to 20,000 cycles per second (extremely high-pitched sounds). However, human speech falls into a much more limited range, generally, from 300 cycles to 4000 cycles per second, although some letters like "S" and "F" have frequencies that range up to 6500 cycles per second. Some men are a little bit lower, some women a little higher.

The telephone company knows all this. So, in order to squeeze more phone calls onto a single wire, they limit the frequencies transmitted during a phone call to a range between 350 and 3500 cycles per second. This is why phone conversations, while still completely understandable, don't sound as nice as listening to someone in person.

In the second part of this exercise, you'll take advantage of this fact to create the illusion of a phone conversation, even though the audio was recorded in-person with a good mic.

Remember, your goal with all filters is subtlety. You want to make an effect believable, not suddenly jolt your audience awake with the feeling someone just turned the echoes on and set them to "stun."

I. ——————————Using Audio Filters

Why, if you are learning compositing, am I starting with audio? Two reasons: first, because this helps make the concept of filters easier to understand and, second, because this is a neat technique to keep in your back pocket for when you need it.

In this exercise, you will first learn how to create the illusion of a speaker moving from a large room into a small room. Then you'll learn how to apply a filter to create the sound of a telephone conversation.

1. If Final Cut is not running, start it and open **Chapter 11 Lesson**. It's in the **FCP Projects/FCP HOT files** folder you created at the beginning of this book.

This Devanas clip shows a weather map, with a meteorologist discussing the upcoming hurricane at a press conference. In point of fact, the commentator is speaking at a press conference from a podium in the same room as the weather map. However, since he is not on camera at this moment, in this effect, you will make him sound like he is moving from a large room to a smaller room.

2. Double-click **Seq – Audio Echo start** to open it.

3. Select the **Razor Blade** tool (press **B**) and cut the clip at the marker. Turn on snapping to help align the **Razor Blade** properly with the marker.

A linked clip is one where the audio and video are synced together. Final Cut indicates this by underlining the clip name in the **Timeline**. *When you use the* **Razor Blade** *to cut a linked clip, both the audio and video will be cut, regardless of which side you click with the* **Razor Blade**.

Cutting the clip, to create a Through edit, makes it easy to apply an effect to one portion of a clip, without affecting other parts of the clip.

4. Select the first portion of the clip and choose **Effects > Audio Filters > Final Cut Pro > Reverberation**. Double-click the clip to load it into the **Viewer** and click the **Filters** tab to make it active.

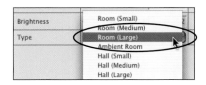

5. From the pop-up menu, choose **Room (Large)**.

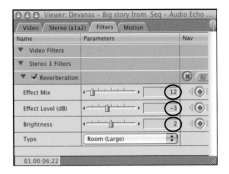

6. The settings in the text boxes are a tad, um, *aggressive*. So, decrease the **Effect Mix** (the percent of the effect compared to the original source) to **12**. An **Effect Mix** of **0** is no effect, all original source; an **Effect Mix** of **100** is all effect with no original source. In this case, we want to sense a light flavoring of the room, not drown in it.

*If you have good speakers, decrease the **Effect Level** to −3. If you have small multimedia speakers, leave this at 0, which will make the effect easier to hear. If I were mixing this for real, I'd set it to −3.*

*Then, increase **Brightness** to +2. This increases the high frequencies, which are a significant component of echoes, to make them easier to hear.*

7. Play the sequence and hear the transition from large room to small. Again, in this case, there's no justification for the movement, but this does illustrate how to prepare a clip for a filter and how to adjust the filter once it's applied.

*You can compare your effect to mine by playing **Seq − Audio Echoes finished**.*

8. Here's another example of using audio filters. Double-click **Seq − Audio Phone start** to open it.

(As usual, it is not a problem to have multiple sequences open at the same time in the Timeline.) In this part of the exercise, you'll create an audio effect to make it sound like the meteorologist is phoning in his report.

9. Select the **Razor Blade** tool (press **B**) and cut the clip at the marker.

In order for this to sound like a phone call, you need to eliminate all frequencies below 350 cycles and above 3500 cycles per second. In fact, to make this effect even more believable, it helps if you cut the low end at 500 and the high end at 2500.

There are several possible filters you could use to limit these frequencies. EQs come first to mind. However, an EQ filter principally enhances or de-emphasizes a range of frequencies. You want to totally eliminate them.

There is no single filter that does this. However, if you use two filters, this becomes very simple.

10. Double-click the *second* half of the clip to load it into the **Viewer**. With the clip still selected, choose **Effects > Audio Filters > Final Cut Pro HD > High Pass Filter**. Then choose **Effects > Audio Filters > Final Cut Pro HD > Low Pass Filter**. Finally, click the **Filters** tab.

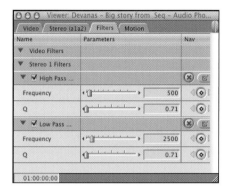

11. See how both filters have been applied to the same clip? You'll work with multiple filters again in Exercise 3.

*However, the frequency settings are wrong. You want the **High Pass** filter to allow (pass) all frequencies above 500 cycles. So, change this setting to **500**.*

*Next, you want the **Low Pass** filter to pass all frequencies below 2,500 cycles. So, change this setting to **2500**.*

*By the way, the **Q** represents the amount of feathering in an audio effect. A high **Q**, greater than 1.0, has very little feathering, and the transition is very sharply defined. A low **Q**, less than 1.0, has more feathering, which softens the transition into the effect.*

12. Play the sequence. Hear how natural the voice is in the beginning, then, after the cut, how it sounds as if he's on the telephone.

*Compare your sequence with mine by playing **Seq – Audio Phone finished**.*

13. As a reminder, to close a sequence in the **Timeline**, **Ctrl+click** the tab containing the sequence name and choose **Close Tab**.

14. Sometimes, even simple effects can be fun! Save your work, if you want. You are done with audio filters; it's time to move to video.

NOTE | Thoughts on Audio Filters

Audio is one of the things I love, and an area that many video editors have limited experience with. Here is a quick summary of the types of audio filters in Final Cut, along with suggestions on how to use some of them.

There are two sets of filters supplied with Final Cut Pro HD: Apple and Final Cut Pro HD. The differences are that the Apple filters are included with the operating system, but the Final Cut filters are only available to people who own FCP. I tend to use the FCP filters, because I like them better.

The Final Cut audio filters fall into four broad categories:

- Equalizers

- Repair

- Dynamic control

- Echo and reverb

Equalizers are designed to alter selected frequencies, either to enhance or eliminate them. The more bands an equalizer has, the more adjustments it can make at one time. Equalizers include 3 Band equalizer, Band Pass filter, High Pass filter (this is the same as the Low Shelf filter), Low Pass filter (the same as the High Shelf filter), and Parametric equalizer. You've already learned how to use the High and Low Pass filters. Try using the Parametric EQ to warm a voice, that is, to enhance the low frequencies. Set it to a **Frequency** of **300**, **Q** of **1**, and **Gain** of **2.5.**

Repair filters are designed to fix problems like hum, or a speaker who is too close to the mic. Repair filters include DC Notch, Hum Remover, Notch, Vocal DeEsser, and Vocal DePopper. Try using the Hum Remover to take out a low hum where power lines are interfering with your audio. Change the **Q** to **20.** Slowly turn on each of the harmonics, one at a time, and listen to your audio to balance between decreasing the hum while causing the least degradation to your dialog.

Dynamic control filters are designed to maximize gain without creating distortion. These filters include Compressor/Limiter and Expander/Noise Gate. I don't particularly like these filters in Final Cut, so I don't have any suggested uses. If I need compression or limiting, which is different than compressing video to go on the Web, I'll move my audio into an audio editing package such as Peak or ProTools (which you'll learn more about in Chapter 12, *"Output Your Project"*) where I have access to better audio tools.

Echo and Reverberation filters are designed to make a singer's voice sound fuller, or give a better sense of the size of a room. Generally, you don't add echo or reverb to a narrator, cool though it may sound.

2. _____Using Video Filters

In this exercise, you will learn how to apply, adjust, and delete video filters to achieve a certain creative look for your sequence. You will also learn how to create a Favorite filter, as well as apply filters to multiple clips simultaneously.

1. If Final Cut is not running, start it and open **Chapter 11 Lesson**. Double-click **Seq – Video Open start** to load it into the **Timeline**. You may need to render it to play it.

This is the same exercise you worked with in Chapter 10, "Motion Effects," a potential open for the Snowboarding sequence. The problem is, the background needs more excitement. You need to create a more unusual look.

2. Play the sequence to get a sense of what it looks like.

Hmmm… To me, the foreground images are so interesting that my eye goes to the text title and the foreground; I'm not seeing the background at all. It feels flat. Since this is the open to my show, this needs to be fixed.

3. Select the clip **Track – Pink Sun** and choose **Effects > Video Filters > QuickTime > Color Tint.**

4. Not ideal. A black-and-white shot of a snow scene just doesn't make it. However, all Final Cut filters can be adjusted, so double-click **Track – Pink Sun** to load it into the **Viewer**. Click the **Filters** tab to make it active.

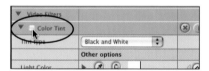

5. To toggle between applying and removing a filter from a clip, uncheck and check the blue check box near the name of the filter.

The benefit of using this check box is that you don't lose any settings on the filter when you toggle it on or off.

*Sigh… the **Black and White** filter just isn't working.*

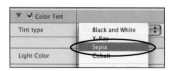

6. Change the pop-up menu from **Black and White** to **Sepia.**

Oh, my goodness! Far worse!! Quick, delete it before somebody sees what you are doing.

7. Click the name of the filter in the **Filters** tab to select it, then press the **Delete** key. (As usual, you "select something, then do something to it.")

Whew! Although sepia tone images are wonderful for giving an image a romantic, nostalgic feeling, extreme snowboarding is not generally considered part of that category. Try again.

8. With **Track – Pink Sun** selected in the **Timeline**, choose **Effects > Video Filters > Stylize > Posterize**.

9. Whoa! Much better. Press **Option+P** to play the sequence without waiting for it to render.

Now, my eye is jumping all over the screen. The background clip is much more predominant, due to this effect. This really makes the beginning of my program seem exciting.

10. Double-click **Track – Pink Sun** to load it into the **Viewer**, if it isn't already. Click the **Filters** tab to make it active, and change the **Red**, **Green**, and **Blue** settings to **5**, **5**, and **5**.

The lower the slider values, the greater the poster effect. The higher the slider values, the more the image looks "real." You can also experiment with different, and unequal, Red, Green, and Blue settings to get an even more pronounced effect.

11. Much better. Select the entire **Timeline** using **Edit > Select All** (or press **Cmd+A**) and render it using **Sequence > Render Selection** (or press **Cmd+R**).

*You could just choose **Sequence > Render Sequence** (or press **Option+R**). That, too, will render your sequence. But I prefer to select what I want to render, rather than always rendering everything. So, for me, my habit has always been to select what I want to render, then just render that selection, whether it's a transition, clip, or group of clips. You can use whichever system you prefer.*

OK. So far, you've learned how to apply a filter, delete a filter, and modify a filter. And, just as you can create a Favorite motion, you can also create a Favorite filter. Here's how.

12. Select **Track – Pink Sun** on the **Timeline**. Choose **Effects > Make Favorite Effect**.

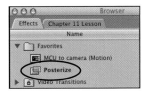

13. Look in the **Effects** tab of the **Browser**. Your Favorite effect is created and stored in this folder.

14. To apply this filter to another clip, select the clip and choose **Effects > (Video Filters) Favorites > Posterize**. (The name of the filter changes, depending upon which effects you are using. The Favorites folder is empty, until you create your first Favorite motion or Favorite effect.) You can apply a Favorite effect to a single clip or a range of selected clips.

15. That's it for this exercise. Save your work, if you wish. Quit Final Cut, if you need to take a break. Otherwise, keep it open; you'll use it again in the next exercise.

NOTE | Favorite Effects vs. Paste Attributes

In Chapter 10, "*Motion Effects*," you learned how to paste attributes for motion effects. The same process applies here: you can paste attributes for filter effects as well.

Favorite effects, like Favorite motions, are convenient, but I rarely use them for all the reasons discussed in Chapter 10.

For me, the biggest negatives are that Favorites always scale keyframes, whereas Paste Attributes gives me the option to scale or not to scale. Also, Favorites are lost when I trash Final Cut's preferences files. Then, again, if the effect doesn't use keyframes, scaling is not an issue.

Just to be clear, when you trash preferences, you are *not* deleting any filters applied to any clip; you are only deleting the *reference* to the filter stored in the **Browser**, under the **Effects** tab, in the **Favorites** folder.

I think Favorites are a great idea and, in the future, when Final Cut preferences are more stable, I look forward to using them more, but for now, I'll stick to Paste Attributes.

NOTE | A Quick Way to Copy a Filter

OK, notwithstanding what I just said about Paste Attributes, here's a fast way to copy a filter to another clip:

Double-click a clip with an effect you like, into the **Viewer**. Grab the name of the filter and drag it on top of the clip you want to copy the filter to. As long as you aren't using keyframes, this technique works great!

3. ——————————Fancy Filter Tricks, Part 1

I was going to call this exercise "Combining Multiple Filters," but how boring is that? In this exercise, you will learn how to combine multiple filters to create an effect, reorganize filters to change an effect, create a filter stack you can apply to other clips, and remove attributes from a clip.

This is an exercise in learning a technique, so you'll need to use only one clip.

1. If Final Cut is not running, start it and open **Chapter 11 Lesson**. Double-click **Seq – Video Fancy Filter 1** to load it into the **Timeline**.

2. Although you can create these effects anywhere you wish in the clip, if you want your screens to match mine, position the **playhead** on the *second* marker.

3. Select **MS Brown coat** in the **Timeline**, then choose **Effects > Video Filters > Border > Bevel**. Double-click the clip to load it into the **Viewer**, then click the **Filters** tab.

4. Click the color tab in the **Bevel** filter and select a light golden color. (Oh, no reason, I just like the color gold.) Notice that the bevel matches the color you selected. Twirl the **Bevel** filter up by clicking the small down-pointing triangle. This provides more room to work in the **Filters** tab.

5. Next, apply a second filter to this same clip. Choose **Effects > Video Filters > Blur > Gaussian Blur**. This blurs the image. (By the way, this is the *only* filter to use when you want to blur a clip. The other blur filters look pretty tacky.) For the purposes of this exercise, crank the **Radius** up to **20**.

6. Finally, apply a third filter to this same clip. Choose **Effects > Video Filters > Image Control > Desaturate**. This removes all the color from the image.

What you have created is a colored bevel around an image, then you blurred the whole image, including the bevel, and removed all the color from the image.

Here's the point of this exercise so far: you can combine multiple filters to create effects not possible with one filter alone. However, and this is an even more important point, the order *of your filters directly affects your effect. Watch this…*

7. Click and drag the title of the bottom filter (**Desaturate**) to the top of the filter stack.

See the change? The image is desaturated first, *then the color bevel is added, then the whole image is blurred.*

NOTE | Filter Processing

Final Cut processes filters from the top down. In other words, the topmost filter is processed first, then the results of that filter are processed by the next filter down, then those results are processed by the next filter, and so on from top to bottom.

This means you can change an effect simply by changing the stacking order of your filters. And you move filters by dragging their names up or down the list.

There is no limit to the number of filters you can apply to one clip, though after you combine more than one or two filters, Final Cut will need to render your effect, rather than play it in real time.

8. One more time to make the point. Drag the bottom filter, **Gaussian Blur**, to the top and watch how the new order changes the image.

9. Just as you can create a Favorite filter, you can also create a Favorite filter stack (or group of filters, such as you've been working on here). To create a filter stack, select the clip containing the effects you like (**MS Brown coat**). Choose **Effects > Make Favorite Effect**.

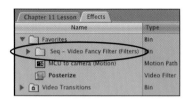

10. Choose **Browser > Effects tab > Favorites** folder. Inside you will see a folder labeled with the name of your clip and **(Filters)**. This is now a Favorite effect that can be applied to other clips.

WARNING | Don't Open a Filter Stack

A filter stack is represented by a folder in the **Effects** tab of the **Browser**. But be careful not to double-click this folder to open the stack. Why? Because the **Browser** sorts files in alphabetical order. Watch…

If you want to see what's in a filter stack, twirl down the folder. That maintains the order of the filters.

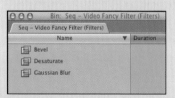

If you open the folder by double-clicking it, the Browser sorts all files in alphabetical order, thus totally rearranging your effect.

There's more to learn about filters, but, first, let me show you another way to remove attributes from a clip. Its called, ta-da! **Remove Attributes**.

11. Select **MS Brown coat** and choose **Edit > Remove Attributes**.

Remove Attributes is smart—it looks at the clip to determine what effects have been applied. In this case, you have only added filters, so only the Filters option is selected. If you had applied other effects, other options would be selected. The benefit to using this window is that you are able to remove some effects without removing all of them.

12. In this case, leave **Filters** checked and click **OK**.

All filters have now been removed from the clip. And this is a good thing, because you are about to work with this same clip in a new way.

13. That's it for this exercise. Don't save your work, unless you feel the need. Quit Final Cut if you want to take a break. Otherwise, leave this sequence open; you'll use it in the next exercise.

4. ————————**Fancy Filter Tricks, Part II**

In this exercise, you will learn how to keyframe a filter.

1. If Final Cut is not running, start it and open **Chapter 11 Lesson**. Double-click **Seq – Video Fancy Filter 2** to load it into the **Timeline**.

2. Select the clip and choose **Effects > Video Filters > Stylize > Posterize**. Double-click the clip to load it into the **Viewer** and click the **Filters** tab.

3. Position the **playhead** at the beginning of the clip and set a keyframe for all three colors (**Red**, **Green**, and **Blue**).

4. Move **30** frames forward (type **+30** and press **Return**) and set a second set of keyframes for all three colors.

5. With the **playhead** parked on the second set of keyframes, change the **Red** value to **6**, the **Green** value to **5**, and the **Blue** value to **7**. (If you have an image that is varying shades of black, white, or gray, you will get a more interesting posterization effect if the three color values are different.)

6. Press the **Home** key to move the **playhead** to the first set of keyframes. Set all three color values to **100**.

7. Play the clip, although you may need to render it first.

Just as you can keyframe motion, you can also keyframe filters—exactly the same way, with exactly the same navigation and control. This provides an enormous amount of control over your effects.

One other note: applying filters is mostly an art, not a science. There is no magic setting *that you should use. If it looks good, in the context of your sequence, it probably is. Just remember to use your scopes (press **Option+9**) to make sure your video levels are within safe boundaries for white level and chroma.*

8. That's it for this exercise. Save your work. Quit Final Cut if you want, but there's lots more good stuff still to come.

5. Nesting Sequences

Sometimes you need to apply the same filter to multiple clips, for example, to create a widescreen look, or display timecode over a series of clips. In this exercise, you'll learn how to nest your clips into a sequence, apply a filter to all of them, then convert them back into individual clips.

1. If Final Cut is not running, start it and open **Chapter 11 Lesson**. Double-click **Seq – Video Nest** to load it into the **Timeline**. This is the open you created in Exercise 2.

What you need to do is apply a widescreen filter to all these clips to make this look as though it were shot 16:9, instead of 4:3. To do this, you need to create a nest. A nest is exactly the same as a sequence, except instead of editing the clips to it, as you would do normally, you create the sequence after all the clips have been edited.

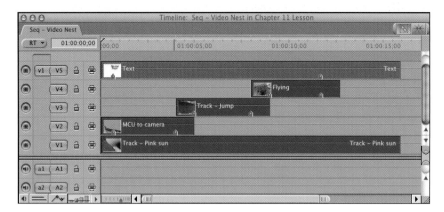

2. Select all the clips in the sequence by choosing **Edit > Select All** (or press **Cmd+A**).

3. Choose **Sequence > Nest Items** (or press **Option+C**).

4. Change the name of the suggested nest to " **Seq – Source Clips**". Remember to use a leading space so all your sequences sort to the top of the **Browser**. Click **OK** to create the new nest.

Notice that all your clips have coalesced into a single, new "master clip," called a **nest**, while in the **Browser**, a new sequence has appeared, called **Seq – Source Clips**. The master clip is the nest, and **Seq – Source Clips** contains all your original clips–intact and available for editing.

5. Select the nest and choose **Effects > Video Filters > Matte > Widescreen**.

This cuts off the top and bottom of the frame to make your images have a widescreen look. However, this isn't a true 16:9 aspect ratio. You need to change the filter settings to get the proportions right.

6. Double-click the nest to load it into the **Viewer**.

Oops, that didn't work. Normally, you double-click a clip to load it into the Viewer, But nests are differ-ent. Double-clicking a nest opens up the nest so you can see, and edit, the individual clips it contains.

*Notice at the top of the **Timeline** there are now two tabs: one containing the original clips (**Seq – Source Clips**) and one that contains the nest itself (**Seq – Video Nest**). Click the **Seq – Video Nest** tab to get back to the nest.*

7. This time, highlight the nest and **Option+double-click** (or press **Return**) to load the nest into the **Viewer**. Click the **Filters** tab, and choose **1.78:1** (which is the correct aspect ratio for 16:9 video) from the **Widescreen** pop-up menu.

8. Play your nest. Given all the effects you are using, you will need to render this before playing it.

The 16:9 filter has been applied to all the clips in the nest. Granted, now that you've changed the aspect ratio, you'll need to change the position of the clips, but that's easy to do.

9. To edit any clip in a sequence, double-click the sequence to open the nest. All your original clips are here, ready for you to edit. Best of all, any changes you make to the clips inside a nest are automatically reflected back to the nest itself.

In this case, you won't make any changes. However, it's nice to know you can. (Oh, OK, make some changes and see what happens.)

Nests are very useful when you want to apply a filter, or motion effect, to a group of clips.

10. That's it for this exercise. Save your work, if you feel so inclined. After a brief discussion of color space, you are going to take a detailed look at a series of specialized filters that all relate to color and keying. Quit Final Cut now, if you need to take a break.

NOTE | Deconstructing a Nest

Although nests are very useful, sometimes you may need to tear them apart and work with the original clips.

You can do this using copy-and-paste, but here's a much cooler, though little known, method:

1. Create an empty sequence, or find an empty spot on an existing sequence.

2. Drag your nested sequence (such as **Seq – Source Clips**) from the **Browser** to the **Timeline**.

3. Once you start dragging, but *before* you get to the **Timeline**, press the **Command** key. This converts your sequence from a nest to a collection of clips.

4. Drop them on the **Timeline**.

Remember, don't press the **Command** key until *after* you start dragging.

Why Color Space Drives Me Nuts

On the surface, computers and video should work well together. They both show movement, audio, and color images, so you'd think they'd be compatible.

You'd think so, but you'd be wrong.

As you first learned in Chapter 9, there are five major areas where computers and video diverge significantly:

Scanning: Computers display progressive images, showing every horizontal line consecutively. Video uses interlaced images, showing first all the even-numbered lines, then all the odd-numbered lines. This has a significant impact when working with movement inside an image.

White levels: Computers create images on a digital scale, ranging from 0 to 255. Digital video creates images also on a digital scale, but broadcast video uses an analog scale, which converts to digital values of 16 to 235. This means it is very easy to create graphics on the computer that are too white, or too saturated, for video.

Pixels: Computers use square pixels. Video uses rectangular pixels. Great-looking images on the computer look tall and thin on video.

Color space: Computers use RGB. Video uses YUV. YUV does not display the same colors as RGB. Video is especially weak displaying saturated shades of yellow and blue.

Color space compression: Computers display all pixels individually at full value. Video compresses color information to reduce file size and make transmission easier.

4:4:4 Color Space

Original image - all pixels accurate

In this example, imagine a block of pixels, showing a blonde actor in front of a green screen. Each of these pixels is defined by three numbers: Y defines the luminance or gray scale value; U and V define the color.

When each of these four pixels is described using its own Y, U, and V values, that image is defined as using 4:4:4 color space; four pixels using four Y values, four U values, and four V values. This is the normal state for your computer, but it is never used in video; the file sizes and transmission requirements are too big. (4:4:4 DV video, if it existed, would require a data rate of slightly more than 31.1 MB per second for playback.)

The human eye is very sensitive to changes in luminance, that is, to changes in brightness. So, a long time ago, video engineers decided not to mess with the luminance value of a pixel, because image quality would suffer too much. However, they still needed to reduce the file sizes of color images, so they started playing games with the color information.

4:2:2 Color Space

Color averaged every two pixels, only row 2 is accurate

What they decided to do was to average the color values of two adjacent pixels. Rather than display them as discrete values, they would blend them. Now, that four-pixel block had four discrete Y values, but only two discrete U and V values, because colors were averaged over two pixels. This reduced the data rate to about 22 MB per second.

4:1:1 Color Space

Color averaged every four pixels, no row is accurate

When it came time to create DV, keeping image quality high was important; however, using small file sizes was even more critical. To do this, engineers again compressed the color space by averaging the color values of four pixels. So, now, each pixel in that group of four pixels had a discrete Y value, but shared one common color value. This is called 4:1:1 color space. This reduced the data rate to about 4 MB per second. And, although DV video uses additional compression techniques to minimize the data rate, this color compression is the one with the most direct impact on effects.

Normally, this color compression is not a big deal. To our eyes, DV video looks pretty good. However, when you start doing color correction, or chroma key, or just messing with colors, you very quickly learn that DV video just doesn't have enough color information in it to create good-looking effects.

So, I'll show you how these tools work. But, if creating high-quality effects is your goal, you'll need to move to a higher-quality color format than DV, such as Betacam SP or DigiBetacam.

6. ——————————Simple Color Correction

The *Advanced Effects for Final Cut Pro* course textbook discusses color for 202 pages. However, in this exercise, we won't go into that much depth. Here, you'll learn a basic approach to solving color problems in four steps.

Although this exercise is designed to teach you how to fix problems, there is a *lot* more that Final Cut can do with color. If you want to learn more, the Appendix lists other resources available to you.

WARNING | Don't Color-Correct Video Using a Computer Monitor

For this exercise, color correcting on your computer monitor will be just fine, because you are learning the process of color correction. However, computer monitors don't display video images using the same colors as your TV set or, even better, a video monitor.

Video displayed to your computer looks dark and muddy. Shown on a TV set, it looks great. Computer images that looks vibrant and colorful on your computer screen look washed out and lifeless on a TV set.

LCD monitors make matters worse.

In Final Cut Pro HD, Apple introduced the idea of Digital Cinema Desktop Preview (**View > External Video > Digital Cinema Desktop Preview**). This is a great way to preview your images, but the colors are still not accurate.

The basic rule is this: if you are color-correcting video for real, you *must* use a calibrated video monitor in order to know what colors look like. Not a TV set. And not a computer screen.

You need three things to properly color correct video: color correction software, accurate video scopes, and a calibrated video monitor. Final Cut provides the first two, and you need to provide the last.

You've been warned.

---

1. If Final Cut is not running, start it and open **Chapter 11 Lesson**. Double-click **Seq – Color Correct** to load it into the **Timeline**.

If you need help in reading the scopes inside Final Cut, please refer to Chapter 9, "Text, Titles, and Graphics."

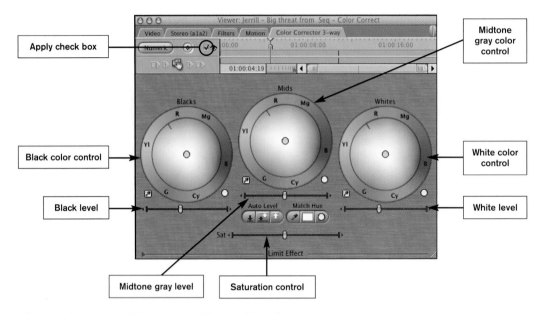

Apply check box

Midtone gray color control

Black color control

White color control

Black level

White level

Midtone gray level

Saturation control

Here are the steps to fixing color problems with a clip:

1. *Apply the **Color Corrector 3-way filter**.*

2. *Set the black levels.*

3. *Set the white levels.*

4. *Color-balance the whites.*

If necessary, you can copy these correction settings to other clips that have the same problem using the same techniques you use to copy other filters or effects.

2. Start by selecting the first clip, **Jerill – Big Threat**, and choosing **Effects > Color Correction > Color Corrector 3-way**.

*The **3-way** filter is used for video and other YUV clips. The **Color Corrector** filter, also in that same collection, is used for RGB and other computer graphics clips.*

3. Put the **playhead** on the marker in the first clip, then double-click the **Jerill** clip to load it into the **Viewer**.

4. Choose **Window > Arrange > Color Correction**. (You can also open the scopes by choosing **Tools > Scopes**, (or by pressing **Option+9**), but using the **Window > Arrange** menu reorganizes all your windows to make color correction easier.)

Again, you can color-correct a clip using video anywhere within the clip; however, if you put your **playhead** *on the marker, your screens will match mine.*

The color in this clip is fine, but the black levels are too high, making it look washed out. Also, the color saturation is a bit low.

On the Waveform monitor, the small white dots represent the grayscale values of all the different pixels in the image. Higher dots represent video levels that are whiter than lower dots. The highest dots are called the white level, and the lowest dots are called the black level.

5. Switch the scope to **Waveform** using the pop-up menu in the top-left corner of the **Scope** window.

See how the black levels, the white dots in the lower third of the scope, are seriously elevated? They are pushing 20%, which is way too gray. Black levels should be down near the line labeled **Black**.

Black level control

Decrease black level

Increase black level

6. You fix this using small increments of change—not huge swipes with the mouse. Click the small left-pointing arrow at the left end of the line below the **Black** color circle on the **3-way color corrector**. This line adjusts black levels. Clicking the left arrow brings them down; clicking the right arrow brings them up. Most often, you are bringing down black levels.

In video, color correction is interactive. Making a change to any color affects all other colors. For this reason, I've found that I get the most consistent results by adjusting levels and colors in a specific order: first, black levels, then white levels, then, finally, color hue and saturation.

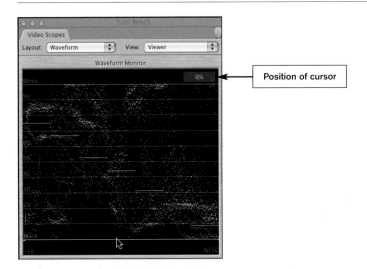

Position of cursor

7. Click the left arrow until the black levels start touching the **Black** line. For me, this was about 37 clicks.

Again, I rarely use the slider because it doesn't have the precision I need. Small increments, slow and steady, work best for color correction.

8. Next, look at the white levels. Again, a little hot (meaning, too high)—around **103%**. Here's a tip to help you quickly set white levels: use **View > Range Check > Excess Luma** (or press **Ctrl+Z**).

NOTE | Using Range Check

Range Check is a very helpful FCP utility that can tell you at a glance if your white levels or color saturation is out of spec.

Here's the basic guideline: if you are outputting to DV, or going directly to DVD, you don't need to worry about white levels. If you are outputting to a higher-quality video format for broadcast, you *do* need to worry.

Video levels for higher quality formats cannot exceed 100%. The Range Check tells you when they do. It has three different settings:

Excess Luma: Check only for white levels that are too high.

Excess Chroma: Check only for chroma levels that are too high (that is, too saturated).

Both: Check for both excess white and chroma levels.

Range Check uses three different icons and two zebra patterns to warn you of problems:

Warning: Video or chroma levels are too hot (depending upon which setting you are using). Use your scopes to determine what needs to be controlled. The red zebra (vibrating lines) pattern shows where the video or chroma levels are excessive.

OK: Video levels are OK with a maximum range between 90% and 100%. The green zebra patterns show where video levels exceed 90%.

OK: Chroma levels are OK, or, if checking for Excess Luma, white levels are below 90%. (Did you notice that the small little arrow in the top left of the green circle is missing in this icon? That's the difference between these two green checkmarks.)

When I am adjusting my white levels, I use both the scope and Range Check. When the Range Check switches from the Warning to the OK icon, I click the white level control down two clicks more and I'm done.

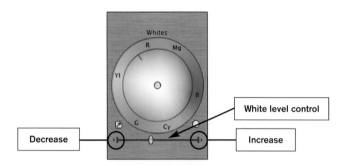

9. To adjust the white levels, click the white level bar underneath the **White** color circle. Click the left arrow to decrease white levels; click the right arrow to increase white levels. In this case, bring the white levels down until the vast majority are below the **100%** line at the top of the **Waveform** monitor. When the **Range Check** switches from the **Warning** to the **OK** icon, click twice more to put your white levels into safe territory. For me, this was three clicks for the warning to disappear, plus two more for safety.

10. Using the pop-up menu, switch to the **Vectorscope** to check your chroma (which means "color") levels.

The chroma levels are well within safe guidelines, so you can safely increase saturation to warm up his skin tones.

11. Adjust saturation by clicking the small arrows at the end of the **Sat** line. The right arrow increases saturation, and the left arrow decreases it. For me, 10 clicks with the right arrow made him look good.

*With saturation, unlike white or black levels, there are no special guidelines. So, make the person look good, while still maintaining safe color saturation levels on the **Vectorscope**.*

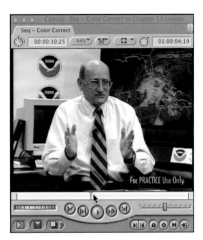

Before (left) and after (right)

12. Play the clip. Compare what he looked like before and after correction by toggling on and off the blue check mark in the top-left corner of the Color Corrector 3-way window. Checked means the filter is on; unchecked means the filter is off.

*In the second clip of this sequence, **Meyers – Bad color**, you need to correct one of the speakers at the press conference who has a decidedly purple skin tone.*

13. Select the second clip, **Meyers – Bad color**, and position your **playhead** on the marker. Choose **Effects > Color Correction > Color Corrector 3-way**, and double-click the clip to load it into the **Viewer.** If you haven't done so already, choose **Windows > Arrange > Color Correction**.

14. First, set the black level. Look at the **Waveform** monitor. The black levels are up near **10%**. Too high.

*Click the black level left arrow to pull the blacks back down to **0%**. (For me, this was about 23 clicks.)*

15. Then, set the white level. Both the **Range Check** and the scope agree the white levels are OK. You might pull the white levels up a few clicks, just to brighten the image a bit. However, if the **Range Check** warning appears, you've gone too far.

Now that both black and white levels are set, it is time to correct the color. Because of how all the different elements of a video signal interact, I've found the most reliable way to do color correction is to follow a strict order of setting black levels, then setting white levels, then adjusting color.

Switch to the **Vectorscope***. The pink line pointing diagonally up left is called the* **flesh tone line***. All skin tones, regardless of race, will appear pretty darn close to this line, because the primary color of human skin is provided by red blood. Since everyone's blood is the same color, all flesh tones are, in the eyes of the* **Vectorscope***, simply different amounts of red.*

By looking at how far someone's skin tone diverges from the **Vectorscope flesh tone line***, it is easy to see what kind of color correction is necessary to bring them back to normal.*

In the case of Mr. Meyers, his skin tone is rolled decidedly toward magenta. This is the last of the three steps to color correction.

16. To color-balance a shot, click the small **eyedropper** in the lower-left corner of the **White** color wheel. Then, click something you believe to be white in the image. Try to pick a part of the image that is not overexposed. In this case, the shoulder of his shirt will work fine.

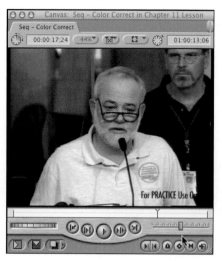

Before (left) and after (right)

As soon as you click the eyedropper, the color is immediately corrected. The skin tones are right on the flesh tone line. And you are done.

There is a school of thought that says color-correcting on a midtone gray is more accurate. Although I don't argue, my point is that finding a clean white in an image is easier than finding a clean midtone gray. This is why I teach this system—it's easy to use and provides dramatically improved results.

However, in this case, you will further improve the image by selecting the mid-gray eyedropper and clicking the gray window immediately to the left of his right ear. In this example, both his skin tone and saturation improve. (I said this was a three-step color-correcting system—I didn't say you couldn't improve on it from time to time.)

---

17. Save your work, or not. As you wish. In either case, you are done with this exercise. Keep things open, though; there's still more to learn.

---

7. ————————Creating a Luma Key

A key is a special effect that removes portions of an image based upon certain values. In the case of a luma key, those values are based on luminance, or grayscale. In the case of a chroma key, those values are based on color. In this exercise, you will learn how to do a luma key.

In Chapter 9, *"Text, Titles, and Graphics,"* you learned how to key Photoshop graphics, which have built-in alpha channels. Luma keys are used when you have a graphic against a black or white background without an alpha, or transparency, channel. They are most often found when you download JPEG graphics off the Web.

1. If Final Cut is not running, start it and open **Chapter 11 Lesson**. Double-click **Seq – Key Luma** to load it into the **Timeline**.

2. This is a color graphic of a snowboarder, **Snowboard Luma.tif**, which you need to key into the background shot on **V1**. To do so, select the clip on **V2**. (Remember, effects are *always* applied to the top clip.) Choose **Effects > Video Filters > Key > Luma Key**.

*Double-click the **Snowboard Luma** clip to load it into the **Viewer**, then click the **Filters** tab.*

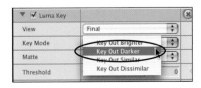

3. Because you want to remove the black background, choose **Key Out Darker** from the **Key Mode** pop-up menu.

4. Since this black background was computer-generated, you can reduce the **Tolerance** to **0**. If you shot this graphic with a camera, you would decrease the **Tolerance** from **100** until the black background completely disappears.

*To minimize the black lines that appear around the image, decrease the **Threshold** to **−65**.*

5. Play the sequence. Because video is bitmapped, some stair-stepping on smooth curves is unavoidable—that's the nature of video. You can minimize these jagged edges by avoiding lines or edges of objects that are almost, but not quite, vertical or horizontal (a rule that I violated in this instance with the edges of the snowboard).

6. That's it. A quick exercise. You don't need to save your work. Quit Final Cut if you want to take a break; otherwise, it's on to chroma keying.

8. ————————**Creating a Chroma Key**

In this exercise, you will learn how to remove a specific color and replace it with the background of your choice in a process called **chroma keying**.

1. If Final Cut is not running, start it and open **Chapter 11 Lesson**. Double-click **Seq – Key Chroma** to load it into the **Timeline**. Double-click **Track – Jump** to load it into the **Viewer**. Click the **Filters** tab to make it active. Position your **playhead** on the marker.

You are going to create a surreal sky as a background for a snowboarder. To do this, you will replace the blue sky with a computer-generated background.

A couple of notes before you start. First, the snowboarder was not shot with chroma key in mind. Because of this, you won't get a perfect key. Don't worry about perfection; concentrate on learning the process.

Second, I knew at the outset that I was not going to get a perfect key, so I selected a background that would hide any blue edges caused by a poor key. Inserting a background with a similar color to your chroma key color is a useful technique when you know that "pulling a clean key" (creating the effect) is going to be difficult.

Third, this effect can be improved by first color-correcting the snowboard shot, then pulling the key. You already know how to color-correct a clip, so you can experiment with it for extra credit at the end of this exercise. I suggest you put the color correction filter in first, then add the chroma key filters.

2. The process of chroma keying involves three different filters, and they need to be applied in a specific order. So, select **Track – Jump**, then choose **Effects > Video Filters > Key > Color Smoothing – 4:1:1**. This filter tries to compensate for the loss of color created by compressing video to DV. This filter is either on or off. Leave it on.

*Next, choose **Effects > Video Filters > Key > Chroma Keyer**. This is the filter that does the heavy lifting.*

*Finally, choose **Effects > Video Filters > Key > Spill Suppressor (Blue)**. This filter compensates for blue halos around your subjects, after you create the key. I've found this filter to be only somewhat useful. For now, turn it off.*

3. Click the **Visual** button on the **Chroma Keyer** filter. This switches the filter from a numeric display to a visual interface.

The chroma key filter is divided into three sections: color selection, edge enhancement, and controls. You'll work with all three in this exercise.

Each of the three bars has two small gray buttons at the top and bottom. The top two gray buttons determine the selection range. The bottom two buttons determine feathering, that is, what amount of adjacent values will be included.

Color bar: *Used to select the Hue of the color to be removed.*

Sat bar: *Used to select the saturation range of colors to be removed.*

Luma bar: *Used to select the luminance range of the colors to be removed.*

Edge Thin: *Use to restrict or expand the edges of the selected color.*

Softening: *Blurs the edges of a key. Use in very small increments (one to three mouse clicks).*

Enhance: *Tries to remove color fringes at the edges of a key by using a complementary color. Use this in very small increments as well (one to three mouse clicks).*

4. The best way to work with this filter is from the top down. Get your color set first, then move to the next row. Don't jump around. Click the **eyedropper** to select the key color. (The "key color" is the color you want to remove.) Then, click in the dark blue sky near the top-right corner.

Instantly, part of your sky disappears and is replaced by the background.

5. Next, extend the range of your selected color by clicking the **eyedropper** again. Hold down the **Shift** key and click near the middle of the frame.

*(Notice how the **eyedropper** has a very small plus sign next to it? This indicates it is adding to the selection.)*

6. Finally, select the **eyedropper** again, hold down the **Shift** key, and click a third time, near the bottom right of the picture.

*The light-gray edge between the trees and the sky is very difficult to remove. Still, there's more you can do to improve this key, so move on to the next two lines: **Sat** and **Luma**.*

7. In order to see how well your key is progressing, click the **Key** icon. The Canvas changes from showing the final key, to a mass of white against the background. The white is the "matte," or the visual information you want to retain for your key. Your goal is to get this white matte as solid and firmly edged as possible. (This is far easier to write than it is to do…)

When you are viewing the matte*, the **Key** icon is a black key on light gray background. When you are viewing the* source video*, the **Key** is red and the background blue. When you are viewing the* final composite*, the **Key** is red on a gray background. Click the **Key** icon to switch between these three variations.*

8. I've also learned that not all three bars are necessary to pull a good key. In this case, turn off **Sat** and see if the matte improves. Nope. Better leave **Sat** on.

9. Turn off **Luma** and see if the matte improves. In most keys, leaving **Luma** off *improves* it. In this case, due to the noise in the lower-right corner, the key is better with **Luma** left on.

Key icon

10. Slowly tweak the buttons at the top of the **Sat** and **Luma** bars until your matte looks as solid as possible. Periodically, click the **Key** icon to switch between the **Matte**, **Source**, and **Final** views. Only when the key looks as good as you can make it should you start adjusting the sliders at the bottom. This screen shot shows the values I came up with when creating this key.

11. Switch back to the **Final** video of your key (click the **Key** icon) and start adjusting the **Edge Thin** slider. Generally, I move this wildly in both directions until I see if things improve. If not, I leave it set in the middle. If so, I gradually narrow down the range of movement until the key looks as good as it can.

*Finally, when everything else is set, click once or twice on the right arrow of **Softening**. This will blur the edges of your key. Any more than three mouse clicks and things deteriorate quickly. I generally use just one mouse click.*

*I'll use **Enhance** when I have a close-up and want to cancel out small blue edges. In this case, it doesn't help a whole lot, so I just used one click.*

Before color correction (left) and after color correction (right)

12. You're done. Render and play your key. The image on the left is my key.

The image on the right is what I came up with after adding color correction. In correcting the image, I pulled down black and midtone levels, significantly boosted the whites, and increased saturation. The image is darker here due to the midtone correction. But this also got rid of the noise in the lower-right corner. You can view my version (without color correction) by playing **Seq – Chroma key finished**.

13. That's it for chroma key. Save your work and quit if you need a break. Otherwise, keep this project open. There's one more exercise to go in this chapter—one of my favorites: creating a travel matte.

9. _____Creating a Traveling Matte

In this exercise, you will learn how to create an effect you've seen most of your life: video inside other video. Often, the video is inside text. In this case, you'll put the video inside a graphic image of a snowboarder. (As an interesting bit of trivia, this is the only effect in Final Cut that requires a minimum of three layers; all the rest require two.)

1. If Final Cut is not running, start it and open **Chapter 11 Lesson**. Double-click **Seq – Travel start** to load it into the **Timeline**. Position your **playhead** at the start of the sequence.

2. If it isn't off already, turn off the visibility indicator for **V3**, so you can see the image on **V2**. Double-click **Snowboard Travel.tiff** to load it into the **Viewer**. (This is a TIFF image with an embedded alpha channel to separate the image of the snowboarder from the background. The problem is, it's too big.)

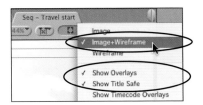

3. In the **Canvas**, turn on **Show Overlays**, **Show Title Safe**, and **Image+Wireframe**.

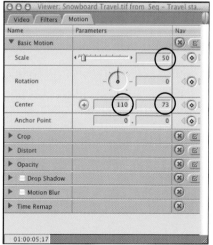

4. Go to the **Viewer**, click the **Motion** tab, and change the **Scale** to **50**. Then, in the **Canvas**, drag the image of the snowboarder to the lower-right corner and align it with the **Title Safe** border. Your **Center** settings should be about **110, 73**.

5. Turn on the visibility indicator for **V3** and double-click it to load it into the **Viewer**.

*You are creating a three-layer effect: **V1** is the background, **V2** cuts a hole into the background, and **V3** fills the hole. To do this, you need to create a traveling matte, where the image on **V3** is inserted into the image on **V2**. Normally, this is done using text. In this case, you'll use a picture.*

6. With the **V3** clip selected, choose **Modify > Composite Mode > Travel Matte – Alpha**.

*The white image of the snowboarder has been filled with video from the **V3** clip. But you need to position the **V3** clip more precisely.*

7. Click the **Motion** tab and change the **Scale** of **Thru trees** to **40**. Then, using the **Arrow** tool, drag the **V3** image so it completely fills the still graphic on **V2**. The **Center** coordinates are about **100, 71**.

Render and play the clip. Very cool, but, somehow, a bit flat. This can be perked up with a drop shadow, but to do that, you need to add one more layer—just to create the shadow.

8. Select both the **V2** and **V3** clips. Press **Option+up arrow** to raise both clips a track and create a new **V4** track, all at the same time.

9. Select *just* the **V3** clip, **Snowboard Travel.tif**, and choose **Edit > Copy** (or press **Cmd+C**).

10. Turn *off* the **Auto Select** button for **V1**, which forces Final Cut to paste the clip to the lowest numbered track with a dark **Auto Select** button; in other words, **V2**.

*Then move the **playhead** to the beginning of the sequence.*

11. Choose **Edit > Paste** (or press **Cmd+V**). A copy of the **V3** clip is pasted into **V2**. Double-click the **V2** clip, also called **Snowboard Travel.tif**, to load it into the **Viewer**. Click the **Motion** tab, and click **Drop Shadow**.

12. The shadow helps a lot, but the **Offset** is too great. Twirl down the **Drop Shadow** triangle to adjust the drop shadow settings and change the **Offset** to **3**.

13. That's it. A four-layer effect! Congratulations. You are done. Save your work, if you wish. Quit Final Cut and take a break. That wraps up this chapter.

NOTE | Other Uses for Traveling Mattes

Traveling mattes are used a lot to put one image inside another image. Here are some other ideas to spark your creativity:

- Put video inside text for an opening title.

- Put video inside a generated shape (click the **Generator** pop-up menu, choose **Shapes**, and then choose a shape (**Circle**, **Oval**, **Rectangle**, or **Square**).

- Put a LiveType texture inside a graphic.

- Put a Photoshop image inside text to provide texture.

In other words, using a traveling matte, you can put any image or video clip inside text, a generated shape, an imported graphic, or anything else with an alpha channel.

Helpful Keyboard Shortcuts	
Shortcut	**Function**
Option+Cmd+W	Toggles audio waveforms on and off in the Timeline
B	Selects the single-clip Razor Blade tool
BB	Selects the multiple-clip Razor Blade tool
Option+P	Plays a clip that needs rendering, without first rendering it
Option+R	Renders a sequence
Cmd+R	Renders the selected clip, clips, or sequence
Double-click	(Nested sequence) Displays nest as series of individual clips
Option+double-click	(Nested sequence) Loads nested sequence into the Browser
Drag (nest), then Cmd	(Nested sequence in Browser) Converts nest into series of individual clips when Cmd-dragged into Timeline.
Cmd+A	(Timeline or Browser) Selects all clips in Timeline, or all elements in Browser
Option+C	Creates a Nest from selected clips or sequence
Option+9	Opens the Scopes window
Ctrl+Z	Toggles Range Checking for excess white levels on and off

Summary

In this chapter, you learned a variety of special effects, all revolving around filters. This only scratches the surface of what Final Cut can do, but you now know everything you need to start creating some really incredible effects. That wraps up our look at effects. In Chapter 12, you'll learn how to output your projects—to the Web, CD, DVD and videotape.

12

Output Your Project

| Techniques for Outputting Long Projects |

| Understanding Pre-Program Material | How to Stripe Tapes |

| Printing to Video | Editing to Tape | Exporting a QuickTime Movie |

| Creating Files for the Web, CD, and DVD |

| Special Cases: Exporting Audio | Special Cases: Exporting Video |

Chapter 12 Lesson

FCP HD HOT DVD

Your project is done and ready to output. This chapter teaches you how to output your project to videotape or to a wide variety of digital formats.

Similar to Chapter 3, "*Gather Your Media*," this chapter is partly an exercise in using your imagination, since your hardware configuration is probably different than mine. So, I'll show you the steps, and you can make the necessary adjustments specific to your system.

Definitions

There is a difference, to my way of thinking, between outputting and exporting. So, let me give you my definitions:

Outputting: Sending a project out of Final Cut Pro HD and onto videotape. Outputting involves converting between the digital files stored in the computer and videotape.

Exporting: Sending a project out of Final Cut, but keeping it in a digital form that can be read by the computer.

Purists will argue that DV is digital by definition, and this is true. Still, for me, I "capture" and "output" to videotape, though I "import" and "export" digital files that remain inside the computer. For me, at least, there's a difference.

Since I use these terms throughout this chapter, I wanted to explain to you at the beginning what they mean to me.

NOTE | Don't Play the Timeline for Final Output

In versions of Final Cut prior to version 4, many users, including me, got used to the idea of playing the Timeline when we wanted to record to tape. This was because the **Print to Video** and **Edit to Tape** functions were not as, um, robust as we would have liked. Many times, playing the Timeline was our only option; nothing else worked reliably.

In Final Cut Pro HD that stratagem no longer works. This is because, in order to reserve more CPU power for real-time effects and audio mixing, the default output options for playing the Timeline are set to a lower quality for both audio and video.

Although these defaults can be changed, my personal feeling is that I like having the extra horsepower for editing. So, for me, it is time to change habits and use the Print to Video and Edit to Tape functions for my final output. In addition, Apple has worked hard to eliminate the bugs that made Print to Video and Edit to Tape unreliable.

Don't spend hours making your projects perfect, only to fall short at the last minute by playing the Timeline to tape. Learn how to do it the right way—read Exercise 1.

Techniques for Outputting Long Projects

Many of the shows I edit are 30 minutes or longer. Although editing a 30- or 60-minute show in a single sequence in Final Cut is possible, I rarely do it.

Instead, I break my show up into acts (or segments) and edit each act in its own sequence. This allows me to see my individual clips more easily, without having to zoom in and out along a huge Timeline.

Then, I create a master sequence with all my acts neatly arranged with room for commercial breaks. Or, if I'm doing something without commercials, I simply butt two segments together with no break.

This practice of creating a master sequence of all the different acts makes final output to tape simple.

> ### NOTE | A Simple Technique to Improve Output
>
> Here's a quick tip that helps improve outputting: before you start the final output, do a **File > Save As** and save your project with a new name; for instance, **My Project v2**. As you will learn in the Troubleshooting section of the Appendix, "*Additional Resources*," **Save As** fixes any internal problems with your files that can mess up output.
>
> Doing a **Save As** every few days during editing is a good idea in general, just to keep project files clean. However, this is an especially good technique to make sure your outputs go smoothly.

Print to Video

In this exercise, you will learn how to output your project to tape. Specifically, this includes learning how and when to use **Print to Video**.

1. Start Final Cut and open **Chapter 12 Lesson**. It's in the **FCP Projects/FCP HOT files** folder you created at the beginning of this book. Double-click **Seq – Snowboard Final** to load it to the **Timeline**.

This is my version of the commercial you've been working on during this book, plus a few extra goodies: a modified nested sequence for the open from Chapter 11, "Filters and Keying," new transitions from Chapter 8, "Transitions–Making Change Beautiful," and audio fades from Chapter 7, "Audio–The Secret to a Great Picture."

It's time to output this to tape. First, though, a note on rendering.

NOTE | Rendering for Output

During editing, a variety of transitions and effects will cause render bars to appear over your video or audio elements. Generally, green bars mean the effect can play in real time.

Generally, that is, but not at output.

When you get ready to output your project, Final Cut renders everything. And, if you have set your render settings to lower quality–a really bad idea, which is why I haven't discussed it in this book–Final Cut will re-render *all* your effects at the highest quality.

This final rendering occurs after you complete the **Print to Video** or **Edit to Tape** dialog. And, sometimes, this rendering can take a while. You can decrease your wait time by rendering your whole sequence first.

Choose **Sequence > Render All > Both** (press **Option+R**) and make sure everything is checked.

When this render is complete, you will notice that **Print to Video** and **Edit to Tape** are ready to output much more quickly than before you did this rendering. This can especially save time if you have multiple tapes you need to create, since you are only waiting to render once, rather than every time FCP needs to output a new tape.

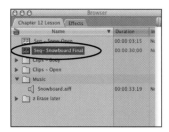

2. Go to the **Browser** and select the sequence you want to output. In this case, choose **Seq – Snowboard final**.

3. Choose **File > Print to Video**, or press **Ctrl+M**.

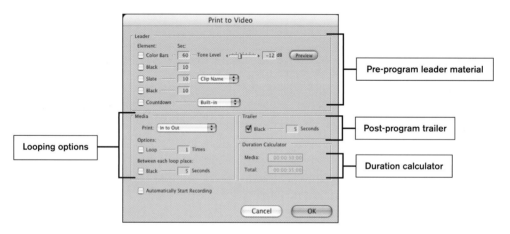

*This is the **Print to Video** dialog. If you are outputting a tape for the Client to review, or for your Aunt Joyce to show to the family, these default settings are fine, with one exception…*

NOTE | Choosing Between "Print to Video" and "Edit to Tape"

How do you decide whether to use **Print to Video** or **Edit to Tape**? Well, it all comes down to timecode.

If all you want to do is output your project to tape, **Print to Video** is your best choice.

If you need to output your project *and* have it start at a *specific* timecode on the record tape, you'll need to use **Edit to Tape**.

For most DV editors, most of the time, **Print to Video** will be fine. For editors of broadcast projects, **Edit to Tape** will most often be a better choice, as you will learn in Exercise 2.

4. Change the **Trailer** from **5** to **60** seconds.

*The **Trailer** setting determines how much black will be output by Final Cut after your sequence is complete. Five seconds is too short a time for someone to get up and turn off the tape. Sixty is more reasonable.*

(If you are outputting to VHS tape, the industry standard is to fill the remainder of the tape with black, so that the viewer never sees "snow" at the end of the tape. That assumes, of course, you are using a tape length close to the length of your program. There's no advantage to outputting two hours of black just to fill the tape.)

*A check box that's new with FCP HD is **Automatically Start Recording**. Rendering can take a long time, in fact, probably more time than you'd like to sit and wait. By checking this check box, if Final Cut has machine control over your deck (as is true with virtually all FireWire-connected decks), then, it will switch your deck into Record mode 3 seconds after rendering is complete. This means you don't need to wait; it can all be automatic.*

Very cool. Except… um, I like watching this last playback to tape. Just to be sure nothing goes wrong. Not, of course, that it ever does. Much. So, I check this box, but I don't leave the room.

5. Click **OK**. Behind the scenes, Final Cut does a final mixdown of your audio to a stereo file and makes sure all video has been rendered.

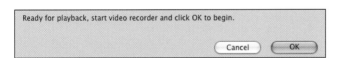

6. This dialog appears when FCP is ready to output. Press **Record** on your deck or camera, click OK in this dialog, and watch your movie.

7. When the recording is done, Final Cut will switch your deck out of Record. Extra black at the tail (end) of your video is *always* a good idea. The amount of black at the end is determined by the number you entered for the Trailer in step 4.

Ta-DA! Finished. Whew!

8. That's it for **Print to Video**. In the next exercise, you'll learn about a more sophisticated way to lay video back to tape, but for now, take a break. Quit Final Cut, if you wish. Otherwise, keep this project open, as you'll use it again. Because you made no changes, there's nothing you need to save to disk.

Pre-Program Material

HOWEVER... if you are planning to take your tape to duplication, broadcast, a trade show, or archiving, there are a few more steps you should complete before pressing the **Record** button on your tape deck or camera.

When I use **Print to Video**, these are the settings I use. Let's take a look at what they do and why you should use them.

In the top half of the screen are the controls for pre-program, or Leader, material. For a long, long time, standard industry practice has organized the beginning of a tape as follows:

- 60 seconds of color bars

- 10 seconds of black

- 10 seconds of slate (keep reading, I'll explain it shortly)

- 10 seconds of black

- Program start

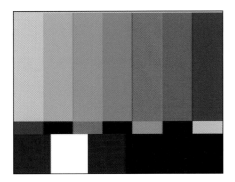

Color bars display an engineering test signal that allows a tape to be configured on playback so that the colors it plays back match the colors you recorded when you output your sequence. Recording 60 seconds of color bars allows an engineer sufficient time to properly set up your tape. Color bars have been used in broadcasting for decades. There's a good reason. Without them, there's no guarantee that the colors that play back from your tape will match the colors you recorded.

In the days of live television and playback from tape decks, the last 10 seconds of black were replaced by a countdown. These days, with everything playing back instantly from servers, countdowns are no longer necessary. (Sigh… I miss them.)

Along with color bars (called "bars" by those "in the know") goes **tone**. Tone is a 1000-cycle tone set at a fixed reference volume level. These reference levels are standardized by tape format, so that an engineer can set the tone at the proper level for playback. The default output level for tone in Final Cut is −12 dB.

Reference Audio Tone Levels	
Recording Tape Format	**Tone Level**
VHS	Output from Final Cut at −12, record at 0 dB.
DV (MiniDV, DVCAM, DVCPRO 25)	−12 dB
DigiBetacam, DVCPRO 50, DVCPRO HD	−20 dB
Betacam SP	Output from Final Cut at −12, record at 0 dB.

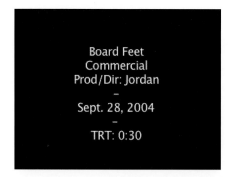

Slate identifies your program. At a minimum, it should include a title and a running time (abbreviated **TRT**, for **T**otal **R**unning **T**ime). Most professional slates also include the name of the client/producer/director, the date the show was finished, and anything else relevant from an engineering point of view.

To create a slate, change the pop-up menu next to Slate to **Text** and type your information in the small text window on the right. Use hyphens (-) when you want to put a space between lines.

Running time is the length your show runs from fade up to fade down, excluding any commercial breaks. The **Duration Calculator** in the lower-right corner of this dialog helps give you the answer. The top line shows actual program running time (30 seconds in the case of this commercial); the second line shows total running time including all the pre-program material, 1:40:02, in this example.

One other neat goodie is the **Media** section. Many times, when I create materials for trade shows, the client wants it to repeat over and over… and over. Using these check boxes means I only need to create the sequence once, and Final Cut will automatically play it back on output as many times (**Loop**) and with as many seconds of black between each repetition (**Black**) as I want. I've used this often and it works great.

Striping Tapes

In order to use **Edit to Tape**, you must first record black and timecode on your tape, in a process called *striping*, or *recording black and code*.

What striping does is feed black video, and silent audio, from Final Cut to your deck, so you can record it to tape. (FYI, Final Cut doesn't supply timecode to the tape; timecode signals are actually created by your deck. Final Cut simply tells your deck to generate and record timecode on the tape.) The benefits to striping your tapes are:

- You have continuous timecode from beginning to end of the tape—no timecode breaks.

- If you are recycling an old tape, all old program material is erased.

- Unlike simply recording a tape with a lens cap on the camera, you record audio black, not extraneous room noise.

- On high-end DV decks (you know if you have one because they cost close to $8000) and professional Betacam videotape decks, you can preset the timecode so it starts at a specific time—most often, 00:58:20:00.

Now there is a raging debate (well, OK, a few of us are kicking the idea around) that striping tapes may not be beneficial to everyone all the time.

So, here's my take on the issue:

- I stripe tapes to be shot by an inexperienced cameraperson. I will not stripe a tape being shot by a professional cameraperson.

- I stripe all tapes that I use for final output of my projects.

Here's how to stripe a tape:

1. Connect your deck and be sure that Final Cut Pro can control it.

2. Put in a blank tape. Be sure the little record-lockout slider is set to **Record**.

3. Choose **File > Edit to Tape**.

4. Click the small square at the top center that looks like a squashed centipede. (It's supposed to be a film frame.)

5. Current Settings matches the video output to the tape to the current video settings of your **Timeline**.

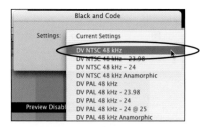

To send a different video format to the tape, select it from the pop-up menu. These settings vary depending upon which deck and capture card you are using. DV NTSC 48 kHz is the DV standard for North America; DV PAL 48 kHz is the default for the rest of the world.

A second dialog appears if you have a deck that allows presetting timecode (which includes virtually all Beta decks and very high-end DV decks). Presetting allows you to specify the starting timecode for the tape, as well as whether you want it to be drop-frame or non-drop-frame. If you can set timecode, a good number to use is 00:58:20:00. You'll understand why in the next exercise.

Virtually no DV camera or deck allows presetting timecode. In this case, all timecode starts at 0:00:00:00. Also, virtually all DV timecode is drop-frame.

6. This dialog appears, giving you one last warning that you are about to erase everything on your tape. When you click **OK**, the recording starts automatically.

7. In the event you need to abort the recording, this dialog reminds you to press the **Esc** key. Otherwise, let the tape record completely. When it's finished, Final Cut will rewind to the beginning of the tape.

2. ————————Edit to Tape

In this exercise, you need to send this snowboard commercial to a broadcast station for airing. They require that your commercial start exactly at timecode 1:00:00:00 on the tape. So, here, you will learn a more advanced way to output your project: **Edit to Tape**.

The key point to keep in mind about Edit to Tape is that it *requires* you to have timecode already recorded on the tape.

1. Start Final Cut and open **Chapter 12 Lesson**, if it isn't open already. Double-click **Seq – Snowboard Final** to load it to the **Timeline**.

2. Using **Edit to Tape** is straightforward. Start by choosing **File > Edit to Tape**.

3. Enter the timecode number of where you want the recording to *start* on the tape (the **In** of the tape) in the lower-left text box. This process and location is identical to entering an **In** in the **Viewer**. In this case, the **In** is set to **1:00:00:00**. (By the way, the **J**, **K**, and **L** keys work in the **Edit to Tape** window, too.)

4. Choose the **Mastering Settings** tab at the top of the window. Set up any pre-program material, similar to **Print to Video**—the settings are the same.

5. Select the sequence you want to output to tape from the **Browser** and *drag* it to the **Edit to Tape** window. Drop it on the **Assemble** overlay.

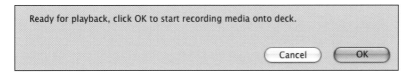

6. Click **OK** in this dialog to start the output process. If you need to abort, press the **Esc** key.

And that's it. Your edit to tape is done.

NOTE | Edit to Tape Options Are Limited for DV

In the world of linear editing, which means tape-to-tape, there are two types of edits: Assemble and Insert. Naturally, the word "Insert" means something different in linear editing than it does in nonlinear editing.

Why should life be easy?

Assemble edit: At the point of the edit, the deck cleanly switches into Record mode and performs a technically invisible edit. Timecode continues without a break. Audio and video edit seamlessly. At the end of the edit, however, there will be a break in timecode, along with a break in video and audio. This is sometimes referred to as a "clean In and dirty Out edit."

An Assemble edit is the only edit a DV deck or camera can make. An Assemble edit edits video, audio, and timecode simultaneously.

Insert edit: At the point of the edit, the deck cleanly switches into Record mode and performs a technically invisible edit. Timecode continues without a break. Audio and video edit seamlessly. At the end of the edit, the audio, video, and timecode switch out of the edit smoothly. This is sometimes referred to as a "clean In and clean Out edit."

A professional-grade videotape deck can make both Assemble and Insert edits. Insert edits are most often used to replace a shot within an already edited and output sequence. An Insert edit can edit any combination of video, audio, or timecode (video-only, audio-only, video and audio, and so on).

"But, Wait A Minute...!"

I hear you exclaim, "There's something wrong here."

Well, yeah. I'm playing a little fast and loose with the truth. Everything I've told you about using **Edit to Tape** is true. *Except*, on all DV decks that cost less than about $8000, you can only start timecode at 0:00:00:00. This means you can't stripe a tape to start at 1:00:00:00.

And why did the broadcast station want 1:00:00:00 in the first place?

All broadcast programs start at 1:00:00:00 on tape because starting at this time makes it very easy for the broadcaster to time the length of a show just by looking at the drop-frame timecode. No calculator required. This has been true for at least the last 50 years.

So, if you need to output a tape for broadcast, you'll need to buy a tape with the correct timecode on it from a professional videotape supply house, or make friends with the engineers at the broadcast station and have them stripe the tape for you.

Also, I mentioned earlier that most professional tapes start at timecode 00:58:20:00. This is because if your show starts at 1:00:00:00, you need to leave room before that for the pre-program leader material, such as bars and tone. Here's the timing of a "normal" broadcast tape:

00:58:20:00	Timecode and audio/video black start
00:58:30:00	Color bars and tone start
00:59:30:00	10 seconds of black starts
00:59:40:00	10 seconds of slate starts
00:59:50:00	10 seconds of black starts
01:00:00:00	Program starts.

In my programs, I sometimes build these pre-program materials into my main sequence, and other times I use the Mastering settings. Depends upon my mood.

If you are editing to a professional deck (specifically for an Insert edit), check in the Final Cut manual about editing settings.

Specifically, you need to set this pop-up to **Editing**.

Then you need to select, using these three control points, the combination of timecode, video, and audio you want to edit.

However, as I said near the beginning, if your medium of choice is DV, most of the time you'll be just fine using **Print to Video**.

So, You Wanna Be an Export Expert?

Whether you want to export your sequence for the Web, CD, or DVD, there are a lot of options, but really only one choice: export as a QuickTime movie (**File > Export > QuickTime Movie**).

Here's the short answer to why.

Using Final Cut to create optimized, compressed files is like using a hammer to drive screws; it will work, but it's the wrong tool for the job. Final Cut does great exports, but other software does better compression.

Creating movies for the Web always involves creating multiple versions (for slow, medium, and fast connections) of multiple formats (QuickTime, Real, and Windows Media). This means exporting the same file from Final Cut over and over again.

You can do it, but life is too short.

Instead, use Final Cut to export one file, at the highest quality, then move that file into Sorenson Squeeze, discreet cleaner, Hip Flix, Compressor, or the compression program of your choice. In all cases, these do a far better job of compression than Final Cut, plus they can create all the versions you need at once through batch processing. While you are out sipping lattes at Starbuck's—or wherever world-class editors hang out in your part of the woods—your computer can be back at the office doing all the work.

Helpful Export Table

What the File Is For	What You Export	Where It Goes
Web	QuickTime movie	Your favorite compression software.
CD	QuickTime movie	Your favorite compression software.
iDVD	QuickTime movie	iDVD will compress it.
DVD Studio Pro (<1 hour)	QuickTime movie	DVD Studio Pro will compress it.
DVD Studio Pro (>1 hour)	QuickTime movie	Compressor will compress it.
LiveType	LiveType export	LiveType (see Exercise 4).
Soundtrack	Soundtrack export	Soundtrack (see Exercise 5).
ProTools	OMF	ProTools or Deck (see Exercise 4).
Other video editing	EDL	Other video editing program.

NOTE | When Should You Use File > Export QuickTime Conversion?

Only when you need to quickly compress a file and don't need the highest quality or the smallest file size. Or when you need to export a still frame. Or when you need to convert a sequence into a special format, like a Targa sequence.

In other words, only in special circumstances.

Exporting a QuickTime movie always exports at the highest quality (8- or 10-bit video). Exporting as QuickTime Conversion limits your video to 8-bit. This will be noticeable if you are doing lots of compositing or gradient color work. DV, by the way, is always 8-bit video, so the effects of QuickTime Conversion will be less with DV source material.

QuickTime Conversion can be very helpful, especially in a pinch. But it should not be your first choice.

3. ——————Exporting a QuickTime Movie

In this exercise, you will learn the best way to export a sequence for the Web, CD, or DVD. And, in all cases, it's the same answer: export your sequence as a QuickTime movie. This exercise explains why and how.

1. Start Final Cut and open **Chapter 12 Lesson**, if it isn't open already. Double-click **Seq – Snowboard Final** to load it to the **Timeline**.

2. There are two ways to select a sequence for export:

• Load it into the **Timeline** and select the **Timeline**.

• Choose the name of the sequence in the **Browser** and select the **Browser**.

Pick one of these two.

3. Choose **File > Export > QuickTime Movie**.

4. Give your movie a name. (QuickTime movies use the extension **.mov**.)

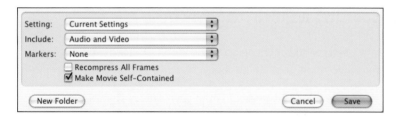

Current Settings will output your movie matching the settings in your sequence.

Unless you have changed your Render Settings, which I do not advise, you do not need to Recompress All Frames.

Make Movie Self-Contained is often confusing. If you are compressing the movie on your system and you haven't deleted any of the assets, uncheck this box. If you are sending the movie to someone else to compress, planning to archive this movie for a long time, or planning to delete some of the media files before compressing, leave this box checked.

When this box is unchecked, you are creating a Reference movie. This is a relatively tiny file that contains all the audio from your sequence, plus pointers that point to the existing media files on your hard disk. Reference movies are about one-twelfth the size of a self-contained movie. Reference movies export 10 to 15 times faster than a self-contained movie, as well. The one trick with using a reference movie is that it must reference the original media files stored on your hard disk, meaning that it will play fine on your machine, but lose the "link" to the referenced media files if you try to play the movie elsewhere.

Checking this box creates a Self-Contained movie, which contains all your media in a single file, which can be played, or compressed on any system (Mac or PC) that can play a QuickTime movie.

By the way, both these formats work fine for compressing a video for the Web. All compressed files are always self-contained. So, whether you start with a Reference movie or a Self-Contained movie, the end result is the same. For this reason, I almost always use Reference movies when outputting for compression to the Web.

5. If you want to export DVD chapter markers for inclusion in iDVD or DVD Studio Pro, choose **Chapter Markers** from the **Markers** pop-up menu.

6. Click **Save**, and you are done. Quit Final Cut if you need a break. Otherwise, keep things open—you will use this file in the remaining exercises.

Special Cases: Exporting Audio

In this exercise, you will learn how to export audio for special cases, such as Soundtrack, OMF files, and AIF files.

1. Start Final Cut and open **Chapter 12 Lesson**, if it isn't open already. Double-click **Seq – Snowboard Final** to load it to the **Timeline**. Leave the **Timeline** selected.

2. You can export a movie to Soundtrack two ways:

• File > Export > **QuickTime Movie**

• File > Export > **For Soundtrack**

The **For Soundtrack** option automatically sets the file output settings for Soundtrack.

As usual, select the sequence in the **Timeline** or in the **Browser**, then choose **File > Export > For Soundtrack**.

The screen that appears is very similar to the **File > Export > QuickTime Movie** screen, except at the bottom.

*Final Cut preset some of the choices for you: it selected **Audio Scoring Markers**, so your Soundtrack markers are included in the export, and made it a **Reference** movie (not **Self-Contained**) since it figured you weren't going to delete any media because the project wasn't finished.*

Audio scoring, or Soundtrack, markers are markers that are created inside Final Cut, and viewed inside Soundtrack. These markers are labels that can indicate where you want music to start, or end, or actually, anything—they are just labels.

3. Open **Soundtrack** and *drag* the movie from wherever you saved it (I generally save my temporary movies to the **Desktop** to make them easy to find) into the **Video** tab at the top center of Soundtrack.

From there, you can watch the movie while you compose the music.

That's how to export from FCP to Soundtrack. But, sometimes, you need to export only the audio files. In this case, you have two choices:

  • *Export an AIF file*
  • *Export an OMF file*

*An **AIF** (or AIFF) file can be played anywhere. It is the native format of the Mac, as well as all CD audio. An AIF file merges all the clips in a track into a single audio file for the entire track. The biggest advantage to AIF is that all audio programs can play them. Plus, an AIF export will include all volume changes and filters in the audio.*

*An **OMF** file is a special-purpose file that is used for transferring audio specifically for mixing from Final Cut into audio programs such as DigiDesign's ProTools or Bias Inc.'s Deck. The key advantage of using OMFs is that all clips remain distinct and editable, each with its own set of handles. The biggest disadvantage to OMF is that only a limited number of audio programs support them. In addition, exporting OMF files from Final Cut does not include any volume changes or filters.*

4. To export AIF files, choose **File > Export > Audio to AIFF(s)**. The standard export dialog box appears, except for different settings at the bottom.

The standard sample rate and sample size (or bit-depth) for DV and broadcast video is 48 kHz, 16-bit. So the initial two choices are fine.

*If you want to export your audio as dual mono, that is with both channels linked and panned to the center, choose **Channel Grouped**. If you want to export your audio with all the odd-numbered channels panned to the left and all the even-numbered channels panned to the right, choose **Stereo Mix**.*

*Final Cut exports all audio tracks whose visibility indicator is **on**. (So, if you want to export individual tracks, turn the visibility light **off** for all tracks you don't want to export.)*

5. To export OMF files, choose **File > Export > Audio to OMF**. The OMF settings dialog appears. Again, the settings of 48 kHz and 16-bit are fine. Generally, I like working with longer handles, so I set **Handle Length** to **5:00**. This provides for more flexibility in the audio mix.

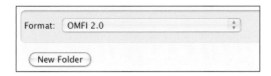

*The default OMF file format is **2.0**, which appears at the bottom of the Save dialog. This, too, is fine.*

6. Give the export file a name, and you are done.

Again, you don't need to save your work in this project, because you haven't made any changes. Quit Final Cut if you need a break. Otherwise, it's time to move on to learning about some special case video exports.

5. ———————Special Cases: Exporting Video

In this exercise, you will learn how to export video for LiveType and Compressor, as well as some suggestions on improving your results with Compressor.

1. Start Final Cut and open **Chapter 12 Lesson**, if it isn't open already. Double-click **Seq – Snowboard Final** to load it to the **Timeline**. Leave the **Timeline** selected.

2. To export a sequence to LiveType, choose **File > Export > For LiveType**.

This dialog is just like the others you've seen earlier, except for the settings at the bottom. Notice that this time, Final Cut is including all the markers in the export. In fact, all four Final Cut marker types display in LiveType:

- *Generic marker*
- *Chapter marker*
- *Compression marker*
- *Soundtrack marker*

*And, again, Final Cut sets the file to be a **Reference** movie (that is, not **Self-Contained**), because you'll be using this movie on your system simply as a reference within LiveType.*

3. Give the export file a name and click **OK**.

4. To import the movie into LiveType, open **LiveType**, choose **File > Place Background Movie**, select your movie and click **Open**. The video from your movie shows up on the **Timeline**, ready for compositing.

5. Exporting a sequence for Compressor is a bit more complex. Again, select your sequence, either in the **Browser** or **Timeline**. Then, choose **File > Export > Using Compressor**.

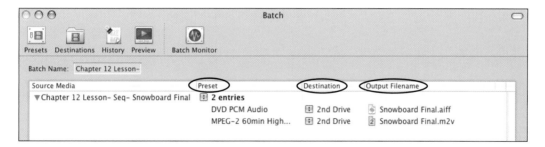

6. Compressor starts, and your sequence automatically loads. From the **Preset** pop-up menu, choose a compression setting. The rule is: choose the setting that is closest to, *but longer than*, the length of your sequence.

So, for a 30-second commercial, choose **60 Minute High-Quality**.

For a 70-minute program, choose **90 Minute High-Quality**.

For a 100-minute program, choose **120 minute High-Quality**.

If your video is in a 4:3 aspect ratio, choose **High-Quality**. *If it is in 16:9 aspect ratio, choose* **High-Quality Widescreen**.

By the way, I always use the **High-Quality** *setting. For me, the length of time it takes to compress a video is never the issue; making it look as good as it can is always far more important.*

---

7. Set the **Destination** to where you want the file stored. On my system, I've created a folder on my second hard disk called **Compressed Files** and use that as the default destination for Compressor.

The main reason to use Compressor is that you want to create high-quality MPEG-2 video files (which is the standard video format for DVD) to import into DVD Studio Pro. (iDVD won't read MPEG-2 files.)

One of the tricks of DVD Studio Pro is that it automatically links audio and video files that have the same file name to the left *of the extension. So, I always change the* **Output** *file name so the audio and video file names match.*

---

8. So, in this case, change the name of each file to **Snowboard Final** and click **Submit**.

The actual compression is done by a background application. Batch Monitor is only there to display the status of your job.

The first half of the job is compressing the audio, the last half is compressing the video. The progress bar displays the amount of the job completed.

While this compression is occurring, Final Cut is exporting each individual frame. It's this dual role of exporting and compressing that makes this take so much time. For me, the benefits of exporting directly out of Final Cut do not outweigh the time it takes.

Instead, I export my sequence as a Reference QuickTime movie, and drag it into Compressor. I can then set my compression settings as I just described and compress the file, without tying up Final Cut. I've found this to be a much, much *faster way to operate.*

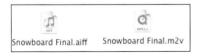

Snowboard Final.aiff   Snowboard Final.m2v

When the compression is done, look on the Desktop and you'll see two files: an audio AIFF and video M2V. These are the files that get imported into DVD Studio Pro for your DVD. These two files get combined in the final stage of creating a DVD, in a process called "multiplexing."

9. And that's it. You've covered all the major elements of outputting and exporting out of Final Cut Pro. Don't save your work, you haven't changed anything. Quit Final Cut if you need to take a break.

NOTE | Exporting a Still Frame

If you need a refresher on how to create and export a still frame of video, please refer to Exercise 5 in Chapter 10.

Helpful Keyboard Shortcuts	
Shortcut	**Function**
Option+R	Renders all clips in a sequence, depending upon what render elements are checked in Sequence > Render All.
Cmd+R	Renders a selected clip, series of clips, or sequence.
Ctrl+M	Opens Print to Video dialog.
Shift+N	Creates a still frame of the frame of video currently under the active playhead. The still frame appears in the Viewer.

Summary

That's it. You've completed a project from beginning to end—capture to output. All that's left is wrapping up the details and archiving your work. And that's next, in Chapter 13, "*Archiving Your Project.*"

I3

Archiving Your Project

| Archiving Your Project | Changing Reel Names |
| Using Save As | Deleting Render Files |
| Backing Up Project Files and Trashing Media |
| Storing Video Tapes | Autosave Vault Files |
| Restoring an Old Project | Exploring Media Manager |

Chapter I3 Lesson
Offline Project

FCP HD HOT DVD

Your project's done. The client's check has cleared the bank. It's time to archive your project and free up some hard disk space.

In this chapter, you will learn how to prepare a project for archiving, what to save and what to throw out, and what to do when you need to restore an old project for reediting. Finally, you'll get an introduction to the Media Manager, along with some examples of how to use it.

Archiving Your Project

Because of the wide variations in system installation and hardware, it isn't possible to provide precise step-by-step instructions on how to archive your project. Instead, I'll show you the process and the screens, so that you can make the necessary adjustments for your system.

The goal in archiving your project is to organize your project file so that sequences are properly named, reel numbers are correct, and the file is in good condition. Then, save everything that can't be easily replaced, and trash everything else.

Here are the steps, all organized in one place:

1. Verify that all sequence names make sense, and delete all sequences not used in the final project.

2. Verify that all reel names are correct, and change those that aren't.

3. Do a **Save As** on the project file.

4. Trash all project-related render files, using **Render Manager**.

5. Back up project files and all non-timecode-based media to CD (or DVD).

6. Trash all project-related timecode-based media, using **Finder**.

7. Remove all project files from the computer.

Now that the heat of battle has passed, take a look at all the different sequences you created. Did you use all of them? If not, delete those that are not necessary to the project. It is easier to delete them now, while they are fresh in your mind, than to spend hours trying to figure out which are the good versions when you return to this project in the future.

In a related vein, be sure your sequence names make sense. Make them less cryptic. If you gave this project to another editor, would the names make sense? Making sequence names easier to understand is a huge help if you need to redo this project in the future.

Once you've reviewed and corrected your sequence names, it's time to make sure all reel numbers are correct. As you will learn later in this chapter, Final Cut makes it easy to recapture material from videotape, using Batch Capture. However, in order for Batch Capture to work, your reel names must be accurate.

 MOVIE | Archive.mov

For a tutorial on using the **Render Manager** and **Media Manager**, please view **Archive.mov**, one of the QuickTime movies included on the **FCP HD HOT** DVD.

I. ───────Changing Reel Names

In this exercise, you will learn how to change reel names in the Browser.

1. Start **Final Cut**, if it isn't running already, and open **Chapter 13 Lesson**. This is the same project you used in Chapter 12, "*Output Your Project.*" This project file may need rendering.

2. Go to the **Browser** and scroll right until you find the **Reel** column. Click the **Reel** column header and drag it *left* until the **Reel** column is next to the **Name** column.

3. Notice that **Blue sky** has no reel name and **Down mountain** has the wrong one.

4. To change a reel name, double-click in the **Reel** field and enter a new name. To start, change the reel name for **Blue sky** to **HOT_01**.

Reel names are part of the timecode data, which is stored permanently in the media file on your hard disk, along with timecode, audio, and video data. This data allows Final Cut to properly identify a media file when it is imported into a new project, by reading both the timecode and reel name. This dialog box appears whenever you modify a reel name, alerting you that the new reel name will be recorded in the media file.

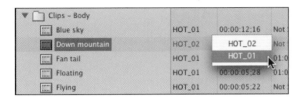

5. Another way to change a reel name is to **Ctrl+click** the **Reel** field and choose the correct reel name from the pop-up menu. Change the **Down mountain** reel to **HOT_01**, as well.

6. Verify that all other reel names are set to **HOT_01**. If not, change them. Once verification is complete, this exercise is done. Keep the lesson file open.

2. _____Protecting Your Project Using Save As

In this exercise, you will learn how to use Save As to create a backup of your project files, and you'll also use it to perform final maintenance before archiving your project.

1. Open **Chapter 13 Lesson**, if it isn't open already. This is the same file you used in Exercise 1.

2. Choose **File > Save As** and save the project using a new name. (I often just use the letters **v2** or **v3**, indicating the version number of the project file.)

The benefit to using Save As is twofold: it provides a backup of your file in case something happens to the first one, and Final Cut uses this as an opportunity to straighten out any internal numbers or pointers that may be flaky.

Although you can easily make a backup of your file in the Finder, this internal repair can only be accomplished when Final Cut does a Save As.

I find myself using this procedure as a backup system during a project, just before final output and just prior to archiving the project.

3. When the **Save As** is done, it's time to delete your render files. Keep everything open for the next exercise.

3. ———————**Deleting Render Files**

In this exercise, you will learn how to use the Render Manager. The Render Manager is a tool inside Final Cut that tracks and deletes render files. One of the benefits to using the organizational system outlined in Chapter 1, "*Get Organized,*" is that it helps the Render Manager track every render file for every project.

1. Open **Chapter 13 Lesson**, if it isn't open already. This is the same file you used in Exercise 1.

2. Choose **Tools > Render Manager**.

3. The current project is always listed separately, along with a folder titled **Additional Render Files**. Twirl down the **Additional Render Files** from time to time to make sure you don't have old render files taking up space.

*As I was writing this chapter, I ran Render Manager to prepare the screen shots for this exercise. And I discovered that I had gigabytes of space tied up with render files of projects that were long gone. I, um, don't check Render Manager as often as I should. Since I was using my system of keeping all my media in one folder (**FCP Media**), Render Manager was happily keeping track of everything, so it was simply a matter of a few mouse clicks and I got 9 GB of space back.*

Sigh... It's nice when I pay attention to my own advice.

4. Clicking the **Size** column header allows you to sort files by size. Click **Size** twice to sort in descending order.

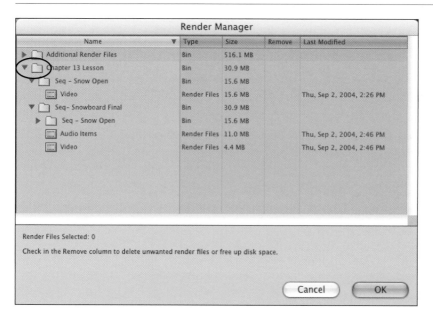

5. In this case, twirl down **Chapter 13 Lesson**. Notice that render files are grouped, first, by project, then by sequence, and, finally, by whether they are audio or video render files.

6. Because you want to get rid of *all* render files related to this project, check once in the **Remove** column in the same line as **Chapter 13 Lesson**. All render files related to that project are flagged (checked) for deletion.

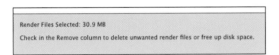

7. At the bottom of the screen is a message explaining how much disk space is involved—in this case, **30.9 MB** of space. (Your file sizes may be different.) Click **OK**, and your render files are gone.

*In the event you made a mistake and trashed the wrong render files, you won't be able to **Undo** this. However, just open your sequence and choose **Sequence > Render All**, and Final Cut will rebuild all missing render files.*

*By the way, for those who are curious, render files are stored near your Capture Scratch folder. If you set your system up as I suggested in Chapter 1, "Get Organized," the path is **[Second hard disk] > FCP Media > Audio Render Files**, for audio render files, and **[Second hard disk] > FCP Media > Render Files**, for video render files.*

8. That's it for this exercise. Now, it's time to back up your project. To do this, quit Final Cut so all open files are closed.

4. Backing Up Project Files and Trashing Media

In this exercise, you will learn what project files to back up and which to trash. However, this system won't work with the exercise files for this book, because I needed to change how they were organized in order to distribute them on the DVD. Rereading Chapter 1, *"Get Organized,"* will be helpful in understanding how this system works.

1. Be sure Final Cut is not running, so that all open project files are closed.

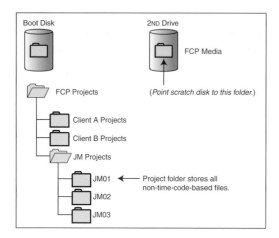

Back in Chapter 1, I described a system where you create a folder, called **FCP Projects**, which serves as the master folder for all your projects.

Inside this folder, I suggested you create a separate folder for each Final Cut project. Here's where that organization system pays off.

If you follow those instructions, inside that project folder you stored all your graphics, music, audio effects, animation, LiveType projects, Soundtrack files… everything related to the project except *timecode-based media*. That is, everything except what is on your video tapes.

2. All you need to do now is copy that project folder from your computer to a CD or DVD, if there isn't enough room on a CD. Generally, these files are very small, compared to media.

Final Cut projects don't contain any media. Instead, all clips are referenced using pointers that "point" from Final Cut's Browser or Timeline to the actual media files stored on your hard disk. Each pointer keeps track of the full path and file name of each media file.

Because all your non-timecode files have been stored in this project folder throughout the project, those pointers, or links, remain unbroken when you copy this project folder. This means that if you need to restore the project, everything is right where Final Cut expects it to be, without reconnecting files.

3. Finally, after all render files are trashed and all projects files safely backed up, you can trash your media files. This too, is easy, if you are using the system outlined in Chapter 1. Go to **[Second hard disk] > FCP Media > Capture Scratch**. Inside it you will find a folder for every project for which you captured media.

Because you set your Scratch Disk to **FCP Media** at the start of the project, and never changed it, every time you captured media it all went into the **FCP Media** folder, sorted into a media folder named the same as your project. Now, when it comes time to trash the media for this project, just select the **FCP Media > Capture Scratch > [project name]** folder for the project and drag it to the **Trash**. All project media clips will be trashed, and you just got a lot of hard disk space back.

4. So, to summarize, all project files go into the project folder, which gets backed up to CD. All render files get trashed, because they can easily be recalculated by Final Cut whenever you need them. All media files get trashed because Final Cut can easily recapture them from the original video tapes whenever you need to reedit the project, as you will learn shortly.

The key point is to archive your media on video tapes, not digital media. Video tapes last longer and are easier to recapture than keeping stacks of hard disks lying around.

NOTE | Storing Video Tapes

Magnetic video tapes have a shelf life of 20 to 25 years, provided you store them away from extremes of heat, light, cold, and moisture.

Tapes will last longer and play back better if they are stored on edge, rather than flat. Storing on edge decreases the effects of gravity on the tape's oxide particles and the earth's magnetic field on the magnetic signals recorded on the tape.

Even better, try to store the tape wound all the way to the head or tail of the tape. First, this assures even winding and stacking throughout the tape; second, over the long term, storing a tape wound all the way to the end offers more protection to the magnetic signals.

NOTE | What Happens to Autosave Vault Files?

```
☑ Autosave Vault
   Save a copy every:    15  minutes
       Keep at most:     20  copies per project
        Maximum of:      15  projects
```

One of the nice features of the Autosave Vault is that you don't need to worry about trashing old Vault files. In Chapter 2, "*Understanding the Final Cut Pro Interface*," you configured the Autosave Vault so that as new projects came in, old projects got trashed automatically. At the time, the setting I was most concerned with was **Save a Copy Every**—and we set it to **15** minutes. This means that Final Cut makes a backup, protection copy every 15 minutes.

Now that you are at the end of a project, the other two settings are more relevant.

Keep at Most 20 Copies means that Final Cut keeps only the 20 most recent protection copies. When it saves the 21st, the first gets trashed, the 22nd trashes the second, and so on. This means that the amount of hard disk space the Autosave Vault needs stays pretty much constant.

Maximum of 15 Projects means that Final Cut keeps only the 15 most recent projects. When the 16th project starts, all of project 1 gets trashed. (Obviously, if you are working on more than 15 projects at the same time, you should increase this suggested level.) Again, this means that the amount of hard disk space required by the Autosave Vault remains fairly constant.

So, set the Vault and don't worry about it. It pretty much takes care of itself.

5. ———————**Restoring an Old Project**

In this exercise, you will learn how to restore a project from backup, how to reconnect media, and how to use Batch Capture.

> **1.** Start **Final Cut**, if it isn't running already, and open **Offline Project**. This is the same file you used earlier in Chapter 13, except all the clips are now offline.

NOTE | Definitions: Offline vs. Online

There are *two* definitions of each of these words, depending upon context. To help you keep them straight, here they are.

Offline (1): A low-resolution version of a videotape format, used in the initial stages of editing to reduce file space requirements. For example, DV is used as the offline file format for editing a DigiBetacam master.

Online (1): A high-resolution version of a videotape format, used to create the final, high-quality version of a project for release.

Offline (2): A clip in Final Cut that is not connected to a media file on the disk, either because the media file has not been captured, or because the media file has been moved or renamed, thus breaking the link between the clip in Final Cut and the media file on disk.

Online (2): A clip in Final Cut that is connected to its media file on disk.

When a clip is offline, meaning it can't find the media file on your hard disk that it is linked to, it shows up in the Browser with a red line through the icon.

An offline clip in the Timeline shows up as white.

If the clips are offline because the media is missing—for instance this is an old project and the media files no longer exist—you need to redigitize the media back into your computer in a process called "recapture."

2. To do this, select the clips you want to recapture, and choose **File > Batch Capture**. This is where having accurate reel names and timecode makes this process dead easy.

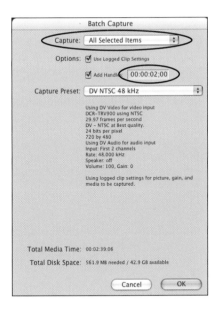

3. The **Batch Capture** window opens. The pop-up menu is set to capture all selected clips. The default handle setting is **0:00**. I always want handles, so I set this to **2:00**. Then click **OK**.

4. This dialog prompts you to put in a tape for capture. Notice that it uses the reel names you entered for each clip. Put in the correct tape and click **Continue**. Final Cut starts at the beginning of the tape and captures clips as fast as it can cue the tape.

Sigh... I love that part.

This batch capture system works great as long as your reel names are correct and there are no breaks in timecode. If you forgot to make sure your reel names are accurate (something you will only do once) or have lots of timecode breaks, you will need to recapture each of these clips manually. And that's such a painful process, I don't even want to think about it. It would be easier to just start over.

5. In this case, though, the media files for this project are on your hard disk, so you just need to reconnect them. Reconnection is necessary whenever Final Cut loses track of a media file. Normally, it doesn't lose track. However, if you move a media file, rename the file, rename the folder it's in, or move a folder containing media files, Final Cut will need your help to reconnect it.

To reconnect the files in the offline project, select all the files you need to reconnect in either the **Browser** *or* **Timeline***.*

6. Choose **File > Reconnect Media**. The dialog that opens asks you to specify what you are looking to find. In this case, you are looking for offline files, so the default setting is correct. Click **OK**.

By the way, I only reconnect an online file when I've made changes to it outside of Final Cut, or if I mistakenly connected the wrong media file to a clip. Also, I never reconnect render files, I always re-render them. It's faster.

Final Cut attempts to find the missing file by looking for its file name on all the hard disks connected to your computer. (The file name is the one you gave it when you first logged, or captured, the clip.) If it finds the missing file, it selects it and displays it in this dialog.

*In this case, all the missing files are stored in the **FCP HOT files > Media > Snowboard** folder, except for the music, which is stored in **FCP HOT Files > Media > Music**.*

7. Reconnect the file by confirming that the name of the selected file (or the file you selected) in the upper portion of this dialog matches the name of the file Final Cut is displaying in the lower-left corner, then choose **Continue**.

*In the event Final Cut can't find the file, it may be because the file name changed. If this is the case, uncheck **Matched Name Only**, select the correct file, and click **Choose**.*

*If there are other missing files stored in the same folder, checking **Reconnect All Files in Relative Path** allows Final Cut to automatically connect all the files it finds in the same folder—provided that their file names match what Final Cut expects.*

*Because the files on the **Browser** are related to the clips in the **Timeline**, in what Final Cut calls a master–affiliate relationship, the offline **Timeline** clips should automatically relink once you finish linking clips in the **Browser**.*

*A **Browser** clip is automatically a master clip the first time it appears in the **Browser**. **Timeline** clips are affiliate clips. An affiliate clip is linked to the master clip via its metadata. In other words, **Timeline** clips are related to the **Browser** based on clip name, reel name, timecode, and auxiliary timecode. Changing one of these attributes in one file changes the same attribute in all related files.*

8. If any Timeline clips don't relink, select the unlinked clips, choose **File > Reconnect Media**, and repeat this process.

9. Once all clips are linked, you are done. Close this project, and don't save changes, since this project was designed to teach reconnection. Quit Final Cut, if you need a break. Otherwise, there's one more exercise left in this chapter.

6. _____Exploring the Media Manager

The Media Manager is one of those tools that should just work. As it is, it's darn near inscrutable, with cryptic check boxes, convoluted documentation, and performance that's somewhat less than breathtaking.

In this exercise, you'll get an introduction to the Media Manager, along with an understanding of when and how to use it.

What the Media Manager Does		
Menu Choice	**Action**	**Risk Level**
Copy	Copies all selected media from wherever it is to wherever you specify. _Option:_ Delete Unused Project Media.	Low
Move	Moves all selected media from wherever it is to wherever you specify. _Option:_ Delete Unused Project Media.	Medium
Use Existing	Removes all project media that is not being used in whatever sequences are selected. Warning: once this process starts, your source files are deleted. If you cancel this operation _prior_ to its completion, both source and modified files may be gone. _Option:_ Delete Unused Project Media.	High
Recompress	Converts existing media from its current compression format to whatever you specify. Recompress will _not_ convert between NTSC and PAL.	Low
Create Offline	Converts a current project into a new project, allowing all clips to be recaptured at a different, generally higher, resolution. _Option:_ Delete Unused Project Media.	Low

1. Open **Chapter 13 Lesson**, if it isn't already open. Select **Seq – Snowboard Final** in the **Browser**. Then, choose **File > Media Manager**.

The Final Cut manual spends 20 pages discussing the Media Manager. I've written an article, which is on my Web site, that takes seven pages just to illustrate Create Offline. (You'll learn more about my Web site, and other resources available to you, in the Appendix, "Additional Resources.") In this exercise, I want to illustrate the two most popular uses of Media Manager: Making a copy of all your project files onto a single hard disk (for example, to take to another Final Cut system) and moving all your project files from wherever they are, into a single location (for example, moving from a collection of FireWire drives to a single RAID).

The two operations are very similar. The first is a Copy, which makes a copy of all your files in a new location, and the second is a Move, which moves all your files into a single location. For both of these, you'll need the Media Manager.

2. The first step is to select what media you want the **Media Manager** to manage:

Media Manager Selection Range	
Select	**Media Manager Processes**
Everything in Browser	The entire project, all sequences, all files
One or more sequences	Only media associated with selected sequences
A section of the Timeline	Only media associated with the Timeline selection
One or more selected clips	In the Browser, Timeline, or Viewer, only the selected clip or clips

3. The pop-up menu determines what operation it will be performing. If you choose **Copy**, all files will be *copied* to their new location, leaving the original project and files intact. If you choose **Move**, all files will be *moved* to their new location, with the ability to create a new project, where all links to moved media are correct.

This dialog illustrates the key settings of Media Manager. **Include Master Clips Outside Selection** *is new with FCP HD. If you check it, Final Cut will include other clips in the* **Browser** *that share similar timecode to the clips in the selected sequence. It is checked by default. I recommend you uncheck it.*

Delete Unused Media from Duplicated Items *will not copy or move media that is* not *part of the sequence you've selected. This is the principal benefit of using the Media Manager: it copies or moves only the material you want, which can save a tremendous amount of space. For instance, in this example, copying* **Seq – Snowboard Final** *and deleting unused media saves over 200 MB of hard disk space. (The dark blue area at the end of the top bar indicates the space taken by render files, which I never move—I always re-render.)*

In concept, this is good. However, if you have another sequence in your project that you need but didn't include as a selected sequence, and it uses media that is also not included as a part of one of the selected sequences, the media for that nonselected sequence will be deleted (or not copied). Further, if you decide later to add a shot that you had previously digitized, it won't be there because it was not part of the original selected sequence.

*If you do decide to delete unused media, be sure to provide handles; I try to use a minimum of **2:00**.*

*The Media Manager provides very useful media management, but it can delete media if you are not careful. Additionally, the language of the check boxes is seriously oblique. I've been using Final Cut for over five years, and I have a hard time understanding what **Include Master Clips Outside Selection** or **Include Affiliate Clips Outside Selection** mean in actual English.*

***Include Master Clips Outside Selection** means that Final Cut will include other clips in the Browser, even if they are not part of your selection, if they have either an **In** or an **Out** set. I generally leave this **off**.*

***Include Affiliate Clips Outside Selection** means that Final Cut will include other clips outside your selection if it has either an **In** or an **Out**, or it falls between two unconnected clips derived from the same master clip, or it appears as an affiliate clip in another sequence. Again, I generally leave this **off**.*

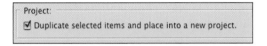

This check box creates a duplicate of the selected sequences or projects and allows you to specify where it is stored. This is a good thing. I always leave it checked.

4. Once you have the settings in place, click **Browse** to select where you want the new project and media files to be saved.

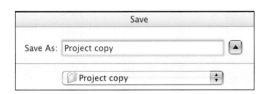

5. I've found it best to create a new folder; in this case, I called it **Project copy**. Final Cut will put all the files into that one folder, making them easy to find or move after this process is complete.

*Click **OK** to begin the process.*

6. If there is insufficient media for your handles, this dialog pops up. Generally, it is OK to click **OK**.

Final Cut provides an ongoing status report as it processes your files. It is really important to let it finish. Canceling in the middle can cause all kinds of problems. Because you are copying huge files, this process can take a long, long time.

*When Final Cut is done, it has created a new project and **Media** folder. Inside the **Media** folder are all the modified clips from the selected sequence or project. Even if you stored your media in multiple folders before, all the media is now combined into this one folder.*

At this point, this is just like any other Final Cut project. You can open it and start editing.

The Media Manager is surprisingly complex and difficult to master. If you plan to use it, create a small test project and practice. Make a point to read the manual, thoroughly, before using it. The Media Manager can do a great job of getting rid of unneeded media and recovering hard disk space, but, good golly, it's tricky.

---

7. That's it. You're done. Save what you want to save and quit Final Cut.

Helpful Keyboard Shortcuts	
Shortcut	**Function**
Cmd+1	Selects the Viewer
Cmd+2	Selects the Canvas
Cmd+3	Selects the Timeline
Cmd+4	Selects the Browser
Shift+Cmd+S	Saves a project file, using a new name (Save As)
Ctrl+C	Opens the Batch Capture window
Cmd+8	Opens the Log and Capture window

Summary

Whew! You've taken a project from beginning to end—from planning through to archiving—and learned a ton about Final Cut along the way. In the appendix, I'll provide you with additional resources you can use to make the most of Final Cut Pro HD.

This appendix provides a variety of additional resources to help you get the most out of your Final Cut Pro HD system.

Additional Resources

Tutorial Movies	Troubleshooting Tips
Helpful Software	Using an External Editor
Online Resources	Other Books from Lynda.com
Apple-Certified Training	One Last Word

No Lesson Files

FCP HD HOT DVD

Tutorial Movies on the FCP HD HOT DVD

Sometimes, it's a whole lot easier to understand a concept if you can see it in action. This is why I've created a series of movies illustrating key Final Cut concepts and included them on the **FCP HD HOT** DVD. These movies cover every major area of Final Cut from capturing video to outputting, from editing clips into a sequence to creating effects.

Best of all, these movies use the same media as the exercises in this book. This makes it easy for you to practice these techniques later on your own system.

For a complete list of all the movies and a brief description, please read **ReadMe.rtf** on the **FCP HD HOT** DVD.

Troubleshooting Tips

Editing is stressful enough, without having to worry about troubleshooting software. Sadly, though, Final Cut is not perfect, and sometimes problems pop up. This section is designed to give you some tips on how to get things back to normal.

Assuming you don't have a hardware failure, there are three principal types of problems:

- Upgrading problems
- Operating system problems
- Final Cut problems

This section provides remedies for all three.

Upgrade Problems

More clients get into more problems due to upgrades than any other issue. Here's my basic rule: Wait *at least* 30 days after a new version of anything is released before upgrading.

Why? Because video editing is about the most taxing task you can perform with a personal computer. Unlike word processing or using a database, video editing pushes every system element to the limit: operating system, CPU, RAM, hard disks, data buses, graphics card, monitor, system I/O… everything. If even one part of your system is not running perfectly, you can't edit.

Software is software. Apple works really hard to release high-quality tools. However, until those tools get released in the real world, it's impossible to check every possible combination of hardware, software, and peripherals.

So, you need to ask yourself: is your role to test software or is your role to edit? If you like being the first one on the block with the latest version of anything, and you can afford to have your edit system down for a while because of incompatibilities, then upgrade as soon as each new version is announced.

I had a client do that when OS X 10.3 and FCP 4.0 were announced. The problem was that, although FCP worked under 10.3, the hard disk drivers for the client's RAID did not. Nor did their capture card.

So this client was dead in the water for four *weeks* waiting for other, crucial, third-party vendors to update their software.

If, on the other hand, your goal is to edit, then wait a while before upgrading. This is *especially* true if your system is working fine now. Make sure that every element of your editing system is approved for the latest version of the operating system and Final Cut. When OS 10.3 came out, I made a list of everything that needed to be upgraded in order for Final Cut to work in a professional setting (items marked with an asterisk are not generally needed for DV video):

• Apple firmware

• System RAM

• Operating system

• SCSI or Fibre Channel I/O cards *

• SCSI software drivers *

• Hard disk drivers

• QuickTime

• Final Cut Pro

• Other Final Cut applications

• Third-party Final Cut plug-ins

• Capture card drivers *

• Device (machine) control drivers *

That's 12 different subsystems of your computer, not all of which are controlled by Apple, that need to work together for you to edit. By the way, this list is in the order you should upgrade your software. If you upgrade out of order, there's a good chance your system will not work properly.

So, my advice is once you've got your system operating properly, turn off Software Upgrade so it doesn't keep beeping you when new versions are announced. Be cautious about upgrading. Wait for new versions to prove themselves before you upgrade. That way, when you do add the latest version, everything should go smoothly, and you'll have a minimum of downtime.

Solving Operating System Problems

If you are seeing the Spinning Beach Ball of Death (SPOD) far more than you'd like, it is generally not a Final Cut problem. More often, it is a problem with the operating system. And the most common problem with the operating system is blown, or corrupted, disk directories.

Unix is a wonderful operating system. However, Apple needed to tweak it to improve its performance. And one of those tweaks was to load disk directories into memory.

A disk directory is like the card catalog in the library. The books on the shelves represent the files on your hard disk. The easiest way to find a book is to go to the card catalog and look it up. Because the cards are alphabetized, finding exactly the book you want is fast and easy.

However, there's a ghost that lives in this library and every so often it sneaks down to the card catalog, pulls out the drawers, and scatters the cards all around the floor. All the cards are still there, but they are no longer in any order. The books are still on the shelf, but with the cards all disorganized, the books are a lot harder to find.

Now, when you want to find a book, you need to go through every card, one by one, to see if it is the book you want. You can do it; it just takes longer.

This is, essentially, the problem with blown disk directories. The operating system only updates disk directories when you shut down your computer. Prior to that, whenever you create, delete, move, or rename a file, those changes are kept in memory. If your computer crashes, those changes will not be written properly to the disk.

Here's a three-step routine that can help fix this problem:

1. Restart (or start up) your computer while holding down the **Shift** key.

2. Continue holding down the **Shift** key while the gear spins on the gray screen until the blue screen appears. (It will take longer than usual for the blue screen to appear. Don't panic.) When the blue screen appears, let go of the **Shift** key. (You'll know you have done this properly when the white box in the middle of the blue screen displays the words "Safe Boot" at the bottom.)

3. Once your system fully boots up, restart it, again, this time without holding down any keys.

This process is called doing a **Safe Boot**. Make a habit to do this once a week.

When you are booting your computer in Safe Boot, you are actually doing two things: you are repairing a significant majority of disk directory problems, and you are also booting your system with a minimalist version of OS X. This limited OS is perfect for system maintenance, but you *cannot* run your system this way.

If you haven't run this routine, you'll be amazed at the performance benefit you get: your system will boot faster and shut down faster, and you will see the Spinning Beach Ball of Death far less frequently.

Now, if your directories are really screwed up, Safe Boot won't fix them. For that you will need a more powerful utility. The best I've found, and recommend highly, is *Disk Warrior X* by Alsoft (**www.alsoft.com**). It is excellent. I use it constantly when maintaining my clients' systems, and encourage all of them to buy it.

The next big problem you will run into are corrupted file permissions. Every file in Unix has 12 "ownership states" that determine who has permission to read to a file, write to a file, read *and* write to a file, or who is not allowed to use the file at all.

In Unix, the operating system and applications are users, just like you and me. And, sometimes, files get confused as to who they can talk to and who they can't. With well over 100,000 files in OS X, that means there are over 1.2 million permission states that can get confused.

To straighten all this out, Apple created **Disk Utility**. I recommend you run this once a week also. Here's how:

Disk Utility

1. With no applications running, except the **Finder**, open **Applications > Utilities** and open **Disk Utility**.

2. When **Disk Utility** starts, select the *name* of the hard disk (not the line with the numbers) that contains your operating system. This is most often, but not always, called **Macintosh HD**.

3. The main **Disk Utility** window appears.

4. Be sure the **First Aid** tab is selected (lighted blue).

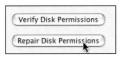

5. Click **Repair Disk Permissions**. (There is no advantage to verifying permissions, so just go ahead and repair them.) Depending upon the size of your hard disk and the speed of your computer, this repair process will take between 2 and 10 minutes.

6. When the utility says **Permissions repair complete**, you may quit. The more lines of text that are displayed in this window, the more likely you were to have problems.

I've found it easiest to run **Safe Boot** and **Repair Permissions** at the same time. That way, all my maintenance gets done together. I run them once a week, *or* when I upgrade the operating system, *or* when I upgrade any application, *or* after a crash. Since I've been running them regularly, my operating system problems have significantly diminished.

NOTE | Leave Your System on for the Weekend

Unix was first written to run servers, which never shut down. Because of this, there are a number of maintenance utilities that run around midnight over the weekend, when server traffic is low. These include

- Daily file maintenance

- Weekly search updating and file maintenance

- Monthly log file maintenance

If you can, leave your Mac on over the weekend once a month or so. If this isn't possible, read the "Helpful Software" section and get a program such as Macaroni or MacJanitor to keep your system optimized.

Solving Final Cut Problems

Final Cut is a wonderful program with an Achilles heel: its preferences files. These preferences are more than the settings you create; they affect the very core of how Final Cut edits and plays media. They exist at the very deepest levels of the application, and sometimes they go south.

Once your preferences files are corrupted, for instance after a Final Cut crash, your only alternative is to trash your preferences files and let Final Cut rebuild them automatically when it restarts.

Although you should run the Safe Boot and Repair Permissions routines frequently, you should only trash Final Cut preferences when the application is not working.

This is because trashing preferences actually removes elements of Final Cut and replaces them with system defaults. The following list is not exhaustive, but here's what gets lost, or reset, when you trash preferences:

- Favorite effects (deleted)
- Favorite motions (deleted)
- Favorite transitions (deleted)
- Default transitions (reset)
- Window layouts that are not saved to disk (reset)
- Browser layouts that are not saved to disk (reset)
- Timeline layouts that are not saved to disk (reset)
- Customized buttons that are not saved to disk (deleted)
- Customized keyboard layouts that are not saved to disk (deleted)
- Capture card settings (reset)
- Scratch disk settings (reset)
- Audio/video settings (reset)
- User preferences (reset)
- System settings (reset)

Trashing Final Cut preferences does not, repeat *not*, endanger any of your media files, nor affect any sequences. But it does reset Final Cut back to a known-good default state, which is what you want. However, you then need to take a few minutes after trashing preferences to reconfigure the system preferences so they meet your specific needs.

To trash Final Cut preferences:

1. Make sure Final Cut Pro is *not* running.

2. Open your **Boot Disk** (the one in the top-right corner of your Desktop that contains the operating system).

3. Open your **User** folder.

4. Open the **Home** folder (the folder with the picture of a house on it).

5. Open the **Library** folder (note, this is *not* the Library folder in your boot disk).

6. Open the **Preferences** folder.

7. Locate and trash **com.apple.FinalCutPro.plist**.

8. Scroll down and open **Final Cut Pro User Data**.

9. Locate and trash **Final Cut Pro 4.5 Preferences**.

10. Locate and trash **Final Cut Pro POA Cache**.

11. Empty the **Trash**.

Remember to trash only files, never trash folders. Also, trash all three preference files, not just one or two.

Oh, one other thing. Those dropped frame warnings that you get at the most inopportune times are, most often, caused when the hard disk cannot play back video at a fast enough rate.

Running these three procedures—Safe Boot, Rebuild Permissions, and Trash Preferences—should, more often than not, solve that problem.

Other Things to Check

Here are some other things to check, from my Web site article, *Troubleshooting Your FCP System*:

- **If you can't see video on your external NTSC monitor:** Make sure *both* the **Viewer** and **Canvas** windows are set to **Fit to Window**. Then, if you are using DV, make sure **View > External Video** is set to **All Frames**.

- **If you've imported a still image, but can't see it on the Timeline:** Make sure all imported images are RGB. CMYK images (frequently used in graphic design and printing) won't display in Final Cut.

- **If you don't have any audio:** Choose **View > Audio Playback** and set it to **Audio Follows Video**. Then, choose **View > Video Playback** and set it to **None** if you are viewing on your computer monitor, or **FireWire** if you are viewing on your deck or camera.

- **If audio and video are out of sync:** If there are red flags at the start of your clip, **Ctrl+click** the **red flag** of your video and choose **Move Into Sync** from the shortcut menu. If there are no red flags at the start of your clip, choose **View > Video Playback** and **View > Audio Playback** and make sure the video and audio playback are both set to the same point. For instance, monitoring video via **FireWire** and audio via **Built-In Audio** will automatically be out of sync by around six frames.

For the complete troubleshooting article (all 28 pages of it) go to **http://www.larryjordan.biz/articles/lj_trouble.html**.

Helpful Software

There are lots of programs that make working with Final Cut fun—from fascinating LiveType animations and Soundtrack loops to tons and tons of special effects plug-ins.

However, because we are in the Troubleshooting section, here are six software packages I've found, and use, that keep my system running smoothly:

- **Disk Warrior X**, published by Alsoft (**www.alsoft.com**). If you buy only one OS X utility, this is the one to buy. It does only one thing—fix and optimize disk directories. But it does it really, really well.

- **FCP Rescue**, written by Anders Holck (**http://fcprescue.andersholck.com**). This free utility provides instant backup, restore, and removal of Final Cut Pro's preferences files. This utility helps you if Final Cut Pro crashes and corrupts its preferences files. It is also very useful if other editors use your login, and you want to be able to go back to your personal settings afterwards. It has a very simple interface.

- **FCP Project**, written by Brian Summa (**http://homepage.mac.com/proeditor/**) This free utility was written after Brian read my article on how to organize FCP files, which I presented in more detail in Chapter 1, "*Get Organized*." First developed for an advertising agency, this utility provides a fast way to automatically create all the folders related to a project.

- **Macaroni**, published by Atomic Bird Software (**http://www.atomicbird.com**), is a tool that handles regular maintenance for Mac OS X, including the Mac OS X repair privileges process as well as Unix-style maintenance. Without Macaroni, some of these tasks normally run in the middle of the night, and don't get run unless you leave your Mac on all night. Others don't run automatically at all, and won't happen unless you remember when they're due.

- **MacJanitor**, written by Brian Hill (**http://personalpages.tds.net/~brian_hill/macjanitor.html**), is a freeware program, similar to Macaroni. I run Macaroni, but others are quite happy with MacJanitor. Either one can help keep your system running smoothly.

- **FCP logging template**, written by me (**http://www.larryjordan.biz/goodies.html**), is a free Excel worksheet that I use for logging tapes. For me, using this file is much faster than using the built-in logger of Final Cut. An additional benefit is that you have an Excel listing of every shot on your tape. I've been using this for years. Instructions are in the template.

Using an External Editor

This falls into the category of advanced topics, but I find myself using it more each day, and I wanted to explain it to you.

Many times, I will create an image in Photoshop or an animation in LiveType, load it into Final Cut, and discover that I need to make changes. In the past, before I learned about this feature, I would

1. Reopen the image in Photoshop.
2. Make corrections.
3. Save it under a different name.

4. Go back to Final Cut.

5. Import the new file.

6. Edit it to a new track on the Timeline.

7. Copy the old file to the clipboard.

8. Paste attributes to the new clip.

9. Delete the old clip.

This is a workable solution, but it took nine steps!

Using an external editor reduces this to just three:

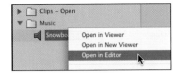

1. **Ctrl+click** a clip in the **Browser** or the **Timeline** and choose **Open in Editor** from the shortcut menu.

2. Final Cut automatically opens the editor application and loads in your file. Make your changes using the other application.

3. Save the file in the editing application (i.e., LiveType or Photoshop).

Final Cut automatically imports the file and replaces it in the **Browser** or **Timeline** with all the settings of the old file copied to the new one.

In order for this to work, choose **Final Cut Pro HD > System Settings** and click the **External Editor** tab, where you can then set your **External Editors** preferences.

In Final Cut Pro HD, you can use external editors for four different types of files:

Still Image Files: Selects a program for editing images, both still frames and imported graphics. Popular programs you can use here include Adobe Photoshop, Macromedia Fireworks, and Graphics Converter. My personal setting is Photoshop.

Video Files: Selects a program for editing video files. Popular programs you can use for this option include Apple QuickTime Player, Discreet Combustion, Pinnacle Systems Commotion, and Adobe After Effects. I rarely take video files out for editing, so I don't have this option set.

Audio Files: Selects a program for editing audio files. Popular programs you can use for this option include QuickTime Player and Bias Inc.'s Peak (a limited version of which is also bundled with Final Cut). Due to how ProTools structures a session, you can't use ProTools for this option. My personal setting is for Peak.

LiveType Movie Files: Selects a program for editing LiveType movies. With the advent, in FCP HD, of importing LiveType projects and allowing Final Cut to render them, the best option for this editor is LiveType itself. As I was writing this book, I used this option a lot to switch between Final Cut and LiveType while creating titles.

Once you've tried using an external editor to quickly "round-trip" a clip, you'll be amazed at how fast you can make changes.

Online Resources

There is a wealth of online resources available to the Final Cut editor. However, here are several that I want to point out that I've found especially useful:

- **Lynda.com** (**www.lynda.com**). Lynda.com offers online video-based tutorials on Apple Compressor, LiveType, Soundtrack, Garage Band, OS X, previous versions of Final Cut, as well as other applications such as Adobe Photoshop, Illustrator, After Effects, Macromedia Flash, Discreet 3ds Max, and other ancillary applications that are a valuable part of your video production toolkit.

- **My personal Web site** (**www.larryjordan.biz**). I started this Web site to provide training and information on Final Cut that I couldn't find anywhere else. It has grown into a full-fledged Final Cut Pro information and support Web site. I also publish a free, monthly Final Cut Pro newsletter packed with useful tips and techniques. Visit my Web site to subscribe. All of the articles referenced in this chapter can be found here.

- **Apple's Final Cut Pro Web site** (**www.apple.com/finalcutpro**). News and tech support on Final Cut from Apple itself. Need I say more?

- **L. A. Final Cut Pro User Group** (**www.lafcpug.org**). Everything you ever wanted to know about Final Cut. Excellent forums for getting your questions answered.

- **Ken Stone.net** (**www.kenstone.net**). Everything you never knew you never knew about Final Cut. Another outstanding site. An incredibly strong international viewership, with excellent forums for getting questions answered.

- **FinalCutProPlanet** (www.finalcutproplanet.com). Arguably the oldest FCP site, predating every-thing else listed here, started by the venerable (and esteemed) Josh Mellicker. Their forums and training programs are excellent.
- **Ripple Training** (www.rippletraining.com). Great training resources from one of Apple's Lead Trainers: Steve Martin.
- **Creative Cow.net** (www.creativecow.net). This site covers virtually every known creative tool. Worth visiting on a regular basis simply for the breadth of tools it covers.

Other Books from Lynda.com

Did you enjoy the hands-on training format of this book? There are other Hands-On Training books on many other subjects. Visit **www.lynda.com** to learn more! See the ads in the back of this book as well.

Apple-Certified Training

As an Apple-Certified Trainer, I would be remiss if I didn't recommend taking a least one Apple-Certified Training course. These hands-on training sessions, taught by an experienced Final Cut instructor, can often help you understand portions of Final Cut that are particularly hazy.

For more information, go to **http://www.apple.com/software/pro/training/**.

One Last Word

I've had a great deal of fun writing this book. It gave me the chance to think through how I edit and how Final Cut works, so that I could make the best possible recommendations to you.

And, although perfection may be unattainable, I've tried hard to make this book accurate. Just as Final Cut will continue to change and grow, my hope is for this book to follow suit, providing you all the latest tips and techniques to make the most of Final Cut.

Feel free to email me suggestions or questions—especially if you find something that's wrong. I'll fix it in the next edition. You can reach me at: **larry@larryjordan.biz**.

In the meantime, come visit my Web site—**www.larryjordan.biz**—and be sure to send me a note when you get nominated for an Oscar...or Emmy...or Clio.

Because when it comes time to tell your stories, Final Cut helps you bring them to life.

Index

\ (backslash), 203
0 dB cross fade, 279
3 Band equalizer, 392
+3 dB cross fade, 277–280, 294, 295–296
3-way filter, 414, 420
3D text, 331
3ds Max, Discreet, 496
4:1:1 color space, 412
4:2:2 color space, 411
4:3 aspect ratio, 406, 461
4:4:4 color space, 411
8-bit video, 323, 454
10-bit video, 323, 454
16:9 aspect ratio, 406, 407, 408, 461

A

A-roll, 241
AAC files, 106, 258
Abort Capture option, 72
absolute audio level, 266
accessories, video-editing, xvi–xvii
Action Safe rectangle, 312, 349
Add Chapter Marker button, 179
Add Compression Marker button, 179
Add Scoring Marker button, 179
Add Track command, 159
Additional Render Files folder, 469
Adobe After Effects, 496
Adobe Illustrator, 496
Adobe Photoshop, 334, 496. See also Photoshop files
Advanced Effects for Final Cut Pro (textbook), 413
affiliate clips, 165, 479, 483
After Effects, Adobe, 496
AIF files, 258, 457–459
AIFF Encoder, 258
AIFF files, 226, 458, 463
alpha channels, 105, 335, 423
Alsoft, 489, 494
analog audio, 223, 224
Angle Table, 380
animation. See also motion effects
  creating with layered graphics, 337–338
  and external editors, 494
  and file-naming conventions, 6, 9
  importing, 101
  and keyframes, 152 (See also keyframes)
  and non-drop-frame timecode, 41
  of simple text titles, 372–376
  and Viewer window, 34

Apple
  Compressor, 496
  Disk Utility, 490
  Final Cut Pro Web site, 496
  FireWire settings, 68
  QuickTime Player, 496
Apple-Certified Training courses, 497
Apple key, xiii
Applications folder, 13
archive.mov, 465
archiving
  basic steps for, 465
  and editing workflow, 7
  storage considerations, 11–12, 473
  tutorial on, 465
Arrange menu, 52
Arrow tool
  keyboard shortcut for, 148
  pros and cons of, 190
  selecting edit points with, 187, 277
  selecting/moving clips to Timeline with, 173
  and transitions, 277, 278
  trimming clips with, 189–190
aspect ratios, 320, 406, 407, 408, 461
Assemble edits, 451
Atomic Bird Software, 494
attributes, Timeline, 57
audio. See also audio files; audio tracks
  capturing, 80
  editing, 222–223, 229–233
  exporting, 457–459
  importance of, 222
  math of, 223–226
  mixing, 265–272
  monitoring, 69
  rendering, 291 (See also audio render files)
  scrubbing, 233, 273
  trimming, 241–246
  troubleshooting, 493
  tutorials, 226
audio buzz, 324, 329
Audio Capture check box, 18
audio capture settings, 80–81
audio files. See also media files
  converting, 258–259
  importing, 106
  stereo vs. dual-mono, 247
  as timecode-based media, 3–4
  using external editors for, 496
audio filters, 388–392. See also filters
audio formats, 258

audio frequencies, 223–225, 387
audio levels, 247–254, 266
Audio Meters
  and audio levels, 248
  on Audio Mixer, 270, 271
  and dynamic range, 225, 226
  and Final Cut interface, 21, 25
  peak indicator on, 248
  zero reading on, 266
Audio Mixer, 265, 267–272
audio mixers, xvi
Audio Peaks, 254
Audio Playback menu, 68, 493
Audio Playback Quality setting, 291
audio preferences, 15, 66
audio production software, xvii
audio render files, 251, 470, 471. See also render files
Audio Scoring Markers, 458
audio speakers, xvi
audio story, building, 227–233
Audio to AIFF(s) command, 459
Audio to OMF command, 459
audio tracks. See also tracks
  adding, 234–235
  exporting, 459
  hearing contents of, 250
  laying out, 256
  muting, 251
audio transitions, 276–282, 294. See also transitions
Audio Transitions folder, 278
Audio/Video Settings dialog, 68–69
audio waveforms. See waveforms
audio.mov, 226
Auto-Aspect Layout option, 52
Auto Kerning setting, 322
Auto Render settings, 72
Auto Select buttons, 156, 163
Automatically Start Recording option, 443
Autosave Vault, 18, 72, 115, 474

B

B-roll
  defined, 84, 227
  editing interviews with, 87
  extending length of, 215
  as illustration for talking head, 234–240
  and multitrack editing, 233, 234
  removing audio from, 241
  sorting from interviews, 237
back-timing, 138–139
Background pop-up menu, 317
backslash key, 203

backups, 472–479. *See also*
    archiving
  automatic, 72, 474
  restoring projects from, 475–479
  storing, 273
  suggested system for, 472–473
  using Save As to create, 468
Band Pass filter, 392
bars, color, 444–445
Basic Motion settings, 348
Batch Capture command, 89–90,
    93, 476–477
Betacam SP, 15, 412
Betacam SX, 15
Bevel filter, 399–400
Bezier controller, 375
Bezier curves, 375, 376, 382
Bias Deck, 458
Bias Peak, 334, 496
bins
  creating, 31, 77, 115
  labeling, 33
  naming, 31, 32
  nesting, 32
  purpose of, 31
bit depth, 225–226
black and coding tapes, 107,
    447–448
Black and White filter, 394
black levels, 323–324, 415–416
Blur filters, 400
boot disk, xviii, xix
booting, in Safe Boot, 489, 491,
    493
bow tie icon, 194, 247
broadcast projects, 442, 444
Broadcast Safe filter, 330
broadcast tape, 452
Browser
  changing reel names in, 466–467
  creating bins in, 31
  customizing, 53
  dragging clips to Timeline from,
      135
  exploring, 27–33
  finding clips with, 141–144
  hiding/showing columns in, 29, 53
  illustrated, 21, 22
  labeling clips in, 55
  moving columns in, 54
  purpose of, 22
  renaming clips in, 94
  reordering columns in, 30
  resizing, 29
  sorting columns in, 30
  using as database, 22, 28, 141
  viewing clips in, 120–121
Browser icons, 28–29
Built-in Audio setting, 68, 69, 493

Burns, Ken, 382
buttons
  converting commands to, 59–60
  deleting, 60
  saving, 60
  and trashing of preferences, 492

C
calibration, monitor, 413
cameras, xiv, 41, 107, 451. *See also*
    decks
Canvas
  exploring, 48–50
  illustrated, 21, 23, 48
  purpose of, 23
  similarity to Viewer, 24, 48
  vs. Timeline, 42, 48
  working with Wireframe mode in,
      353–358
Capture Audio and Video to
    Separate Files check box, 18
Capture Now, 92–96
  capturing clips with, 92–93
  and DV Start/Stop Detection,
      94–95
  and renaming of clips, 94
  vs. Log and Capture, 84–85, 93,
      94
Capture Scratch folder, 97–98, 264,
    473
Capture Settings tab, Log and
    Capture, 82
capture.mov, 82
capturing
  basic steps for, 63
  with Batch Capture, 89–90, 93,
      476–477
  with Capture Now, 92–93
  defined, 62, 63
  getting ready for, 66–73
  with Log and Capture, 83–91
  terminology, 63–64
  tutorials on, 82
CD
  backing up to, 473
  exporting to, 453, 454, 455
  life expectancy, 12
  players, 259
  storage considerations, 12
CD audio, 259
CD rot, 12
Channel Grouped option, 459
channel strip, Audio Mixer, 272
chapter markers, DVD, 179, 456
checkerboarding, 256
Chroma Keyer filter, 426
chroma keying, 425–431
chroma levels, 417

"Civil War" PBS series, 382
clamping video levels, 324, 330
client folders, 10
clip collisions, 160, 201
Clip Enable option, 251
clip markers, 95, 174–177. *See also*
    markers
Clip Overlays button, 292
Clip Settings tab, Log and Capture,
    79
clips
  affiliate *vs.* master, 165
  applying Favorite effects to, 397
  back-timing, 138–139
  Browser *vs.* Timeline, 165
  building sequences of, 127–134
  capturing with Capture Now,
      84–85, 92–93
  capturing with Log and Capture,
      76, 83–91
  changing opacity of, 292–293
  changing speed of, 168, 346–347,
      379
  copying and pasting, 161–163
  creating still frames from, 377–378
  creating subclips from, 180–182
  defined, 4, 22
  deleting, 150–157
  distorting, 357
  dragging from Browser to Timeline,
      135
  editing to Timeline, 127–135 (*See
      also* editing)
  fading to black, 370–371
  finding, 141–144
  fixing color problems with, 414
      (*See also* color correction)
  importing, 101–107
  labeling, 33, 54, 55
  linking/unlinking, 242–243, 246,
      389
  loading into Viewer, 35–36
  locating record points in, 94
  logging, 76, 84
  marking, 84, 118–126, 152–153
  moving around in, 37
  moving on Timeline, 158–162
  moving to Viewer, 121
  naming/renaming, 32, 78–79, 87,
      88, 94
  nesting/unnesting, 406–409
  offline *vs.* online, 475
  out-of-sync, 242–243, 493
  playing, 37–38
  previewing, 374
  removing attributes from, 403
  replacing, 166–168
  reversing, 347

clips *(continued)*
running at variable speeds, 379–381
scrubbing, 84, 233, 273
selecting/deselecting, 147–149
setting Ins/Outs for, 118, 121–124, 152–153
stacking, 341–342, 365
trimming (*See* trimming)
viewing, 120–121
Close Gap command, 156
Cmd key, 19. *See also* keyboard shortcuts
collisions. *See* clip collisions
Color bar, Chroma Keyer, 427
color bars, 444–445
color correction, 413–422
with 3-way filter, 414
basic steps for, 414
with chroma keying, 425–431
with Color Corrector filter, 414, 419, 420
hardware/software requirements, 413
interactive nature of, 416
and Range Check utility, 417
resources, 413
of skin tones, 419–422
color-correction software, 413
Color Corrector 3-way filter, 414, 419, 420
color levels, TV-safe, 329
color saturation. *See* saturation
Color Smoothing filter, 426
color space, 410–412
Combustion, Discreet, 496
Command key, xiii. *See also* keyboard shortcuts
commands. *See also* specific commands
converting to buttons, 59–60
entering from keyboard *vs.* mouse, xii–xiii, 34
Commotion, Pinnacle Systems, 496
compositing
and audio filters, 388
defined, 386
and Export > For LiveType, 460
and Export QuickTime Conversion, 454
in Image+Wireframe mode, 349
and track stacking, 238
Compressed Files folder, 461
compression, color, 319, 410, 412
Compression markers, 179
compression programs, 453
Compressor, 453, 460–463
Compressor/Limiter filter, 392
computer. *See also* Macintosh
accessories, xvi–xvii

booting in Safe Boot, 489, 491, 493
color-space considerations, 410–412
file maintenance, 491
optimizing, 491
organizing, 9
requirements, xiv
sharing with multiple users, xvii
troubleshooting, 487–491
video considerations, 319, 410–412
contextual menus, xiii
Control key, xiii. *See also* keyboard shortcuts
Controls window, Viewer, 307, 316, 322
Convert to AIFF command, 259
coordinates
entering into Center text boxes, 364
entering into Origin, 309
for exact center of image/video frame, 310, 348
Final Cut *vs.* Photoshop, 310
timecode, 136
copy-and-paste technique, 161–163, 409
Copy command, Media Manager, 480, 481, 482
copyrighted materials, 259
corrupted file permissions, repairing, 489–491
CPU requirements, xiv
Create Offline command, 480
Creative Cow.net, 497
credit rolls, 321–322
Crop menu, 351
Crop tool, 356
cross dissolves, 283, 285, 294–295
cross fades, 277, 278, 279, 280
Cross Stretch transition, 297–298
Ctrl key, 19. *See also* keyboard shortcuts
Ctrl+click, xiii
custom layouts, 52
customization settings, 53, 492. *See also* customizing
customize.mov, 51
customizing, 51–60
Browser, 53
keyboard layout, 57–59
labels, 54
Timeline, 56
tutorial on, 51
window layouts, 52
Cut command, 161

D

data rates, 65
database
using Browser as, 22, 28, 141
videotape, 9
dB, 226, 266
DC Notch filter, 392
decibels, 226, 266
Deck, Bias, 458
decks
and Assemble edits, 451
and black levels, 324
and Edit to Tape settings, 452–453
as editing accessory, xvi, 83
giving Final Cut control over, 443
and starting timecode, 108, 447, 448
Delete key, 150, 153
Desaturate filter, 400–401
DigiBetacam, xv, 15, 412
DigiDesign, 458
digital audio, 224, 225. *See also* audio
digital distortion, 226
digital video, xi, xv, 3–4. *See also* DV; video
directories, disk, 488–489
Discreet 3ds Max, 496
Discreet Combustion, 496
disk directories, 488–489
disk space, xiv–xv
Disk Utility, 490
Disk Warrior X, 489, 494
displays, xvi, 413, 493
dissolves, 283, 285, 294–295
Distort tool, 357
Dock
hiding/showing, 13
moving FCP icon into, 13
parking windows on, 22
starting program from, 14
documentaries, 208, 227
dots per inch, 382
double-clicking, 36
dpi, 382
dragging
clips, 135
nested sequences, 409
transitions, 315
drop-frame timecode, 41
drop shadows, 317–318, 322, 352, 435–436
dual-mono files, 247
Duplicate Sequence command, 116
Duration Calculator, Print to Video, 446
Duration dialog, 198–199, 280

DV cameras, xiv, 41, 107, 451. *See also* decks
DV decks, xvi. *See also* decks
DV formats, 4, 64, 412. *See also* specific formats
DV-NTSC, 66
DV-PAL, 66
DV Start/Stop Detect, 94–95, 182–183
DVCAM, xi, xv, 4, 15
DVCPRO-25, xi, xv, 4, 15
DVCPRO-50, 15
DVCPRO-HD, xiv, 15, 65
DVD
  chapter markers, 179, 456
  drives, xiv
  exporting to, 453, 454, 455
  life expectancy, 12
  storage, 12
  this book's companion, xviii, 487
  and white levels, 417
DVD Studio Pro, 454, 461
Dynamic Control filters, 392
dynamic range, 225–226
Dynamic Trimming check box, 220

E

Ease In/Ease Out keyframe, 382, 384
Easy Setup command, 14–15, 66
Echo filters, 392
echoes, 387
Edge Thin slider, Chroma Keyer, 427, 430
Edge Wipe transition, 286, 288
Edit Marker dialog, 175, 176
edit points. *See also* Ins/Outs
  applying transitions to, 278
  moving, 245
  selecting, 187
  three sides to, 187
Edit Selection tool, 149
Edit to Tape, 447–453
  render considerations, 441
  and tape striping, 107–108, 447–448
  and timecode, 442, 449
  vs. playing Timeline to tape, 439
  vs. Print to Video, 442
editing. *See also* trimming
  accessories, xvi–xvii
  with Assemble edits, 451
  audio, 222–223, 229–233
  defined, 3
  with Extend edits, 214–215, 239
  with Fit to Fill edits, 168–169
  "inclusive," 147
  with Insert edits, 133, 134, 451

linear *vs.* nonlinear, 451
mantra, 146
  with match frame technique, 164–166
  with mouse *vs.* keyboard, xii, 34
  multitrack, 208–211, 234
  with Overwrite edits, 127–129, 133, 162
  power techniques for, 164–169
  with Replace edits, 166–168
  software/plug-ins, xvii, 494
  with Split edits, 245–246
  with Storyboard edits, 170–173
  with subclips, 181
  system requirements, xiv–xv
  tape-to-tape, 451
  three-point, 136–140
  with Through edits, 194, 389
  to Timeline, 127–134
  trying to reach perfection in, xi
  tutorials on, 135
  two-track, 233
  workflow, 4–7, 26, 222–223
Editing tab, User Preferences, 73, 203, 338
editing.mov, 135
EDL files, 454
effects. *See also* filters
  importance of precision in, 363
  motion (*See* motion effects)
  picture-in-picture, 343–352
  plug-ins, xvii
  previewing, 290, 374
  and QuickView window, 373–374
  rendered *vs.* real-time, 289–290
  resetting, 358
  sound (*See* sound effects)
  three-layer, 432, 433
  tips for creating, 342
  vertical nature of, 341–342
Effects menu, 277, 284, 295
Enhance slider, Chroma Keyer, 427, 430
Enter key, 19
EQ filter, 390
equal gain cross fades, 279
equal power cross fades, 279
Equalizer filters, 392
Escape key, 19
Excel, 494
Excess Chroma setting, 417
Excess Luma setting, 416, 417
Expander/Noise Gate filter, 392
Export table, 454
exporting
  audio, 457–459
  for Compressor, 460–463
  keyboard layouts, 59
  for LiveType, 460

projects, 439
QuickTime movies, 453, 454, 455–456
still frames, 378, 454, 463
video, 460–463
Exposé feature, Mac OS X, 130–131
Extend edits, 214–215, 239
external editors, 334, 494–496
eyedropper tool, 421–422, 427–428

F

Fade Size setting, 322
fade to black, 370–371
Favorites
  effects, 397–398
  filter stacks, 402
  filters, 397–398
  motions, 367–368
  transitions, 297–298
  and trashing of preferences, 492
  vs. Paste Attributes, 367–368, 397
Favorites folder, 298, 367, 397
FCP HOT files folder, xviii, xix
FCP icon, 13
FCP keyboard, xvi
FCP logging template, 494
FCP Media folder, 10, 97, 470, 473
FCP Project, 494
FCP Projects folder, xviii, xix, 10
FCP Rescue, 494
feathering, 391, 427
file footage, 318
file-naming conventions, 7–9
file permissions, repairing corrupted, 489–491
files
  archiving (*See* archiving)
  backing up, 11, 72, 468, 472–474
  importing, 101–107
  installing, xviii
  naming, 7–9
  opening, xix, 27
  reconnecting, 96, 97–100, 478–479
  reverting, 151–152
  sorting by size, 470
  trashing, 493
film, frame rate for, 41
filter stacks, 402
filters, 386–409. *See also* specific filters
  Apple *vs.* Final Cut, 392
  applying, 394, 406–409
  audio, 388–392
  changing order of, 401
  combining multiple, 399–401
  copying, 398

filters *(continued)*
  creating Favorite, 397–398
  how Final Cut processes, 401
  importance of subtlety in, 387
  keyframing, 404–405
  and nested sequences, 406–409
  removing, 394, 395, 403
  tutorials, 387
  and video levels, 405
  vs. motion effects, 386
filters.mov, 387
Final Cut keyboard, xvi
Final Cut Pro HD
  and Apple Exposé feature,
    130–131
  computer knowledge required for,
    xi
  customizing, 51–60
  editing workflow, 4–7, 26
  interface, 20–25, 34 (*See also*
    specific interface elements)
  and multiple users, xvii
  newsletter, 496
  online resources, 496–497
  plug-ins, xvii, 494
  purpose of, xi
  quitting, 19
  setting preferences for, 13–15
  starting, 14
  survey regarding use of, xii
  system requirements, xiv
  troubleshooting tips, 492–493
  windows, 21, 50 (*See also* specific
    windows)
Final Cut Pro User Group, L.A., 496
FinalCutProPlanet, 497
Find command, 141
Finder, 465, 468
FireWire, xv, 17, 64
FireWire DV setting, 68, 69
Fireworks, Macromedia, 496
Fit to Fill edits, 168–169
Fit to Window menu/command, 49,
    58–59, 353, 358, 493
Flash, Macromedia, 496
flesh tones, color-correcting,
    419–422
floating palettes, 21, 25
floating windows, 22
folders. *See also* specific folders
  creating, 10
  importing, 103
  trashing, 493
fonts, 309, 331
frame rates, 41, 64
frames per second, 41
freeze frames, 377
frequencies, audio, 223–225, 387
frequency response, 223, 225

G

Gap Width setting, 322
gaps, 153–157
  closing/deleting, 150–151, 154,
    155, 156
  defined, 153
  finding, 155, 157
  and lift deletes, 150, 153
  and ripple deletes, 150–151, 153,
    200
  zooming in on, 154
Garage Band, 496
Gaussian Blur filter, 400, 401
General tab, User Preferences,
    71–73
Generator menu, 305, 314
Get Info command, 18
gigabytes, 19
Gradient Wipe transition, 300–302
Graphic Image Sizes table, 320
graphics. *See also* images
  and black/white settings, 323–324,
    330
  changing default duration for, 105
  design considerations, 313
  importance of, 304
  importing, 104–105, 320
  layered Photoshop, 335–338
Graphics Converter, 496
graphics software, xvii
grayscale, 319, 327, 423
green bow tie icon, 247
Group Selection tool, 149

H

Hand tool, 172
handles, 188, 281, 483, 484
Hands-On Training books, 497
hard disks
  creating scratch disks for, 18
  determining size of, 18
  determining space available on, 18
  internal *vs.* external, xv, 65
  repairing corrupted directories on,
    488–491
  system requirements, xiv
  and video editing, xv, 65
HD 720i/720p, 15
HD 1080i/1080p, 15
HD video, 64
hearing, human, 223, 226, 387
Hide Column command, 29, 53
High Definition video, 64
High Pass filter, 391, 392
High-Quality settings, Compressor,
    461
High Shelf filter, 392

Hill, Brian, 494
Hip Flix, 453
Histogram, 325
historical footage, 318
Holck, Anders, 494
HOT DVD, xviii, 487. *See also* tutorial
    movies
hue, 328, 427
Hum Remover filter, 392
human hearing/speech, 223, 224,
    226, 387

I

iDVD, 454, 461
Illustrator, Adobe, 496
Image mode, 349
Image Scaling pop-up menu, 353
images. *See also* graphics
  altering shape of, 353
  color-correcting (*See* color
    correction)
  combining two or more, 386 (*See
    also* compositing)
  creating, 320
  cropping, 356
  distorting, 357
  interlaced *vs.* progressive, 410
  moving, 310, 359–369, 382–384
  positioning, 356
  removing portions of, 423
  resizing, 320
  rotating, 355
  scaling, 354–355
  single- *vs.* multilayer, 320
  size considerations, 382
  washed out, 326
  zooming in/out on, 358
Image+Wireframe mode, 308, 349,
    354
iMovie, 382
importing
  defined, 63
  keyboard layouts, 59
  layered Photoshop files, 105
  LiveType files, 332
  media, 101–107
  music, 106
  sound effects files, 106
  speeding up, 107
In indicator, 123
In points. *See* Ins/Outs
Ins/Outs
  adjusting in real time, 216
  clearing, 125
  defined, 118
  for edit points, 187
  and Replace edits, 168

setting, 118, 121–124, 126, 152–153
and three-point editing, 136–139
Insert edits, 133, 134, 451
Insert Tracks command, 158, 234
installing project/media files, xviii
interface
  floating palettes, 21, 25
  main windows, 21–24
  rules, 34, 36, 147
  tutorial, 21
interface.mov, 21
interlaced video, 319, 410
IRE, 323, 327
iTunes, 258–259

J

J-edits, 245–246
J-K-L keys, 38, 219–220
job codes, 8–9
jog wheel, 37
Jordan, Larry, 496, 497
JPEG files, 423
jump cuts, 231, 233

K

K key, 38, 219–220
Ken Burns Effect, 382
Ken Stone.net, 496
kerning, 322
Key icon, 429
keyboard
  customizing, 57–59
  importing/exporting layouts for, 59
  navigation tips, 147–148
  selecting edits with, 212–214
  special Final Cut, xvi
keyboard shortcuts, xiii, 34
  Chapter 1, *"Get Organized,"* 19
  Chapter 2, *"Understanding FCP Interface,"* 61
  Chapter 3, *"Gather Your Media,"* 111
  Chapter 4, *"Build Your Story,"* 145
  Chapter 5, *"Organize Your Story,"* 184–185
  Chapter 6, *"Trim Your Story,"* 221
  Chapter 7, *"Audio–The Secret to a Great Picture,"* 273
  Chapter 8, *"Transitions–Making Change Beautiful,"* 303
  Chapter 9, *"Text, Titles, and Graphics,"* 339
  Chapter 10, *"Motion Effects,"* 384–385
  Chapter 11, *"Filters and Keying,"* 437

Chapter 12, *"Output Your Project,"* 463
Chapter 13, *"Archiving Your Project,"* 485
Crop tool, 356
Distort tool, 357
  positioning, 356
  rotation, 355
  scaling, 355
  timecode, 140
keyframes
  changing clip speed with, 379, 380–381
  controlling audio levels with, 265
  creating, 361
  creating transitions with, 292–293
  defined, 252, 361
  deleting, 361
  and filters, 404–405
  and motion effects, 361
  moving, 361
  moving images with, 359–369, 382–384
  moving text with, 372–376
keys
  chroma, 425–431
  luma, 423–424

L

L-edits, 245–246
L key, 38, 219–220
L.A. Final Cut Pro User Group, 496
Label command, 33
labeling
  bins, 33
  clips, 33, 54, 55
  videotapes, 9
Labels tab, User Preferences, 54
Landsberg, Cleve, 265
larryjordan.biz, 496, 497
Lawson, Dr. Richard, 341
layered Photoshop files, 105, 335–338
LCD monitors, 413
Leader material, 444–446
leading, 309
lesson files, xvii, xix, 27
Lessons folder, xix
lift deletes, 150, 153
Lift edits, 200
linear editing, 451
Link button/command, 241, 242–243, 246
linked clips, 242–243, 246, 389
LiveType
  disk space required for, xiv
  exporting for, 454, 460
  and external editors, 496

importing files from, 105, 332–334
  tutorial, 496
locking tracks, 201
Log and Capture
  Capture Settings tab, 82
  Clip Settings tab, 79
  exploring, 74–82
  illustrated, 75–76
  opening, 74
  vs. Capture Now, 84–85, 93
Log Clip button, 88
logging, 74, 84. *See also* Log and Capture
Logging Columns layout, 53
Logging Info window, 110
logging template, 494
Loop option, Print to Video, 446
Low Pass filter, 391, 392
Low Shelf filter, 392
lower-third titles, 314–318
Luma bar, Chroma Keyer, 427, 429–430
luma keys, 423–424
luminance, 411, 423, 427
Lynda.com, 496, 497

M

M2V files, 463
Mac OS X. *See also* Macintosh
  and CD audio, 259
  Exposé feature, 130–131
  and Final Cut system requirements, xiv
  multiple-user capabilities, xvii
  tutorial, 496
  upgrade problems, 487–488
  utilities, 494
Macaroni, 491, 494
machine control messages, 75, 76
Macintosh. *See also* computer; Mac OS X
  file maintenance, 491
  optimizing, 491
  single- *vs.* two-button mouse, xiii
  system requirements, xiv–xvii
  utilities, 494
Macintosh HD disk, xviii, xix
MacJanitor, 491, 494
Mackie audio mixer, xvi
Macromedia Fireworks, 496
Macromedia Flash, 496
Make Favorite Effect command, 397, 402
Make Favorite Motion command, 367
Make Movie Self-Contained option, 456
Make New Clip option, 72
Make Subclip command, 181

Mark In button, 123
Mark Out button, 124
markers, 174–179
  Audio Scoring, 458
  deleting, 176, 177
  and DV Start/Stop Detect,
    182–183
  moving between, 175, 178–179
  naming/renaming, 95, 175
  repositioning, 179
  setting, 175, 177
  types of, 174
  and video export, 460
  yellow *vs.* pink, 95
Markers pop-up menu, 456
marking clips, 84, 118–126,
    152–153. *See also* markers
master-affiliate relationship, 479
master clips, 165, 407, 479, 483
Master Fader, 271
master sequence, 440
Mastering Settings tab, Edit to Tape,
    450
match frame technique, 164–166
Matched Name Only option, 479
mattes, 429, 432–436
media. *See also* media files
  capturing (*See* capturing)
  copying, 480, 482
  deleting unused, 483
  importing, 101–107
  locating missing, 98–100
  logging and capturing, 83–91
  managing (*See* Media Manager)
  moving, 480, 482
  recompressing, 480
  reconnecting, 96, 97–100,
    478–479
  removing unused, 480, 482
  timecode-based, 4, 10, 11, 16
Media End, 37, 118, 181, 188
media files. *See also* media
  archiving (*See* archiving)
  defined, 3–4, 22
  disk space required for, 11
  installing, xviii
  storing, 10, 16
  trashing, 4, 11, 473
  and trashing of preferences, 492
media limits, 36
media management, 7. *See also*
    Media Manager
Media Manager, 480–484
  drawbacks to, 480, 483, 484
  menu choices, 480
  opening, 481
  selecting media in, 481–482
  tutorial, 465
Media section, Print to Video, 446
Media Start, 37, 118, 181, 188

megabytes, 19
Mellicker, Josh, 497
memory
  building effects into, 373
  and open sequences, 42, 136
  system requirements, xiv
  and Undo levels, 72, 162
Memory & Cache tab, 71
menu commands. *See* commands
metadata, 28
microphones, 260
MiniDV, xi, xv, 4, 15
Minimum Allowable Free Space on
    Scratch Disks setting, 18
mixers, audio, xvi. *See also* Audio
    Mixer
mixing audio, 265–272
modifier keys, xiii
monitors, xvi, 413, 493
motion effects, 340–385
  compositing with, 386
  copying, 365–367
  defined, 341
  and Fit to Window menu, 353, 358
  freezing, 377–378
  and Image+Wireframe mode, 349
  moving images with keyframes,
    359–369
  moving still images, 382–384
  moving text with keyframes,
    372–376
  picture-in-picture, 343–352
  and QuickView window, 373–374
  resetting, 358
  tutorials, 343
  types of, 341
  variable-speed clips, 379–381
  vs. filters, 386
Motion menu, 348
motion paths, 375, 376
Motion tab, 309, 340, 343,
    348–350
motion.mov, 343
mouse
  accessing shortcuts with, xiii
  creating transitions with, 276
  editing with, xii, 34
  single- *vs.* two-button, xiii
.mov extension, 455
.mov files, HOT DVD. *See* tutorial
    movies
Move command, Media Manager,
    480, 481, 482
movies
  compressing, 453, 456
  creating, 453
  exporting, 453, 454, 455–456
  Reference, 456, 458, 460, 463
  Self-Contained, 456, 458
  tutorial (*See* tutorial movies)

Movies folder, xviii. *See also* tutorial
    movies
MP3 files, 106, 258
MPEG-2 files, 461
Multi-Frame Trim Size setting, 220
Multi-Spin Slide transition, 284, 285,
    286
multiplexing, 463
multitrack editing, 208–211, 234
Murch, Walter, 216
music
  adding to sequences, 255–257
  importing, 106
  libraries, xvii
Mute button, 251, 272, 280

N

naming conventions, 7–9
narration, recording, 260–264
natural sound, 84
Nest Items command, 406
New Bin button, 77
New Bin command, 31
New Project command, 74
newsletter, Final Cut Pro, 496
"No communication" message, 76
non-drop-frame timecode, 41
nonlinear editing, 451
Notch filter, 392
NTSC monitors, xvi, 493
NTSC video, xii, 15, 41
Nyquist Theorem, 225

O

offline clips, 475, 476
offline file format, 475
Offline Files dialog, 98, 100
OMF files, 454, 457–459
one-sided trimming, 196–201
online clips, 475
online file format, 475
online resources, 496–497
opacity, changing clip's, 292–293
Open command, xix, 27
Open Recent command, xix, 27
operating system. *See also* Mac OS
    X
  Final Cut system requirements, xiv
  solving problems with, 488–491
  upgrading, 487–488
Option-dragging, 315
Option key, xiii, 19, 243–244
organize.mov, 169
organizing-story tutorials, 169
Origin control, 309
OS X. *See* Mac OS X
Out indicator, 124
Out marker, 125

out-of-sync flags, 200, 493
Out points. *See* Ins/Outs
outputting, 438–453
    to CD/DVD, 453
    defined, 439
    with Edit to Tape, 447–453
    long projects, 440
    with Print to Video, 441–446
    rendering prior to, 441
    saving prior to, 440
    for use on Web, 453
    vs. exporting, 439
Overwrite button, 128, 132
Overwrite edits, 127–129, 133, 162

P

padlock icon, 201, 208
PAL monitors, xvi
PAL video, xii, 15, 41
palettes, 21, 25
Pan slider, 252–254
Parametric equalizer, 392
Paste Attributes command, 366,
        367–368, 397
Paste command, 162
Paste Insert command, 162
patch panel, 234, 235–237, 238
PBS "Civil War" series, 382
Peak, Bias, 334, 496
peak indicator, 248
Pen tool, 253, 266, 276
permissions, repairing corrupted file,
        489–491
perspective, 357
phone-call sounds, 390
Photoshop files, 105, 320, 335–338
picture-in-picture effect, 343–352
Pinnacle Systems Commotion, 496
pinning, 357
pixel aspect ratios, 320. *See also*
        aspect ratios
pixels
    color-averaging, 411–412
    Final Cut's internal limit on, 382
    luminance values of, 411
    square *vs.* rectangular, 319–320,
        410
    viewing in Waveform monitor, 326
Place Background Movie command,
        460
Play In to Out button, 125
playback controls, 36–37, 38, 219–220
Playback Preview settings, 203
playback rates, 64
playhead
    in Canvas, 48
    in Timeline, 44
    in Viewer, 36
Playhead Sync menu, 48, 49

plug-ins, xvii, 494
PNG files, 378
pointers, 4, 22
positioning
    images, 356
    markers, 179
    text, 309–310
    Timeline, 46
poster frames, 121
Posterize filter, 395–396, 397, 404
power supply, uninterruptible, xvi
preferences. *See also* User
        Preferences dialog
    audio/video, 15, 66–71
    External Editors, 495
    for professional users, 12
    saving, 19
    setting, 13–15, 66–73
    storing, xvii
    trashing, 299, 492–493
presets, 69–70
Print to Video, 441–446
    and pre-program/Leader material,
        444–446
    recommended settings for,
        442–443, 444–445
    render considerations, 441
    vs. Edit to Tape, 442
    vs. playing Timeline to tape, 439
processor requirements, xiv
progressive video, 319, 410
project files. *See also* projects
    backing up, 468, 472–473
    installing, xviii
    managing (*See* Media Manager)
    opening, xix
    purpose of, 3
    saving, 72, 468
    storing, 10
project folders, 10
projects. *See also* project files
    archiving (*See* archiving)
    backing up, 11, 72, 468, 472–473
    breaking up long, 440
    creating, 74, 114
    creating bins for, 115
    defined, 3, 22
    exporting, 439
    gathering media for, 5
    mixing, 265–272
    naming, 7–9, 115
    outputting, 439 (*See also* outputting)
    planning/organizing, 5
    protecting with Save As, 117, 468
    restoring from backup, 475–479
    saving, 114, 115, 117, 468
    steps for editing, 4–7
ProTools, 454, 458, 496
PSD files, 320. *See also* Photoshop
        files

Q

Q values, 391
Quality settings, Compressor, 461
quantizing, 224
QuickTime
    and Final Cut system requirements,
        xiv
    movies, xviii, 22, 453, 454,
        455–456
    Player, 496
QuickTime Conversion, 378, 454
QuickView window, 290, 373–374
Quit command, 19

R

RAIDs, xv, xvi, 17, 65
RAM, xiv, 71, 136. *See also* memory
Range Check utility, 417, 418, 420
Range Selection tool, 149, 151
Range slider, 374
Razor Blade tool, 191–194, 230,
        389
ReadMe.txt, 487
Real format, 453
real-time effects, 290, 291
Rebuild Permissions procedure,
        493
Recompress command, 480
Reconnect Media command, 478,
        479
Reconnect Options window, 99
Reconnect window, 99–100
reconnecting media
    demo, 97–100
    for projects restored from backup,
        478–479
    purpose of, 97, 478
    tutorial on, 96
reconnect.mov, 96
Record button, 262
Record Keyframes button, 269
recording tape formats, 445
red bow tie icon, 194
Reduced... Large option, 57
Reel column, Browser, 30, 109
reel IDs, 64, 109. *See also* reel
        numbers
reel names, 465, 466–467, 477
reel numbers, 30, 64, 78, 109–110
Reference Audio Tone Levels table,
        445
Reference movies, 456, 458, 460,
        463
relative audio level, 266
Remove Attributes command, 403
Render All command, 291, 471
render bars, 289, 290, 441

render files
and archiving process, 465
deleting, 251, 468, 469–471
grouping of, 470
rebuilding missing, 471
reconnecting, 99, 478
space required for, 11, 470, 482
storage location for, 16, 469, 471
tracking, 469
and visibility indicators, 251
Render Manager, 465, 469–471
Render Selection command, 291, 396
Render Sequence command, 396
rendering
defined, 289
prior to outputting, 441
and render bar colors, 290
and Safe RT *vs.* Unlimited RT, 291
Repair Disk Permissions option, 491
Repair filters, 392
Replace edits, 166–168
Reset button, 358
resolution, 313, 384, 475
resources, online, 496–497
Restore Column Layout command, 54
Restore Project option, 73
Restore Track Layout option, 56
Restore Window Layout command, 53
Reveal Master Clip command, 165
Reverberation filter, 389, 392
Revert command, xix, 27, 151
Revert Project option, 73
RGB colors, 319, 323, 410
RGB Parade, 325
right-mouse-click, xiii
ripple deletes, 150–151, 153, 200
Ripple edits, 213, 217
Ripple tool, 196–198, 217, 230
Ripple Training, 497
Roll edits, 213, 214, 217, 218
Roll tool, 202–204
rotating images, 355
round-tripping, 334, 496
RT Extreme, xiv
RT pop-up menu, 291
rubber bands, 249–250, 266
running time, tape, 446

S

Safe Boot procedure, 489, 491, 493
Safe RT setting, 291
sample rates, 106, 224–225, 258
Sat bar, Chroma Keyer, 427, 429–430
saturation, 328, 329, 417, 418–419, 427

Save... Restore option, 57
Save As command, 117, 440, 468
Save Project As command, 117
Save Track Layout option, 56
Save Window Layout command, 52
Scale Attribute Times option, 366, 367, 368
Scale command, 309
scaling images, 354–355
Scanned Graphics Sizes table, 382
scanning, 410
scopes, video, 325–329
Scoring markers, 179
scratch disks
importance of, 17
maximum number of, 17
purpose of, 16
setting, 16–19
and trashing of preferences, 492
scrolling text clips, 321
scrubbing, 84, 233, 273
SD video, 64
Selection rectangle, 149
selection tools, 149
Self-Contained movies, 456, 458
Sepia filter, 394–395
Sequence Presets tab, 69
sequences
adding music/effects to, 255–256
creating, 116
defined, 22
duplicating, 116, 189
exporting, 455–456
inserting tracks in, 158
looping, 446
maximum number of tracks in, 43, 208
memory considerations, 42, 136
nesting, 406–409
purpose of, 114
rendering, 396
serifs, 313
Set Custom Layout commands, 52
Set Logging Bin command, 77
shadows. *See* drop shadows
Shift key, xiii, 19. *See also* keyboard shortcuts
shortcuts. *See* keyboard shortcuts
Show Audio Waveforms option, 43, 57
Show Clip Labels option, 57
Show Duplicate Frames option, 57
Show Through Edits option, 57
Show Thumbnail command, 120
Show Video Filmstrips option, 57
shuttle bar, 37
shuttle controllers, xvii
skin tones, color correcting, 419–422
slate, 444, 446

Slide tool, 202, 206–207
Slip tool, 202, 204–206
slugs, 370, 371
snapping, 161, 195, 279
Softening slider, Chroma Keyer, 427, 430
software
accessories, xvii
Final Cut system requirements, xiv
upgrade problems, 487–488
Solo button, 251, 272, 280
Sorenson Squeeze, 453
SOT, 84
sound, perception of, 265
Sound Cues, 263
sound effects. *See also* audio
adding to sequences, 255–256
importing, 106
libraries, xvii
Soundtrack, xiv, 454, 457–458, 496
speakers, xvi
special effects. *See* effects
speech, human, 224, 387
speeds, running clips at variable, 379–381
Spill Suppressor filter, 426
Spinning Beach Ball of Death, 488, 489
Split edits, 245–246
sprocket holes, 122, 165
square pixels, 319–320
stacking
clips, 341–342, 365
filters, 401, 402
staircase effect, 337
Standard Columns layout, 53
Standard Definition video, 64
Start/Stop Detect. *See* DV Start/Stop Detect
stereo files, 247
Stereo Mix option, 459
Stereo Pair command, 243, 247
Still Cache setting, 71
still frames
creating, 377–378
exporting, 378, 454, 463
Still/Freeze Duration setting, 338
still images
moving, 382–384
troubleshooting, 493
using external editors for, 496
Stone, Ken, 379, 496
storage devices, xv, 17
Storyboard edits, 170–173
storytelling, 3, 113
striping tapes, 107–108, 447–448
subclips, 180–183
subwoofers, xvi
Summa, Brian, 494
super-white levels, 324, 326, 330

Superimpose overlay, 306
synchronization problems, 200, 242, 243, 493
system requirements, xiv
System Settings dialog, 16, 70–71

T

Tab key, 19
talking heads, 84, 208, 227, 233, 234
tape. *See also* videotape
    black and coding, 107, 447–448
    color bars, 444–445
    formats, 445
    logging, 494
    outputting to, with Print to Video, 441–446
    playing Timeline to, 439
    pre-program/Leader material, 444–446
    storing, 12, 473
    striping, 107–108, 447–448
"Tape not threaded" message, 76
tape-to-tape editing, 451
Targa, 454
technical support, Final Cut Pro, 496
terminology
    capturing, 63–64
    digital video, 3–4
    marking, 118
text. *See also* titles
    3D, 331
    adding drop shadows to, 317–318, 322
    adjusting leading/tracking for, 309
    applying color to, 316–317
    changing background color for, 317
    changing font size for, 309
    design considerations, 313
    entering, 308
    formatting, 307
    importance of, 304
    moving, 306, 372–376
    positioning, 309–310
    scrolling, 321
text clips, 306–307. *See also* text
text generator, 305
text supers, 306
three-layer effect, 432, 433
three-point editing, 136–140
Through edits, 194, 389
Thumbnail Cache file, 18
thumbnails, viewing, 120–121
TIFF files, 104, 320, 378
Time Remap tool, 379
timecode
    coordinates, 136

dealing with breaks in, 107–108
defined, 40
and Edit to Tape, 442, 449
how Final Cut uses, 41
how to read, 40
positive *vs.* negative numbers for, 196
power of, 41
and Print to Video, 442
shortcuts, 140
and tape striping, 447
trimming with, 212–215
types of, 41
using to mark clips, 126
timecode-based media, 4, 10, 11, 16
Timeline
    attributes, 57
    changing horizontal scale of, 46
    creating transitions in, 276
    customizing, 56
    deleting clips/gaps from, 150–157
    dragging clips from Browser to, 135
    editing clips to, 127–135
    exploring, 42–47
    finding gaps in, 155
    illustrated, 21, 24, 43
    labeling clips in, 55
    moving clips around on, 158–162
    navigating, 147–149
    playing for final output, 439
    positive *vs.* negative numbers in, 196
    purpose of, 4, 24
    repositioning, 46
    track controls, 45
    turning off waveforms in, 43, 229
    using Ins/Outs in, 168
    vs. Canvas, 42, 48
    zooming in/out on, 47
Timeline controls, 46
Timeline gaps. *See* gaps
Timeline markers, 174, 177–179
Title 3D generator, 331
Title Safe rectangle, 312, 349
titles. *See also* text
    creating lower-third, 314–318
    creating main, 305–311
    creating upper-corner, 318
tone levels, reference audio, 445
Tool palette, 21, 25
track controls, Timeline, 45
Track Gap command, 156, 157
track visibility indicators, 45, 250–252
tracking, character, 309
tracks
    closing gaps in, 155
    creating, 158–159

defined, 43
finding gaps in, 157
how Final Cut handles, 208
how Final Cut reads, 342
inserting, 158
locking, 155, 201
maximum number of, 43, 208
Trailer setting, 443
training resources, 496–497
Transition Editor, 286–289
transition plug-ins, xvii
transition.mov, 289
transitions, 274–302
    aligning, 288
    changing default, 294–296
    changing duration of, 279, 280, 284, 287
    creating, 276–289, 292–293
    creating favorite, 297–298
    defined, 274
    deleting, 278, 283
    examples of, 275
    and handles, 281–282
    Option-dragging, 315
    and rendering, 289–291
    tutorial, 289
    vs. keyframes, 279
    ways of applying, 284, 286
transparency, changing clip's, 292–293
transparency channels, 423
trashing
    media, 4, 11, 473
    preferences, 299, 492–493
traveling mattes, 432–436
Trim Edit window, 216–220
trimming, 187–207
    with Arrow tool, 189–191
    audio, 241–246
    defined, 118, 187
    with Duration dialog, 198–199
    and editing workflow, 6
    general-purpose tools for, 189–194
    one-sided, 196–201
    power techniques for, 212–215
    with Razor Blade tool, 191–194, 230
    with Ripple tool, 196–198, 230
    with Roll tool, 202–204
    with Slide tool, 206–207
    with Slip tool, 204–206
    with Timecode, 212–215
    toggling snapping off during, 195
    tutorial on, 187
    two-sided, 202–207
trimming.mov, 187
troubleshooting tips, 487–494
TRT, 446

tutorial movies
archive.mov, 465
audio.mov, 226
capture.mov, 82
editing.mov, 135
filters.mov, 387
interface.mov, 21
Media Manager, 465
motion.mov, 343
organize.mov, 169
reconnect.mov, 96
Render Manager, 465
transition.mov, 289
trimming.mov, 187
TV-safe color levels, 329
TV-safe video levels, 327
TV video, 319, 413
two-sided trimming, 202–207
two-track editing, 233

U

Undo levels, 72, 162
Unix, 488, 491
Unlimited RT setting, 291
upgrade problems, software,
487–488
upper-corner titles, 318
UPS, xvi
Use Existing command, 480
User Group, L.A. Final Cut Pro, 496
User Preferences dialog
Editing tab, 73, 203, 338
General tab, 71–73
Labels tab, 54

V

variable-speed clips, 379–381
Vault files, 474. *See also* Autosave
Vault
Vectorscope, 81–82, 325, 327–329,
418, 421
VHS tape, 12, 443, 445. *See also*
videotape
video. *See also* video tracks
8- *vs.* 10-bit, 323
color-correcting, 413–422
computer *vs.* TV, 319, 413
and computers, 410–412
distorting, 357
exporting, 460–463
monitoring, 69

putting forced perspective into,
357
troubleshooting, 493
video editing. *See also* editing
and RAID storage devices, xv, 17
and software upgrades, 487–488
system demands, 487
and timecode, 40, 140
two-track, 233
video effects software, xvii
video files, 3–4, 496. *See also*
media files
video filters, 393–398. *See also*
filters
video formats, 15, 64, 65
video graphics, 313. *See also*
graphics
video-in-video effect, 432
video levels
clamping, 324, 330
and filters, 405
TV-safe, 327
Video Playback menu, 68
video preferences, 15, 66
video render files, 251, 291, 470,
471. *See also* render files
video resolution, 313, 475
video scopes, 325–329, 413
video tracks. *See also* tracks
adding, 234–235
closing gaps in, 155
finding gaps in, 157
how Final Cut reads, 238, 342
viewing contents of, 250
video transitions, 283–289, 294.
See also transitions
videotape. *See also* tape
archiving files on, 11, 473 (*See
also* archiving)
converting information stored on,
62
high- *vs.* low-resolution, 475
labeling, 9
lifespan of, 12
storing, 12, 473
timecode breaks in, 107
videotape decks. *See* decks
View controls, Audio Mixer, 271
Viewer
exploring, 34–39
illustrated, 21, 23, 35
loading clips into, 35–36
moving clips to, 121
playback controls, 36–37

purpose of, 23, 34
similarity to Canvas, 24, 48
visibility indicators, track, 45,
250–252
Vocal DeEsser filter, 392
Vocal DePopper filter, 392
Voice Over tool, 260–264
volume rubber bands, 249–250, 266
VTR in Local message, 76
VTR OK message, 75, 76

W

Warn After Capture option, 73
WAV files, 226, 258
Waveform Cache file, 18
Waveform monitor, 81, 325–327,
415
waveforms
purpose of, 228
turning on/off, 43, 229
viewing, 81, 325–327, 415
Web, exporting to, 453, 454, 455
white levels, 323–324, 330, 410,
415–421
Widescreen filter, 406, 407–408
window layouts, 52, 492
Window Scaling menu, 48–49
Window View menu, 48, 50
windows. *See also* specific windows
hiding/showing, 22
identifying selected *vs.* unselected,
31
moving, 22
resizing, 51
saving arrangement of, 52, 492
specialized, 50
Windows Media format, 453
Wipe transitions, 300–302
Wireframe mode, 349, 353–358,
376

Y

YUV colors, 319, 410–411

Z

Zoom In/Out tools, 47, 154, 358
Zoom slider, 46, 47

THIS SOFTWARE LICENSE AGREEMENT CONSTITUTES AN AGREEMENT BETWEEN YOU AND, LYNDA.COM, INC. YOU SHOULD CAREFULLY READ THE FOLLOWING TERMS AND CONDITIONS. COPYING THIS SOFTWARE TO YOUR MACHINE OR OTHERWISE REMOVING OR USING THE SOFTWARE INDICATES YOUR ACCEPTANCE OF THESE TERMS AND CONDITIONS. IF YOU DO NOT AGREE TO BE BOUND BY THE PROVISIONS OF THIS LICENSE AGREEMENT, YOU SHOULD PROMPTLY DELETE THE SOFTWARE FROM YOUR MACHINE.

TERMS AND CONDITIONS:

1. GRANT OF LICENSE. In consideration of payment of the License Fee, which was a part of the price you paid for this product, LICENSOR grants to you (the "Licensee") a non-exclusive right to use the Software (all parts and elements of the data contained on the accompanying DVD-ROM are hereinafter referred to as the "Software"), along with any updates or upgrade releases of the Software for which you have paid on a single computer only (i.e., with a single CPU) at a single location, all as more particularly set forth and limited below. LICENSOR reserves all rights not expressly granted to you as Licensee in this License Agreement.

2. OWNERSHIP OF SOFTWARE. The license granted herein is not a sale of the original Software or of any copy of the Software. As Licensee, you own only the rights to use the Software as described herein and the magnetic or other physical media on which the Software is originally or subsequently recorded or fixed. LICENSOR retains title and ownership of the Software recorded on the original disk(s), as well as title and ownership of any subsequent copies of the Software irrespective of the form of media on or in which the Software is recorded or fixed. This license does not grant you any intellectual or other proprietary or other rights of any nature whatsoever in the Software.

3. USE RESTRICTIONS. As Licensee, you may use the Software only as expressly authorized in this License Agreement under the terms of paragraph 4. You may physically transfer the Software from one computer to another provided that the Software is used on only a single computer at any one time. You may not: (i) electronically transfer the Software from one computer to another over a network; (ii) make the Software available through a time-sharing service, network of computers, or other multiple user arrangement; (iii) distribute copies of the Software or related written materials to any third party, whether for sale or otherwise; (iv) modify, adapt, translate, reverse engineer, decompile, disassemble, or prepare any derivative work based on the Software or any element thereof; (v) make or distribute, whether for sale or otherwise, any hard copy or printed version of any of the Software nor any portion thereof nor any work of yours containing the Software or any component thereof; (vi) use any of the Software nor any of its components in any other work.

4. THIS IS WHAT YOU CAN AND CANNOT DO WITH THE SOFTWARE. Even though in the preceding paragraph and elsewhere LICENSOR has restricted your use of the Software, the following is the only thing you can do with the Software and the various elements of the Software: THE ARTWORK CONTAINED ON THIS DVD-ROM MAY NOT BE USED IN ANY MANNER WHATSOEVER OTHER THAN TO VIEW THE SAME ON YOUR COMPUTER, OR POST TO YOUR PERSONAL, NON-COMMERCIAL WEB SITE FOR EDUCATIONAL PURPOSES ONLY. THIS MATERIAL IS SUBJECT TO ALL OF THE RESTRICTION PROVISIONS OF THIS SOFTWARE LICENSE. SPECIFICALLY BUT NOT IN LIMITATION OF THESE RESTRICTIONS, YOU MAY NOT DISTRIBUTE, RESELL OR TRANSFER THIS PART OF THE SOFTWARE NOR ANY OF YOUR DESIGN OR OTHER WORK CONTAINING ANY OF THE SOFTWARE on this DVD-ROM, ALL AS MORE PARTICULARLY RESTRICTED IN THE WITHIN SOFTWARE LICENSE.

5. COPY RESTRICTIONS. The Software and accompanying written materials are protected under United States copyright laws. Unauthorized copying and/or distribution of the Software and/or the related written materials is expressly forbidden. You may be held legally responsible for any copyright infringement that is caused, directly or indirectly, by your failure to abide by the terms of this License Agreement. Subject to the terms of this License Agreement and if the software is not otherwise copy protected, you may make one copy of the Software for backup purposes only. The copyright notice and any other proprietary notices which were included in the original Software must be reproduced and included on any such backup copy.

6. TRANSFER RESTRICTIONS. The license herein granted is personal to you, the Licensee. You may not transfer the Software nor any of its components or elements to anyone else, nor may you sell, lease, loan, sublicense, assign, or otherwise dispose of the Software nor any of its components or elements without the express written consent of LICENSOR, which consent may be granted or withheld at LICENSOR's sole discretion.

7. TERMINATION. The license herein granted hereby will remain in effect until terminated. This license will terminate automatically without further notice from LICENSOR in the event of the violation of any of the provisions hereof. As Licensee, you agree that upon such termination you will promptly destroy any and all copies of the Software which remain in your possession and, upon request, will certify to such destruction in writing to LICENSOR.

8. LIMITATION AND DISCLAIMER OF WARRANTIES. a) THE SOFTWARE AND RELATED WRITTEN MATERIALS, INCLUDING ANY INSTRUCTIONS FOR USE, ARE PROVIDED ON AN "AS IS" BASIS, WITHOUT WARRANTY OF ANY KIND, EXPRESS OR IMPLIED. THIS DISCLAIMER OF WARRANTY EXPRESSLY INCLUDES, BUT IS NOT LIMITED TO, ANY IMPLIED WARRANTIES OF MERCHANTABILITY AND/OR OF FITNESS FOR A PARTICULAR PURPOSE. NO WARRANTY OF ANY KIND IS MADE AS TO WHETHER OR NOT THIS SOFTWARE INFRINGES UPON ANY RIGHTS OF ANY OTHER THIRD PARTIES. NO ORAL OR WRITTEN INFORMATION GIVEN BY LICENSOR, ITS SUPPLIERS, DISTRIBUTORS, DEALERS, EMPLOYEES, OR AGENTS, SHALL CREATE OR OTHERWISE ENLARGE THE SCOPE OF ANY WARRANTY HEREUNDER. LICENSEE ASSUMES THE ENTIRE RISK AS TO THE QUALITY AND THE PERFORMANCE OF SUCH SOFTWARE. SHOULD THE SOFTWARE PROVE DEFECTIVE, YOU, AS LICENSEE (AND NOT LICENSOR, ITS SUPPLIERS, DISTRIBUTORS, DEALERS OR AGENTS), ASSUME THE ENTIRE COST OF ALL NECESSARY CORRECTION, SERVICING, OR REPAIR. b) LICENSOR warrants the disk(s) on which this copy of the Software is recorded or fixed to be free from defects in materials and workmanship, under normal use and service, for a period of ninety (90) days from the date of delivery as evidenced by a copy of the applicable receipt. LICENSOR hereby limits the duration of any implied warranties with respect to the disk(s) to the duration of the express warranty. This limited warranty shall not apply if the disk(s) have been damaged by unreasonable use, accident, negligence, or by any other causes unrelated to defective materials or workmanship. c) LICENSOR does not warrant that the functions contained in the Software will be uninterrupted or error free and Licensee is encouraged to test the Software for Licensee's intended use prior to placing any reliance thereon. All risk of the use of the Software will be on you, as Licensee. d) THE LIMITED WARRANTY SET FORTH ABOVE GIVES YOU SPECIFIC LEGAL RIGHTS AND YOU MAY ALSO HAVE OTHER RIGHTS, WHICH VARY FROM STATE TO STATE. SOME STATES DO NOT ALLOW THE LIMITATION OR EXCLUSION OF IMPLIED WARRANTIES OR OF INCIDENTAL OR CONSEQUENTIAL DAMAGES, SO THE LIMITATIONS AND EXCLUSIONS CONCERNING THE SOFTWARE AND RELATED WRITTEN MATERIALS SET FORTH ABOVE MAY NOT APPLY TO YOU.

9. LIMITATION OF REMEDIES. LICENSOR's entire liability and Licensee's exclusive remedy shall be the replacement of any disk(s) not meeting the limited warranty set forth in Section 8 above which is returned to LICENSOR with a copy of the applicable receipt within the warranty period. Any replacement disk(s)will be warranted for the remainder of the original warranty period or thirty (30) days, whichever is longer.

10. LIMITATION OF LIABILITY. IN NO EVENT WILL LICENSOR, OR ANYONE ELSE INVOLVED IN THE CREATION, PRODUCTION, AND/OR DELIVERY OF THIS SOFTWARE PRODUCT BE LIABLE TO LICENSEE OR ANY OTHER PER-SON OR ENTITY FOR ANY DIRECT, INDIRECT, OR OTHER DAMAGES, INCLUDING, WITHOUT LIMITATION, ANY INTERRUPTION OF SERVICES, LOST PROFITS, LOST SAVINGS, LOSS OF DATA, OR ANY OTHER CONSEQUENTIAL, INCIDENTAL, SPECIAL, OR PUNITIVE DAMAGES, ARISING OUT OF THE PURCHASE, USE, INABILITY TO USE, OR OPERATION OF THE SOFTWARE, EVEN IF LICENSOR OR ANY AUTHORIZED LICENSOR DEALER HAS BEEN ADVISED OF THE POSSIBILITY OF SUCH DAMAGES. BY YOUR USE OF THE SOFTWARE, YOU ACKNOWLEDGE THAT THE LIMITATION OF LIABILITY SET FORTH IN THIS LICENSE WAS THE BASIS UPON WHICH THE SOFTWARE WAS OFFERED BY LICENSOR AND YOU ACKNOWLEDGE THAT THE PRICE OF THE SOFTWARE LICENSE WOULD BE HIGHER IN THE ABSENCE OF SUCH LIMITATION. SOME STATES DO NOT ALLOW THE LIMITATION OR EXCLUSION OF LIABILITY FOR INCIDENTAL OR CONSEQUENTIAL DAMAGES SO THE ABOVE LIMITATIONS AND EXCLUSIONS MAY NOT APPLY TO YOU.

11. UPDATES. LICENSOR, at its sole discretion, may periodically issue updates of the Software which you may receive upon request and payment of the applicable update fee in effect from time to time and in such event, all of the provisions of the within License Agreement shall apply to such updates.

12. EXPORT RESTRICTIONS. Licensee agrees not to export or re-export the Software and accompanying documentation (or any copies thereof) in violation of any applicable U.S. laws or regulations.

13. ENTIRE AGREEMENT. YOU, AS LICENSEE, ACKNOWLEDGE THAT: (i) YOU HAVE READ THIS ENTIRE AGREEMENT AND AGREE TO BE BOUND BY ITS TERMS AND CONDITIONS; (ii) THIS AGREEMENT IS THE COMPLETE AND EXCLUSIVE STATEMENT OF THE UNDERSTANDING BETWEEN THE PARTIES AND SUPERSEDES ANY AND ALL PRIOR ORAL OR WRITTEN COMMUNICATIONS RELATING TO THE SUBJECT MATTER HEREOF; AND (iii) THIS AGREEMENT MAY NOT BE MODIFIED, AMENDED, OR IN ANY WAY ALTERED EXCEPT BY A WRITING SIGNED BY BOTH YOURSELF AND AN OFFICER OR AUTHORIZED REPRESENTATIVE OF LICENSOR.

14. SEVERABILITY. In the event that any provision of this License Agreement is held to be illegal or otherwise unenforceable, such provision shall be deemed to have been deleted from this License Agreement while the remaining provisions of this License Agreement shall be unaffected and shall continue in full force and effect.

15. GOVERNING LAW. This License Agreement shall be governed by the laws of the State of California applicable to agreements wholly to be performed therein and of the United States of America, excluding that body of the law related to conflicts of law. This License Agreement shall not be governed by the United Nations Convention on Contracts for the International Sale of Goods, the application of which is expressly excluded. No waiver of any breach of the provisions of this License Agreement shall be deemed a waiver of any other breach of this License Agreement.

16. RESTRICTED RIGHTS LEGEND. Use, duplication, or disclosure by the Government is subject to restrictions as set forth in subparagraph (c)(1)(ii) of the Rights in Technical Data and Computer Software clause at 48 CFR § 252.227-7013 and DFARS § 252.227-7013 or subparagraphs (c) (1) and (c)(2) of the Commercial Computer Software-Restricted Rights at 48 CFR § 52.227.19, as applicable. Contractor/manufacturer: LICENSOR: LYNDA.COM, INC., c/o PEACHPIT PRESS, 1249 Eighth Street, Berkeley, CA 94710.